THE ROOTS OF THE REFORMATION

Tradition, Emergence and Rupture

Second Edition

G. R. EVANS

IVP Academic

An imprint of InterVarsity Press
Downers Grove, Illinois

InterVarsity Press
P.O. Box 1400, Downers Grove, IL 60515-1426
World Wide Web: www.ivpress.com
E-mail: email@ivpress.com

Second edition: ©2012 by G. R. Evans
First edition: ©2012 by G. R. Evans

InterVarsity Press® is the book-publishing division of InterVarsity Christian Fellowship/USA®, a movement of students and faculty active on campus at hundreds of universities, colleges and schools of nursing in the United States of America, and a member movement of the International Fellowship of Evangelical Students. For information about local and regional activities, write Public Relations Dept., InterVarsity Christian Fellowship/USA, 6400 Schroeder Rd., P.O. Box 7895, Madison, WI 53707-7895, or visit the IVCF website at <www.intervarsity.org>.

Scripture quotations, unless otherwise noted, are from the New Revised Standard Version of the Bible, *copyright 1989 by the Division of Christian Education of the National Council of the Churches of Christ in the USA. Used by permission. All rights reserved.*

Cover design: Cindy Kiple
Interior design: Beth Hagenberg
Images: procession of the Catholic league: Procession of the Catholic League on the Ile de la Cite at Musee de la Ville de Paris, Musee Carnavalet, Paris, France. Giraudon/Art Resource.

> *procession of the Catholic league: Procession of the Catholic League on the Place de Greve in Paris. Detail: A baker's stall; background: medieval Paris and the cathedral of Notre-Dame at Musee de la Ville de Paris, Musee Carnavalet, Paris, France. Erich Lessing/Art Resource.*

> *old page with border: © peter zelei/iStockphoto*

ISBN 978-0-8308-3996-4

Printed in the United States of America ∞

Library of Congress Cataloging-in-Publication Data

Evans, G. R. (Gillian Rosemary)
 Roots of the Reformation: tradition, emergence, and rupture / G. R. Evans.
  p. cm.
 Includes bibliographical references (p.) and index.
 ISBN 978-0-8308-3947-6 (pbk.: alk. paper)
 1. Reformation. I. Title.
 BR305.3.E93 2012
 270.6—dc23

                                                                    2012000264

P	20	19	18	17	16	15	14	13	12	11	10	9	8	7	6	5	4	3	2	1
Y	30	29	28	27	26	25	24	23	22	21	20	19	18	17	16	15	14	13	12

CONTENTS

PART 2: CONTINUITY AND CHANGE IN THE MIDDLE AGES

PREFACE

WHAT HAPPENED AT THE REFORMATION? What did it "reform"? We see the sixteenth century now as a time of radical change, but looked at in the context of the history of disputes among Christians, it turns out to be an episode in a much longer story. Similar objections and criticisms had been raised for centuries, and some of them since the earliest Christian times. Many of them can still be heard today. Yet in the sixteenth century the questioning prompted an unprecedented event: the lasting fragmentation of the church in the West.

We can make sense of all this only if we know something of the reasons why the key questions first occurred to people and what happened when people kept on asking about them in different times and places. Beliefs have been held by individuals down the ages in the social environment of their times, in a complex of other ideas and assumptions which have given them color and point and emphasis, and made some things seem important at one time and other things at another.

The picture which emerges if we look at the story as a whole is of immense honest endeavor by believers well aware of the importance of protecting the essential character of the faith, and frequently infuriated by what others were saying precisely because it all mattered so much. There were mutual slanging matches, accusations of conspiracy and corruption (not always unjustified, it has to be said). Groups formed allegiances and clung to particular opinions, which were condemned by other groups who said they were heretics. The resulting divisions or "schism" between Christian communities seemed to some commenta-

tors to be a heresy in itself, because it did not take the need for unity
seriously enough.

Throughout this colorful story run certain threads that reappear
through the weave as topics of importance century by century. The difficulty is to spot the ends so as to tug them and begin the unraveling.
This book is written as an aid to understanding the way continuities
have run through the changes of Christian history. It offers a history of
the changes of the Reformation seen as episodes in that continuity, and
as a complement to the series of recently published modern studies of
the Reformation and its immediate background.[1]

A NOTE ON THE SECOND EDITION

I am grateful to Brannon Ellis for his support in producing in this second edition a revision of this book which it is hoped will meet the needs
of readers seeking to use it as a textbook for relevant courses. The book
has been streamlined somewhat to allow its major themes to come to
the fore for these readers. All dates for people and places have been
conformed to the *Oxford Encyclopedia of the Reformation*, or else the
Oxford Dictionary of the Christian Church, unless there was good reason
to depart from these. The argument remains the same—while the Reformation and its effects were in many ways something new, many of the
significant questions and concerns at its roots are as ancient as the
church itself.

---

[1]A number of these studies are mentioned in the footnotes and bibliography by way of providing
references for further reading.

ACKNOWLEDGMENTS

I AM GRATEFUL TO NUMEROUS FRIENDS and colleagues who have been willing to talk about the topics of this book, its purposes and the complex task of drawing it together. I am especially grateful to Michael Gibson and the editorial staff of IVP for their professionalism and their patience with authorial vagaries and to Brannon Ellis for his invaluable work on the present edition.

ABBREVIATIONS

Augustine, *Confessions*	Augustine's *Confessions* is available in numerous Latin editions and English translations. References are to standard sections, and for convenience page references are given to Augustine, *Confessions*, ed. James J. O'Donnell (Oxford: Oxford University Press, 1992).
Calvin, *Institutes*	John Calvin, *Institutes of the Christian Religion*. 1559 edition. Edited by John T. McNeill. Translated by Ford Lewis Battles. 2 vols. Philadelphia: Westminster, 1960.
CCCM	Corpus Christianorum: Continuatio Medievalis (Turnhout: Brepols, 1966-).
CCSL	Corpus Christianorum: Series Latina (Turnhout: Brepols, 1953-).
CSEL	Corpus Scriptorum Ecclesiasticorum Latinorum (Vienna: Austrian Academy of Sciences, 1866-).
EETS	Early English Text Society
fl.	flourished
c.	*circa*
d.	died

Homilies   *Certain Sermons or Homilies Appointed to Be Read in Churches in the Time of the Late Queen Elizabeth of Famous Memory: And Now Thought Fit to Be Reprinted by Authority from the King's Most Excellent Majesty* (Oxford: Oxford University Press, 1832).

Hooker, *Laws*   Richard Hooker, *The Laws of Ecclesiastical Polity*, ed. William Speed Hill, 8 vols. (London: Sidgwick & Jackson, 1977-1998).

Luther, *Table Talk*   Martin Luther, *The Table Talk of Martin Luther*, trans. William Hazlitt (London: George Bell, 1883), www.ccel.org/ccel/luther/tabletalk.html.

PL   Patrologia cursus completus. Series Latina. 221 vols. Edited by J.-P. Migne. Paris, 1844-1864.

Tanner   Norman P. Tanner, *Decrees of the Ecumenical Councils* (Washington, D.C.: Georgetown University Press, 1990).

Wilkins   David Wilkins, *Concilia magnae Britanniae et Hiberniae* (London, 1737).

1

SETTING THE SCENE

The "Fair Field of Folk"

THE POET KNOWN AS WILLIAM LANGLAND (c. 1332-1386) had a vision of a "fair field of folk," which he used as a motif in a hard-hitting analysis of the society of his day.[1] Medieval poets were fond of using pretend dreams as a literary device. This particular image of the "field of folk" may have been prompted by the real view from the Malvern Hills near the Welsh border, down into the Severn Valley, where Worcestershire and Warwickshire and Gloucestershire still lie spread for miles before the observer of the English scene today. In *Piers Plowman* Langland sketches the contemporary world in all its variety from his vantage point on these hills.

Despite its rural setting, most of Langland's poem is about the behavior and attitudes of an urban community. He describes London's people, the way they lived and the way they thought, at about the time when Geoffrey Chaucer (c. 1343-1400) wrote *The Canterbury Tales*, with its similarly sharp social satire and digs at the misbehavior of the clergy.[2] This urban way of life was a relatively new medieval phenomenon in Europe, except in Italy, where some of the towns of the ancient Roman Empire had persisted. There citizenship had remained a vivid reality, at least for those lucky enough to be well-born (and male).

---

[1] J. A. W. Bennett, "Chaucer's Contemporary," in *Piers Plowman: Critical Approaches*, ed. S. S. Hussey (London: Methuen, 1969), pp. 310-24.
[2] *Piers Plowman: A New Translation of the B-text*, trans. A. V. C. Schmidt (Oxford: Oxford University Press, 1992), www.courses.fas.harvard.edu/~chaucer/special/authors/langland.

Elsewhere in Europe the opportunity of active participation in public affairs by a good proportion of the population had given way to a top-down way of running things. In most of northern Europe the last few centuries had been feudal. This was a hereditary aristocratic system and highly military in character. In the feudal system kings and emperors owned the lands of their realms and allowed the great nobles to hold and use them during their lifetimes as vassals, in return for an oath of fealty (loyalty or faithfulness) and the provision of a certain number of days of military service ("knight days") a year. The nobility ran their estates by farming the land with the aid of their peasants, some of whom were freemen but many of whom were serfs bound to the land in slavery. From the same aristocratic families were drawn the senior churchmen, whose elevation to bishoprics also involved holding land from the monarch, in the form of the estates of the diocese. Bishops too had to provide their quota of knight days. Church and state were intimately bound together in a power structure in which baron and bishop were often brothers.

So the emergence in twelfth-century northern Europe of towns full of tradespeople with marketable skills created a new class of articulate and inquiring people, the sort of people who ran businesses and behaved like entrepreneurs. There was even the beginning of a new middling gentry as they aspired to a social mobility which had not been possible for many centuries. They asked searching questions about social arrangements and conventional religious teaching, and wanted to have their say when they heard the answers. Langland's prospective readership in this new middle class was evidently quite considerable, to judge from the number of manuscripts of his poem which survive, so we can assume that the grudges he expresses struck a chord at least with the literate. And more of them, of both sexes, were becoming literate.[3]

A good deal of fourteenth-century England of all social classes was spread out before the poet for inspection:

---

[3]It is not possible to establish statistics; the evidence consists in the multiplication of books intended for the use of the laity, such as the Books of Hours. We cannot know whether the women who had such volumes mainly looked at the pictures, but the very fact of creating books for those who did not belong to the clerical classes is evidence of a growing interest in being able to read among such people.

All manner of men / the rich and the poor,
Working and wandering / as the world asketh.

"Barons and burgesses and bondmen also I saw in this crowd"; "bakers and brewers and butchers a-many"; "woollen-websters and weavers of linen"; "tailors and tinkers toll-takers in markets"; "masons and miners and men of all crafts." He contrasts the hardworking laboring classes with the greedy "wasters." There are the fashionable, leading lives of conspicuous luxury, and there are those "such as anchorites and hermits" who out of sight in their "cells" quietly lead lives of self-denial, "in hope for to have heavenly bliss." There are retailers, who seem to do rather well ("such men thrive"). Then there are entertainers, some who just "make mirth" ("as minstrels know how") and earn an honest living that way, but others defraud the public. Some are "tramps and beggars" who make a good living begging for their food and then create disturbances by getting drunk at inns, "the thieving knaves!"

Langland is particularly shocked by the corruption and fraudulent activities going on in the name of religion. "Pretend" pilgrims and "palmers" (pilgrims who carried a palm to show they had visited the Holy Land) told tall tales in order to get money from the gullible. "Hermits, a heap of them with hooked staves, were going to Walsingham and their wenches too." Langland sees them as work shy:

Big loafers and tall / that loth were to work,
Dressed up in capes / to be known from others
And so clad as hermits / their ease to have.

He is equally disgusted by the friars of every kind "preaching to the people for profit to themselves":

Explaining the Gospel / just as they liked,
To get clothes for themselves / they construed it as they would.

The friars who belonged to the Dominicans, Franciscans and other mendicant orders founded since the early thirteenth century were professional itinerant preachers, but they had also gained an entrance to the courts of Europe as personal confessors, the "life coaches" of their time. They behave like "chapmen," or tradesmen, says Langland, and make a nice living from the invitation "to shrive lords." The friars and the professional peddlers of penitential aids will feature prominently in the medieval story told in part two.

The ordinary clergy come in for Langland's criticism too. Since the "pestilence time" of the Black Death (with its climax in Europe in 1348-1350), they complain that they cannot live on the income from their parishes and they ask "leave and licence in London to dwell." There they "sing requiems for stipends[,] for silver is sweet." They neglect their pastoral duties: to hear their parishioners' confessions, grant them absolution and "preach and pray for them and feed the poor."

Langland was evidently confident that his descriptions would strike a chord. What did the general population know of the tides of opinion and discussion which are now apparent to us as we look at the records of these events and the theological controversies they prompted? The truth seems to be that the ordinary faithful were involved, to a greater degree than they perhaps realized, in setting those tides running and putting pressure on theologians to make theological sense of their pastoral demands. Langland could see the effect of this popular pressure clearly enough as he wrote his sketch. But the routes by which they could exchange views and gain up-to-date information were naturally limited by the very restricted means of communication then available, even for the literate. Satirical verses were distributed by traveling ballad sellers like the one in Shakespeare's *A Winter's Tale*, Act 4, Scene 4:

> *Servant:* O master, if you did but hear the pedlar at the door, you would never dance again after a tabour and pipe; no, the bagpipe could not move you: he sings several tunes faster than you'll tell money; he utters them as he had eaten ballads and all men's ears grew to his tunes.

> *Clown:* He could never come better; he shall come in. I love a ballad but even too well, if it be doleful matter merrily set down, or a very pleasant thing indeed and sung lamentably.

Shakespeare's examples in this play are ribald and poke simple fun, but some of the surviving medieval ones were highly political and socially aware.

If an inquiring population was beginning to ask awkward questions about the way the institutional church was running religious affairs, could it turn for answers to the Bible? Practical impediments stood in the way for the "fair field of folk" if they wanted to know what the Bible said about the matters which concerned them. Copies were expensive in the centuries before the invention of printing. In any case, even if they could have afforded Bibles, the medieval laity were mostly illiterate. And even if some learned to read or had someone to read the Bible to them, most of them could not read for themselves what the Bible actually said, because it was not widely available in any language except Latin until attempts were made in the late Middle Ages and the early Reformation to produce vernacular versions.

These impediments to Bible study were accidents of history, not deliberate attempts to keep Scripture from the ordinary Christian. It was, however, natural for the church authorities to become protective about the Bible, since the educated who could read it in Latin also had the knowledge to read the body of respected commentary which survived from the early Christian centuries, for example the work of Augustine of Hippo (354-430), Gregory the Great (c. 540-604) and Bede (672/3-735). The educated could be expected to understand the theology too. The laity lacked this background and context, and there were fears that without the necessary educational preparation they might misinterpret the Bible and be led astray in their faith. These barriers between the inquiring layperson and the Bible lasted until the late Middle Ages, when one by one they began to be resolved. But those who called for the changes that took place were looked at askance and made themselves objectionable to the authorities of church and state alike. It all became something of a power struggle for ownership and control of the Bible.

Other great themes emerged, which we shall see as recurring problems again and again throughout this book. One was the relationship of spiritual and secular, church and state, as they affected the people in their daily lives. Another was the way in which people's lives were shaped by the teaching of the institutional church, its claim to hold the keys to heaven through the ministry of the sacraments, and its demands about behavior.

The story that follows traces these themes and their subthemes, and seeks to point to the patterns as they reappeared in the Reformation debates. Parts one and two tell the story of the way in which key Christian doctrines were formed and gave rise to concerns about various topics as they appeared to reformers in the sixteenth century. The way reformers and others tackled these concerns is explored in part three. At the end of the book is a "map," in the form of a "Handlist of Reformation Concerns and Their History."

PART ONE

BIBLE AND CHURCH
The Questions Begin

2

THE IDEA OF CHURCH

A NEW IDEA

How the story began. To the Reformers of the sixteenth century, "church" was an idea only too familiar; it connoted a monolithic institution corrupt and oppressive and urgently in need of reform. But at the outset it was a novelty. There had been nothing like it until the early Christians began to form themselves into communities for worship and "fellowship," expressed by the Greek word *koinōnia.*

The New Testament was written within this early community of Christians, and in the same community the discussions took place which would decide which Old Testament writings were to be included in the collection that became the Bible. This forming of what is sometimes called the "canon"—which came to mean the authentic Scriptures—took place among a body of people who were also busy forming a community and organizing the life of that community. The two processes were interconnected and reciprocal. The emerging Scriptures were searched for guidance about the life of the church. The church decided which books were to be received as scriptural.

"Church" was something without exact precedent.[1] The word *ekklēsia* (Latin *ecclesia*) itself came from a Greek verb meaning to "call out"; the ancient Greeks used it for a political assembly of the sort used to govern Greek city-states. That was a bare starting point. A good deal

---

[1]J.-M.-R. Tillard, *Eglise d'églises: L'ecclésiologie de communion* (Paris: Cerf, 1987); G. R. Evans, *The Church and the Churches* (Cambridge: Cambridge University Press, 1994).

of thought and experiment were going to be needed to create a Christian "church."

The first question may well have been why a church was needed at all. One key answer, of course, was that Jesus had declared his intention to found one, when he said that Peter was the rock on which he would build his church (*ekklēsia*, Mt 16:18). That naturally led to the question what the church should be like.

One, holy, catholic and apostolic Church (Niceno-Constantinopolitan Creed of 325/381)

The holy catholic Church (Apostles' Creed)

These descriptions in the creeds (later sometimes called the "notes" or marks of the church) tell us what Christians of the first centuries took to be the defining characteristics of the church, and also emphasize the significance attached from the first to maintain its unity.

In this list of "notes," *catholic* (from the Greek *katholikos*) meant "universal." *One* stressed the importance of maintaining unity throughout this universal church. The emphasis from the beginning was on the need to keep the church together as one single great community with one faith, for it was obvious early on that quarrels were tending to tear it apart.

There was never any dispute that the church ought to be *holy*. That became a difficulty only when in a fragmented church the fragments claimed that each was alone the true church because rival fragments had ceased to be holy; that if there had been a breach of unity, it was the others who had broken away.

Apostolic had two distinct strands of meaning. One sense focused simply on faithfulness to the apostolic tradition, the teaching of the disciples or apostles who had recieved it directly from Jesus. The same ideal of keeping close to the beginning and its fresh vision inspired the founding of medieval religious "orders" (societies or communities who took vows to follow a particular rule of life), who felt a special calling to live lives of poverty and simplicity—to go out and preach the gospel just as Jesus had instructed.

When Richard Hooker (c. 1554-1600), lawyer and English theologian, took stock of the meaning of *apostolic* at the end of the sixteenth century, he put the same emphasis on the poverty and simplicity of the apostolic life. He still saw it as a model:

> In proposing the Apostles' times as a pattern for the Church to follow ... the chiefest thing which lay reforms yawn for is, that the Clergy may through conformity in state and condition be Apostolical, poor as the Apostles of Christ were poor.[2]

But by then the medieval orders who had set out to live like this had gained a reputation for failing, because of the various sorts of reprehensible behavior William Langland had satirized. And there had been a Reformation. There was Hooker, writing from the other side of the Reformation and in a Protestant church, highly conscious of the irony that the Church the Reformers had rejected was the same Church "which hath such store of mendicant Friars," the Franciscans and Dominicans and others, for whom apostolic poverty was basic to their way of life.[3]

The other meaning of *apostolic* linked it with a "succession of ministry," through a line of transmission from the apostles by the laying on of hands. The problem of demonstrating the continuity of Jesus' commission from the apostles themselves arose several times over the centuries when there was a claim that a group or community had allowed a break to occur. It lay at the heart of the Donatist controversy of the fourth century and the Hussite controversy of the fifteenth. The Donatists claimed that those who disagreed with them had an invalid ministry because they had allowed ordination—episcopal succession through the laying on of hands—to be conducted by *traditores*, "traitors," who had given up (literally "handed over") the Scriptures in time of persecution (see p. 72). The Hussites, followers of John Hus (c. 1372-1415; see pp. 225-28), had made "emergency" ordinations using priests, when they had no bishop in sympathy with their party, and the resulting ministers were declared to have been invalidly ordained.

Apostolic continuity became contentious again at the Reformation and once more when Anglican orders were declared null and void by the

---

[2]Hooker, *Laws*, pref., 4.3.
[3]Ibid., 4.4.

papal bull *Apostolicae Curae* in 1896 because the Roman Catholic Church held that there had been a break in the sequence of Anglican ordinations in the sixteenth century.[4] The difficulty of establishing a basis of "mutual recognition of ministry" is still the most common reason for ecumenical conversations between divided churches to fail to reach agreement.

This has been held to be important, because if it is claimed that ministry is not valid, the efficaciousness of the acts of ministers in administering the sacraments comes into question, and that can threaten the sense of security of Christian people and their hope of heaven. *Validity* was taken to be an assurance of authenticity and proper authorization; *efficaciousness*, a guarantee that the sacraments would work.

Uncertainties about the status of the ministry were also taken to undermine ecclesial standing; this could give rise to the claim that the community in which ministry is a mere pretense cannot really be the church. Arguments of this sort are contentious in themselves. They beg many questions about what church is and what sacraments are and whether there is a way of salvation outside the church and not dependent on these technical questions. Not everyone would agree this is an appropriate way to think about church. But that has made these matters immensely important and divisive precisely because so much is as stake.

A practical necessity. Another reason for founding a church or churches was that it turned out that something of the sort was a practical necessity. Jesus' disciples and Paul and some others got on with the missionary work of preaching the gospel as Jesus had instructed. (They came to be known as the apostles simply because the underlying Greek word means "messengers" or "sent ones.")

The result of their energetic activity in spreading the gospel was the creation of gatherings or communities of Christians all over the eastern Mediterranean and around the Aegean and Ionian seas. It is evident from the Acts of the Apostles and the letters of Paul to the young churches which were coming into being that this missionary work, partly because it was so successful, began to create organizational difficulties. Christians have always had heated arguments. There were squabbles; factions formed.

---

[4]Dom Gregory Dix, *The Question of Anglican Orders*, rev. ed. (Westminster: Dacre Press, 1956).

As the New Testament epistles show, the communities soon began to need some guidance on the conduct of their community life.

One of the first attempts to create a framework of rules within which to conduct the business of the infant Christian community is described in Acts 15. Some itinerant preachers were teaching that Christians could not be saved unless they were circumcised according to Jewish custom; Paul and Barnabas protested (Acts 15:1-2). So it was agreed that it would be sensible to go to Jerusalem and convene a meeting to discuss the matter. For this raised the larger question whether the whole law of Moses applied to Christians too and even whether Gentiles as well as Jews could be Christians. Peter had already had a vision, recorded in Acts 10:1–11:18, in which he saw animals regarded by the Jews as "clean" as well as those which were "unclean" and forbidden as food, lowered in a great sheet. Peter heard God telling him to kill and eat *both*, and he interpreted it as a sign that Gentiles as well as Jews were now welcome in God's kingdom. In Acts 15:6-11, Peter is recorded as reminding the meeting of this new inclusiveness. He said the Christian calling was a calling to freedom and believers should not have to be burdened with the yoke of regulations that Israel itself could not bear. The agreement of the meeting was to be communicated throughout the local churches.

That account of finding a way to reconcile opposing positions contains many lessons about the way to organize a church and what sort of leadership works best. We see the first Christians learning to work by consensus, through meetings of the sort which eventually became councils, but also by appointing leaders and deciding what their responsibilities should be. The Reformers of the sixteenth century went back to these precedents in search of a truly scriptural model for the church. But anxious to cast aside what they perceived as the "corruptions" of more recent times, they tended to be selective in what they approved.

The Emergence of Ministers as Leaders

The nature of the job. Ministerial leadership, the apostle Peter insisted, should not be managerial or dictatorial; the authority of a minister should come from the example he sets.

> Now as an elder myself and a witness of the sufferings of Christ, as well
> as one who shares in the glory to be revealed, I exhort the elders among
> you to tend the flock of God that is in your charge, exercising the over-
> sight, not under compulsion but willingly, as God would have you do
> it—not for sordid gain but eagerly. Do not lord it over those in your
> charge, but be examples to the flock. (1 Pet 5:1-3)

The New Testament shows the young church working out—under
the pressure of events—how to appoint and authorize its leaders, and
how to decide on the range of their responsibilities. In the early church
there were already arguments about the tasks for which the communities' leaders ought to be responsible. Were they to be overseers, teachers,
ministers of the sacraments; or helpers of widows and orphans and the
needy in general; or all those things? What exactly were their appointed
tasks, and who gave them authority to carry them out?

Paul emphasized the importance of the authority of the Holy Spirit
in commissioning a minister. He sent a message from Miletus to Ephesus, asking the elders of the church there to meet him (Acts 20:17). He
explained that he wanted to leave them instructions for their future
ministry. "Keep watch over yourselves and over all the flock, of which
the Holy Spirit has made you overseers, to shepherd the church of God"
(Acts 20:28). Paul saw that there could be a need for a firm hand when
there were quarrels or when dissidents mounted a challenge to the community's faith. Local churches are to expect "wolves" to come among
their sheep. Even their own members will "come distorting the truth in
order to entice the disciples to follow them" (Acts 20:30).

This perceived need for what might now be called management skills,
and with it the definition of the scope of something rather like execu-
tive power, was also going to be worked out in a relationship with secular government in every period and throughout Christendom in the
ensuing centuries. Churches had to do this locally. Every secular authority, whether empire, kingdom or city-state, had its own arrangements to be accommodated. But in every type of relationship with governments, the church found itself struggling to assert strong leadership

against the secular authority. The balance of power between church and state is a constant concern in the story told in this book.

To Titus, Paul wrote a comprehensive list of desirable personal qualities to go with the list of ministerial duties, which closely resembles the list he sent to Timothy (1 Tim 3:1-7).

> I left you behind in Crete for this reason, that you should put in order what remained to be done, and should appoint elders in every town, as I directed you: someone who is blameless, married only once, whose children are believers, not accused of debauchery and not rebellious. For a bishop, as God's steward, must be blameless; he must not be arrogant or quick-tempered or addicted to wine or violent or greedy for gain; but he must be hospitable, a lover of goodness, prudent, upright, devout, and self-controlled. He must have a firm grasp of the word that is trustworthy in accordance with the teaching, so that he may be able both to preach with sound doctrine and to refute those who contradict it. (Tit 1:5-9)

Paul did not think every minister would necessarily have to have all the relevant gifts or necessarily had to exercise all these forms of ministry. There are different gifts. Some should be "apostles, some prophets, some evangelists, some pastors and teachers, to equip the saints for the work of ministry, for building up the body of Christ" (Eph 4:11-12).

Decisions about special responsibilities and the best way to divide them up, taken at the very beginning and recorded in Acts, were thus to have an influence for centuries. When there were complaints that the practical needs of the widows and orphans of the community were being neglected, it was decided to appoint men with a special responsibility for practical pastoral matters, looking after the finances of the community and making sure the helpless and the poor were looked after (Acts 6). These were to be the deacons.

Those specially appointed ministers who were to exercise leadership were also to teach and preach. These individuals were to be chosen by the whole community because it was important that they could be trusted to preserve the faith and not mislead the faithful. Reformers of the sixteenth century warmed to the tone of all this, because it seemed so free of the formalities and restrictions and power play of the institutional church in the West during the later Middle Ages.

Bishops or elders? Were the church's leading ministers to be called bishops (*episcopoi*) or elders (*presbyteroi*), and what was the difference? Probably there was no intended difference at first, and the New Testament authors used either word indifferently, but a difference emerged, and it grew to be important. In succeeding centuries two distinct categories emerged: *bishops*, as overseers of dioceses, and *priests*, as their deputies or vicars. The ancient diaconate lost its distinctive tasks and deacons became absorbed into a single hierarchy or ladder of ministry, where, mounting the first rung, a candidate would become a deacon, on the second rung a priest (elder?), with the episcopate (bishops) at the top.

There were sharp distinctions of function and powers for those in the process of climbing this ladder. Deacons were not allowed to celebrate the Eucharist or to "absolve" penitents; priests could celebrate the Eucharist, and from the early Middle Ages they were allowed to grant absolution too. Only bishops were allowed to ordain, and in the first centuries, the centuries of public penance for serious sins, they were also the ministers of absolution.

The allocation of these powers was to be of great concern to the Reformation's leaders of opinion. They claimed that the balance of tasks and personal qualities outlined in the New Testament had been lost sight of, that the preaching and teaching and pastoral care described in the New Testament had given way to a sacerdotal conception of a priest's role, in which a minister's chief duty was to make "sacrifices" rather than to be a shepherd to his flock.

Whether to have bishops or not to have bishops became a church-dividing issue for many sixteenth-century Reformers. The Lutheran *Treatise on the Power and Primacy of the Pope* of 1537 explained the history thus. "Formerly" it claimed, "the people elected pastors and bishops." The role of the bishop of the local church (or a neighboring church if the election was of a bishop), was, it claimed, merely to confirm that choice by the laying on of hands. This was a mere ratification. Texts apparently of an early date—such as the writings of Clement, bishop of Rome, or those of Dionysius—appearing to support any other requirement, are dismissed as spurious or fictitious. It is only by human authority that the grades of bishop and elder or pastor are distinct, the treatise argues.[5]

The reformer Martin Bucer (1491-1551) claimed in his *Commonplaces* that there was and should be no difference between a bishop and a priest. They held the same ministerial office, and deacons held the second:

> The Holy Spirit has appointed two distinct degrees in the Church's ministry. . . . The one comprises the senior pastors, whom the Holy Spirit styles overseers and elders, . . . the other . . . comprises those who are to aid the elders in all their pastoral ministry and in feeding Christ's sheep, . . . and . . . helping the needy.[6]

Elders, as the followers of John Calvin (1509-1564) understood their role, should run their local churches by committee. Elders could even be laymen, some said, and therefore not infected with the high claims to special personal powers which bishops made. In Scotland, as we shall see, presbyterianism became the preferred form of church government. Richard Hooker recognized this as still a point of serious controversy at the end of the sixteenth century, when England was riven by factions wanting no more bishops and calling for a presbyterian style of church government instead:

> It is a matter of biblical interpretation to say "it is probable that in the Apostles' times there were lay-elders . . . or to affirm that Bishops at the first were a name, but not a power distinct from presbyters."[7]

Vocational dramas. It also became important to be sure that those who exercised pastoral ministry had been properly instructed and "called" and "sent" for the purpose—and were not self-appointed or chosen by breakaway groups which admired charismatic leaders who might not be teaching the true faith. One of the reasons for the practice of sending a letter of introduction with priests who moved elsewhere was to ensure that this could not happen.

---

[5]*A Treatise on the Power and Primacy of the Pope: A Treatise Compiled by the Theologians Assembled at Smalcald* (1537), *Triglot Concordia: The Symbolical Books of the Evangelical Lutheran Church: German-Latin-English*, ed. F. Bente et al. (St. Louis: Concordia Publishing House, 1917), http://bookofconcord.org/treatise.php.

[6]Martin Bucer, *A Brief Summary of Christian Doctrine (Commonplaces)*, trans. D. F. Wright (Abingdon, U.K.: Sutton Press, 1972), p. 83.

[7]Hooker, *Laws*, pref., 4.6.

The "calling" by the people could be dramatic. In the early centuries the shortage of good candidates, particularly for bishoprics, led to the practice of press ganging, where a likely subject would be seized by force, carried off and thrown down on the floor of the church to be forcibly ordained. Sometimes the new bishop was far from reluctant (though it was etiquette to look it, protesting unworthiness at one's ordination). Augustine describes in his *Confessions* how he was brought by God's guidance by means of "exhortations" and "terrors" and "consolations" to "preach the word" and minister the sacraments to God's people.[8] For when he returned to North Africa after his baptism, he justifiably feared that he too would be captured for the ministry, though what he really wanted to do was to spend time living a monastic life with a group of friends, thinking about God.

And so it fell out. First he was persuaded to allow himself to be ordained priest, as an assistant to the bishop of Hippo, and then a few years later he became bishop of Hippo himself. The ordination of the captured candidate, like that of every new minister, involved the laying on of hands in token of the calling of the Holy Spirit. This was God's part of the "calling," and it was soon held to be, like baptism and confirmation, permanent and unrepeatable, imposing a "character" or indelible stamp on the individual. So a new minister was thought to be set aside for ministry for the rest of his life, though able to serve other congregations than the one which first called him.

The final element was the tie to a particular church, and with it, ministry to a particular congregation. This was later known as "title," partly because as the church began to acquire property rights, holding a particular pastoral ministry provided the minister with a living and the local secular authorities with a vested interest in conferring these temporalities on the new incumbent. Medieval kings fell into the practice of leaving bishoprics vacant for a year so as to help themselves to the income. It was a convenience they began to view as perfectly proper.

The increasingly formal set of requirements about ministry which evolved in the West by the end of the Middle Ages could give rise to

[8]Augustine, *Confessions* 11.2.2.

a serious crisis, as happened with the Hussites, if one of these required elements was seen to be compromised. But the Reformers, as we shall see, took an altogether more radical approach. They were concerned not only with the authenticity of a succession but with the very nature of the ministry and its purpose.

LOCAL CHURCHES AND THE UNIVERSAL CHURCH

The church. The medieval and Reformation perception of the importance of the church's unity were strongly colored by the assumptions about its institutional structure, many of which the Reformers rejected. All this was very Western. Of the five ancient patriarchates—Jerusalem, Antioch, Alexandria, Constantinople and Rome—only Rome was in Western Europe, the part of the Roman Empire where Latin, not Greek, was the dominant language. There it had had no rivals during all the centuries since there had first been a bishop of Rome, until the Reformation. It had developed a complex and hierarchical institutional structure within which archbishops throughout Europe were subordinate to the jurisdiction of the bishop of Rome, and under them served the bishops of individual dioceses, each with his priests or vicars and their local congregations. So the structural unity of the church in the West was made up of parts, each in its hierarchical place in the whole.

In the Greek-speaking East the churches which came to be known as the "Orthodox" were familiar from an early stage with the difficulty of defining their areas of authority in relation to this fourfold structure. The solution they arrived at was to hold fast to one faith but allow variation of practice. Each patriarchate was "autocephalous," having its own primate or patriarch, and running its own affairs. Churches, whether very local indeed or the size of the patriarchate, saw themselves not as parts, but as microcosms of the whole church.

The overarching questions of primacy, including which of the five patriarchs was *first*, and in what sense, constituted a contentious subject from the end of antiquity. Medieval debate aimed at mending the schism which occurred in 1054 took place from time to time (see pp. 102-8), but by the Reformation most of those involved in the debates had lost sight of the huge difference in attitude and understanding. Lutherans made overtures to Constantinople, in the belief that a shared dislike of the papacy would be enough to enable them to form an alliance, and were surprised to be roundly rejected.[9] The distinction between "local and visible" and "universal and invisible" is an inheritance of these debates.

The real practical problem at first, as the New Testament makes clear, was to keep a jumble of only too visible local churches together in the faith. Can anyone start a new local church? The New Testament answer is evidently yes. The missionaries who converted groups of Christians across the Roman Empire were doing precisely that. But Paul's letters show that too much loyalty to the person who had converted the local community could cause problems. Apollos was a Jew from Alexandria who became an assistant to Paul at Corinth and preached with him at Ephesus before going on to Achaia. He was, it seems, a powerful and persuasive preacher, though it was suspected that he was creating not followers of Jesus but followers of John the Baptist. In any case, his grasp of the Christian gospel seems to have been incomplete. Priscilla and Aquila had to take him home and explain the difference to him (Acts 18:26).

In 1 Corinthians, Paul found himself responding to a letter from a worried community which had become divided in its personal loyalties. First Corinthians 1:10-12 describes the emergence of factions with personal loyalties, some to him, some to Apollos. This tendency to adhere to a human leader who has preached an attractive gospel reappears throughout Christian history. It is the same instinct that has led to Christians calling themselves Benedictines, Franciscans, Dominicans, Lutherans, Calvinists and Wesleyans, and which can still bind a congregation to a charismatic pastor, and blind it to what threatens to be the creation of a new sect around a figure commanding adulation.

Even if there were no such special focus of loyalty to a particular individual, in growing local churches it soon became impossible for

---

[9]E. Benz, *Die Ostkirche im Lichte der Protestantischen Geschichtsschreibung* (Frieburg: K. Alber, 1952), pp. 17-20.

the leader of the community to be pastor to so many, perhaps over a considerable geographical area. A local bishop could not lead worship every week throughout a large diocese; there would have to be smaller local worshiping communities. The bishops could not be constantly traveling to run all their parishes on a daily basis; priests were chosen to be the bishop's deputies or vicars. This, rather than forming a team of equal elders, became the preferred solution to the problems created by missionary success throughout Christendom in the first centuries.

A priest remained with his bishop in his diocese unless there was a reason to move, and then his bishop would send him to his new bishop with a letter of recommendation, testifying to his suitability and good character and stating that he had been properly ordained.

What was the church in each place? What *was* the "church in each place"? Was it a fragment or complete in itself? Was it a part of the whole or a microcosm of the macrocosm? How were these units or entities related to one another, and how could they hold together in the unity of one church? A controversy divided Europe again and again over the centuries about fixing the date of Easter. This did not appear at the time to be just an unimportant difference of dating. It seemed a church-dividing matter, fragmenting the Easter moment of commemoration of the resurrection and therefore the church.

It certainly seemed like that at one of the high points of the controversy, recorded by Bede in his *Ecclesiastical History.* At the synod called at Whitby in the north of England in 664 to discuss the domestic and political difficulties caused by a king and a queen of different persuasions celebrating Easter on different days, King Oswiu of Northumbria "began by declaring that it was fitting that those who served one God should observe one rule of life and not differ in the celebration of the heavenly sacraments, seeing that they all hoped for one kingdom in heaven." The Synod ruled against the local Ionan tradition of calculating the date of Easter, in favor of conformity to the practice of Rome.[10] The problem became controversial again in the late sixteenth century when

---

[10]Bede, *Ecclesiastical History* 3.25, ed. B. Colgrave and R. A. B. Mynors (London: Oxford University Press, 1969), p. 299.

the West moved to the Gregorian calendar decreed by Pope Gregory XIII in 1582, and the Orthodox found themselves celebrating Easter on a different day from Western Christians, as still happens.

3

THE IDEA OF FAITH

WHAT DO WE BELIEVE?
TRYING TO PUT THE FAITH IN A NUTSHELL

Centuries before the exact parameters of Scripture were officially acknowledged, the Christian community found it needed not only to reach agreement about how to make decisions together about the way to live as a community, but also to frame an agreed statement of the essentials of the faith. That need did not disappear with the emergence of the Scriptures. The Bible is neither a textbook of systematic theology nor a short guide for beginners (though as we shall see, some seventeenth-century critics thought it might be just a starting place for Christian thought, ready to be expanded).

Christians found from the earliest times that they needed approved statements (creeds) of manageable length, which new converts could study with an instructor so that they could come to an informed understanding of their new faith. *Creed* comes from the Latin *credo*, meaning "I believe." Those who were baptized would then confess—"declare their faith"—before the gathered congregation using such a formula as a sign that they shared the common faith.

The Apostles' Creed in the version it has come down to us was certainly not made up by the apostles contributing a clause each, as the old story went. The Creed probably took its present form no earlier than the seventh century. But long before it evolved into its final form in the West, a version was in use in the liturgy, and the basic structure and contents of the Creed had been acknowledged as the Christian 'rule of faith (*regula fidei*)' since the days of Ignatius of Antioch (c. 35-c. 107), Irenaeus (c. 130-c. 200), and Tertullian (c. 160-c. 225).

Credo was also *credimus* (*we* believe) when the congregation declared its faith together in worship. It was a short step from there to a different sort of creed, an official statement of orthodox views specifically designed to reject those of heretics. The earliest of these which is still in common use in worship is the Nicene Creed of 325. This was slightly amended in 381 by another council held at Constantinople.

So the Niceno-Constantinopolitan Creed was the product of formal meetings of representatives of local churches which tried to address the threat to the faith posed by the teachings of Arius (c. 260-336). He was a priest from Alexandria who had been attracting a lot of attention and interest, and who was feared to be misleading the faithful. The Council of Nicaea was called together by the emperor Constantine, the first Christian emperor. The emperor, as a layman, took no part in the debate or decision making. It met near what is now Iznik in Turkey. The emperor summoned the bishops of both Eastern and Western Christendom, each of whom was allowed to bring a retinue of two priests and three deacons, though only bishops had the right to vote. Far more seem to have come from the East than from the West, which sent only five or six; although the pope sent two legates, he did not go himself. Nevertheless, this was the first comprehensive attempt to assemble an ecumenical (world) council, and it helped to establish the principle that bishops, as leaders of their local churches, represented their people at such meetings.

The problems the Arian popular movement had created were real enough, and the church would have needed to address them officially in any case. Early Christianity had to work out its doctrinal framework in the context of a world of thought where Plato's ideas were dominant. Plato considered that a God who was so high as to be in a sense even beyond "being" was the only God worthy of worship by philosophers; and intellectuals of the late antique world, especially the Greek-speaking ones, were brought up to be philosophers. So intellectual respectability was at stake. Just as Augustine had had to write a book about the nature of the church that educated and philosophically trained Latin-speaking readers would respect, so at the Greek-speaking end of the empire, it was necessary to describe God in a way similarly educated readers could respect.

As Christianity began to attract interest in the late Roman world, it entered into a dialogue with Platonism, and Platonic forms of expression began to permeate Christian thinking. The Platonist philosophers had a conception of a divine "trinity." But in their way of thinking this was hierarchical, God being utterly transcendent, with his Word or Logos inferior to him as an intermediary between God and the cosmos. Another entity, a "Soul of the World," stood lower still in the sequence. This World Soul was able to come into contact with the material world and realize the ideas or "forms" in matter, thus bringing into being a physical world. It was therefore hard for Platonists to accept both that the Word or Son of God is truly God, just as the Father, and that at the incarnation he also truly became man. Just as with Arius's subordinationist alternative to the divinity of the Son, many alternative ways of understanding and qualifying the humanity of the Son—more like the donning of a garment or the wearing of a mask—were tried out.

The Nicene Council produced the Nicene Creed, whose great achievement was to establish both the concept and the terminology which have defined orthodox trinitarian theology ever since. In 381 a follow-up council was held at Constantinople. They agreed to slight revisions to the Nicene Creed and agreed to the form in which it is still used in worship. The essential principle established was that Christ is "of the same substance" (*homoousios*) with the Father, while having a distinct *hypostasis*, which the Latins translated as *persona*.

It had become apparent that concentration on the themes of the Arian controversy had left the definition of the Holy Spirit incomplete and his divinity uncertain. So it was emphasized that he "proceeds from the Father" and is therefore of the same being or "substance." This council also helped to establish the Christian doctrine of the Trinity as involving the three divine Persons as equally God, and not forming a hierarchy of descending levels of divinity. This idea involved debates of immense philosophical and theological sophistication and was to be challenged repeatedly in succeeding centuries.

Arianism outlasted these councils and became a political preference as much as a theological standpoint. Eventually being an Arian became partly a matter of where one lived, with some parts of Europe following an Arian tradition, and the Goths and Visigoths and Vandals, who helped bring the Roman Empire to destruction, conquering it as long-standing Arian tribes. So one of the lessons of the Nicaea experiment was the persistence of mistaken opinions among Christians, especially when they became entangled with politics.

Some big issues for the faith: One Almighty God? This first "official" statement of faith to be accepted by a council that claimed to represent the whole church certainly bears the marks of being framed to rebut heretical challenges. It emerged in times of huge conflict, and its wording reflects the battles which had been going on. But it also took account of known longstanding disputes. For example, the opening statement deals with the most fundamental question of all. Is there only one God and is he all powerful?

> I believe in one God, the Father Almighty, Maker of heaven and earth, and of all things visible and invisible.

This phrase counters the teaching of the *dualists* who had been challengers of Christianity from the very beginning. They claimed that there were two opposing primal powers in the universe, neither omnipotent. One was good and the other evil. Dualists also claimed that all material things, the physical and visible world, were the creation of a second God, the ultimate source of evil in the universe, while the good God ruled only the spiritual and invisible realm. So the framers of the wording of the creed needed to stress that there is only one God and that he made everything, matter as well as spirit. The Apostles' Creed begins with the same emphasis on the almightiness of the Father and his making of earth as well as heaven:

> I believe in God, the Father Almighty, the Maker of heaven and earth.

The first dualists, who were teaching before Christianity began, were the Gnostics. Then came the Manichees, to whom Augustine belonged for a decade in his youth. In the Middle Ages, a variety of groups known as Bogomils, Cathars, Albigensians and so on took up the dualist cause. All these tried to solve the problem of evil (how can there be evil in the world if it was made by an all-powerful and perfectly good God?) in essentially the same way.

The Nicene Creed also attempts to resolve the other long-running debate, about the *hierarchical* versus the *equal* Trinity, with its statement of belief

> in one Lord Jesus Christ, the only-begotten Son of God, begotten of the Father before all worlds; God of God, Light of Light, very God of very God; begotten, not made, being of one substance with the Father, by whom all things were made.

The emphasis on the belief that Jesus is begotten of the Father and of one substance with him, not inferior in any way, was a necessary rebuttal of Platonist assumptions. Christian orthodoxy was crystallized in the process of defining the difference, and then fixed its position in a creedal statement. The resulting Nicene definition was also sharply contemporary and topical because it addressed the very reason for the calling of the council. It was designed to refute the followers of the priest Arius (the Arian heretics) who, influenced by Platonism, seemed to be saying that Christ was not coeternal with the Father or of the same substance. The same intellectual struggle was stretching the capacity of the Greek language, as it was to do for Latin, when a new exactness was required in expressing concepts previously unheard of.

The creedal legacy. The Niceno-Constantinopolitan Creed was the product of two ecumenical councils responding to heretical controversy.[1] The Apostles' Creed is historically much more difficult to pin down, but even after it began to be realized that it was not the work of the apostles themselves but probably a Carolingian construct based on a creed used in early liturgies, it kept its place in worship. The sixth- or late-fifth-century Athanasian Creed, with its emphasis on the doctrine of the Trinity and on Christology, has also kept a toehold in the liturgies of many churches—including the Lutheran, Anglican and Roman Catho-

---

[1] J. N. D. Kelly, *Early Christian Creeds*, 3rd ed. (London: Continuum, 2006).

lic—despite or perhaps because of its unequivocal anathemas condemning those who think differently. The creeds (the Apostles' and Nicene in
particular) formed a body of foundational texts whose authenticity and
importance was not seriously questioned in the Middle Ages.

Reformers of the sixteenth century saw the creeds as profoundly reliable, sometimes as inspired texts. In his *Table Talk*, the conversations at
meals noted by John Aurifaber, which show Martin Luther (1483-1546)
at his most informal and sharp-witted, Luther is recorded as taking a
very high view of the Apostles' Creed as divinely inspired:

> I believe the words of the Apostles' Creed to be the work of the Holy
> Ghost; the Holy Spirit alone could have enunciated things so grand, in
> terms so precise, so expressive, so powerful. No human creature could
> have done it, nor all the human creatures of ten thousand worlds. This
> creed, then, should be the constant object of our most serious attention.
> For myself, I cannot too highly admire or venerate it.[2]

Calvin, born half a generation later and educated in a new Renaissance
approach to early texts, could be critical about historical origins. He perhaps saw further than Luther into the puzzle about the origin of this text.
He was aware of some of its ancestry in early liturgy. In discussing the
statement that Christ "descended into hell," he comments that "it appears
from the ancient writers that this phrase which we read in the Creed was
once not so much used in the churches."

He balances this difficulty against what to him is a far more important certainty:

> But it matters little by whom or at what time this clause was inserted.
> Rather, the noteworthy point about the Creed is this: we have in it a sum-
> mary of our faith, full and complete in all details; and containing nothing
> in it except what has been derived from the pure Word of God.[3]

The enduring value of the creeds for the Reformers lay in their brev-
ity and comprehensiveness. They were of a sufficiently small compass to
be committed easily to memory. They could become familiar through
use in worship. They could form a basis for catechetical instruction.

---

[2]Luther, *Table Talk*, 264.
[3]Calvin, *Institutes*, 2.16.8.

ONE FAITH AND DIFFERENT RITES

Where was the line to be drawn between *faith* and *rites?* It was never disputed that the faith was one (Eph 4:5), and all Christians everywhere should hold the same faith, though there was often disagreement about what that faith essentially included. Sometimes groups of Christians, particularly in the Reformation, claimed that they alone had the true faith, but they still held to the principle that Christianity was a single faith. It was not suggested that other communities could differ on these essential points without being heretics.

On the other hand, most Christians did not insist that all communities follow exactly the same pattern of worship. Rites or ceremonies could to some extent legitimately vary, said the councils and synods of the early church. First Corinthians 8:8-9, where Paul speaks of the conditional freedom Christians have not to adhere strictly to the dietary restrictions of the Old Testament, provided a scriptural warrant. In fact the proper scope of ritual variety was a more frequent preoccupation than matters of faith.

In the Reformation the possibility was canvassed that some things are indifferent, *adiaphora*.[4] This was not taken to mean that they did not matter, but that holding a particular view or following a particular practice beyond the essentials of the faith was not in itself a condition of salvation. The basis of this apparent permissiveness in the later Middle Ages and the Reformation was something relatively new. It rested on claims that the institutional church had been adding unnecessary requirements and burdening the faithful with the fear that in order to be saved they must comply with mere "human impositions," which is what John Wyclif (c. 1330-1384) called many of the ritual and ceremonial requirements of the late medieval church.

Luther wholeheartedly agreed. The debate about ceremonies concentrated the anger of Reformers of many colors about the human impositions of which the Church stood accused at the end of the Middle Ages. These Martin Luther had considered oppressive and

---

[4]See Bernard J. Verkamp, *The Indifferent Mean: Adiaphorism in the English Reformation to 1554* (Athens: Ohio University Press, 1977).

likely to "terrify the consciences" of the faithful. Lutherans debated the point energetically. The Augsburg Confession says that "it is not necessary for human traditions, that is, rites and ceremonies, to be everywhere alike."

The legitimate variability of rites, "traditions and ceremonies" is also asserted in Article 34 of the Thirty-Nine Articles of the Church of England. But it could also be claimed there that deeper matters of good order are involved. For "he that offendeth against the common order *of* the Church, and hurteth the authority of the Magistrate, and woundeth the consciences *of* the weak brethren" is in breach of good order because he harms others. Each "particular or national Church" is held to have "authority to ordain its own rites" as well as "authority to ordain, change, and abolish, ceremonies or rites of the Church ordained only by man's authority, so that all things be done to edifying."

Of ceremonies, thought the sixteenth century Church of England, "some are good although man-made as well for a decent order in the Church . . . as because they pertain to edification." The principle to be followed is to find a middle way between those who "think it a great matter of conscience to depart from . . . their old customs" to which they are "addicted" and those who are "so new-fangled, that they would innovate all things, and so do despise the old, that nothing can like them but that [which is] is new." "And besides this, Christ's gospel is not a ceremonial law, as much of Moses' law was, but it is a religion to serve God, . . . in the freedom of spirit."[5] There were important related dimensions such as the old question whether Christians were still obliged to obey the law of Moses, the point raised in the text about freedom to eat, from 1 Corinthians 8. Article seven of the Thirty-Nine Articles tackles the question whether the Old Testament's ritual requirements should still be binding on modern Christians. "The Old Testament is not contrary to the New" is the starting-point. Then the article makes a distinction between "Ceremonies and Rites," which "do not bind Christian men," the "Civil precepts," which "ought of necessity to be received in any commonwealth," and the "Commandments which are called Moral,"

---

[5]Book of Common Prayer, 1559, ed. John E. Booty (Charlottesville: University of Virginia Press, 1976), pp. 18-19.

which are deemed still to be binding. In this discussion, the controversy at issue is one we shall meet throughout this book—whether the church can make human impositions a requirement for the faithful.

In the end, when Elizabethan England was consumed by debates about the wearing of clerical vestments, Richard Hooker complained in some exasperation that the whole question was taking up so much time and energy that it was distracting theologians from more important matters: "This unhappie controversie, about the received ceremonies and discipline of the Church of England, which hath so long time withdrawne so many of her Ministers from their principall worke, and imployed their studies in contentious oppositions."[6]

Those Protestant communities that retained the basic liturgical patterns of worship, notably the Lutherans and the Anglicans, and particularly for the celebration of the Eucharist, tended to adopt and carefully modify their practices for orthodoxy, as they held it. The wording which was traditional in the now quite localized patterns of worship of the Western Middle Ages, they retained in differing sequence, key stages or episodes, such as the ministry of the Word, confession and general absolution, the recitation of the creed, prayer, the thanksgiving, the consecration of the bread and wine, the receiving of the consecrated elements by the individual. There seems to have been little in this process which was felt to require a comprehensive study of the development of rites in the Eastern Church.

Calvin and other Reformers similarly minded preferred to dispense with much of this inherited detail. In worship at Strasburg or Geneva there would be confession and general absolution or a statement of God's forgiveness at the beginning; and there would be reading from Scripture, preaching, prayer and intercession, singing of psalms and use of the creed, with considerable variation of order allowed.

[6]Hooker, *Laws*, 1:346.

4

WHERE WAS THE BIBLE?

ADDING TO THE OLD TESTAMENT

When the Christian faith began to spread, it was obvious at once that it was not going to be easy to maintain unity of faith in an enormous empire where the fastest means of transport was still the horse. And in the first Christian centuries it was not possible simply to turn to the Bible as it would come to be known. As yet the Bible was a series of separate books. It was not even universally agreed which books were parts of the Bible and which were not, although only a few of the writings that came to be received as canonical were ever widely debated. It was not practical to expect local church communities—let alone individuals—to own copies even of those. Copies would have been far too costly.[1]

The creation of an agreed "canon" or authoritative list of the Old Testament texts took place within Judaism over several centuries, ending as late as the second century A.D. Even then it does not seem to have been regarded by all as fixed. Communities such as the Samaritans and the Sadducees had their own independent views of the acceptability (or not) of particular texts. Although we know from Acts that there were controversies at the very beginning about the status of the Old Testament's rules for living, the Christians and their satellites are not recorded as having begun the task of determining the precise limits of

---

[1] For example, Augustine says he was converted to Christianity when he was prompted by a child singing in a neighboring garden to "take up and read," not a copy of the entire Bible, but the copy of Romans he had in hand, when he fell upon the passage, "Let us walk honestly . . . not in chambering nor in wantonness." Augustine, *Confessions* 8.12.29, referencing Rom 13:13.

which were to be their own sacred books until the second century. Then, about 140, Marcion (c. 85-c. 160), the son of the bishop of Sinope on the Black Sea, and a wealthy contributor to Christian funds, suggested making a list. He wanted to include some letters of Paul and portions of what became Luke's Gospel, but he rejected the Gospel of Matthew and the Gospel of John. He also took a stand against the Old Testament, which he seems to have claimed to be the book of an inferior God, the God of justice and punishment portrayed there, in contrast with the book of the supreme God of the Christians, whose gospel Christ had come to earth to bring his people. This was not quite full dualism, but it was possibly Marcion who introduced the germ of an idea which became familiar in later centuries, that the Old Testament tells of the evil God, the God who made the material world, while the New Testament is the book of the good God, the God of spirit.

Marcion was roundly rejected as a heretic in 144 at a hearing in Rome, but seeds had been sown. The Christian community as a whole began to realize that deciding which books to approve formally as God's Word and which to reject was a matter of some importance. It was agreed that the Old Testament in the Greek version known as the Septuagint should be adopted. For what was to become the New Testament, some Pauline epistles were already circulating in collections before the end of the first century, and Gospels which were understood to preserve the memories of Jesus' disciples are mentioned in the early second century.

Origen (185-254) was the first leading authority to draw up a working list of all the books now found in the New Testament, except for the epistles of James, 2 Peter and 2–3 John. He also included writings which it was eventually agreed ought to be left out, notably the *Shepherd* of Hermas, a second-century collection of visions, instructions and parables urging Christians to defend the purity and integrity of the church.

It was not until the empire became officially "Christian" with the conversion of Emperor Constantine early in the fourth century that the task of deciding the boundaries of the New Testament came close to completion. In 367 Athanasius (c. 296-373), bishop of Alexandria, included a list in his Easter letter which includes all the books now in the New Testament canon. His list for the Old Testament, however, did not quite match. He included the book of Baruch and the Letter of Jere-miah, but he left out Esther. In 382 Pope Damasus issued a list at a council of Rome. In 393 a synod held at Hippo in North Africa, where Augustine was now bishop, formally approved the content of the mod-ern New Testament and the Septuagint. The decision was ratified by Councils of Carthage in 397 and 419. In 405 a later pope, Innocent I, sent a list of canonical books to the bishop of Toulouse. In Augustine's time the Scriptures were still copied in separate books and not by any means always bound as a single volume, so listing of books could be a practical help to those forming a collection of canonically accepted texts. The only substantial difference between the list now becoming accepted in the Latin-speaking West and that of the Greek-speaking East was whether or not to include the book of Revelation. By the fifth century that seems to have won acceptance in the East as it had long before in the West.

This fourth- and fifth-century discussion is an important historical witness to the complexity of the relationship between the writing of the books of the Bible and their approval and acceptance by the community of Christians under the guidance of the Holy Spirit, during the forming of the canon of the Scriptures in the first Christian centuries.

What recommended the writings included in the canon of Scripture? Con-sidering the underlying principles of canonicity, Augustine advises the reader to rely on the "authority" of as many "catholic churches" as pos-sible. Those local (that is, diocesan or provincial) churches which con-sider themselves to be in unity with the whole church are "catholic." Best of all for reliability are the opinions of those churches which are known to have received "apostolic letters"—letters from Paul or Peter or James—or were apostolic sees.[2]

This is a different approach from asking what evidence there is that a given writing was inspired by God. What understanding of the idea of divine inspiration did the early church hold? The idea was certainly in the mind of Jerome (c. 345-420), for he said he did not consider himself inspired when he made the Latin translation that became the Vulgate

---

[2] Augustine, *De doctrina Christiana* 2.8.12.24, ed. and trans. R. P. H. Green (London: Oxford Uni-versity Press, 1995), p. 66.

and replaced the many versions of the Old Latin translation for general use in the West. A standard way of depicting the Evangelists in medieval iconography was to show the Gospel-writer writing his Gospel with a dove speaking into his ear (compare Acts 4:25).

This patristic conception of inspiration as a form of divine whispering in the ear, a direct implanting in the human author's mind of the exact words to be written down as the Word of God, remained strong. It outlasted the Middle Ages. It still seemed appropriate to Zwingli in the sixteenth century. But meanwhile there had been a growing recognition of the fact that Scripture also had human authors, and their role could be complex and even uncertain. A favorite medieval example was the prophet Amos's statement "I am no prophet" in Amos 7:14. Did he mean that he was not always prophesying but sometimes just talking about ordinary things as other human beings did? If so, did he himself know when what he said was God's word, not his own? And how were his listeners to tell the difference?[3] Reformation scholars were highly conscious of such difficulties, as we shall see.

The patristic period and the earlier Middle Ages had seen the evolution of a loose hierarchy of authoritative texts. Jerome, in his *De viris illustribus,* had begun to draw up the list, and Gennadius of Marseilles (fl. 470) had continued it, with a tradition of such list making continuing through the Middle Ages, growing steadily longer as more recent authors were added. This process perhaps helped to crystallize the understanding which eventually became defined that there had been a special period during which God had continued to speak directly to certain human authors of the texts which became the Scriptures. This had come to an end, and the early Christian writers such as Augustine and Gregory the Great, although they were felt to have authority, were not inspired in the same way.

Medieval academe gave considerable thought to the role of the human authors of Scripture—Moses (who was believed to be the author of the first five books of the Old Testament), the prophets, the Gospel writers and the authors of the New Testament epistles—and to

---

[3]J. P. Torrell, *Théorie de la prophétie et philosophie de la connaissance aux environs de 1230,* Etudes et Documents 40 (Louvain: Spicilegium Sacrum Lovaniense, 1977).

trying to distinguish the ways in which God spoke through them.[4] A sophisticated, many-layered understanding emerged. Nicholas of Cusa (1401-1464), for example, notes that when the author of the letter to the Hebrews acknowledges that "God spoke through the prophets in many ways" (*Multifarie multisque modis olim Deus loquens patribus in prophetis* [Heb 1:1-2]), he was seeking to open the Scriptures (*aperire scripturas*) and prove (*probat*) that Christ is the Son of God.[5]

Such guiding principles were going to be important when it came to the Reformation debates about whether Scripture had a unique authority, and thus whether any equally authoritative text could be created by the church or by any individual with prophetic visions (or delusions).

Reformation debates about the canon of Scripture. The canon question settled down during the Middle Ages, largely no doubt because the completion of the Vulgate provided a fixed and accepted Latin version. But some of the sixteenth-century Reformers raised it again. Martin Luther included in one of his attempts to put down Johannes Eck a robust dismissal of 2 Maccabees, on the grounds that this and other apocryphal books were not cited by the New Testament writers as other Old Testament books were. But Luther also argued that certain books which seemed to counter the doctrines that God justified only through faith (*sola fide*) and that only Scripture was a reliable source of teaching for the Christian (*sola scriptura*) could not be canonical. He originally tried to get Hebrews, the epistle of James as well as Jude and Revelation removed from the canon. He did not succeed, but in Luther's German translation of the Bible these books still come last.

The Reformers, including Zwingli and Calvin, continued to reject the apocryphal books; Protestant Bibles have omitted them. And Zwingli, like Luther, was uncertain about the inclusion of Revelation. Such reopening of these old questions may have been a factor in prompt-

---

[4]On medieval exegesis see Beryl Smalley, *The Study of the Bible in the Middle Ages*, 3rd. ed. (Oxford: Basil Blackwell, 1983); H. de Lubac, *Exégèse médiévale* (Paris: Aubier-Montaigne, 1959); and G. R. Evans, *The Language and Logic of the Bible*, 2 vols. (Cambridge: Cambridge University Press, 1984-1985).

[5]Nicholas of Cusa, "Sermo 258," *Sermones* 4 (1455-1463), ed. H. D. Reimann, H. Schwaetzer and F. B. Stammkötter (Hamburg: Meiner, 2005), p. 377. Nicholas, like the great majority of premodern exegetes, attributed Hebrews to Paul.

ing the Council of Trent to list the apocryphal books explicitly among the canonical books of the Bible.

Part of the problem was the difficulty of establishing common ground as to what constituted proof or authority when it came to defining the canon. For Rome the answer was straightforward: the Church had decided. In book 1.7 of the *Institutes of Christian Religion*, however, Calvin asserts that the authenticity of Scripture is attested by the Holy Spirit and not fundamentally by a formal act of recognition by the institutional church. This almost amounts to arguing that Scripture is self-authenticating, its own witness.

CREATING A STANDARD TEXT OF THE BIBLE FOR USE IN THE WEST

The version of the Bible used almost exclusively in the West from the fifth century to the sixteenth was the Vulgate (meaning "common" or "standard") translation of Jerome. The Vulgate was not meant to present a barrier to understanding for ordinary Christians, quite the opposite. It was the vernacular translation of its day, made for a Latin-speaking population.

When Jerome made this translation it was urgently needed for two reasons. The first was that the Roman Empire was beginning to decay and split into two parts, the Greek-speaking East and the Latin-speaking West. The Greek in which the New Testament and the Septuagint version of the Old Testament had been written was no longer easily understood in the West. Even in Augustine's youth, boys had been expected to learn Greek, though he complains that he never really mastered it. The second reason was that a confusing variety of independent translations into Latin had been made (known as the Old Latin versions). Jerome seemed the ideal choice as a translator because he had studied Hebrew as well as Greek, and he was commissioned by Pope Damasus I in 382 to produce a new, single, reliable translation.

The concept of "inspiration" was already important when Jerome made his translation. He was confident that the Bible was the Word of God. But as we have seen, when he asked himself whether his translation was *itself* inspired, he said he thought not. He did not have a sense that the Holy Spirit had dictated to him word by word as he worked at the translation. That did not prevent students of the Bible in succeeding centuries from treating the Vulgate as though it was directly inspired, for this was "the Bible" as they knew it, and endless effort was put into discussing the finest points of detail of Jerome's wording.

Latin and the emergence of new vernaculars. As the "barbarians" took over the decaying Roman Empire, knowledge of Latin diminished in Western Europe, except among the educated. In much of the old empire Latin decayed and developed over the centuries into the Romance languages of today, producing Italian, Spanish, Portuguese, French, Romanian and (in part, and with a large contribution from French) modern English. Elsewhere the Teutonic or Germanic languages became dominant, as in Anglo-Saxon England.

At the same time, Latin itself remained a living language. Knowledge of Latin did not disappear. During the same centuries, up to the sixteenth century and beyond, it was still developing and maturing into a stylish vehicle of expression of sophisticated Christian thought.[6]

But it became a learned language used only by monks and clerics. From the sixth century Latin speakers were mainly the monks and nuns who spent their lives in prayers and reading. The study of the Bible had always been central in medieval theology. But the formal study of theology was now to be confined for centuries to a small clerical class, and once universities were invented at the end of the twelfth century, it became even more the special prerogative of a highly educated specialist class of scholars engaged in advanced and sophisticated studies.

In an earlier era when the three "biblical languages" were in active use, Augustine already understood the need to take careful note of linguistic differences in studying the text of the Bible: "Users of the Latin language ... need two others, Hebrew and Greek, for an understanding of the divine scriptures, so that recourse may be had to the original versions if any uncertainty arises from the infinite variety of Latin translators."[7]

---

[6]Christine Mohrmann, *Mélanges* (Utrecht: Het Spectrum, 1973).
[7]Augustine, *De doctrina Christiana* 2.11.16.34.

With this in mind, Augustine discusses the principles on which authorities in different languages are to be compared with one another. "To correct any Latin manuscripts, Greek ones should be used and among these the Septuagint is supreme when it comes to the Old Testament." Whether it is true that each of the seventy worked independently in a separate cell and all their versions agreed, or whether they discussed and collaborated, as Augustine clearly believes, he takes this version to be the result of a divine dispensation. He stresses that very literal (word-for-word, *de verbo ad verbum*) translations may be of value when trying to explain a passage.[8]

All this notwithstanding, "there are certain words in particular languages which just cannot be translated into the idioms of another language" and "translators often meet not only individual words but also whole phrases which simply cannot be expressed in the idioms of the Latin language, at least not if one wants to maintain the usage of ancient speakers of Latin."[9] Translation had in some earlier periods involved a painstaking word-for-word approach, though it was well enough understood that that was not guaranteed to work as a method of conveying the sense. In the expanding university syllabus the emphasis remained upon learned languages and their differences, although pragmatically speaking there was at least as much need to think about the ground rules for making the numerous translations of the Bible into the vernacular which were underway from the fifteenth century (and in pockets, earlier).

There was a further complex of considerations here. *Translation, paraphrase* and *interpretation* are closely connected in Latin, conveying as a group every nuance of the process of turning a passage from one language into another, including the use of modes of speech (*modi loquendi*) within a single language. The Latin *interpres* means both "translator" and "interpreter." When Jerome made the new translation of the Bible into Latin, which became the Vulgate, he described himself as *interpres*. Jerome acknowledges in his *Commentary on the Pauline Epistles* that a passage which is clear in the Greek may become obscure if it is translated

---

[8]Ibid., 2.15.22.53.
[9]Ibid., 2.11.16.35; 2.13.19.44.

into Latin *de verbo ad verbum*, that is by simply substituting a word in the first language by a word in the other.[10] A "translator" must embrace a wider spectrum and not only find the most appropriate counterpart words between languages or modes of speaking, but also try to place them in the juxtapositions and contexts that will best assist speakers of the second language to understand what the words in the first language really mean. From the moment a word gets into a sentence it has what medieval logicians called a "supposition," that is, a particular coloring which it takes from that specific use in context.

THE MINISTRY OF THE WORD
IN THE EARLY CHURCH

The Bible has always had its place in worship, both in "readings" and in exposition by the minister, who might talk to the congregation to explain the readings and draw attention to particular lessons to be drawn from the Lessons. But read aloud in Latin portions, the Bible had a limited role in teaching the medieval laity about their faith. And sermons became rarities in ordinary parish churches in the Middle Ages. In any case, those too would normally be in Latin, though some late medieval sermons were "macaronic," in a mixture of Latin and the vernacular. Bible stories in pictures were often provided on the walls of medieval churches for the congregation to use as visual aids to help them learn the Christian story and the message of the gospel.

This simplified and rather homely medieval ministry of the Word with occasional homilies contrasts with the sophisticated preaching that evolved during the early Christian centuries, before the fall of the Roman Empire brought down with it much of the culture of antiquity. At the end of antiquity one of the most important duties of a bishop was to preach on the Bible. As bishop of Hippo, Augustine would preach lengthy sermons to rapt congregations in which—in a serial, sermon after sermon—he would comment on a selected book of Scripture (for example, St. John's Gospel or the Psalms).

---

[10]Jerome, *Commentary on the Pauline Epistles*, PL 26.534; *Letters to Pammachius* 57, PL 22.568-79; and see *Commentarius in Ecclesiasten* 8.6, CCSL 72, p. 316.

He must have done this rather well to command such audiences. But then he was a professional orator. In Augustine's generation and before, rhetoric was the high point of the education of the leaders of society. The study of grammar, literature, logic and even philosophy were all designed to ensure that an educated man could argue a case persuasively and elegantly. Augustine discussed an aspect of the use of rhetorical skills in book 4 of *On Christian Learning* (*De doctrina Christiana*). God uses different figures and styles in the Bible. Do not feel that as a Christian you must avoid the use of rhetorical skills, he says (4.2.3.4). If you do, you will give the devil all the best tunes and confine yourself to dull and uninviting language. Those with the skill should not hesitate to use their knowledge of rhetoric either to help them identify the stylistic devices the Bible uses in order to understand it better, or to aid in their own preaching and teaching.[11]

Rhetoric was understood to be the "art of persuasion," because it involved framing an argument in such a way as to exhort or encourage listeners. Preachers needed to do that if they were to bring their hearers to live better Christian lives. But complex rules emerged about how best to achieve it. In the *De doctrina Christiana*, Augustine tackled several questions which were urgent in his time but which turned out to be important later too. In his discussion of the use of stylistic devices, for example, he licensed the energetic technical explorations of many succeeding centuries.[12] The influence of Augustine remained huge throughout the Middle Ages in the West, long after these rhetorical studies had ceased to be the usual equipment of every educated man. In the modest surviving collection of popular medieval sermons, the print of Augustine's theories is still visible.

In North Africa, Augustine found he had to deal with highly edu-

---

[11]Rhetoric became one of the neglected areas of study after the fall of the Roman Empire because it removed most of the need for rhetorical skills throughout much of Europe. There was no emperor to flatter with sophisticated speeches, no courts requiring forensic oratory, none of the old-style politics.

[12]In the Middle Ages grammatical studies overlapped not only with logic but also with rhetoric when it came to the use of figurative language. For the study of "figures of speech" and "figures of thought" the first medieval universities had the *Rhetorica ad Herennium*, which was mistakenly believed to be the work of Cicero and was normally paired with his *De inventione* as a set book for the course. See p. 157.

cated exiles from Italy, who were running from the threat of the barbarian invasions which were progressively destroying the empire. One of
the key events, the sack of Rome by Alaric the Visigoth and his armies
in 410, fell in Augustine's lifetime. It was seen as symbolic, and it was
also an indication that the device of meeting the invaders on their terms
and allowing them pieces of the empire, which had been used by Rome's
administrators, was not working.

These angry intellectuals-in-exile pointed indignantly to the fact that
this collapse had begun only after the emperor Constantine had declared
himself a Christian in 312. They said they had read the Christian Scriptures and thought them badly written and naive. Augustine had felt the
same as an arrogant young student, preparing to be a professor of rhetoric
in Carthage and later in Italy, in Milan. He admits as much in his *Confessions*. "It seemed to me unworthy in comparison with the dignity [*digni-
tas*] of Cicero," he writes. "My arrogance recoiled from its modesty
(*modum eius*) and my sharp wits did not penetrate to its inwardness" (3,
v. 9). So he wrote the *De doctrina Christiana* to discuss the literary claims
of the Scriptures and the ways in which rhetorical knowledge ought to be
used in connection with reading and preaching. This book was immensely
influential and important in the centuries which followed, not only because it asked some of the most demanding questions of the age but also
because it included a first attempt to work out how many ways there
might be to interpret a particular passage of Scripture.

FINDING MANY MEANINGS IN SCRIPTURE

Can a given passage in the Bible have more than one meaning? No sophisticated educated reader of Augustine's time could fail to be aware
that language is used in many ways which go beyond the making of
plain statements. It was by no means a new idea that some passages of
Scripture were meant to be taken figuratively. An obvious example is
Jesus' parables. When Jesus told the parable of the sower, he did not
mean his listeners to believe that he was describing a real sower of real
seeds. He was telling a story, a story with a message, so the "literal"
meaning of the story was the message, not what the narrative related.

This question about the literalness of what seems clearly to be intended figuratively was recognized down the centuries. Luther commented on it too:

> Dr. Luther was asked whether the history of the rich man and Lazarus was a parable or a natural fact? He replied: The earlier part of the story is evidently historical; the persons, the circumstances, the existence of the five brothers, all this is given in detail. The reference to Abraham is allegorical, and highly worthy of observation. We learn from it that there are abodes unknown to us, where the souls of men are; secrets into which we must not inquire. No mention is made of Lazarus' grave; whence we may judge, that in God's eyes, the soul occupies far more place than the body. Abraham's bosom is the promise and assurance of salvation, and the expectation of Jesus Christ; not heaven itself, but the expectation of heaven.[13]

But what were the rules? Here Augustine faced a difficulty because in his time the solutions known to his successors remained to be devised. The most useful recent book about the interpretation of the Bible had been written by Tyconius. Tyconius was a fourth-century Donatist.

Despite the discomfort of using the ideas of a schismatic (and Augustine believed that schism was the worst form of heresy, so he considered that Tyconius was a heretic as well as a schismatic), in book 3 of the *De doctrina Christiana* Augustine sets out the rules of Tyconius the Donatist by which the text of Scripture is to be searched for literal and figurative interpretation according to established principles. He makes some modifications[14] but essentially he gives Tyconius's seven rules for reading puzzling passages of Scripture because he thinks they are useful.[15] They are far from clear and represent a relatively primitive attempt to resolve the question. For example, the relationship of Christ and church is that of head and body. Sometimes the Bible speaks of the head meaning the body and vice versa. In the visible church on earth as Augustine believed, "wheat and weeds" grow together until harvest (Mt 13:30). So sometimes the Bible speaks of the church in a way which

---

[13]Luther, *Table Talk* 29.
[14]Robert A. Kugler, "Tyconius's Mystic Rules and the Rules of Augustine," in *Augustine and the Bible*, ed. Pamela Bright (Notre Dame, Ind.: University of Notre Dame Press, 1999), p. 142.
[15]Augustine, *De Doctrina Christiana* 3.32.45.100.

sounds inaccurate unless that is remembered. Although Tyconius's rules as discussed by Augustine are formidably difficult to grasp and to apply, they went on being taken seriously, for example by Hugh of St. Victor (1096-1142) in the twelfth century.[16]

Much of book 2 of Augustine's *De doctrina Christiana* is concerned with the need to understand the words Scripture uses so as not to miss the subtler implications and figurative senses which Augustine the rhetorician is confident are to be found there. His training had taught him that language works on the understanding in complex ways. In book 3 Augustine encourages the student to apply himself to discussing and resolving the ambiguities in Scripture (*discutienda atque solvenda*), equipping himself with a knowledge of languages, using reliable texts based on the manuscripts and an awareness that sometimes there may even be a need for emendation.[17] He is to look to punctuation and to try reading aloud, for example to test the length of the syllables, and some ambiguities will disappear in that way.[18] The reader should keep very close to the words of the text and look constantly for the lessons to be learned from reading those words as applying figuratively to something more than their surface appearance suggests.

> The words, "I slept, and took rest; and rose, for the Lord will take me up," lead us to believe that this Psalm is to be understood as in the Person of Christ; for they sound more applicable to the Passion and Resurrection of our Lord, than to that history in which David's flight is described from the face of his rebellious son. And, since it is written of Christ's disciples, "The sons of the bridegroom fast not as long as the bridegroom is with them" [Mt 9:15] it is no wonder if by his undutiful son be here meant that undutiful disciple who betrayed Him.[19]

For Augustine the most important feature of figurative language is that it is surprising. It departs from the expected meaning (e.g., from "lion" as a beast to Christ as "Lion of Judah"), though it must be said,

---

[16]See Hugh of St. Victor, *Didascalicon*, ed. C. Buttimer (Washington, D.C.: Catholic University Press, 1939).

[17]Augustine, *De doctrina Christiana* 3.1.1.1.

[18]Ibid., 3.2.5.9.

[19]Augustine, *Homilies on the Psalms* 3, CCSL 38, pp. 9-10, www.ccel.org/ccel/schaff/npnf108 .ii.III_1.html.

always in accord with the rule of faith. The Latin *translatio* was used in ancient rhetoric for the "transference" or sideways movement from the literal to a figurative or metaphorical meaning of a term or expression. In the European languages that derive from Latin, the tendency has been for such shifts of meaning to move from the concrete to the abstract, though it took until the twelfth century for *abstractio* to progress from meaning an actual "taking away" to the taking of an idea into one's head involved in abstract thought. Augustine was not yet tackling this in quite such a technical way, but he was clearly grappling with the main question whether a word or phrase in Scripture may mean something beyond what it seems to say on the surface.

Psalm 3:7 speaks of "the teeth of the wicked." On the presumption that the Bible's words are all true and if properly understood never in conflict or contradiction with one another, Augustine proposes a number of interpretations, cross-referring to other passages. One meaning, he suggests, is that the teeth are the "chiefs" of sinners. These teeth are in opposition to the church's teeth, or leaders. With these teeth Peter was told to eat the animals that had been sacrificed, and in doing so he killed that in the Gentiles which made them what they were and incorporated them into what he himself was, the "rock" on which the church was founded. These teeth are mentioned again in Song of Songs 4:2; 6:6, where, Augustine suggests, the passage "thy teeth are as a flock of shorn sheep, coming up from the bath, whereof every one beareth twins and there is not one barren among them" has many further meanings. It has more to tell us about than shorn sheep and their teeth.[20] These "shorn sheep" have put away their earthly cares and they come up from the waters of baptism (the "bath"), in which their sins are washed away, to fulfill the "twin" commandments on which Jesus said "hang all the law and the prophets" (Mt 22:40). That is to say they are not "barren" if they love God and their neighbors.

Augustine's minutely close scrutiny of the text is apparent everywhere. His rhetorical training takes him to "modes of speaking" (*modi loquendi*) in the Bible, taking the Latin text as though it were the original and

---

[20]Ibid., p. 11.

inspired text. Though Jerome insisted that he did not regard himself as inspired in making his translation, that did not prevent generations of readers in succeeding centuries weighing every word exactly as they would have done if the words they were reading had been dictated by God in Latin.

Gregory the Great identifies the four senses. The real achievement in creating a system of interpretation for the West that was practical and easy to use is that of Gregory the Great (c. 540-604). Clement of Alexandria (c. 150-c. 215) was well ahead of him in identifying four, but he wrote in Greek and for many centuries his direct influence in the West was slight. Gregory said that Scripture has, first and foremost, a *literal* sense (sometimes described as the historical sense). The events described actually happened. But not every passage can be read in that way, and from an early stage some interpreters thought it possible that certain passages had no literal sense, for they appeared, if taken literally, to present an unacceptable face or behavior of God.

Gregory also identified three "spiritual" senses, the *tropological*, the *anagogical* and the *allegorical*. The tropological was the moral sense. If a passage of Scripture deals with the way to live a good Christian life, it is to be read in a moral sense. The anagogical was the prophetic sense. Some books of the Bible, such as Daniel and Revelation, were clearly books of prophecy. The allegorical transferred or shifted the literal meaning. For example, where Christ is called the Lion of Judah (Gen 49:9) the reader is not expected to think Jesus was an actual lion. The characteristics of a real lion are transferred to Christ to arrive at the meaning of the expression. Allegory includes metaphor, simile and other figurative expressions. Gregory taught that a single passage often has more than one level of meaning.[21] The underlying idea was that any meaning which was consistent with the passage and the rest of Scripture, and was in accordance with the faith, was a true meaning, for it could be taken as certain that it had been put there by God. No human reader could possibly think of anything that God had not thought of first.

---

[21]Henri de Lubac, *Exégèse médiévale*, 2 vols. (Paris: Aubier-Montaigne, 1959-1964); G. R. Evans, *Language and Logic of the Bible: The Early Middle Ages* (Cambridge: Cambridge University Press, 1983).

Gregory continued the tradition of preaching serial sermons on whole books of the Bible (such as Ezekiel—on which he preached with the barbarians once more at the gates of Rome),[22] and writing an intimate commentary searching out the moral lessons of the book of Job, which he shared with the monks in his community. He describes in his dedicatory epistle how beneficial he found it to enter monastic life and spend time with the brothers, while he was living in Constantinople on imperial public business, "in a sea of secular matters" (and incidentally failing to improve his Greek). They asked him to expound the book of Job for them in all its senses, but especially the moral sense. This was pioneering work, "for noone had commented on it fully before" and he found the stimulus of his brothers' interest essential.

The dedicatory letter also tells us something about Gregory's working methods. He dictated his commentary and revised it at his leisure, paying attention to points of style. But he found toward the end that his "brothers" raised so many points and made him digress so much that he was not able to maintain this discipline throughout. So this evidently became a collaborative effort, a sort of seminar on Job as Bible study session at home in the monastery rather than a sermon from a public pulpit.[23]

Gregory begins with general questions about the book of Job. Who wrote it? Could it have been Moses? What was its date? What historical reference points are there? But for Gregory these questions were not ultimately what mattered. The Holy Spirit is the author. He dictated to whatever human author wrote it down. The distinction came naturally in late antiquity, especially to someone who had been a senior civil servant. If, he says, we read a letter from "some great man," we do not ask what scribe actually wrote the letter or what kind of pen he used. We attribute what we read to the great man, not his secretary (compare Rom 16:22).

He, like Augustine, seeks to explain the "behaviors" of Scripture by wider reference to its customs of expression. It is true that we read "Job

---

[22]Gregory the Great, *Homilies on Ezekiel*, CCSL 142 (1971), p. 3.
[23]Gregory the Great, *Moralia in Job*, ed. M. Adraien, CCSL 143, 143A, 143B (1979), www.lectionary central.com/GregoryMoraliaIndex.html.

said" in the third person, which might seem to suggest that Job did not write the book of Job himself, but we find the same convention in Numbers (believed to be the work of Moses) in such passages as "Now the man Moses was very humble" (Num 12:3). Similarly, the movement between authorial statements by God and authorial statements by human authors of Scripture should not worry us. A reader in church may read the passage from Exodus, "I am the God of Abraham, the God of Isaac, and the God of Jacob," but we do not therefore confuse the reader with God.

In the *Moralia* Gregory deals first with the literal, then with the allegorical and finally with the moral sense. Without abandoning the "historical truth," he claims, we are free to follow out the spiritual implications of what our ears receive in a "bodily" way. So, just as Job really had seven thousand sheep, so we have seven thousand spiritual sheep when we "feed" on innocent thoughts in our hearts.[24] Gregory also poses in his preface the great question raised by the book of Job. Why do bad things happen to good people? Job was humble, hospitable, generous. The answer is that God tested him in order to increase his merits.[25] This is the great "moral" question.

Some later scholars teaching in the medieval universities took these three figurative senses to be far older, going back even to apostolic times. It was the belief of the leading Dominican, Thomas Aquinas (1225-1274), that the four senses of Scripture, the literal and the three spiritual or figurative ones, had been in use since the time of the apostle Paul.

In his *Summa Theologiae* (completed 1274), Thomas appeals to Hebrews 10:1 in support of the contention that the *sensus spiritualis trifaria* goes back so far.[26] He cites Gregory the Great's claim that when Scripture says something, it not only says what it seems to say but also hints at a mystery. God the Word is the author of language, so he can make

---

[24]Ibid., bk. 1.15.21, CCSL 143, pp. 34-35, www.lectionarycentral.com/GregoryMoralia/Book01 .html#moral.

[25]Ibid., pref., 3.7, 143, pp. 12-13, www.lectionarycentral.com/GregoryMoralia/Preface.html.

[26]Aquinas, *Summa Theologiae*, 1a q. 1 a. 10. "Since the law has only a shadow of the good things to come and not the true form of these realities, it can never, by the same sacrifices that are continually offered year after year, make perfect those who approach (Heb 10:1)." The *Summa Theologiae* is available in numerous Latin and English editions, in print and online.

words means what he chooses, and he can make one word point to another. Thus in the literal sense a word may have its obvious meaning, but the same word may have other *kinds* of meaning. An Old Testament expression may signify something in the New Testament. Aquinas gives the example of Moses hitting a rock, from which water flows. This was an actual rock but it also signifies allegorically that Jesus is the source of living water (as Paul himself interpreted it in 1 Cor 10:4). When Jesus told his listeners that whoever was without sin might throw stones at the woman taken in adultery (Jn 7:53–8:11), he was also making a moral or tropological point, which is that no one is without sin. Finally, the prophetic or anagogical sense is when the words of the Bible refer to our eternal glory, so when the Israelite prophets refer to the restoration of Jerusalem, the literal meaning is the actual city of Jerusalem, but the anagogical sense is the kingdom of God (compare Heb 11:10, 16).

What were the implications for those who wish to emphasize the simplicity and clarity of Scripture? Can the Bible be read in a literal sense that makes all this subtlety unnecessary or even misleading? We shall watch the Reformers and their heirs wrestling with this question and arriving at some surprising answers. Though these ideas about multiple meanings were scoffed at by some of the Reformers, they were often carefully adopted and quietly used.

5

BECOMING AND REMAINING A MEMBER OF THE CHURCH

THE DOCTRINE OF BAPTISM EMERGES

Jesus was baptized by John the Baptist. He told the disciples to go and teach the nations, "baptizing them in the name of the Father, the Son and the Holy Spirit" (Mt 28:19; Jn 3:5). Acts and the New Testament epistles mention the baptism of believers who repent of their sins (Acts 2:38). The baptized are said to be cleansed (1 Cor 6:11) and united with Christ as members of his body, Jews and Gentiles, slaves and free; they are said to taste the Holy Spirit (1 Cor 12:13).

Nevertheless, the way baptism was to be understood raised important questions for the early church. Was baptism necessary to salvation? If baptism conferred membership of the church, was it necessary to join the church to be saved? If so, what were the implications for the place of the church in the life of a Christian?

A widespread, though controversial, custom in the early church was to defer baptism until late adulthood. Since it could be administered only once—to ask to be baptized again would, it was claimed, be like putting your hand to the plough and turning back (Lk 9:62)—the prudent were anxious not to be baptized too soon and inevitably give themselves more opportunities to sin again and dirty the shining cleanliness of the newly baptized state.

In any case, baptism for adults was held to be something that required preparation and the serious study of the faith. Only an informed believer should come to be baptized. Philip had set a precedent when he instructed the Ethiopian eunuch before baptizing him, according to the account in Acts 8:26-40. Both the *belief* (faith in the sense of trust in God) and the *knowledge* (faith in the sense of holding a certain content to be true) were emphasized.

For the first few centuries catechumens, postulants for baptism, would attend study sessions for a lengthy period before coming to baptism at Easter or Pentecost in a great public ceremony. This period of study was partly a test of the seriousness of a person's calling to be a Christian. He or she was expected to put in a good deal of effort. It was also needed in order to provide a level and detail of instruction which educated people needed in order for them to take Christianity seriously as an intellectually respectable replacement for their philosophical training.

This early prebaptismal training was also the first time the question of faith and works became controversial, but for different reasons from those which gave it heat in the sixteenth-century controversy. In the early centuries, as Augustine complained, the problem was that catechumens sometimes said that they did not intend to change their way of life until baptism. First they would learn about the faith. They thought they could start to be good once they were baptized. In his writings on faith and works, Augustine told them smartly that that would not do: "Some think it acceptable to admit anyone to baptism . . . even if they are unwilling to change their manifestly evil and wicked life beforehand."[1] Being good mattered in the sense that it ought to flow from Christian faith. Works ought to stand alongside faith from the outset. That is of course quite different from suggesting that good works would get them to heaven. Among the Reformers many centuries later, reading Augustine on the subject with startling misunderstanding, the burning question of the moment was whether it was possible to earn a place in heaven by good works, and Luther answered that question in his doctrine of

---

[1] Augustine, *De fide et operibus* 1.1, CSEL 31 (1900), p. 35.

justification by faith with a resounding no.

Infant baptism. The late fourth century in the West saw the church increasingly coalesce around the practice of infant baptism. This was partly a response to the growing conviction that baptism was necessary to salvation, that without the purging of sin it brought, a person inevitably died a sinner and could not hope for heaven. In an age when infant mortality was high, parents wanted to ensure the eternal safety of their infants, and it gradually became the normal thing to baptize babies, and as soon as possible after birth.

This coincided, ironically, with the Pelagian controversy, in which Augustine became embroiled, as he regularly did in the debates of his time. Pelagius (c. 354-420/440) was rumored to be of British origins, but he first came to notice as a popular teacher among lay aristocratic Christians in Rome. He commanded large congregations who warmed to his teaching that anyone could reach heaven by practicing self-discipline and living a good life. Sin could be dealt with in that manner, he said, and there was consequently no inherent need for baptism. Augustine reacted vigorously, writing numerous anti-Pelagian works, in which he developed the important counterdoctrine of original sin.

Every child, he claimed, is born infected with original sin inherited from Adam, so that from birth the infant deserves to be sent to hell. This inherited sin engenders all actual sins (though they are committed willingly nonetheless), for which a just God will punish him or her. The human will to do good is hopelessly damaged, he said, and can do nothing toward salvation without the assistance of divine grace. It follows that God's grace poured out in baptism itself seems essential to cleanse the sinner of the guilt and corruption of original sin as well as the consequences of all the actual sins everyone inevitably commits.[2] The same urgency to rescue the newborn from danger of eternal hellfire could allow a nonordained person to baptize, even a midwife if a newborn child seemed likely to die, and baptism therefore never became associated as closely with the inalienable powers of priesthood in the West which attached to the doctrine of the Eucharist.

[2]The Eastern church's doctrine of original sin would develop somewhat differently, affirming that corruption is inherited from Adam, but not personal guilt.

The position by the Middle Ages was that infant baptism was ortho-dox, and initiating all babies into the church as well as the Christian society with this rite became the universal practice. In the West, only the small number of Jews living in Western Europe and the Muslims on the fringes, for example in southern Spain, were exceptions. Most of the sixteenth-century Reformers, with the exception of some extrem-ists such as the Anabaptists, kept to the traditional teaching about bap-tism. They too baptized infants born into Christian families, where they could be confident they would be brought up to understand the faith and accept it for themselves when they were old enough. For ex-ample, Martin Bucer wrote in his *Commonplaces* in support of baptism when it was done "with water, in the name of the Father, the Son, and the Holy Spirit, on behalf of the whole Church" for "all those who have been converted to the Lord through the preaching of the Gospel . . . and have also been sufficiently instructed in the faith by means of the special catechism." Those to be baptized must make "confession of such faith before the congregation of Christ, renouncing the devil and the world, and submitting themselves wholly to the obedience of Christ and all the discipline of the Church."[3] Children are to be baptized too, then taught the faith by catechism, so that they may make their per-sonal declaration of faith when they are old enough to be confirmed. This is baptism "of regeneration and renewal in the Holy Spirit" and remission of sins, says Bucer.[4]

Catechizing beginners in the faith. About A.D. 400, Augustine wrote *On Teaching the Faith to Beginners* (*De catechizandis rudibus*) in re-sponse to a request he had been sent by a deacon at Carthage who was responsible for providing such teaching to local converts. His advice is sophisticated. It concerns itself with the skills in communicating ideas of the sort he had learned as a professional teacher of rhetoric. In-struction should be thorough, but the catechist should not lose sight of the importance of helping the catechumens to keep their eye on what really matters:

---

[3]Martin Bucer, *A Brief Summary of Christian Doctrine (Commonplaces)*, trans. D. F. Wright (Abing-don, U.K.: Sutton Press, 1972), p. 84.
[4]Ibid., appealing to the language of Tit 3:5.

In all things, indeed, not only ought our own eye to be kept fixed upon
the end of the commandment, which is "charity, out of a pure heart, and
a good conscience, and faith unfeigned," to which we should make all
that we utter refer; but in like manner ought the gaze of the person
whom we are instructing by our utterance to be moved toward the same,
and guided in that direction.[5]

After Christianity was well established, when almost every child was
baptized in infancy, catechism and elementary teaching were mainly for
children, and they needed to encompass a wide range of abilities and educational levels—and increasingly of views and opinions, for there were
many stances and loyalties and shades of reforming or conservative opinion.

Luther's ideas about catechisms were expressed with characteristic
forcefulness in his *Table Talk:*

Sermons very little edify children, who learn little thereby; it is more
needful they be taught and well instructed in schools, and at home, and
that they be heard and examined what they have learned; this way profits
much; 'tis very wearisome, but very necessary. The papists avoid such
pains, so that their children are neglected and forsaken.[6]

In the catechism, he said:

We have a very exact, direct, and short way to the whole Christian religion.
For God himself gave the ten commandments, Christ himself penned
and taught the Lord's Prayer, the Holy Ghost brought together the articles of faith. These three pieces are set down so excellently, that never
could any thing have been better; but they are slighted and condemned by
us as things of small value, because the little children daily say them.[7]

The catechism is the most complete and best doctrine, and therefore
should continually be preached; all public sermons should be grounded
and built thereupon. I could wish we preached it daily, and distinctly read
it out of the book.[8]

He lists the key texts with which the young must become familiar, in
just the terms we find being encouraged in the Middle Ages in the work

---

[5]Augustine, *De catechizandis rudibus* 3.6, CCSL 46 (1969), p. 125.
[6]Luther, *Table Talk* 265.
[7]Luther, *Table Talk* 267.
[8]Luther, *Table Talk* 265.

of John Peckham (c. 1225-1292) as archbishop of Canterbury:

> The catechism must govern the church, and remain lord and ruler; that
> is, the ten commandments, the creed, the Lord's Prayer, the sacraments,
> etc. And although there may be many that set themselves against it, yet
> it shall stand fast, and keep the pre-eminence, through him of whom it
> is written, "Thou art a priest for ever:" for he will be a priest, and will
> also have priests, despite the devil and all his instruments on earth.[9]

Calvin's *Institutes* was an up-to-date compendium of Christian faith
and practice as well as an apologetic for the Protestant cause, something
quite new in itself. Since the late twelfth and early thirteenth centuries,
there had been systematic theology books, but they were meant for the
few advanced (graduate) students who studied theology in the universities, not for the general population.

Martin Bucer seems to have intended to contribute a short summary
of essentials in a similar spirit in his *Commonplaces*. It presented key
points in a pithy way and in terms which people were expected to grasp
and accept immediately because they seemed so self-evidently true. For
example: "Nothing is to be taught unless it is either expressly set out in
the Scriptures, or may be truly and certainly proved from the same";
"God wants us to do good works but he does not reward us for them."
And "since we are helpless to do them without him, he is rewarding his
own work in us. The church is 'all who have been born anew in Christ
the Lord and possess justifying faith.'"[10] This was a popular format in
the sixteenth century.

Insiders and Outsiders:
Cyprian and the Rigorist Approach
to the Problem of Apostasy

Cyprian (d. 258), bishop of Carthage, like Augustine a century later,
was a professional teacher of rhetoric who had been converted and
baptized in his maturity. Soon after his baptism he was ordained as
a deacon, then a presbyter and then, possibly in much the same way

---

[9]Ibid.
[10]Bucer, *Brief Summary*, p. 83.

as happened to Augustine, he found himself being chosen to be bishop of Carthage in 248 or 249. In Cyprian's case, in sophisticated urban Carthage, it was a contested election and he continued to have enemies.

The emperor Decius (emperor of Rome 249-251) handled an outbreak of plague—the kind of thing that could cause unrest in a frightened population and unseat an emperor—by blaming it on the Christians. Periods of state persecution of Christians had begun in the first century, with the emperor Nero, between A.D. 64 and 68, and were still occurring. The Decian persecution began in 250 with the demand that all must offer a sacrifice in favor of the emperor and the Empire and obtain a certificate of compliance. For ordinary citizens in a polytheist pagan society, this was not a problem of conscience. But Christians and Jews said there was only one true God, who was clear about his exclusive rights to his people's worship. Cyprian's response to this threat would have long-term effects. It would help to crystallize one of the most important questions about the integrity of the church and its ministers.

Cyprian fled before the imperial enforcement officers arrived in Carthage. Some of his flock who stayed behind gave in and worshiped the emperor. He continued to encourage the steadfast and exhort the lapsed (*lapsi*) while in exile, although his enemies called him a coward for removing himself from the scene. As the threat of punishment by the state receded, many of the lapsed were allowed to return to full communion without much disciplinary action. Upon his return Cyprian took a harder line with the defectors.

At a council held in Carthage in 251, it was agreed that those who had not only foresworn their faith but actually sacrificed to idols could never be absolved and fully restored to the church until they were on their deathbeds. This rigorism was modified in due course, and all those who repented and sought to be welcomed back into the church were absolved and returned to full communion after a prescribed course of penance. But the strict view was that those who had been clergy could never have the authority to exercise their functions as clergy again. So frequent were episodes like this in the first Christian centuries that apostasy was included in the list of the three most serious sins with murder and adultery, and provided for in the early penitential process.

Purity and ministerial authority: Baptism outside the true church. This clarification of principles emphasized two things. The first was the importance of the purity of the church. The second was that for this purity not to be compromised, the authenticity and integrity of ministerial authority mattered.

The early church was especially concerned in this regard with the validity of "heretical" baptisms and whether the work of "unworthy" ministers was valid and "efficacious." Some Christians had been baptized within communities deemed heretical by the mainstream church. They presented a problem. If they had been truly baptized, they could not be baptized again. And if they had not, they must be baptized or they could not be purged of their sins and become members of the visible church. But it might not be possible to be sure.

Cyprian baptized such incoming converts for safety's sake. This was in effect a "conditional baptism." But if it was known that they had been baptized in the church originally, had fallen away into a heretical group and then wanted to return, he did not baptize them again. He was thus inclined to place a strong emphasis on the ecclesial integrity of the community within which baptism took place.

Others said that baptism's efficacy did not depend on the community's integrity or on its being carried out by a validly ordained minister, but simply on its being done in the name of the Trinity and with water. That was enough, decreed the Council of Arles in 314. Augustine agreed and pressed the argument firmly in his own writings. This would automatically exclude the "baptism" of any group which was heretical in that it did not accept the doctrine of the Trinity and the saving work of Christ. But did it dispose of the question whether persons baptized outside the one true church were really baptized and (perhaps, some suggested) the baptism, already valid, became efficacious when they were restored to the true church?

Rigorist communities would not accept the efficacy of the ministry of lapsed-and-returned ministers, even if there was no dispute that they had originally been validly ordained. Other forms of unworthiness included dishonesty and various forms of personal moral turpitude. The emerging consensus of the early church was that the grace of God could take care of such failures of personal conduct and that God could make sacraments efficacious provided the minister was validly ordained and therefore acting in and through the church, even if he himself was not worthy. The minister was thus a mere instrument of God's grace operating in the church.

The question was important not only to individual ministers whose ministry was brought into question but also to the faithful. If the sacrament of baptism was important to salvation, it mattered a great deal that a person who had been baptized had really been the recipient of divine grace and was forgiven his or her sins.

Another highly significant long-term legacy of Cyprian was the phrase *Nulla salus extra ecclesiam*, "There is no salvation outside the church." But then of course it depends what the church is and who is "in" it.

Augustine, the Donatists in North Africa and the problem of unworthy ministers. North Africa was still a hotbed of problems about the nature of the church, its ministry and its membership during the lifetime of Augustine—all problems arising out of the Donatist controversy. It will be remembered that the Donatists believed the sacraments could not be valid if they were celebrated by clergy who had become *traditores* (who "handed over" the Scriptures in times of persecution, see p. 25), who might be restored to the fellowship but could never again be ministers.

The Donatists claimed that this meant that any ordinations such a bishop subsequently carried out would be void and the whole church in North Africa was consequently infected.[11] They alone preserved the true church. There was a schism.

In Augustine's time as bishop of Hippo there followed intense debate and episodes of violence. It all made Augustine think out his position. He was confident that the Catholic Church, the mainstream church in which he was himself a bishop, was the true church and he came to believe that dividing the church was itself a heresy.

But he was also confronted by articulate argument from the exiles who were fleeing Italy in the hope of escaping the barbarian invaders

---

[11]This is not unlike the situation where some Anglicans or Episcopalians claim that ordinations by a woman bishop can never be valid because a woman cannot be a bishop.

who were steadily destroying the Roman Empire. Like many of Augustine's writings, *The City of God* was a serial composition, lengthening as he thought his position out in response to these critics. The task prompted him to claim that the true church, the very "city of God" has as its citizens all Christians, the dead, the living and those not yet born but known to God as his own for all eternity. On the other hand, since only God knows who his chosen are, it does not follow that one's baptized friends and neighbors, even one's regular fellow worshipers, are members of the city. "Wheat and tares" grow together until harvest.

Augustine approached the question of the church's purity by asking whether divine providence is ultimately in charge of everything that happens. This had long been a topic of great interest to philosophers. Accordingly, he considered the question of the fall of the Roman Empire from a cosmic point of view. Looked at on that scale it appeared a minor blip in the history of the world. That gave him his context for the church and its membership. For, important though he thought baptism was, Augustine believed that true membership in the church was not guaranteed by baptism.

For Augustine the true church in the ultimate sense is understood as reaching backward and forward in time and across the world. It is itself the very "city of God" he described in his book on the subject.

> [The] Church is [Christ's] body, wherewith also are united and numbered all the saints who lived in this world, even before His advent, and who believed then in His future coming, just as we believe in His past coming. For (to use an illustration) Jacob, at the time when he was being born, first put forth from the womb a hand, with which also he held the foot of the brother who was taking priority of him in the act of birth; and next indeed the head followed, and thereafter, at last, and as matter of course, the rest of the members: while, nevertheless the head in point of dignity and power has precedence.[12]

Augustine's visible church, then, is a far from pure and exclusive body. The church in certain key respects is invisible to us. Only God knows

---

[12]Augustine, *De catechizandis rudibus* 3.6.

who are his own. The visible church, with its communities and worship and buildings, may include sinners who do not really belong to
God at all.

For Augustine, membership of the church and the certainty of
heaven then rest most fundamentally on God's choosing me in Christ
rather than on anything I do, or on anything the church does for me, by
way of sacramental aid or even what I believe. He adopted Cyprian's
dictum that there is no salvation outside the church, but inevitably
with a different slant, since *the church* is not simply coextensive with the
visible institution.

6

PENANCE AND THE
RECURRING PROBLEM OF SIN

NOT ALL COMMUNITIES IN THE EARLY CHURCH took a rigorist position with straying sheep. In communities that were more forgiving, what was to be done in the case of those who had been baptized as adults who knew what it meant and had made lengthy preparations, but had lapsed, or sinned, again? The only answer for those who wanted to return to the fold was that they must follow the penitential route. Early penance was public penance, and it assumed a strong doctrine that God is just and that his very nature means that he is bound to take sin seriously.

Even in accommodating communities that allowed it, penance began as an exceptional provision, to retrieve the situation for the few Christians who committed one of a small number of serious sins—murder, adultery and apostasy. It provided a public event proportionate to the equally public manner in which adult baptism was administered (with a long period of preparation and instruction, and then a great community celebration at Easter when the catechumens were baptized at last). Such penitents faced a period of very public humiliation. They had to make the sincerity of their repentance publicly manifest in the church for an appropriate period, appearing at worship in sackcloth and ashes and sitting apart from the congregation with the other penitents.[1] They had to come before the bishop after they had served their sentences and obtain his absolution. Even then they suffered permanent disabilities in

---

[1] Bernhard Poschmann, *Penance and the Anointing of the Sick* (New York: Herder & Herder, 1964).

the life of the church. For example, the previously ordained who sinned and repented (just like the returned apostates) were no longer allowed to perform certain priestly functions.

Martin Bucer, in his *Commonplaces*, describes this ancient practice of public penance with approval, affirming that "God has prescribed and ordered a medicine of penitence." He describes a patristic model, involving brotherly correction, the public disciplining of sinners followed by readmission to the congregation, with absolution allowed if the penitent asks for it. There is reference to the easing of "troubled consciences" by this means and the call for both public and private processes.[2]

From public to private penance. From the basic assumptions attaching to the sacrament of baptism, the conviction of its importance and the certainty that it could not be repeated, developed a sacrament of penance, which became increasingly complicated as the medieval centuries progressed. It seems that this pattern of "public and exceptional" penance decayed naturally after the end of the Roman Empire, when the pattern of society changed radically throughout Europe and the baptism of infants all born into Christendom became the norm. Something much smaller and cozier began to emerge to meet the resulting pastoral needs of a population baptized as infants and likely to have been regular sinners ever since. Ordinary people were well aware that they had sinned, yesterday and today, and were going to sin tomorrow. But their routine sins of selfishness, greed, petty dishonesty and unkindness to their neighbors were more modest. Private pastoral support from local clergy gradually took the place of big public demonstrations of disapproval and the intervention of the bishop.

Priests in parishes now began to discharge the dual roles of "judge" and "physician" in the penitential process, telling people clearly when they had done wrong but also helping them to heal. The penitent was expected to be sincerely sorry and to show it. "Doing penance"—traditionally by prayer, fasting or almsgiving—was seen as the way to demonstrate the sincerity of repentance and also to help with the healing. In the latter sense, it was rather like the modern notion of "closure."

---

[2]Martin Bucer, *A Brief Summary of Christian Doctrine* (*Commonplaces*), trans. D. F. Wright (Abingdon, U.K.: Sutton Press, 1972), pp. 88-89.

But the penance, which was quantitative and related to the seriousness of the offense, could also be seen as a way of serving a sentence or carrying out a punishment so that a just God could be thought to consider the matter closed. The underlying belief in a just and justly angry God who takes sin seriously was important, and the more seriously it was all taken by the people of God, the more significant became the role of the priest.

What was absolution, and was it enough? What gave the priest the authority to do all this, to absolve and to impose penances? The public absolution of penitents had originally been a task for the bishop. The scriptural foundation of the theology of ministry which underpinned the medieval explanation was the passage where Jesus entrusted to Peter the power of "binding" and "loosing" (Mt 16:19). This was universally read as a gift of authority to turn the keys of heaven so as to unlock or to lock its door. But not everyone agreed about Jesus' intention in giving this power to Peter or whether he had intended it to pass on to Peter's successors, or, if he had, who those successors were. Did Jesus mean that the power was to belong to future popes and be exercised on delegated authority from the papacy? Did he mean that it would pass to all his disciples? Did he mean that all Christians would have it and could use it to discipline and support one another (as in Jas 5:16)? And was the absolution an act of forgiveness by the pope, or a priest who was acting on his authority, or was it merely a declaration of God's forgiveness to the repentant sinner?

These questions were in Langland's mind in *Piers Plowman*, and he evidently expected his readers to be familiar with them too. "I perceived of the power / that Peter had to keep, / To bind and to unbind /as the Book telleth." The four cardinal virtues—prudence, justice, fortitude or courage, and temperance or moderation—are, he explains, so called after the Latin *cardo*, a hinge.

> They hinge the gates
> Where Christ is in glory / to close and to shut
> And to open it to them / and show heavenly bliss.

But, with heavy irony, he tells his readers that he is not going to say anything at length about

cardinals at Rome / that received that name
And power presumed in them / a pope to make,
That they have Peter's power / deny it I will not.

In Langland's time the question of the power of priests was not yet as
central as it became immediately before and during the Reformation
period. But it seems that claims to priestly power had already become
an irritant in this important area of penitential practice. It caused outrage in those who thought they saw corruption and excess among the
clergy all about them. Even the most self-conscious and sorry sinner
could feel indignant at being expected to confess and receive absolution
from an "unworthy priest."

Although the early church had made up its mind that grace could be
received from God even through the dirtiest hands, this seemed so contrary to the ordinary person's sense of fairness and decency that late
medieval dissidents were prepared to open the question up again, as we
shall see.

Confessor's manuals. So strong was the demand for pastoral support
for worried sinners that in the late twelfth century manuals began to be
produced to guide local clergy, many of whom had limited education.
"Confessor's manuals" were written to guide parish priests in dealing
with parishioners who were anxious to confess their sins and receive
absolution and in setting appropriate penances for them in proportion
to their wrongdoing. The emphasis was on straightforward calculations
of penances, with much detail about the variety of special kinds of wick-
edness to which those in particular trades and professions were subject.
This approach belonged to a well-established tradition. Earlier peniten-
tials had, for example, gone into great detail about the fair apportion-
ment of penances for soldiers returning from war. Someone who knew
that he had killed a certain number of the enemy could have his penance calibrated with exactness, but an archer who discharged his arrows
into the enemy lines could not know how many he had killed and must
do penance on a different basis.

It will be apparent that a shift had taken place since the early centuries, not only from public penance for a few serious sins rarely committed to private penance for a multitude of sins everyone commits all the

time, but also in the direction of a potentially unhealthy preoccupation with remaining sin as a barrier between the Christian and a just and angry God.

To the eyes of sixteenth-century Reformers these manuals were highly undesirable because they encouraged what Luther was to call the "terrified conscience," an intense anxiety to ensure that one had done all that was necessary to make up for one's sins. It was Luther's insight that there was as great a pastoral need for liberation from all that, as there had been for the provision of such manuals to reassure people that they had calculated their debt correctly and paid it sufficiently.

The changes the Reformers proposed did not seek to diminish belief in God's anger about sin. Luther took that very seriously. But the Reformers sought to place the remedy elsewhere by reminding believers that when Christ died on the cross he had done everything that needed to be done. His sacrifice was more than enough for all the sins of humanity, including those which were going to be committed in the centuries that followed.

Purgatory. The doctrine of purgatory emerged fully in the twelfth century. This was the belief that there is a place or state after death between heaven and hell in which the souls of the dead can linger for a time until they have completed their penances and are fit to enter heaven. Purgatory was by no means pleasant, but it could paradoxically be seen as a comforting doctrine, for it taught reassuringly that everyone who passed through death and found him- or herself in purgatory could be sure of entering heaven eventually.

Dante Alighieri (1265-1321) was the author of a different sort of social and ecclesiastical satire from the pretended peasant's-eye view of the poet we know as William Langland. His took the form of an epic poem, the *Divina Commedia*. Here is the universe in a hierarchical arrangement with punishments and rewards meted out as deserved. He wrote it between 1308 and 1320, while he was in political exile from his native Florence; it became a vehicle of sharp criticism of contemporaries as well as famous names of old. As in Langland's *Piers Plowman*, the narrative takes place in a vision. Dante passes through hell and purgatory on a journey to heaven, noting the many different levels to be seen in each and who is to be found there. The idea was evidently to surprise the readers as they came upon familiar characters in unexpected places.

Purgatory is "that second realm / where man's soul goes to purify itself / and become worthy to ascend to heaven" (canto 1). It contains only "those souls worthy to climb to God" (canto 7). It is both a painful and an edifying place to find oneself. In canto 13 Dante describes the singing of the souls "in tones inspiring a sweet blend of joy and pain" from "shades loosing the knot of their great debt to God." Canto 19 reminds the reader that "blessed are those who mourn."[3]

There are vignettes. Dante's companion in the dream at this stage is Virgil. Virgil, the Roman poet, had famously written about the descent into Hades in book 6 of his *Aeneid*, beginning with the much-quoted line, "It is easy to go to hell but hard to get out again." He was therefore the ideal literary guide. As they continue their climb through purgatory toward heaven, they observe souls "stretched out upon the ground, weeping and sighing" and reciting the Psalm *adhaesit pavimento anima mea*, "My soul cleaveth unto the dust" (Ps 119:25 KJV). These are the avaricious. Dante notices a pope among them, Adrian V, who was pope in 1276. Dante asks him why he is there. The pope explains that what the avaricious have done wrong is to turn their backs on heaven and fix their eyes on earthly riches. It is only just that they be bound now with their faces to the ground. He asks Dante if he would kindly warn his niece, who is surrounded by corruption, to save her from a similar fate.

Popular belief in purgatory seems to have become embedded very thoroughly after the theological concept emerged in the twelfth century, perhaps because it so neatly met a perceived pastoral need.[4] It was very reassuring to think that it might not be too late after death to put your record straight with God. But Dante's merciless satire brought purgatory into the realms of social comment with the rest of the contemporary lived-in world. If the church was behaving badly, there were critics to tell it so.

Indulgences. The development of a doctrine of purgatory encouraged the evolution of the old doctrine of indulgences with its many appurte-

[3]Dante Alighieri, *Purgatory*, trans. Mark Musa (Bloomington: Indiana University Press, 1981).
[4]Jacques Le Goff, *The Birth of Purgatory*, trans. A. Goldhammer (London: Scolar Press, 1984).

nances. Indulgences were not part of the penitential process. They came in afterward, in the form of the remission of the temporal penalty for forgiven sin, that is a "letting off" of part of this debt of undischarged penance on the authority of the church which had imposed the penances in the first place. But it was easy for people to get confused about what they were buying when they bought an indulgence, and Luther's accusation that the confusion extended to the church magisterium and to theologians too was not without foundation.

The claim was that if the church allocated penances through its priests at confession, the church could also lift or remit them. Any such remission of a penalty would lie outside the penitential process itself. It would involve some form of buyout so that the "books" balanced. On this understanding, human enough but ultimately destructive to the very rationale of the process, it became acceptable for the church to offer indulgences in return for money or actions.

The theology that underpinned this practice was grounded in the infinite worth of Christ's merits and the abundance of the acquired merits of the saints, and assumed that such remissions ought to be granted only by senior clergy, the pope or a bishop. The call to go on the First Crusade was accompanied by one of these offers, which took the form of the first total or plenary indulgence. Those who joined the crusade and died on the way or stayed with the army all the way to Jerusalem were promised a complete remission of all their undischarged penances. This was seen as an exceptional offer for a quite exceptional reason. But as is the way with such bending of the rules, it then began to look quite unexceptional. As the Middle Ages progressed, the church did not resist the temptation to use indulgences even as a fundraising measure for building projects, though some saw this as a scandal. The expansion of this practice in the case of the building of St. Peter's basilica in Rome, which began in 1506, particularly offended would-be Reformers of the sixteenth century, especially Luther.

For those who wanted to help dead friends and relatives out of purgatory as well, there was a doctrine that vicarious satisfaction was possible. This was in itself a very ancient and entirely respectable belief. Jesus died on the cross for our sins, and thus he himself had made a vicarious satisfaction. So the doctrine of vicarious satisfaction under-lies the claim that when Christ died on the cross he made a full and sufficient satisfaction for the sins of the whole world, though he him-self was sinless and owed no satisfaction at all. In the smaller compass of my daily life, if it is possible for one person to pay another's debt, why should I not try to purchase satisfaction on behalf of my dead parents in purgatory, so that they may enter heaven sooner? People thinking in this way in the late Middle Ages could buy indulgences on behalf of others.

Linked with the selling of indulgences to shorten the time in purga-tory was the practice of saying masses for the dead or private masses. One of the fiercest denunciations of the Reformers was the practice of turning the Eucharist, which they said should be an action of the com-munity, into the act of a single priest acting alone without a congrega-tion. Priests would do this for a fee, and the faithful came to believe that each Mass (from the concluding words *missa est*) dedicated in this way was itself a sacrifice and added to the sum total of sacrificial benefit which could be deployed for the assistance of the faithful departed. Rich men sometimes set up private "chantry chapels" in which prayers would be said and Masses celebrated specifically for their own souls or those of their families.

The theory of a transferability of merit to enable penances to be offset depended on two concepts, one very old and the other an invention of the thirteenth century. The ancient idea was that of a "communion of saints," coined in the third or fourth century. *Saints* did not have its modern meaning here. It referred to the *sancti*, the Latin word which simply meant "holy ones," which included all Christians. The idea was that the whole community of Christ's people, living and dead, formed a union which was the body of Christ, the church.

This does not mean that the idea of "the saints" as a category of the specially holy was not well developed by the patristic period and cer-tainly by the Middle Ages.[5] The merits of certain individuals stood out. Bede has a good deal to say in his *Ecclesiastical History* about the tokens

---

[5]Peter Brown, *The Cult of Saints: Its Rise and Function in Latin Christianity* (London: SCM Press, 1981).

and evidences of this notable holiness of the exceptional few, the miracles performed, the healings at the touch of a relic, such as a piece of cloth the saint had worn or a bone of the saint.[6] The holiness of such a saint was felt to be immanent in his or her physical remains, to linger, to be available to the less holy to meet their spiritual and physical needs. By the late eleventh century a monastery whose abbot had been admired and respected by his monks would often arrange for his *Life* to be written, evidences of miracles collected and canonization sought (see p. 132). Having a local saint was to have a tourist attraction, and that could mean substantial income.[7]

The idea that this "body," particularly the specially holy saints, possessed a treasury of merits seems to have been devised by Bonaventure (c. 1217-1274), a leading Franciscan scholar, to try to provide a theological explanation for the growing practice of allowing the faithful to pay for indulgences. His idea was that there exists in the custody of the institutional church a reservoir of goodness, composed of Christ's own infinite merits, together with the surplus merits of the saints, which were more than enough to benefit themselves, so that some of their merits were left over and kept in a reservoir by the church to benefit others. That this might be taken to imply that the merits of Christ were not abundantly sufficient did not cause offense until the Reformation, when it formed part of a backlash against the whole theology of sainthood. It is not hard to see how these developments occurred, how natural they were, how they responded to pastoral needs as the church then saw them; nor how easily they became infected with corruption when money came into the equation.

Langland also points a finger at the "pardoners" who sell indulgences, so that people can buy off some of the time they believed they would otherwise have to spend in purgatory serving a sentence for the sins for which they had not done the appointed penance before they died. The pardoner impresses the people by bringing out "a brief with bishops'

---

[6]Bede, *Ecclesiastical History*, ed. B. Colgrave and R. A. B. Mynors (London: Oxford University Press, 1969), p. 299.
[7]Ronald Finucane, *Miracles and Pilgrims: Popular Beliefs in Medieval England* (London: J. M. Dent, 1977).

seals thereon," and plays on their ignorance, for they do not know that he is not a priest and cannot absolve them but only sell them ready-made indulgences for the temporal penalties of already forgiven sin:

> Laymen believed him / welcomed his words,
> And came up on their knees / to kiss his seals.

He takes their "rings and brooches" on false pretenses and keeps contributions intended for church collections, which "the parish poor would have / if he were not there." These were the characters whose successors in a later generation so offended Luther when he encountered them in Germany.

Good works and bad: How the penitential system got out of hand.

> *Nullum bonum irremuneratum / nullum peccatum impunitum*
> ("No good act will go unrewarded, no sin unpunished")
> —Piers Plowman

There was of course a theological dimension to all this development of pastoral practice. It was not unheard of for the practices to get ahead of the theology, with theologians seeking to make sense of what was happening only in retrospect. Of no area of theology was this more true than the penitential system. Ordinary people could not avoid being affected by the way this developed. In 1215 the Fourth Lateran Council had decreed that everyone, men and women alike, must make confession at least once a year, and for a century before that there had been a growing emphasis on the development of the duty of parish priests to help their people deal with the consequences of their sins. The consciousness of sin was strong. People feared for their eternal futures and those of their families and friends. What everyone wanted was a strong hope of heaven, or better still, a certainty, not only for themselves but for those they loved. It was obvious enough that few of those who died were so conspicuously holy that their friends and relations need have no anxiety about their eventual destination. There was a strong popular wish for a means of doing something about the uncertainty.

The representatives of the church in the "fair field of folk" who are singled out by Langland for attack are all peddling pardon in some way, or trying to make money out of the gullible worried faithful, or both. This is largely true of the "clerical frauds" we shall meet among Chaucer's pilgrims too.

This is not surprising given the immense expansion of the penitential system and its baggage since the twelfth century, partly at the instigation of the ecclesiastical authorities but partly, too, in response to a popular pressure which grew with the growing fear. To a certain extent, people were getting what they had asked for.

Why did people assume they needed all this help to get to heaven, and that it had to come from the church? This was a question which was to be addressed with vigor by the Reformers. Why people gave their money so readily to charlatans and rogues claiming to offer them a shortcut is another question. The Reformers tended to approach this by seeking to reassure the faithful that they did not need this sort of help. The requirements the church set before them were merely human impositions.

7

THE EUCHARIST AND
THE IDEA OF SACRAMENTS

EUCHARIST

From time to time in the earlier history of the church there had been
controversy about the meaning of Jesus' words at the Last Supper when
he took bread and wine and said "this is my body" and "this is my blood"
before sharing them with his disciples and telling them to "do this in
remembrance of me" (1 Cor 11:24-25). Was he actually making the bread
and wine into his real body and blood, and telling them to eat and drink
on that understanding? And if that is what he meant, who would have
the power or authority to "do this" after he had gone, so as to turn bread
and wine into his body and blood down the ages? And would that mean
that he would be physically or only spiritually present with believers
when the bread and the wine were shared? Writers of the first few centuries, such as Cyril of Jerusalem (c. 315-387) and Ambrose of Milan (c.
339-397), made various efforts to explain what occurred, but these efforts
were framed largely in terms of the spirituality of the time. Rather than
engaging in the technical theological analysis possible in later centuries,
they focused on encouraging the faithful to approach Christ's real presence in the Eucharist with awe.[1]

Disputes about the mode of Christ's presence. In Carolingian times, Paschasius Radbertus (c. 790-c. 860), John Scotus Eriugena (c. 810-c. 877),

---

[1]Cyril of Jerusalem, *Catecheses Mystagogicae* 4, 3-6 PG 33, pp. 1098-1106; Ambrose, *De mysteriis* 9,
54, 58, ed. Otto Faller, CSEL 73 (1955), pp. 92, 111, 114.

Hincmar of Rheims (c. 806-882) and Rabanus Maurus (c. 780-856) all became involved in trying to tease out the relationship of the visible bread and wine to the body and blood of Christ himself, and the "effect" of a priest speaking the words of consecration which Jesus himself had used.[2] The question was still what exactly happened when the minister took the bread and the wine and repeated Jesus' words at the Last Supper, "This is my body," and "This is my blood." Was he merely commemorating the event and following Jesus' instructions to his disciples to "remember him" when they did the same? Or was the bread really Christ's body and the wine really his blood after the words had been spoken by someone authorized by ordination to speak them? Again, the discussion, though full of complex refinements, lacked the scholastic crispness it would acquire when the study of logic became more technically advanced from the eleventh century.

In the late eleventh century the grammarian Berengar of Tours (c. 1010-1088) caused a crisis by claiming, as Paschasius Radbertus had done in the ninth century, that Christ is really present to us in the Eucharist, but there is no need to explain this by positing any change in the nature of the sacramental elements themselves. Berengar and his opponents, who included Lanfranc (c. 1010-1089), later archbishop of Canterbury, with the increasingly advanced knowledge of Aristotelian logic of their time, were able to explain his objections and seek to counter them in a novel way, which was to have an immense impact on the thinking of the later medieval centuries.

For Greek philosopher Aristotle (384-322 B.C.), each thing has a "substance" but it also has "accidents," qualities which may vary without the substance ceasing to be what it is. For example, you may be a redhead but if you dye your hair black you will still be yourself. A boy of ten will grow taller but still be the same person. I am here and you are there, but if we change places we do not become one another. Bread grows moldy if it is kept too long, but even when it looks green and furry it is still

---

[2] "Exegesis in the Ninth-Century Eucharist Controversy," *The Study of the Bible in the Carolingian Era*, ed. Celia Chazelle and Burton Van Name Edwards (Turnhout: Brepols, 2003), pp. 167-87; Celia Chazelle, "Figure, Character, and the Glorified Body in the Carolingian Eucharistic Controversy," *Traditio* 47 (1992): 1-36.

bread. Against Berengar, Lanfranc and others were claiming that the faithful are being asked to believe that the contrary happens when the words "This is my body" are said over a piece of bread by a priest celebrating the Eucharist. The bread continues to look exactly as before, but it is now in reality the body of Christ. The substance has altered but not the accidents. There is a trans-substantiation, a change of substance. That is to turn Aristotle on his head.

Therefore a great deal turned on the meaning of the Latin *hoc est corpus meum*, "this *is* my body." That "is" took on a new significance in the eleventh century with the revival of the study of logic. Syllogisms, or formal arguments, were made up of two premises, or propositions, and a conclusion. They followed (with many sophisticated variations) the basic form:

All A is B
B is C
Therefore A is C

It is obviously very important what the "is," or *copula* which links the A, B and C, is doing. A could be identical with B or a member of a class of B or another word for B and so on. Which of these was the *est* doing in *hoc est corpus meum*? If Jesus meant that the bread became identical with his body as he said the words, what was the explanation of that fact that as far as the eye could see, there was no change? Here arose another norm of contemporary thinking to help. In the ordinary course of events a bread's appearance can change. It may grow stale or moldy, but it will still be bread, the same substance. It was as if the miracle of the Eucharist occurred in reverse: while the accidents of the bread remained the same, the substance changed. This is why it was natural to use these assumptions in trying to explain what happened when the bread and wine were "changed" in the Eucharist, and to describe the change in the language of substance and accidents. So it remained a miracle but had a logical explanation.

Why was the Eucharist so important? The Eucharist had always been important in the life of the church, but when it became officially accepted that the real body and blood of the historical Jesus were present, living and real, at the Mass, the celebration gained a new seriousness in the popular imagination. Baptism was experienced by the individual only once, though parents would see their children baptized, and probably other infants in their local community. The celebration of the Eucharist touched lives in a quite different way because it took place throughout the Christian's life.

It remained a rare and special event. It was not usual in the Middle Ages for Christians to receive the consecrated bread and wine every week, and the custom grew up of allowing the laity only the bread. The terminology was made official by its use at the Fourth Lateran Council in 1215. The decree of 1215 requiring everyone to confess once a year recognized that for many the Easter Eucharist was their annual occasion for participating.

Transubstantiation also fostered a strong doctrine of the power of the priesthood, for if it was true, priests could in a sense "make God." And if the body and blood of Christ were constituted anew at each celebration, the Mass could be seen as a reenactment of his sacrifice on the cross, which helped to elevate the status of the priest who "celebrated" often, well above that of the laity who rarely participated.

As the word *transubstantiatio* came into widespread use during the twelfth century and the doctrine of transubstantiation was formulated as the orthodox teaching of the church, there was further elaboration, some of which has the stamp of popular questioning.[3] For example, it was asked what happened if a mouse ate a crumb of the body of Christ. Would it be saved? (Most theologians said no, the Eucharist was salvific only for human beings.) It was asked how the enormous total quantity of bread which had been consecrated throughout the world over the centuries could all be one human body. It was asked how Christ could be physically present in so many places at once. (To neither of these was a satisfactory answer found, at least none which could end the debate.) But the doctrine held, and it had the effect of enhancing the perceived powers of priests and bishops, and of creating for the laity a focus of devotion. Caesarius of Heisterbach (c. 1180-1240) told the story of a woman who carried the consecrated bread

---

[3]See in general Marilyn McCord Adams, *Some Later Medieval Theories of the Eucharist: Thomas Aquinas, Giles of Rome, Duns Scotus, and William Ockham* (Oxford: Oxford University Press, 2010).

home in her mouth in order to use it for magical purposes. But her bees built it a little wax shrine, for they recognized God and accorded him the proper respect.[4]

Thus perhaps the most important development for popular religion was the institution of the Feast of Corpus Christi—"the body of Christ"—at the instigation of Juliana of Liège (c. 1192-1258), who claimed to have had visions in which Christ appeared to her and told her to press for the establishment of this new feast as a regular part of the church's year. She told her confessor and petitioned leading ecclesiastics, and local celebrations began. In 1264 Pope Urban IV made the feast official throughout the church, as a moveable feast, one of those which follow the date of Easter each year. It was to be celebrated on the Thursday after Trinity Sunday.

It became the season for the performance of mystery plays, for processions and for emotional devotion by the people as Christ was carried through the streets for all to see.[5] At the beginning of the fifteenth century, the archbishop of Canterbury Thomas Arundel (1353-1414) saw clearly that the processions celebrating this feast had a capacity to encourage popular piety and also respect for the clergy on the part of the laity (see pp. 205-6).

SACRAMENTS

The early Christians did not have a general doctrine of sacrament. They practiced baptism and celebrated the Lord's Supper or Eucharist (which takes its name from the Greek for "thanksgiving"). It was not until the time of Augustine that serious thought seems to have been given to the question whether there was something these celebrations shared as instruments of or aids to salvation, which gave them a special holiness and importance. In his *De catechizandis rudibus* (26.50), Augustine proposed a distinction which proved immensely useful in later centuries and was often used to explain the character of sacraments and what they did.

---

[4]Caesarius of Heisterbach, *Dialogue on Miracles*, trans. C. C. Swinton Bland (London: G. Routledge, 1929).

[5]Miri Rubin, *Corpus Christi: The Eucharist in Late Medieval Culture* (Cambridge: Cambridge University Press, 1991).

The "apparatus" of a sacrament—the words and the water in baptism, the bread and the wine in Holy Communion—are visible, he said, but those visible things are simply signs. They have an invisible spiritual significance to which the sign points.

This left much room for further debate about the exact link between the outward and visible sign and the inward and spiritual realities signified. Did baptism and the Lord's Supper have an actual salvific effect? For example, was there a cause-and-effect pathway between the visible sacramental actions and the spiritual consequences? This puzzled Isidore of Seville (c. 560-636). "A sacrament," he said, "is when in a celebration something is done in order that something may be understood, which is to be accepted as holy." The "sacraments are so-called because beneath the covering of bodily things the saving act may be done more secretly by divine power."[6]

The word *sacrament* comes from the Latin *sacramentum*, which meant "mystery." It had a connotation of "holiness" derived from the Latin *sacer* (from which English derives *sacred*). The word *sacramentum* was used too for the ceremony when a Roman soldier took his oath and was branded behind the ear with a number that showed which legion he belonged to, so it also had a link to an idea of a permanent marking of an individual. Here may have been one of the origins of the idea of an indelible "character."

When Hugh of St. Victor found himself discussing the subject in his *On the Sacraments of the Church* (*De Sacramentis Ecclesiae*) in the twelfth century, he gave the term a very broad meaning. A "sacrament is a sign of a holy thing," he said (*sacramentum est sacrae rei signum*).[7] He distinguished three types of sacrament: baptism and the Eucharist, "in which salvation is chiefly to be found" (*in quibus principaliter salus constat*); those which although not "necessary to salvation" are useful for promoting holiness (*proficient tamen ad sanctificationem*), such as scattering water and ashes; and those which were instituted to make possible the

---

[6]Isidore of Seville, *Etymologiae*, 6.19.39-40, trans. Stephen A. Barney (Cambridge: Cambridge University Press, 2006).
[7]Hugh of St. Victor, *De Sacramentis Ecclesiae*, bk. 1.9.1, PL 176, 317.

administration of the sacraments, such as the ordination of ministers.[8] This discussion was still vague about the meaning and purpose of sacraments, and how many there are, but clearly the two instituted by Jesus himself stand out.

---

[8]Ibid., bk. 1.9.7, PL 176, 327.

8

ORGANIZATION, MAKING DECISIONS AND KEEPING TOGETHER

COUNCILS AND OTHER WAYS OF MAKING DECISIONS

The *consensus fidelium*, the "agreement of the faithful" as a whole, has expressed itself only gradually and with revisions, or even complete changes. Sometimes a position which looked very firm at one time has imperceptibly shifted. The Roman Catholic Church set its face against allowing the Bible to be translated into the vernaculars of Europe in the sixteenth century, but saw no difficulty at the Second Vatican Council, in the middle of the twentieth century, when it became evident that the "agreement of the faithful" had moved on.

To hold a meeting and record a decision was quickly found to be a sensible way to resolve disputes. The model for this was set in the events recorded in Acts 15. The early centuries saw the development of a number of expectations about such *councils* or *synods* (the words are largely synonymous, derived from the Latin and Greek terms respectively). These basics seemed uncontroversial in the first centuries, though that changed later. One such rule was that councils convened to make decisions on matters of morals and practice were intended to be binding only on the local churches whose representatives had participated. The representatives would normally be the leaders of those churches, their bishops, and the appropriateness of limiting the voting to these leaders was also accepted without controversy from an early stage.

Most councils and synods were local, and in practice most of the business of such meetings had to do with disciplinary matters (misbehaving clergy) or decisions about which rites (patterns of worship) were to be acceptable locally.[1] Only occasionally did a council—usually one seeking to represent the whole church—address matters of faith, and the consensus was always that that there must be no variation there. There was to be one faith in one church. Councils regularly reaffirmed what their predecessors had said in order to ensure continuity over time as well as consistency in the present. Difference of belief was not only heresy, it meant schism.

The first ecumenical councils. For the purposes of addressing questions affecting the whole church, a universal (from the Latin *universalis*) or ecumenical (from the Greek *oikoumenē*) council was needed. A series of these was held, beginning with the Council of Nicaea of 325 (whose Creed was elaborated slightly at the Council of Constantinople, 381). Nicaea was—as we have already seen—convened by the first Christian emperor, Constantine the Great, to address the dangers to peace among the churches in the empire presented by what would come to be regarded as the Arian heresy.[2]

Three more of the early ecumenical councils concentrated on resolving further disputes. A cluster of disputes had emerged as the consequences of the Arian controversy rumbled on and forced further active discussion of what exactly happened when God became man in Jesus. Were there two natures and two Persons, as Nestorius (c. 386-c. 451) seemed to teach; or one nature and one Person, as Eutyches (c. 380-456) said; or two natures, divine and human, in one Person, as orthodoxy came to describe things? In 431 a council was held at Ephesus to address, among other concerns, the problem of Nestorianism, which had become "the controversy of the day," and condemn it. The second Council

[1] Norman P. Tanner, *Decrees of the Ecumenical Councils* (Washington, D.C.: Georgetown University Press, 1990).
[2] See in general R.P.C. Hanson, *The Search for the Christian Doctrine of God: The Arian Controversy, 318-381* (Edinburgh: T & T Clark, 1988).

of Ephesus in 449 and the Council of Chalcedon (451) tried to articulate a position on Eutyches. The Oriental Orthodox Churches, the Copts and Armenians and Jacobites and others, did not accept the Chalcedon decision and remained "one naturists" (Monophysites), creating the first great and enduring schism in the unity of the church. They accepted as ecumenical only the first three councils.

Even then disagreement was not at an end among the rest, as the Second Council of Constantinople showed in 553, for it was still actively rejecting Nestorianism. Did the incarnate Christ have one will or two? One will, said the Monothelites. The Third Council of Constantinople (680-681) condemned their teaching.

Now further divergence began to threaten. The Quinisext Council, which is also known as the Council in Trullo (692), was not accepted by the West as ecumenical. It decided that the church should be ruled by a "pentarchy" of primates or patriarchs of the great metropolitan sees: Rome, Constantinople, Antioch, Alexandria and Jerusalem. The metropolitan sees had formed in great cities, and they were to become the leaders of the autocephalous churches of the ancient and medieval worlds. It was foreseeable that who was to be chief would be bone of future contention.

Iconoclasm. The Second Council of Nicaea (787) officially ended the "iconoclasm controversy" which had been dividing the Greek churches. One party maintained that the veneration of pictures of the saints was idolatry, and there was physical destruction of icons. The other said that the veneration of icons was an aid to faith, and did not supplant the true worship due to God alone. This issue was largely confined to the Eastern empire. This meant that when controversy about images became fierce in the late Middle Ages and Reformation, the legacy of these discussions was not familiar in the West.

These councils marked divisions as well as endeavoring to settle disputes. They were in reality responses to problems and grew out of the political structure of the late Roman Empire, and were shaped by its preoccupations. The guidance of the Holy Spirit was believed to underpin and to be the source of each council's authority. Nevertheless, they established some important principles of conciliar theory and practice, as each council carefully confirmed the decrees of the one before, so as to establish not only the unity of the faith but also its continuity and consistency over time.

The emergence of a universal primacy. The five ancient patriarchates had become something more than an administrative convenience. In the East the bishops of the four great metropolitan sees of ancient foundation had come to be recognized as "first" among their local fellow bishops (primates) and as presiding over autocephalous churches, united in faith, but each a complete microcosm of the whole church. In the West, Rome had a claim to stand beside them as a principal see because of Peter's visit there and Jesus' promise that Peter would be the rock on which he would build his church. The church in the West never saw itself as autocephalous in the same way, but it seemed natural for the bishop of Rome, as Peter's successor, to acquire a primacy of jurisdiction over the other bishops of the West.

This became fully apparent in the reign of Gregory the Great, who had been a civil servant and administrator before he became pope (590-604) and who remained an invaluable support to the collapsing food distribution system and administrative arrangements of the decaying empire. He engaged in vigorous exchanges with the Eastern patriarchs, asserting the primacy of Rome over all of them.

1054 and after: The schism with the Greeks. In 1054, for reasons as much political as theological, certain tensions over several centuries between the Greek and the Roman Churches came to a head in a breakdown of communication between the then pope, Leo IX (1002-1054), and Michael Cerularius (d. 1058), patriarch of Constantinople. Legates were sent to Constantinople from Rome to inform the patriarch that he was required to recognize the universal primacy of the bishop of Rome. He refused. Cardinal Humbert of Silva Candida (d. 1061), the leader of the Roman party, excommunicated him, and the patriarch in turn excommunicated Cardinal Humbert and his party. The anathemas exchanged in 1054 were not lifted until 1965.

The de facto breach was rationalized theologically—and somewhat after the event—by claiming that significant differences divided Greek and Latin Christians in matters of faith. One of these issues was the difference in the kind of bread used at the Eucharist. The Latins used unleavened bread, and the Greeks, bread with yeast in it. Then there was the *filioque* clause, which amended the Nicene Creed in the West (offically at the Third Council of Toledo in 589, but in practice well before then). The creed now said that the Holy Spirit "proceeds from the Father *and the Son.*" This was added for clarity, the Latins said, but the Greeks said that even if it were correct, it was unacceptable because it was a unilateral decision and an innovation. And in any case it was not correct, because it implied that there were two "first principles" or origins in the Godhead. The *filioque* debate has continued between East and West ever since.

The schism of 1054 meant no truly ecumenical councils could be held during the later medieval centuries, but a series of "Lateran Councils" took place, of which the most important for the indignation it later caused among Reformers was the Fourth Lateran Council of 1215.

The Fourth Lateran Council was designed as a major political event, deliberately engineered by Pope Innocent III (1160/1161-1216) to have a considerable impact. He invited observers from the Greek churches to make it as much of an ecumenical council as possible. It put out a declaration of faith that included a claim that there is no salvation outside the Church. It condemned various contemporary heresies, some of them overlapping with claims dissidents were already making, but which were going to be important in the Reformation.

It laid down a requirement that "everyone of either sex should make confession at least once a year":

> All the faithful of both sexes shall after they have reached the age of discretion faithfully confess all their sins at least once a year to their own (parish) priest and perform to the best of their ability the penance imposed, receiving reverently at least at Easter the sacrament of the Eucharist, unless perchance at the advice of their own priest may for good reason abstain for a time from its reception.[3]

This came to be seen as the foundation stone of the hated penitential

---

[3]Fourth Lateran Council, canon 21, in *Decrees of the Ecumenical Councils*, pp. 244-45, www.fordham .edu/halsall/source/lat4-select.asp.

system as it rose up in the later Middle Ages into the immense system of requirements Wyclif and Luther condemned as "human impositions" on the faithful.

There was also a conciliar statement of the doctrine of transubstantiation containing a strong claim about priestly power:

> There is one Universal Church of the faithful, outside of which there is absolutely no salvation. In which there is the same priest and sacrifice, Jesus Christ, whose body and blood are truly contained in the sacrament of the altar under the forms of bread and wine; the bread being changed (*transsubstantiatio*) by divine power into the body, and the wine into the blood, so that to realize the mystery of unity we may receive of Him what He has received of us. And this sacrament no one can effect except the priest who has been duly ordained in accordance with the keys of the Church, which Jesus Christ Himself gave to the Apostles and their successors.[4]

In a sermon given at Erfurt on April 7, 1521, Luther claimed that what dissidents since at least Wyclif had called the "human impositions" of the modern church, particularly of the papacy, were adding to the list of requirements for salvation and burdening the faithful.

> The papal authorities . . . issue decrees about fasts, prayers, and butter-eating, to the effect that whoever observes these papal orders will be saved, and that he who does not observe them will be seized by the devil. Thus the people are led astray by the delusion that their piety and salvation depend upon their own works.[5]

THE FIFTEENTH-CENTURY BID FOR CONCILIARISM INSTEAD OF PRIMATIAL GOVERNMENT OF THE CHURCH

Between the Fourth and the Fifth Lateran Councils, nearly three hundred years elapsed. These were the years when a papal monarchy developed (see pp. 110-14); it became a matter for discussion whether a pope

---

[4]Ibid.
[5]Martin Luther, *Reformation Writings of Martin Luther*, trans. Bertram Lee Woolf (London: Lutterworth, 1956), 2:111.

could rule on his own authority in a way which bound the church or whether decisions should continue to be made by councils, as the would-be conciliarists maintained.

In the fifteenth century a series of councils were held in which the papacy and conciliarists were engaged in a power struggle. The first was the Council of Constance (1414-1418). It had urgent business, the ending of the Great Schism in the Western church, which lasted from 1378-1417.

This was not a schism of the sort which had occurred in 1054 and which cleft the church down the middle. It was about the problem of rival claimants to be the true pope. That was nothing new, for popes and antipopes had often been rivals in previous centuries. Lists of popes and antipopes show that this was far from uncommon. The monarchical papacy, which had emerged since the twelfth century, had not by any means been monolithic. But this time there had been a rival papacy based at Avignon for too long for comfort—from 1309 to the late 1370s. The fact that it had set up camp outside Rome and seven successive popes had been Frenchmen defiantly remaining in their own country was in itself a factor making the division seem exceptional. At last in 1377 Gregory XI (1329-1378) brought the papal court back to Rome. Schism continued, however, because a fresh line of antipopes began at Avignon and continued until the Council of Constance brought things to a head and ended the story.

The degree of uncertainty involved in the Great Schism now began to draw in the politicians of Europe. The Council of Constance deposed the current rivals, Gregory XII (c. 1326-1417, supported by the Romans), Benedict XIII (d. 1423, the Avignon party's favorite) and John XXIII (d. 1419), who had succeeded Alexander V (c. 1339-1410), the preferred candidate of a council held at Pisa in 1409. Constance unanimously chose Martin V (1368-1431) as pope. Its ecclesiological authority to do so was clearly open to challenge, but in fact the time was ripe for a resolution, and during his tenure the Great Schism ended, in 1429.

The council reflected on the benefits to church life and sound ecclesiology of holding regular councils and the drawbacks of failing to do so:

The frequent holding of general councils is a pre-eminent means of culti-

vating the Lord's patrimony. It roots out the briars, thorns and thistles of
heresies, errors and schisms, corrects deviations, reforms what is deformed
and produces a richly fertile crop for the Lord's vineyard. Neglect of councils, on the other hand, spreads and fosters the aforesaid evils.[6]

It decreed that councils should be held regularly and frequently, at
least every ten years in the long term:

> For this reason we establish, enact, decree and ordain, by a perpetual edict,
> that general councils shall be held henceforth in the following way. The
> first shall follow in five years immediately after the end of this council,
> the second in seven years immediately after the end of the next council,
> and thereafter they are to be held every ten years for ever.[7]

Before the end of any council, the pope, or failing the pope, the council itself, was to identify a place for the next council to be held, and that
arrangement was not to be changed without good reason.

It was envisaged that the problem of rival popes was likely to arise
again in the future. If that happens "the date of the council, if it is more
than a year off, is to be brought forward to one year ahead; calculating
this from the day on which two or more of them publicly assumed the
insignia of their pontificates or on which they began to govern." Everyone who ought to attend the council is to come in such an emergency
without a summons—avoiding the difficulty which would arise if a
pope must summon a council and it is disputed who the pope is. All
claimants to the papacy at the time are suspended from office by the
council until it has been "settled by the Council" who is the true pope.[8]
Taken together these two provisions clearly tend to put council above
pope. The council, in its fifth session of April 6, 1415, made an unequivocal statement to that effect in the *Haec sancta* decree:

> First it declares that, legitimately assembled in the Holy Spirit, constitut-
> ing a general council and representing the catholic church militant, it has
> power immediately from Christ; and that everyone of whatever state or

---

[6]Council of Constance, pt. 5, in *Decrees of the Ecumenical Councils*, pp. 437-38, www.dailycatholic
.org/history/16ecume5.htm.
[7]Ibid., pt. 1, pp. 404-5, www. dailycatholic.org/history/16ecume1.htm.
[8]Ibid.

dignity, even papal, is bound to obey it in those matters which pertain to the faith, the eradication of the said schism and the general reform of the said church of God in head and members.[9]

The Council of Constance also attempted to tackle the pervasive corruption in the church, which it was claimed had grown worse during the schism. One of its decrees, on how to behave at a council meeting, gives a picture of the conduct which was causing disquiet even during the conduct of council business: "Nobody should shout at or in any way disturb the Lord's priests when they sit in the place of blessing. Nobody should cause disturbance by telling idle stories or jokes or, what is even worse, by stubborn disputes." This was partly a plea for the dignity of the proceedings to be respected. "For, justice loses its reverence when the silence of the court is disturbed by a crowd of turbulent people. As the prophet says, 'the reverence due to justice shall be silence'":

> Therefore whatever is being debated by the participants, or is being proposed by persons making an accusation, should be stated in quiet tones so that the hearers' senses are not disturbed by contentious voices and they do not weaken the authority of the court by their tumult.[10]

Anyone who disturbs the quiet tenor of the proceedings "with noise or dissensions or jests" shall be ejected and stripped of the right to be present. It seems to have been accepted with resignation that people may not sit where they are not supposed to, so "since it may happen that some of the participants will not be in their rightful seats, we decree, with this sacred council's approval, that no prejudice shall arise to any church or person as a result of this seating arrangement."[11]

The other area of widespread concern to which the Council of Constance gave attention was the spread of heresy. The call for unity and the fear of schism was in the forefront of minds in confronting this problem of heresy too. In May 1415 the council declared itself a "general council" which represented the "catholic Church" and was "legitimately assembled in the Holy Spirit" for the eradication of the present schism

---

[9]Ibid., pt. 1, pp. 408-9, www.dailycatholic.org/history/16ecume1.htm.
[10]Ibid.
[11]Ibid.

and the elimination of the errors and heresies which were sprouting beneath its shade and for the reform of the church. It is an irony perhaps that Reformation hatred of the papacy and its monarchical claims should have been so strong when the monarchy of a given pope at the time had been so regularly challenged by an antipope, and popes tended to be to some degree puppets or preferred appointees of political factions in Rome or in Europe at large. One of the prompters of the habit of thinking like that was John Wyclif, whose antipapal diatribes had been numerous and impassioned, and who after his death was condemned at Constance, along with his followers (see pp. 214-25).

Trying to restore unity: The Council of Basel-Ferrara-Florence, 1431-1445. The Council of Basel, which transferred to Ferrara and then to Florence (therefore usually simply called the Council of Florence), was held in the context of a strong and optimistic conciliarist movement. This went naturally enough with an energetic drive to restore unity throughout the Christian church, not merely by suppressing heretical and dissident opinions, but also by bringing together long-divided communities through revisiting old schisms with the churches of the East. One by one these churches were allegedly brought to see the error of their ways and to agree with the Roman position, though none of the agreements lasted. The points of disagreement were of course old quarrels, and there was not much heat in most of them in the fifteenth century, a thousand years on from their beginnings. Nevertheless, the contrast with the repressive way the church treated dissidents in the West itself is striking. A pattern of suppressions was being set here which was to continue in the sixteenth century when it came to dealing with the emerging Reformers in the West.

The passage of arms between conciliarists and papacy set a context. The council that began at Basel, with lively intentions of keeping the papacy in its place, divided early on into a remnant which stayed behind and still claimed to be the true council, and the bulk of the council delegates. These transferred to Ferrara in a climate of European warfare and continuing concern about the popularity of dissident opinions in the wake of Wyclif and Hus. The breakdown of the council was regarded as unfortunate by those who feared the dissidents would read it as a statement of the weakness of the institutional church.

The first and most urgent task was to make it plain which group was now the true council. The transferred council identified heretical views held by the remnant at Basel that could be taken to disqualify them. Basel, they said, had misrepresented the intention of the Council of Constance when it made its pronouncement about the authority of a General Council. Ferrara, by contrast,

> is already legitimately assembled, and . . . the continuation of this trans-lated synod has been effected . . . and the synod is and ought to be con-tinued from today onwards for all the purposes for which the synod of Basle was convened, including being the ecumenical council at which the union of the western and the eastern church is treated and with God's help achieved.

For the avoidance of doubt:

> This holy synod . . . quashes, invalidates and annuls, and declares to be invalid, quashed, null and of no force or moment, each and all of the things done in the city of Basel in the name of a general council after the said translation, and whatever may be attempted there or elsewhere in the future in the name of a general council.

Although "if in the matter of the Bohemians (the Hussites) something useful has been achieved by the said people assembled at Basel after the said translation, it intends to approve that and supply for defects."

The transferred council thus chose to incorporate into its business some meetings which had been arranged with the representatives of the Greeks, whose Church had been divided from that of the West at the schism of 1054. The Greeks, bishops and some theologians, attended the council from April 1438, and went with it when it was once more trans-ferred, this time to Florence in 1439.[12] These stages of the council took place under the presidency of the pope, and their decisions therefore took the form of papal bulls rather than the conciliar decrees which had been envisaged when the council first met at Basel. It was the pope who stated the official reason for this further transfer, which was that a coun-

---

[12]On July 6, 1439, the decree of union with the Greek church was approved and the "decrees of union" which followed were approved shortly afterward.

cil needed "healthy air" and the city was full of plague, making it difficult for the delegates to concentrate with minds free from anxiety for
their personal safety. "Assuredly it is right that those who come together
at synods to treat of difficult questions should be free from every anxiety and fear, so that they may be able in greater peace and freedom to
give their attention to the matters of public concern."

Despite the optimism of the pope's address, the agreement with the
Greeks was never to "take"; when the Greek bishops and scholars got
home they found their autocephalous churches unwilling to ratify what
they had agreed.

Of particular interest with hindsight was not the ecclesiological na-
ivety of the attempt but the identification of the topics of disagreement
which had proved church-dividing. The first thing was the procession of
the Holy Spirit. "Texts were produced from divine scriptures and many
authorities of eastern and western holy doctors, some saying the holy
Spirit proceeds from the Father and the Son, others saying the procession is from the Father through the Son." The conclusion was that if
these texts were correctly understood, there was no substantial disagreement. "All were aiming at the same meaning in different words."

On the subject of the use of leavened or unleavened bread in the
Eucharist, they simply agreed to differ: "Priests should confect the body
of Christ in either, that is, each priest according to the custom of his
western or eastern church."

A universal papal primacy was "agreed," with the rider that "the patriarch of Constantinople should be second after the most holy Roman
pontiff, third should be the patriarch of Alexandria, fourth the patriarch
of Antioch, and fifth the patriarch of Jerusalem, without prejudice to all
their privileges and rights."[13]

Encouraged by this success, the council moved on to discussions with
other Eastern Christian churches, whose continuing existence does not
seem to have been much in Western minds for many centuries. With
the Armenians, divided from Rome for nearly a thousand years, the
Romans once more nominated scholars and academics to give expert

---

[13]"Ecumenical Council of Florence," in *Decrees of the Ecumenical Councils*, pp. 454-55, www.ewtn
.com/library/councils/florence.htm.

help. ("We nominated from every rank of this sacred council experts in divine and human law to treat of the matter with the envoys with all care, study and diligence.") The objective was "that they should think in every way like the apostolic see and that the union should be stable and lasting with no cause for hesitation whatsoever."[14] The agreement involved settling which of the early councils the Armenians would accept and persuading them that they had been mistaken all these centuries. The

> Armenians have accepted no other later universal synods nor the most blessed Leo, bishop of this holy see, by whose authority the council of Chalcedon met. For they claim that it was proposed to them that both the synod of Chalcedon and the said Leo had made the definition in accordance with the condemned heresy of Nestorius. So we instructed them and declared that such a suggestion was false and that the synod of Chalcedon and blessed Leo holily and rightly defined the truth of two natures in the one person of Christ, described above, against the impious tenets of Nestorius and Eutyches.

A "brief scheme" of the seven sacraments now recognized in the West ("namely baptism, confirmation, Eucharist, penance, extreme unction, orders and matrimony") was provided, for the avoidance of future uncertainty.

The Armenians accepted all this and other points "in their own name and in the name of their patriarch and of all Armenians" in a spirit of obedience to the Roman see.

In the case of the Copts, the available representative at the council was abbot Andrew. He was "examined by some outstanding men of this sacred council on the articles of the faith, the sacraments of the church and certain other matters pertaining to salvation." The key topics in the case of the Copts were the doctrine of the Trinity, especially the procession of the Holy Spirit. Also important was the outlawing of dualism (God is the creator of the material world and the author of the Old Testament as well as the New): "Hence it anathematizes the madness of the Manichees who posited two first principles, one of visible things, the other of invisible things, and said that one was the God of the new Testament, the other of the old Testament."

---

[14]Ibid.

A complex of patristic debates on the incarnation seem to have been considered in this review of the Copts and their ideas at a level of detail which reveals a sophisticated understanding of the issues. The agreement rejected the following heretical opinions of the early centuries, those of "Manes and his followers who, imagining that the Son of God took to himself not a real body but a phantasmal one completely rejected the truth of the humanity in Christ"; those of "Valentinus, who declared that the Son of God took nothing from his virgin mother but that he assumed a heavenly body and passed through the virgin's womb like water flowing down an aqueduct"; those of "Arius, who by his assertion that the body taken from the virgin had no soul, wanted the Deity to take the place of the soul"; those of "Apollinarius who, realizing that if the soul informing the body were denied there would be no true humanity in Christ, posited only a sensitive soul and held that the deity of the Word took the place of the rational soul." It anathematizes also Theodore of Mopsuestia and Nestorius and Eutyches. And for safety's sake, the major heresiarchs of the early centuries are listed (the Arians, the Eunomians and the Macedonians, Ebion, Cerinthus, Marcion, Paul of Samosata, Photinus).

The agreement was that there is no salvation outside the Church, and that "outside" included all heretics, pagans and Jews and all schismatics.

The ecumenical councils (up to the sixth) accepted by the Copts were listed, and it was agreed that the Coptic Church "embraces, approves and accepts all other universal synods which were legitimately summoned, celebrated and confirmed by the authority of a Roman pontiff, and especially this holy synod of Florence." "After all these explanations the aforesaid abbot Andrew, in the name of the aforesaid patriarch and of himself and of all the Jacobites" declared the conformity of the Copts with "whatever the holy apostolic see and the Roman church holds and teaches" and undertook always to obey the regulations and commands of the said apostolic see.[15]

Coptic differences with Rome on the subject of Eucharistic bread were declared unimportant, as long as transsubstantion is affirmed.

---

[15]Ibid.

"Whether the wheat bread, in which the sacrament is confected, has been baked on the same day or earlier is of no importance whatever. For, provided the substance of bread remains, there should be no doubt at all that after the aforesaid words of consecration of the body have been pronounced by a priest with the intention of consecrating, immediately it is changed in substance into the true body of Christ."

The council moved on to the Syrians in discussions with "our venerable brother Abdala, archbishop of Edessa and legate of our venerable brother Ignatius, patriarch of the Syrians, and of his whole nation," who had come to Rome "devoutly to petition that we give to them the rule of faith which the holy Roman church professes." So once more these ecumenical conversations were directed toward persuading the non-Roman participants that they were in substantial agreement with the Roman position:

> They found him orthodox on all points of faith and practice except three articles: namely, the procession of the holy Spirit, the two natures in Jesus Christ our saviour, the two wills and principles of action in him. They laid before him the truth of the orthodox faith, opened up the meaning of the sacred scriptures, adduced the testimonies of holy doctors and added telling and pertinent reasons.[16]

The representative of the Syrians was won over in his turn:

> When the archbishop had understood the doctrine on these points, he affirmed that all his doubts had been completely answered. He professed that he thought he fully understood the truth of the faith as regards both the procession of the holy Spirit and the two natures, two wills and two principles of action in our lord Jesus Christ. Moreover he declared that he would accept, in the name of the aforesaid patriarch and of the whole nation and of himself, the whole faith and all the teaching which we, with the approval of this sacred council, would propose to him.[17]

There was a follow-up visit to Cyprus to bring in the Chaldeans and the Maronites there to the newly unified church. The talk here was with

> our venerable brother Andrew, archbishop of Kalocsa, to eastern lands and the island of Cyprus. He was to confirm in the faith which had been

---

[16]Ibid.
[17]Ibid.

accepted by the Greeks, Armenians and Jacobites living there, by his sermons and his expositions and explanations of the decrees issued for their union and return. He was also to try to bring back to the truth of the faith, using our warnings and exhortations, whoever else he might find there to be strangers to the truth of faith in other sects, whether they are followers of Nestorius or of Macarius.[18]

The Chaldeans "who have been called Nestorians in Cyprus until now" then sent an envoy, "to make to us a solemn profession of the faith of the Roman church, which by the providence of the Lord and the aid of blessed Peter and the apostle has always remained immaculate." He too promised agreement with and obedience to Rome, and in particular that

in future I will always hold and profess that the holy Spirit proceeds from the Father and the Son, as the holy Roman church teaches and holds. Also, in future I will always hold and approve two natures, two wills, one hypostasis and two principles of action in Christ. Also, in future I will always confess and approve all seven sacraments of the Roman church, just as she holds, teaches and preaches. Again, in the future I will never add oil in the sacred eucharist.[19]

---

[18]Ibid.
[19]Ibid.

9

The Church
and the State

The Two Swords

They said, "Lord, look, here are two swords." He replied, "It is enough."
(Lk 22:38)

In periods when meaningful images were looked for everywhere in
Scripture (which means most periods), the "two swords" were readily
interpreted as representing the spiritual and the secular powers. Pope
Gelasius (d. 496) seems to have been the first to use this passage in a
letter of 494 as a basis for the idea that the two swords represent the
spiritual and the temporal or secular powers.[1]

The secular and spiritual powers were henceforth generally understood to be the two fundamentally distinct powers in the world, under
God. But which was to be dominant?

This image was relied on again and again from patristic times to
make the same distinction. It spoke to the times. The period of the late
Roman Empire and the centuries that followed, at least until the end
of the Middle Ages, were warlike. Most persons of consequence in
church and state had experience of the sword in its literal form. Sword
imagery also raised the question whether the spiritual authority of the
church could properly be exercised through the use of force, that is

---

[1] "To the Emperor Anastasius," in Francis Dvornik, *Pope Gelasius and Emperor Anastasius* (München:
C. H. Beck'sche, 1951).

physical violence. The usual view was that it could not, but nevertheless in feudal Europe bishops were generally also barons and had to provide their annual requirement of "knight days" to the king like any other landholder (see p. 16).

The Donation of Constantine. For much of the Middle Ages, until Lorenzo Valla (1406-1457) exposed it as a forgery, it was believed that by the "Donation of Constantine" the first Christian Roman emperor (c. 272-337) had granted supreme authority in the Western half of the Roman Empire to the pope. The real origins of the Donation were probably Carolingian. It was written for a different age when the papacy was more of a power in the West. Pope Hadrian I (d. 795) wrote to Charlemagne (c. 742-814) to encourage him to follow his predecessor's example. This was also an age much more conscious of the value of authentic documentation in lending legal authority to claims. In the ninth century the letter was included by Pseudo-Isidore in a collection of purported canon law materials, along with many pseudo-letters of pseudo-popes.[2]

A contest about investiture and papal claims to plenitude of power. Medieval thinkers began from the assumption that ultimately all power comes from God.[3] Only if God has given power to a monarch or a prelate can it be lawful and not usurped or stolen. But did God give both swords to the church, so that the pope could lend one to the temporal power of a king or emperor at a coronation, or did he give both to the secular power, which lent one to the spiritual power? Or did he perhaps give them one each? On all these matters there was much disagreement among medieval academics, as we shall see. They struggled to construct a principled rationale for the raw power struggles of real life.

The investiture contest of the late eleventh and early twelfth centuries was prompted by another power struggle between church and state, and the two-swords analogy began to be used again. That started the theme on a long medieval career.

Part of the trouble lay at the close family relationships of the leading figures in European politics. In a feudal society the bonds between a man

---

[2] *Decretales Ps-Isidorianae*, ed. P. Hinschius (Leipzig, 1863).
[3] *Authority and Power: Studies on Medieval Law and Government Presented to Walter Ullmann*, ed. Brian Tierney and Peter Lineham (Cambridge: Cambridge University Press, 1980).

and his secular lord were not those of slavery, except in the case of the serfs, but they were, even among the nobility, very nearly a relationship of ownership. A lord "owned" the serfs who actually farmed his lands. At higher levels of society the king would form a relationship of vassalage with each of his barons. The baron knelt and placed his hands between those of his lord in an act of fealty (from *fidelitas,* faithfulness).

The nobility of northern Europe had only two professions open to them, the military and the clerical. By the high and late Middle Ages the sons of great families either fought their "rent days" for the King as knights or they held "livings"—sometimes bishoprics—as ordained ministers. This meant in practice that a few families shared the exercise of the two powers in each land among them. In the feudal system the monarch owned all the land and granted parcels of it to his vassals in return for their acceptance of his ultimate ownership and his rulership over the realm in question. So land was power in both church and state. It was easy to confuse the spheres and boundaries of spiritual and temporal influence when you were a baron and your brother was a bishop. That began to happen to a troublesome degree in the late eleventh century.

As a baron, a bishop's lands were on loan from the king. Kings and emperors were tempted to exploit the advantage of their control of the granting of land to enhance their revenues. Every see had "temporalities," lands and property which went with the bishopric, and while the see was "vacant" the king could take the revenues from these lands. It became the custom to leave a see vacant for a year for this reason.

In reality, the ruling classes of these areas of northern Europe were relatively small. The same few leading families produced the bishops as well as the barons. The king had to entrust the estates or lands of a bishopric to the bishop just as he would grant lands to his brother the baron. A bishop easily came to be seen as a "spiritual baron." The emperors of Germany and successive popes struggled for supremacy over one another in Europe. One of the effects was the development of a culture of top-down management in the church, the assertion of overmounting claims of primacy and supremacy of jurisdiction.

Then kings and emperors began pushing the boundaries of the rules even further in replacing bishops. A bishop could be *consecrated* or promoted to the office only by the church, but the person who was to be bishop could be *selected* in various ways, some of which involved royal or imperial patronage. Kings and emperors had every reason to try to make their own relatives and friends bishops, for a bishop was likely to feature actively at court in the future. This sort of patronage and nepotism was tolerated, but not when the king or emperor went so far as to seek to *invest* or install his chosen bishop in the position, with the ring and staff of episcopal office. This too was solely the church's prerogative. It belonged to the "spiritualities," not the "temporalities," of the office of bishop.

A serious dispute began and the papacy took the opportunity to try to enforce the superiority of the spiritual over the temporal power. To this end, Pope Gregory VII (d. 1085) jotted down a list of papal powers in 1075, which was preserved among his papers in the official register. These *Dictatus Papae* form a list of twenty-seven articles or assertions.[4] They represent the first moves in an aggrandizement of papal power, which was eventually to become one of the main prompters of the Reformation.

Gregory VII's contention was first "that the Roman church was founded by God alone," and second that only its bishop can rightfully be called "universal." This assertion comes high up his list because for some centuries, particularly since the time of Gregory the Great, the bishop of Rome and the four other holders of patriarch office in the church, the patriarchs of Alexandria, Antioch, Constantinople and Jerusalem, had been struggling for supremacy as primate of the whole church. Constantinople claimed with justice to have been the city of Constantine; Rome claimed with justice to have been the city where Peter, whom Jesus called the rock on which he would found his church, was the first bishop. The dispute helped to develop thinking about the role of the supreme bishop of the West and his hierarchical relationship to other bishops. In the Eastern, Greek-speaking half of the church as it had emerged in the last centuries of the old Roman Empire, the custom had grown up of agreeing on a special role for the metropolitan bishops, bishops of cities of especial political importance. Higher still came the patriarchs.

---

[4]Brian Tierney, ed., *The Middle Ages, Vol. I: Sources of Medieval History*, 4th ed. (New York: Alfred A. Knopf, 1983), pp. 142-43.

Ecclesiologically, "primacy" came to be seen in the West as a matter of jurisdiction rather than of honor. It meant, as Gregory VII put it, that the primate of Rome "alone can depose or reinstate bishops" (3). He also insisted that in a council of the church, where historically each bishop had a vote and an equal voice on behalf of his local church or diocese, the pope's own legate—even if he was not himself a bishop—was "above all bishops" (4). This was important because it sought to replace collegiality and the forming of consensus with monarchical aspirations for the papacy. He claimed in the *Dictatus Papae* that "no synod shall be called a general one without his order" (16).

Gregory was chiefly concerned in 1075 to clarify and strengthen the pope's position in relation to the state. He claimed "that he alone may use the imperial insignia"; "that of the pope alone all princes shall kiss the feet." He also enlarged his claims into areas where the faith is determined and into judicial and juridical territory. "The Roman church has never erred; nor will it err to all eternity, the Scripture bearing witness." "No chapter and no book shall be considered canonical without his authority." "He himself may be judged by no one," and if anyone appeals to him against the sentence of a lower church authority, no one shall dare to condemn the appellant but the pope. In essence he was claiming that he *was* the church, and when there was general acceptance that there is no salvation outside the church that was a very important claim. "He who is not at peace with the Roman church shall not be considered catholic" (26) is how he put it in the *Dictatus Papae*.

Emperors also went too far in another direction, by seeking to interfere in Italian affairs. Italy was still full of city-states, which took a hostile view of claims to overarching authority above them. The emperor Henry IV (1050-1106) tried to choose the next bishop of Milan when a different candidate was already favored by Rome. Gregory excommunicated him in 1076, a year after he had asserted the right to "absolve subjects from their fealty to wicked men" and that "among other things, we ought not to remain in the same house with those excommunicated by" the pope (*Dictatus Papae* 27 and 6).

Popes successfully asserted the church's rights not only against those of the state but also over those of other authorities in the church, during the decades of the ensuing investiture contest. It was an opportunity to test the extent of the "spiritual power." This had its advantages. A pope could excommunicate several monarchs at the same time without stretching his resources. Excommunication affected the whole kingdom and could lead to uprisings by angry subjects. But, although emperors made a bid to choose popes as well, a secular ruler had only armies with which to fight back, and although there were several forays by the German emperors over the Alps and into Italy, it was manifestly unwise to try to fight on too many fronts at once. And it proved to be ineffectual too, for Italy had city-states, not feudalism, and the capacity of those cities to resist was discomfiting to the emperor. This was an era of intense competitive struggles among the cities and factions within cities in Italy in which the papacy was a significant prize. A glance at the list of popes and antipopes for the period tells its own story.

The Concordat of Worms provided a rough settlement of the "contest" in 1122. A separation of "temporalities" and "spiritualities" in the appointment of bishops was agreed. A king or emperor could invest a bishop "by the lance" with secular control of the lands of the see, but he could not intrude on the investment by "ring and staff," which the church alone could make because this conferred sacramental authority and the pastoral charge.

Bernard of Clairvaux and "considerations" for popes. Bernard of Clairvaux (1090-1153) was the main reason for the huge success of the Cistercian order. These were reformed Benedictines, whose founder, Robert of Molesme, had started a monastery at Cîteaux in 1098 with the idea of creating a community that would return to the original vision of Benedict. He was himself of noble birth and had been a monk since he was a boy; he had become disillusioned with the difficulty of reforming what he saw to be serious corruptions in existing houses. To this new foundation came Bernard with thirty other young men whom he had drawn to the idea of living this new, reformed, more dedicated monastic life. He turned out to have great natural powers as a preacher, and he was soon bringing in crowds of new members. He was sent to start a new monastery at Clairvaux three years after entering Cîteaux, and the numbers continued to grow with a series of new foundations.

Bernard never moved on from the abbacy of Clairvaux, but he was much in demand as a diplomat and emissary in the church and moved in influential circles. One of the monks he had known when young became Pope Eugenius III (d. 1153). It was brought to Bernard's notice that Eugenius was allowing too much of his time to be taken up in hearing appeals to the papal court; there were plenty of ambitious young lawyers keen to take advantage of his naiveté. So Bernard wrote him a book which he titled *On Consideration* (*De consideratione*), probably choosing a word Gregory the Great had used in his own guidance for the church's leaders (*Regula Pastoralis*). This had much the same message: that a busy administrator must not to forget to make time for his spiritual and intellectual life. He must learn to strike a balance.

Bernard also had something to say on the subject of the two swords, the spiritual and the temporal or material. One is wielded *by* the church and the other *for* the church. One is a priestly, one a knightly sword, exercised by the orders of priest and emperor respectively.[5]

His contemporary John of Salisbury (c. 1120-1180) used the image too:

> This sword, then, the prince receives from the hand of the Church, although she herself has no sword of blood at all. Nevertheless she has this sword, but she uses it by the hand of the prince, upon whom she confers the power of bodily coercion, retaining to herself authority over spiritual things in the person of the pontiffs. The prince is, then, as it were, a minister of the priestly power, and one who exercises that side of the sacred offices which seems unworthy of the hands of the priesthood.[6]

Bernard originally meant *De consideratione* to be a single book, but he was soon drawn into preaching the Second Crusade and then he found he was writing further sections, until *De consideratione* was in five books, completed close to the end of his life. He had expanded his advice to include a review of the full extent of the powers of the pope. The pope, he claimed, was supreme above everything in the created world and had nothing above him but the hierarchy of heaven. *Sacerdos magnus, summus pontifex.*[7]

---

[5]Bernard of Clairvaux, *De Consideratione*, 4.3.7, *Opera Omnia*, 3, p. 454.
[6]John of Salisbury, *Policraticus* 4.3, ed. K. S .B. Keats-Rohan, CCCM 118 (1993).
[7]Bernard of Clairvaux, *De Consideratione*, 2.8.15, p. 423.

These were strong encouragements to the further development of monarchical aspirations in the papacy. The success of the moves to claim supremacy over the secular powers went with assertions of special primatial powers over against the other ecclesiastical authorities. Bishops in a properly constituted council where the Holy Spirit was held to preside could run the church collegially, and in earlier centuries that had been the accepted method of decision making. The *plenitudo potestatis*, the pope's "plenitude of power," ordained by God (who alone has absolute power), had been asserted in the pontificate of Leo I (440-461). But its full expansion of meaning came now, in the Middle Ages, and especially under Innocent III.

John of Paris and Dante. John of Paris (d. 1306), a Dominican and author of *On Royal and Papal Power*, took this discussion about the distinction of temporal and spiritual power further in the late thirteenth century.[8] The writing of the book was prompted by a dispute between Philip IV (1268-1314), king of France, and Pope Boniface VIII (c. 1234-1303) over some currently contentious aspects of the old argument about the positioning of the boundaries between the spiritual and the secular or temporal realms of jurisdiction or *dominium*, "lordship." He weakened the likelihood that his views would have long-term influence by tending to favor the king. He suggested that in certain circumstances a pope might even be deposed.

There were several running questions. If all property is essentially "secular," perhaps the church has no property rights at all. If all power comes from God, does it come "through" the pope, when the church plays its part in the coronation of a monarch? If that is the case, then the church has jurisdiction, under God, over everything, and ultimately controls the temporal as well as the spiritual. That was certainly what Bernard of Clairvaux had claimed. John of Paris knows that some

> "say that the pope and bishops have no power in temporal affairs, and that it is unlawful for the clergy to have any temporal property"; some "say that the pope has power over the properties of laymen and jurisdiction over them,

---

[8]John of Paris, *On Royal and Papal Power* 7, trans. Arthur P. Monahan (London: Columbia University Press, 1974).

and say that the pope 'has primary authority, derived directly from God, whereas the prince has his power mediately from God through the Pope.'"[9]

John of Paris's own position was "separatist." He favored a form of subsidiarity in which temporal and spiritual have their own distinct realms. Secular government is not subordinate to the church; the church has no temporal power from Christ. Church property belongs to the Christian community; the property of laymen belongs to them as individuals, though property owners may be required to make contributions for the common good.

However, the structures of power seem to favor the notion of a hegemony by the church. In John of Paris's eyes the pope is a monarch. He is the single supreme priest at the head of the whole church. He is the focus of unity. On the other hand, there is not a single secular ruler who can stand as his counterpart. The emperor does not control the whole of Europe. There are many kings too.

It follows that a world empire is not desirable, though Dante took the opposite view in his *De Monarchia*. In 1301 he was in political exile from his beloved Florence and seeking revenge on those of an opposing faction who had driven him out. Italian city states were rife with factions. He put forward a theory which would, if it caught on, have provided a much higher authority to knock heads together. In this work he asks three questions, of which the third is whether the supreme secular power derives its authority directly from God or from God through the church. He wanted to show that the powers are separate, that it is not true as papal advocates claimed that the pope held both swords (as Peter had done at Jesus' arrest), and merely lent one to the emperor; that the Donation of Constantine merely lent authority to the pope to look after what remained the emperor's domain.

THE BODY POLITIC, THE CITY, THE CORPORATION AND THE CHURCH

The rationalizations that began with Bernard's treatise and were carried forward in these later debates soon began to engage the interest of the

---

[9]Ibid., p. 71.

lawyers. Here the Italians were prominent. The great early law school of Europe was in Bologna, and it maintained its preeminence in law as universities invented themselves all over the continent.

Italian cities were still run in a way which the ancient Romans would have found familiar. Bartolus of Sassoferrato (1313-1357) made an especially important contribution to the understanding of the city-state and the way it can operate as a political entity. He published his *Treatise on City Government* about 1330. He began with Aristotle, as medieval writers on political thought usually did from the thirteenth century onward, when Aristotle's *Politics* became available in Latin. Aristotle says there are six ways of governing. There is government by the many, in its good form (polity) and its bad form (democracy, by which he means mob rule). There is government by the few (oligarchy, which is bad, and aristocracy, which is good in its Greek sense of rule by the best). There is government by one ruler, in a good form, monarchy, and a bad form, tyranny. Of these, polity is the best of all.

Bartolo disagreed with Aristotle here. He thought monarchy was the best because it helped to focus the many on a single objective of living in unity, maintaining peace and harmony. He looked at Old Testament passages for biblical guidance on the benefits of benevolent kingly rule.

Baldus de Ubaldis (1327-1400) lectured in a number of Italian universities and developed a theory of the fundamental nature of society which had features with special appeal to the church. Societies are like bodies, he said. The basis of "corporation" theory is the understanding of the way people unite in a common purpose. This he derives from the analogy of the human body. Bodies are complex organisms in which the parts of the body have different functions and which need the direction of a head. In the state the head is the king or prince or emperor. In the church it is Christ, though the papal monarchists would say that Christ has a vicar on earth.

This is of course a scriptural idea, one which had been explored in the twelfth century too. First Corinthians 12:12-14 emphasizes the unity of the body, although it is made up of many members (cf. Rom 12:5; Eph 3:6; 5:23; Col 1:18, 24). Each member knows its place. The foot does not complain because it is not a hand. These are doctrines that strengthen social stability and discourage social revolution, particularly important considerations in the turbulent, faction-ridden cities of Italy.

It was still important to be able to say where power comes from. There were two main schools of thought. The one which gave rise to variants of the two swords theory insisted that all power comes from God and the only question is the route of transmission. The other, a view derived in part from the structure of classical city-state, said that the consent of the people made a state legitimate. They had to agree to be ruled, or the ruler was a tyrant and usurper. John of Salisbury had already asked whether it can be lawful to overthrow a ruler in his *Policraticus* in the 1160s:

> Between a tyrant and a prince there is this single or chief difference, that the latter obeys the law and rules the people by its dictates, accounting himself as but their servant. . . .
>
> Whereas private men are held responsible only for their private affairs, on the prince fall the burdens of the whole community. . . . [T]he prince is the public power, and a kind of likeness on earth of the divine majesty. . . . For all power is from the Lord God. . . . The power which the prince has is therefore from God, for the power of God is never lost, nor severed from him. . . . Who, therefore, resists the ruling power, resists the ordinance of God [Rom 13:2].[10]

Baldus proposed a compromise. A free people, he said, might choose their monarch. But God must legitimize the people's choice by a grant of power because ultimately all power comes from God.

This view of things was compatible with various forms of government, from the collegial to the monarchical and with the government of both church and state. It could also accommodate a problem vexing the church, which was the framework of jurisdiction over the many parts of the Holy Roman Empire, the medieval revival of the classical empire, and the Roman Church in the West. The bishop of Rome claimed ultimate spiritual jurisdiction over all the dioceses of Western Europe. The main problem with attempting to generalize the principle to all forms of government was that a city-state (in Italy at least) had no prince, no "head."

---

[10] John of Salisbury, *Policraticus* 4.1.

The questions what is a tyrant and whether tyrants can be legitimate rulers did not die away with the Reformation. Juan de Mariana (1536-1624), a Spanish Jesuit, was involved in a number of controversies with both church and secular authorities. In 1610 Henry IV of France (b. 1553) was assassinated, and the question whether a tyrant ceased to be a legitimate ruler became a practical and no longer just an academic one. Juan distinguishes the usurper from the lawful ruler who behaves badly: "The prince who has taken possession of a republic by force and arms and, moreover, with no right and no public consent of the citizens can be killed by anyone and be deprived of his life and dominion, . . . he may be removed by any method."[11]

But in the case of "the prince who holds power by the consent of the people or by hereditary right," the people must put up with him unless "he destroys the republic, considers public and private fortunes as his own booty" and so on. It may be legitimate to get rid of him, but that does not mean that violence is allowable. If possible, there should be a public meeting and a warning, and only if that does not work should there be resort to arms.[12]

How, then, is a tyrant to be identified? Is a ruler a tyrant "when the capacity for public meeting has been taken away from the citizens"? "Upheavals in the republic must be avoided. Care must be taken."[13] And if a ruler is a lawful ruler, any attempt to topple a king or resist the authority of a bishop is an affront to God, who appointed the individual in question.

An ideal of order. The reaction of the authorities in church and state in the later Middle Ages to any challenge to peace and good order reflects a much more practical reality than these academic treatises presented. The authorities feared popular discontent and uprising, even suspected that not all those present in church every week were truly orthodox in their opinions. There was good enough reason for that. It was a well-known fact that in the south of France the Albigensian heretics of the

---

[11]Juan de Mariana, cited in *Early Modern Catholicism: An Anthology of Primary Sources*, ed. Robert S. Miola (Oxford: Oxford University Press, 2007), p. 88.
[12]Ibid., pp. 88-89.
[13]Ibid., p. 90.

early thirteenth century often went to church as well as to their heretical meetings, just to be on the safe side.

The threat that dissident religious views might lead to disorder grew with the Reformation, especially in the anarchic and sometimes violent challenge posed by Anabaptist and other extreme revolutionary Reformers (see pp. 275-76, 311-12).

The medieval appeal to order (*ordo*) had many dimensions. It entailed that a social hierarchy was integral to God's plan for his creation (see p. 128). God created angels, human beings, animals, vegetables, rocks and stones, with distinct functions and places in the world, and it did not behoove them to try to move up to a higher level of being. Within the stratum of human society, there were servants and masters, and here too the right thing for the Christian to do was to accept the position he or she was born into and seek to be a good servant, not to become a master, if that was his or her intended place.

The ideal of *ordo* assumed that those who had power—either because they had won fair and square in battle or they had become rulers by a legitimate process such as inheritance of a kingdom or election as emperor—were approved by God and held rightful authority from him. It held that people ought to obey their superiors and that uprising against legitimate authority was wicked. Scholars discussed in a worried way whether there could be justification for disobeying or even seeking to overthrow a tyrant or a usurper.[14]

So disorder presented a direct social challenge and also a challenge to political stability. It had the potential to overturn established hierarchies of social class and to overthrow rulers.

TITLES AND BENEFICES AND THE GROWING PROBLEM OF THE CHURCH'S WEALTH

One of the results of the establishment of local churches was the need to come to an arrangement about the possession or holding or use of physical property by the community. That was bound to be a different

---

[14]John of Salisbury, *Policraticus* 4.1, ed. K. S. B. Keats-Rohan (Turnhout, Belgium: Brepols, 1993), p. 232ff.

question in different places, for property rights, and especially those which related to land, were also a matter of interest for the secular authorities, and they had their own local laws and practices and expectations in different parts of Europe.

Northern Europe was mainly feudal, with lands held by the ruler and granted to barons or other nobles and to the bishops by the current ruler. The rent took the form of a number of days of military service each year, which even church holders of lands had to provide, and a proportion of the yield of the lands in the form of meat and vegetables produced. It was because of this assumption that all lands were the property of the ruler that kings and emperors had been able to withhold the lands of vacant sees for a year or two and keep the revenues, until they were ready to nominate a new bishop—a scandal that had helped to prompt the investiture contest.

In southern Europe the survival of Italian city-states created a quite different environment in which the politics might be more sophisticated, but the fighting over property was no less intense, and where, again, the members of a few influential families or factions often controlled power and property in church and state alike. In Italian cities there were powerful factions engaged in a form of gang warfare, where a similar pattern of small groups seeking power and control tried to trade appointments to bishoprics and even the papacy. Dante experienced the consequences in his own life in the painful exile from his native Florence, which prompted him to write a book about monarchy.

When a priest was entrusted with a parish, he was given a location within this complex environment of taxation on land. The church exacted its tax on lands too, in the form of a "tithe." The practice was based on the tithe of the Old Testament (Deut 14:22; Num 18:31-32), and its continuation justified by the reference to tithes in the New Testament (Mt 23:23; Lk 11:42). Parishes were expected to provide an income for their priest through the tithe. Exceptional emergency tithes were also possible, such as the "Saladin tithe" exacted to raise funds for the Third Crusade, which was assessed in dioceses and not in counties.

Reformers of the sixteenth century found it hard to separate the question what is of the essence of church from the practicalities of the way it is run in the local political and economic framework, or as Richard Hooker put it, "What the Church is and in what respect lawes of politie are thereunto necessarily required."[15] Reformers in some communities, including the Church of England, were willing to continue the system because it provided parish priests with "livings," and the *advowson*, or right to grant a "living," became an important power of patronage in succeeding centuries.

Popular protest begins to emerge. Any undercurrent of popular questioning about the way things were run emerged into resistance in ways which made the authorities in church and state nervous of mob rule. English chronicler Ranulf Higden (c. 1285-1364) wrote a *Polychronicon*. In it he describes the exciting times in London when John Northampton was Lord Mayor for two years in the reign of Richard II (1367-1400). Northampton was elected with known reforming ambitions and a reputation as a troublemaker. He was arrested and accused of being the cause of much of the trouble in the city.[16] A cobbler "drove the people to rise up." But "the just and merciful God" did not approve of sedition; the authorities thought it better that one should die than that there should be general bloodshed, so he was captured, executed and his head fixed in a public place as an example to others. The effect was not what the authorities anticipated. The people were angry and resentful. More trouble was threatened.[17]

The troublesome were often members of a new middle class of tradesmen, articulate, able, and conveniently closely in touch because they were working in a city (or in the growing towns) and not in a rural area. Tradespeople resented attempts at government control of their activities, especially when Parliament tried to take away their privileges and enact legislation to allow everyone to buy and sell freely anywhere.[18]

The Paston letters, exchanged by members of an East Anglian family in the fifteenth century, frequently reveal the fear of disorder and even violence. William Paston (1378-1444) wrote to the representative of the

---

[15]Hooker, *Laws*, bk. 3.1.
[16]Ranulf Higden, *Polychronicon*, Rolls Series, ed. J. B. Lumby (1886), 9:30.
[17]Ibid., p. 31.
[18]Ibid., p. 179.

abbot of Cluny in England in 1430 to express his concerns about the
local community of young monks "that have abiden there" for a decade
without an abbot. He is worried that unless they are taken in hand and
properly professed, "many inconvenients are like to fall."[19] In a letter of
May 1448, Margaret Paston (d. c. 1479) wrote about an episode on the
previous Friday: "the parson of Oxnead being at mass in our parish
church, even at the levation of the sacring," when a fight broke out in
the street outside.[20]

Reports of Lollard preaching were as disturbing as rumors of popular unrest. Both were thought to have a tendency to spread. In the
case of the preachers, the accusation was that they "perverted" the
thinking of *idiotas et simplices* with their "wicked doctrines" in many
ways, and the infection was spreading throughout England. Called to
answer for their behavior, they said the local bishop had no right to
send for them and they had no duty to respond because he was a friar
(*frater*) and an apostate.[21]

We are back in the landscape about which Langland was writing, and
ready to look at the medieval scene.

---

[19]*The Paston Letters*, ed. Norman Davis (Oxford: Oxford University Press, 1963), p. 1.
[20]Ibid., p. 10.
[21]Higden, *Polychronicon*, 9:171.

PART TWO

CONTINUITY AND CHANGE IN THE MIDDLE AGES

10

MONASTIC LIFE, MONASTIC EDUCATION AND AWAKENING SOCIAL CONCERNS

GUIBERT OF NOGENT:
MONK AND SOCIAL COMMENTATOR

In his autobiography *On My Life (De vita sua)*, the monk and historian Guibert of Nogent (c. 1053/1065-c. 1125) expresses his indignation about the corrupt clerical practices of the day as they had affected his own family. Deals were done for family advantage but contrary to the church's (canon) law:

> A brother of mine, a young knight and a citizen of Clermont . . . situated between Compiègne and Beauvais was waiting for the payment of money by the lord of that town, either a gift or a feudal due. And when he deferred payment, probably through want of ready money, by the advice of some of my kinsmen it was suggested to him that he should give me a canonry, called a prebend, in the church of that place, which, contrary to canon law, was in his gift, and that he should then cease to be troubled for the payment of his debt.[1]

There was also indignation that too many priests were known or suspected to be keeping mistresses. A rash of treatises appeared, advocating clerical celibacy. There were children of these unions, and it was becom-

---

ing common for a local priest to try to ensure that his children or other family members inherited his "living" or benefice. Guibert was not the only contemporary to be scandalized by this sort of "simony," the purchase of clerical office named after Simon Magus, who tried to buy for himself apostolic power and position (Acts 8:18-24). Numerous treatises against simony also appeared.

By the late twelfth century the group of articulate townspeople—followers of Waldes or Waldo of Lyons (c. 1140-c. 1218)—who were beginning to lead movements of dissent, were expressing disgust at the sight of bishops on fine horses and wearing rich clothes. This attitude of resentment of undeserved privilege was to develop during the later medieval centuries into what is now recognizable as a form of class warfare.

Yet the Middle Ages was a period when it was almost universally accepted that God had created a universe with a built-in hierarchy, explored in some detail in the work of the fifth- or sixth-century Greek author Pseudo-Dionysius (see pp. 198-99), with Western borrowings by the Carolingian author John Scotus Eriugena.[2] God stood at the apex, with the angels below him, then human beings, animals, vegetables and at the bottom inanimate rocks and stones. Within the human sphere—uncontroversially to the medieval eye—were rulers and ruled, those born to high places and those born to serve. The New Testament seemed clear about the duty to accept one's position and be a good servant if that was one's lot.

Almost the only route to social mobility in the Middle Ages in Western Europe lay through the church. It was possible—just—for a humbly born boy to make his way to eminence through the monastic life or through the priesthood. As the universities came into existence it was also possible for an able young man to get into the civil service through higher education and eventually by becoming a graduate. But Guibert was born too soon for that. His mother had high educational ambitions for him, but she also felt a pull toward the monastic life for herself and for her son. As we shall see in a moment, in an experiment in autobiog-

[2]See John Joseph O'Meara, *Eriugena* (Cork: Mercier, 1969).

raphy, rare for its time, Guibert describes what this meant for him with an eye fully alive to the social context.

What did monastic life involve? The first painful self-denials. Some Christians had always felt a special vocation to a dedicated Christian life. In the East in the early centuries they often lived this life by retreating to the deserts of the Middle East and North Africa to live alone and pray in extreme poverty. The faithful were fascinated by them and would bring them gifts in the belief that they would themselves get the benefit of a share in their holiness in that way. In times of state persecution, which were frequent in the first centuries, those who had suffered (the term was not then restricted to martyrs who actually died for their faith) gained a reputation for special holiness. People with troubled consciences would go to them, confess and ask for their prayers and spiritual support. They were the Christian heroes of their time.

In reality many of them were inwardly in torment. This sort of special calling was immensely hard work. One of the fundamental beliefs of these would-be ascetics was that there was a war between body and soul, with the body and its fleshly lusts on the side of evil, but full of fight and desperately attractive. Jerome, translator of the Bible into the Latin version known as the Vulgate, which was used throughout the Middle Ages and beyond as an authorized version of Scripture, tried several times to live this sort of life and found himself thinking about dancing girls instead of God. In 374 he wrote to Theodosius and his fellow anchorites in the Syrian desert:

> How I long to be a member of your company, and with uplifting of all my powers to embrace your admirable community! Though, indeed, these poor eyes are not worthy to look upon it. Oh! That I could behold the desert, lovelier to me than any city! Oh! That I could see those lonely spots made into a paradise by the saints that throng them! But since my sins prevent me from thrusting into your blessed company a head laden with every transgression, I adjure you (and I know that you can do it) by your prayers to deliver me from the darkness of this world.[3]

---

[3]Jerome, "Letter 2," *Nicene and Post-Nicene Fathers*, Second Series, ed. Philip Schaff and Henry Wace, rev. Kevin Knight (Buffalo, N.Y.: Christian Literature Publishing, 1893), www.newadvent .org/fathers/3001002.htm.

Jerome found his inner conflicts got worse when he tried to be good. He put that down to the work of the devil: "And because it is only a little while since I have begun not so much to abandon my vices as to desire to abandon them, the devil now ensnares me in new toils, he puts new stumbling-blocks in my path, he encompasses me on every side."[4]

Benedict institutionalizes monasticism in the West. The "inventor" of Western monasticism was Benedict of Nursia (c. 480-543). Benedict's biography appears in the *Dialogues* of Gregory the Great (published c. 593), along with many colorful stories about hermits. Much of the color derives from the behavior of people who went to see them, especially women who regarded them as a challenge and did their best to seduce them.

The authenticity of this part of the *Dialogues* is by no means certain, but this is an important early account of what Benedict's *Rule* was trying to do in encouraging the living of humble, quiet, prayerful lives of withdrawal from the world and its fleshly temptations. Benedict's *Rule* was not his original invention; it owes a great deal to the anonymous *Rule of the Master*, which was already in use. But Benedict's work became the *Rule* for Western monasticism from the sixth to the twelfth centuries, adopted by community after community and order after order. It emphasized poverty, chastity and above all obedience to the abbot and to God. The Eastern emphasis on the solitary hermit life, where even in communities monks rarely ate together and spent most of their time in their cells alone, was replaced in the West by a form of community life in which a group of monks lived together under a "rule," spending their time in prayer, reading and manual labor. He founded several experimental communities, but the great mother house of the Benedictines was at Monte Cassino in southern Italy.

Communities of nuns grew up too, and it occasionally happended in Anglo-Saxon times in England that a double house was founded, with nuns and monks in linked communities, sometimes with an abbess presiding over both.

However, things did not work out quite as intended. Social pressures shaped this developing Western monasticism, which mirrored the social

---

[4]Ibid.

hierarchy of the time. The monastic life became the preserve of the nobility. In the later Middle Ages, noble families with family members in a
monastery naturally still assumed that when the position of abbot was
vacant it would be filled by a nobleman among the monks, whether or
not he was equipped for the job by talent or vocation. Chaucer's Ma-
dame Eglantine, in "The Prioress's Tale," is an example of a noblewoman
who has had similar promotion in a community of nuns. She is very
genteel, with a "coy" little smile. She sings in chapel with a restrained
nasal "tune." She has never been to France, but she speaks French—with
an East London accent. Her table manners are exquisite for the times.
Morsels of food never fall from her lips onto the plate. She belches most
elegantly after her meals. Her manner is stately. She weeps tender-heart-
edly at the sight of a small animal caught in a trap, and she carries spoiled
lap dogs. She is rather well-dressed for a nun, and her brooch bears the
legend "Love conquers all." In short, she is indistinguishable from a fine
society lady, which is what she was brought up to be.

Wealthy families could be very generous to local religious houses, giving them land in the form of gifts to purchase their prayers and any surplus merits the house might produce for the benefit of the benefactor or
his family. But wealth tends to corrupt, and some houses ran themselves
like luxury hotels. By the end of the Middle Ages there had been several
cycles of reform. Each time new corruptions appeared. The Cluniacs at
the Abbey of Cluny tried to return to the original rigor of the monastic
life from the tenth century, but new distortions crept in. They made things
overcomplicated with new detailed customs. The rule about silence at
meal times could conveniently be got round by using sign language. Then
a hungry monk could say "pass the bread" or "pass the fish," and even be
specific as to the kind of fish he fancied a little more of. The Cistercian
reform of the early twelfth century, led by Bernard of Clairvaux, tried to
make space for lay brothers from the lower social classes, but they were
not full "choir monks" and were left to do the menial domestic tasks.

There was another reason why it was easy for religious houses to
decay into bad practice. Not all those who found themselves in monastic houses felt a personal call to the life. Leading families often found it
convenient to make some of their children monks or nuns to take the

pressure off the family land when it came to inheritance. This need have no reference to any vocation to the religious life on the part of the children. Indeed until the end of the twelfth century, it was usual for children to be given up to be monks or nuns as infants.

From child oblate to retirement choice. The custom of putting tiny children into monasteries began to change, however, at the end of the eleventh century, just as Guibert was observing the scene. Now retired military men, who had fought as knights all their lives, began to long for a change of lifestyle, and it was not uncommon for such people to make an agreement with their wives, who would become nuns as their husbands became monks. This led to a significant change, because it began to bring adult perception and lifetime experience in the world into the enclosed religious houses of Europe, hitherto mainly populated by individuals who had never known the outside world, were discouraged by the expectation of stability from leaving their monasteries, and who might not live on one of the travelers' routes which brought monasteries guests bringing a glimpse of the ways of the world.

As mentioned earlier, Guibert of Nogent called his autobiography *On My Life.* This is an unusual book for its time. Biographies were common enough, in the form of hagiographies, so common in fact that a late-eleventh-century monastic house which had had a notable member could hire a professional hagiographer to write his life story when he died in the hope that that might lead to his canonization; if he became an official "saint" there might be visits from pilgrims in search of miraculous cures and an income for the monastery. Guibert was not seeking to make himself a saint. He seems to have been imitating Augustine's *Confessions,* exploring his own spiritual growth in close-up. He even uses some of Augustine's favorite stylistic devices and emphasizes, as Augustine does, the importance of his mother in his religious formation.[5]

The book is a mine of information about this transition from the admission of infants to the welcoming of the middle-aged and elderly in search of retirement at the end of active lives "and the conversions to it that I have seen":

---

[5]Guibert, *De Vita Sua* 1.17.

In our day in the oldest monasteries, numbers had thinned, although they had an abundance of wealth given in ancient times and they were satisfied with small congregations, in which very few could be found who, through scorn of sin, had rejected the world, but the churches were rather in the hands of those who had been placed in them by the piety of their kinsmen early in life. And these, having little to fear on account of their own sins, as they imagined they had committed none, therefore lived within the walls of the convents a life of slackened zeal.[6]

Recently, by contrast, older recruits have emerged, he says, people with true vocations:

A certain Count of the Castle of Breteuil, which is situated between the borders of Amiens and Beauvais, came forth to arouse enthusiasm in many others. He was in the prime of life, a man of most pleasing refinement, noteworthy for the nobility of his family and the power it exercised in other towns as well as its own, through the remarkable splendour for which it was conspicuous, and widely renowned for its riches. Set for some time on a pinnacle of pride, at last the man came to his senses and turned to reflect on the wretchedness of the life which he had begun to live in the world.[7]

Discussing his new vocation with his friends, this Everard of Breteuil helped to attract others to share his "ardent desires":

Without telling those he left behind, but in company with others whom he had induced by his secret persuasions to form a brotherhood and adopt a religious life, he fled to foreign parts to live where his name was utterly unknown. There he employed himself in burning charcoal to pay for his living by hawking it with his friends through the country and the towns. In this way he imagined he had won the greatest riches, the contemplation, that is, of the daughter of the king, allglorious within. Now I will add another example, the one followed by him.[8]

Such do-it-yourself experiments with the monastic life were taking

---

[6]Ibid., 1.8.
[7]Ibid., 1.9.
[8]Ibid.

place alongside the new habit of entering an existing monastery as a retirement home.[9]

Some of these experimenters were much younger, and some were a little wild. There were, it was rumored, extremely eccentric and unorthodox examples.[10] Guibert goes on to explain that Everard had got his ideas from another nobleman:

> Theobald, now universally called Saint and renowned for the number of churches dedicated to him, was before that a young noble. In the midst of his military training, conceiving a distaste for arms, he fled, barefooted, from his friends, to take up the occupation mentioned above, living in this for some time a life of indigence to which he was unaccustomed. Inspired by his example, I say, Everard had resolved to support himself in the same humble occupation.[11]

These descriptions tell us something about the extent of the popular discussion about the best way to live the Christian life that was now going on. And according to Guibert the tale of these heroic bids by rich men to live a simple and apostolic life soon had pretenders seeking to cash in on what they were doing. Everard met "a man in a scarlet cloak and silken hose that had the soles cut away in a damnable fashion, with hair effeminately parted in front and sweeping the tops of his shoulders looking more like a lover than a traveler" who claimed to be Everard. Everard rethought his plans. He did not want accidentally to lead others astray or be a "stumbling block."

So he and his group decided it would be better to enter an established monastery. They went to Marmoutiers and became proper Benedictines.

As to Theobald, he seems to have become classless. Guibert notes that "the meanness of his apparel, the humility of his looks and the emaciation of his limbs would have proclaimed him, not a Count, but a country boor." He says that when he was sent on errands for an abbot "he could never be induced of his own accord to endure even once to set foot in the castles which he had relinquished." This sort of thing was an

---

[9]See *Libellus de diversis ordinibus*, ed. Giles Constable and Bernard Smith (Oxford: Oxford University Press, 1972).
[10]As the *Libellus de diversis ordinibus* makes clear, pp. 40-45.
[11]Guibert, *De Vita Sua* 1.9.

implicit challenge to social norms and potentially to a settled order which was reassuring the rulers of both church and state.

Guibert gives another example of a prominent nobleman with a late-in-life vocation, whose choice of the religious life set a conspicuous example to others:

> For Simon, the son of Count Ralph, enriched the religion of our time by the renown of a sudden conversion. How famous was the power of this Ralph throughout France, the cities which he attacked, the towns which he took and held with wonderful skill, many can testify who survived him and have remembered his deeds.[12]

Simon's example was therefore noticed because of the contrast it provided:

> The purity of his conversation, with the humility of spirit evident in his looks, inspired so many men and women of consequence that dense crowds of both sexes gathered to escort him on his way, and everywhere numbers were incited by the example of his fame to a similar resolve, since a great swarm of men of knightly rank was won over by this man's zeal.[13]

Women find their vocation too. Guibert's ambitious, pushy mother was widowed and brought him up as best she could. She had procured a schoolmaster for him when he was a boy, and he says that he and this strict and demanding master formed the *studium generale* of the town.[14] But she found she had a vocation for the religious life. Noble women were already to be found forming small communities in houses adjacent to churches and monasteries, and this is what she did. But she developed a longing for a more permanent commitment and decided to live at the monastery of Fly. She found a companion, an experienced woman "religious" whose extreme severity of life she began to imitate, to adopt her simple "diet, to choose the plainest food, to give up the soft cushions in her bed, to which she had been accustomed, to sleep in contentment on cornstraw covered with a little linen sheet." She tried to make herself look old and ugly, though she

---

[12]Ibid., 1.10.
[13]Ibid.
[14]A striking choice of phrase, because *studium generale* was later to become the term for a university.

was still beautiful.[15] Here are attitudes which chime both with the later
Puritan rejection of many sensual pleasures and with the earlier attitudes derived from dualism, which saw the body, matter, all physical
things, as evil and only the spiritual as good.[16]

This new life did not make Guibert's mother happy. She suffered
mental torment as Jerome had done. Guibert stresses her anguished
state, her sense of sin, her "confession, almost daily renewed" for

> her mind was for ever occupied in searching out her past deeds, what as
> a maiden of tender years, what in her married life, what as a widow with
> a wider range of activities she had done or thought or said, ever examin-
> ing the seat of reason and bringing what she found to the knowledge of
> a priest and to God through him. Then you might have seen the woman
> praying with such sharp sighs, wearing herself with such anguish of spirit
> that, as she worshipped, there was scarcely ever a pause in the heartrend-
> ing sobs that went with her entreaties.[17]

She was an attractive, clever and witty woman, and visitors "took pleasure in conversing with her because of her wondrous wit and modesty." As
soon as they had left, her soul was thrown into "indescribable anguish
until she reached the customary waters of penitence or confession." Yet
however hard she tried "she could win for her soul no confidence, no
certainty of salvation to stay her unceasing lamentations, her earnest and
tearful questionings whether she could ever earn pardon for her offences."[18]

There is a complex of assumptions here which was important to one
strain of monasticism throughout the Middle Ages and was continuous
with the motivation of the first desert hermits. Here was the enormous
sense of sin, of the importance of sin, of the need to struggle with sin
and try to shed its load, for in no other way could one hope for heaven,
coupled with an oppressive belief that one must work hard to be good
under this heavy burden. Here was no light yoke (Mt 11:30).

The troubles of a young man called to the religious life. While "she, as I have

---

[15]Ibid., 1.14.
[16]Cf. Leland Ryken, *Worldly Saints: The Puritans as They Really Were* (Grand Rapids: Zondervan,
   1991), pp. 41-42, 44.
[17]Guibert, *De Vita Sua* 1.14.
[18]Ibid.

described, was thus divorcing herself from the world," Guibert reports, "I was left deserted by mother, guide and master." His schoolmaster, of whom more in a moment, had himself decided to become a monk and gone to live in the monastery at Fly. Guibert's mother needed to make arrangements for the care of little Guibert who would thus be left an "orphan." Guibert, apparently now an adolescent, responded as might have been predicted:

> And I, now possessed of a baneful liberty, began most immoderately to abuse my power, to laugh at churches, to hate school, to love the company of my young lay cousins devoted to knightly pursuits, and, whilst cursing the clerk's garb, to promise remission of sins, to indulge in sleep in which formerly I was allowed little relaxation, so that by unaccustomed excess of it my body began to waste. Meantime the agitating news of my doings fell on my mother's ears, and surmising from what she heard, my immediate ruin, she was halfdead with fear. For the fine clothing which I had in the church processions, provided by her in the hope that I might be the more eager for the clerk's life, I wore everywhere in wanton pursuits natural at my age.[19]

He imitated the "boldness of older youths, utterly careless and intemperate." No doubt his confidence in being so honest about this regrettable behavior was bolstered by the fact that Augustine admits to very similar conduct in his youth.

His worried mother begged the abbot of Fly to allow his former schoolmaster, now one of his monks, to resume his responsibilities as Guibert's schoolmaster. Family influence can be seen again: "The Abbot, brought up by my grandfather and under obligation for benefits received from his house, gave me a ready welcome, when I went to him, and followed up his kind reception with still kinder treatment thereafter."

The schoolmaster was not allowed by the abbot to go back to his old job but he "at least took care to urge me to search diligently those holy books which I was reading, to study those less known by more learned men, to compose short pieces of prose and verse, warning me to apply myself the more closely because less care was being expended by others on my instruction."[20]

---

[19]Ibid., 1.15.
[20]Ibid.

So here we see family and society interacting with trends in professional Christianity. As he grew up, Guibert was experiencing, in a less dramatic fashion, the "conversion" he describes in the case of late entrants to the monastic profession, who chose to give up the military life at the end of successful careers as knights. Being a "religious" involved giving up the world and concentrating one's whole being on God and one's relationship with him. This was not conversion from unbelief. It was conversion from a vague, undemanding cradle Christianity to a serious commitment. It meant doing something about one's newfound faith by giving up secular ambition.

These were times of shakeup for the monastic life. In those years, orders of canons, the Victorines and Premonstratensians, emerged, allowing a degree of active life in the world for their members, as priests or teachers. The Cistercians challenged Benedictine complacency by setting out to lead lives of poverty and dedication in accordance with what they conceived to be the original vision of Benedict of Nursia. The mendicant orders, first the Franciscans and Dominicans, grew out of the perceived need for traveling preachers.

MONASTERIES AS
POWERHOUSES OF EDUCATION

In the Middle Ages some of the houses of monks ran schools for the children and any adult recruits, to equip them at least with Latin so that they could read and sing with understanding. These could be excellent schools or very inadequate ones. It all depended on the quality of the monks available to do the schoolmastering in what might be a very small community (and the communities could be as small as twenty).

We have close-ups of some of these schools. One is the school run by Aelfric (c. 955–c. 1020) at Eynsham near Oxford. He used to teach the small boys Latin by means of a pretend dialogue in which he asked them what their fathers did for a living so that they could enlarge their vocabulary by learning the words for shepherd and ploughman and so on.[21]

A much more sophisticated school was run at the abbey of Bec in Normandy by Anselm (c. 1033–1109), who later became archbishop of

---

[21]Aelfric of Eynsham, *Colloquy*, ed. G. N. Garmondsway (Exeter: University of Exeter, 1978).

Canterbury.[22] Orderic Vitalis (1075-c. 1142), the contemporary chronicler, said his students were all "seeming philosophers."[23] Learning with Anselm as schoolmaster was a spiritual exercise as well as an intellectual one. In the biography of Gundulph, one of these monk students who later became bishop of Rochester, is a description of the way Anselm would talk and Gundulph would weep with emotion, as though he were watering the seeds Anselm was sowing, says his biographer.[24]

In his first book, the *Monologion*, Anselm discusses the basic doctrines about God—his oneness and the Trinity of Father, Son and Holy Spirit—and tries to make it clear to the monks how it all works from the point of view of human reason. He begins by explaining that he has written the book because his fellow monks and students have begged him to, so that they may have a record of the discussions they have had and can look up his solutions in writing and reflect on them:

> Some of the brothers have kept asking me to write down the ideas I have discussed with them in our discussions, about meditations on the being of God, and other topics connected with that subject. . . . I have done this because they have asked me to rather than because I am confident that I can do it well that they have asked for me to write this as a meditation and in plain language with proofs everyone can understand and with a simple rational argument. They also wanted me to deal with any objections which struck me in the course of the exposition. I have been reluctant for a long time to agree to do this. I could see how difficult it would be. But I have given in because they have been so persistent in asking me.[25]

This is a very different matter from teaching schoolboys the Latin names for shepherds and ploughmen. And it is not without its literary sophistications. Anselm knew well that it was conventional to say one had written a book only because one's friends had insisted. This "modesty topos" could be a mere cover for authorial vanity. But in his case, he

---

[22]See R. W. Southern, *Anselm: A Portrait in a Landscape* (Cambridge: Cambridge University Press, 1990).

[23]Orderic Vitalis, *Historia Ecclesiastica* 4, ed. Marjorie Chibnall (London: Oxford University Press, 1969), 2:296-97.

[24]*Vita Gundulfi*, PL 159.817.

[25]Anselm, *Monologion, Epistola ad Lanfrancum* and *Prologus, Anselmi Opera Omnia*, ed. F. S. Schmitt (Edinburgh: Thomas Nelson, 1946), 1:6, 7.

wants his readers to see, he really means it. Much to his surprise the book has been a success and many copies have been made and it is circulating widely through the monasteries of northern France. He has reread it and thought hard about the great responsibility of seeming to speak to a readership beyond his immediate circle of pupils. He says he is confident that he has not said anything which disagrees with the views of the respected early Christian writers, particularly Augustine. If anyone thinks otherwise, he is encouraged to read his Augustine carefully and think about it.[26]

This example reveals something of importance about the attitudes with which the early medieval monastic theologians approached their task. It was, as Anselm put it, "faith seeking understanding" (*fides quaerens intellectum*).[27]

The contrast between Aelfric's school for little local boys and Anselm's academy for philosophers flags up a recognized challenge. Schools outside monasteries were probably still few at this date. Guibert's mother had to find him a personal tutor. John of Salisbury a generation later began his education in a local school for two, with a schoolmaster who dabbled in the occult and was not a good example intellectually or morally.[28] Grown-up nobles who had vocations for the monastic life would not be able to enjoy the benefits of a clerical education in the same way as the children brought up in monasteries, but they could be hungry for food for their minds and souls. Guibert describes how Theobald would ask anyone he met whom he knew to be learned "to write something in prose or verse for his amusement in a little book which he often carried about with him for the purpose; so that while collecting the maxims of all who had fame in particular studies, he might from these weigh their several opinions."[29] This enabled him to educate himself and form his own views.

Guibert is eloquent on the subject of his own intellectual development. He comments that once he had entered the monastery he felt he

---

[26]Anselm, *Monologion, Prologus, Anselmi Opera Omnia*, 1:8.
[27]Anselm, *Proslogion, Proemium, Anselmi Opera Omnia*, ed. F. S. Schmitt (Edinburgh: Thomas Nelson, 1946), 1:94.
[28]*The Letters of John of Salisbury*, ed. C. N. L. Brooke (London: Oxford University Press, 1986), 1:xiii.
[29]Guibert, *De Vita Sua* 1.9.

saw things much more clearly. He read and he composed "short pieces of prose and verse" as his former master encouraged him to do, and he even read under the bedclothes: "How often did they think me asleep and resting my little body under the coverlet, when my mind was concentrated on composition, or I was reading under a blanket, fearful of the rebuke of the others."[30] But once asleep he had bad dreams and liked to have a night-light to comfort him.

In time, as Guibert moved through adolescence, "carnal life began to stir," and his mother questioned him about his new sexual feelings and gave him advice on the best way to control them. There are hints here of the contemporary style of parenting and indications that young Guibert was able to see his mother reasonably easily. He was restless because he felt that although he had once been much less knowledgeable than the other monks now, through his assiduous studies, he surpassed them and he thought they were jealous. He asked for family help in arranging for him to move to another house of monks. But his mother had a vision and was able to persuade him that this was a wrong desire and he should stay at Fly.[31] Having read Ovid and the *Bucolics* of Virgil, he developed a taste for poetry so strong that he found himself composing immodest verses and more immodest fleshly stirrings were the result. He grew up at last and gave himself to serious reading of the Bible and Gregory the Great.[32]

Here we see an intelligent youth, with books and guidance available to him—and nowhere but in monasteries and cathedrals were such libraries to be found in the eleventh century—inventing his own syllabus of reading and largely educating himself, but falling into recognized dangers. Secular classics were full of undesirable contents, and Jerome had famously regretted the strength of their temptation when he castigated himself for being "more a Ciceronian than a Christian."

Conversion was taken by many to mean having to give up intellectual pursuits of this sort. It is commonplace in the hagiographies of the period to read that the saint had been well versed in the liberal arts but had given all that up for the spiritual life. A sort of "learned ignorance"

---

[30]Ibid., 1.18.
[31]Ibid., 1.16.
[32]Ibid., 1.18.

(*docta ignorantia*) was favored by the school of thought which took it
that simplicity and casting oneself on God were all that was needed, and
thinking was a dangerous distraction, still worse writing books. This line
between fostering the spiritual life and enjoying intellectual challenge
and freedom of thought was going to become increasingly important in
the later medieval story.

Guibert met Anselm, who visited Fly (he says quite regularly) while
Guibert was a monk there:

> In this work I had to encourage me Anselm, the Abbot of Bec, after-
> wards Archbishop of Canterbury, an Italian from across the Alps the
> country of Augustus, a man of sublime example and holiness of life.
> Whilst still holding office as Prior in the aforesaid convent, he admitted
> me to his acquaintance and, utter child as I was in knowledge as well as
> age, he readily offered to teach me to manage the inner self, how to con-
> sult the laws of reason in the government of the body.[33]

He gives us another glimpse of Anselm the teacher. "He taught us
then to divide the mind into three or four parts, to treat the whole of the
operations of this inner mystery under sensation, will, reason and perception." "And after he had discussed certain chapters of the Gospels on
this principle and most clearly explained the difference between will
and sensation," Guibert himself was led to write scriptural commentaries and "to imitate his methods in similar commentaries, so far as I
could and everywhere in the Scriptures to examine carefully with all the
energy of my mind anything that was morally in agreement with those
ideas."[34] Anselm also encouraged him to preach sermons.[35]

As a monk, Guibert was under obedience, so he had to ask his abbot's
permission to continue his work on the Bible. He was nothing if not
ambitious in literary matters. He did not stop at writing a commentary;
he wrote a book about how to write a commentary.

> Now I had in mind to attempt a moral commentary on the beginning of
> Genesis, that is the Six Days. To the Commentary I prefixed a treatise of

---

[33]Ibid., 1.17.
[34]Ibid.
[35]Ibid.

moderate length shewing how a sermon ought to be composed. I followed up this preface with a figurative exposition at length of the six days with poor eloquence, but such as I was capable of.[36]

When the Abbot realized the extent of this work, he forbade it. He belonged to the anti-intellectual old school of monastic life:

But when my Abbot saw that I was commenting on a chapter of that sacred history, he no longer took a reasonable view of the matter and when he with much anger warned me to put an end to these writings, I, seeing that such works only put thorns in his eyes, avoided both his presence and that of any who might report it to him, and completed my task in secret. For I made no notes in my tablets for the composition and writing of this or any other of my works, but committed them to the written page without alteration, as I thought them out. In that Abbot's time therefore my studies were carried on in complete secrecy.[37]

As soon as this Abbot was no longer in charge, Guibert finished his work:

This was contained in ten books arranged according to the above-mentioned four activities of the inner man and I so carried out the moral treatment in all of them that they went from beginning to end with absolutely no change in the order of the passages. Whether in this little work I helped any one, I know not, although I have no doubt that some learned men were pleased with it; but this is certain that I gained no little profit from it myself, insomuch as it saved me from idleness, that servant of vice.[38]

Once he had the taste for authorship, Guibert continued exploring the Scriptures and considering how best to write about them. His approach continued the assumptions developed by Gregory the Great in the sixth century. The Bible, Gregory suggested, has its literal meaning. But in some passages that meaning seems at odds with what Scripture says in other places. It also has figurative meanings. For instance, when Jesus told the parable of the sower, he meant his listeners to understand

---

[36]Ibid.
[37]Ibid.
[38]Ibid.

that this was a story with a moral. They were not supposed to think he was describing a real farmer with a name and address.[39] As discussed previously (pp. 56-63), Augustine had grappled with the same notion of the multiple meanings of Scripture, but he had not succeeded in producing a neat working system, as Gregory did when he proposed four possible kinds of meaning. This simple set of four kinds of meaning was adopted almost universally in the West for the next thousand years. Guibert accordingly explained his experiments in biblical commentary in these terms:

> In most of these I followed a figurative, in a few an allegorical treatment in the same manner as in Genesis. Moreover, in Genesis I gave my attention chiefly to morals, not that there was wanting matter for thought on the allegorical side, had I equally worked that out, but because in my opinion morals were in these times more important than allegory, when faith by God's help stands intact, but morals are universally debased by the many forms of vice.[40]

[39]Ibid.
[40]Ibid.

11

THE BEGINNING OF
ACADEMIC THEOLOGY
AND THE INVENTION
OF UNIVERSITIES

THE INVENTION OF UNIVERSITIES

Should a "saving faith" be simple, something open to anyone willing to trust in Christ? It is striking how complicated the Reformers of the sixteenth century and their opponents made it, as they met for disputations and colloquies and exchanged blasts of pamphlet warfare. Christian education was important from an early stage of Christian history. In the early centuries catechumens were required to attend regular study sessions in order to be instructed in the faith. But the sophisticated knowledge of the sixteenth-century combatants went far beyond that.

Between those early teaching experiments and the beginning of the Reformation came more than a thousand years of Christian education, and with that the emergence of new emphases and priorities. New environments for learning tended to sideline what even the best monastic schools could offer. An academic theology was born which in its technical complexity went beyond anything Guibert could have gleaned from his personal study of the books available to him. With the invention of universities, self-conscious intellectuals arrived and gained a certain authority. At the Fourth Lateran Council of 1215 the church was portrayed not only as mother (*mater*) but also as *magistra* (teacher).

The postantiquity doldrums. How did this happen? After the sixth century there was, for some centuries, no regular continuation of the traditions of the early centuries when bishops such as Augustine and Gregory would preach long, meaty sermons, sometimes in series that made up a serial study of a book or books of the Bible. Their sermons came to be regarded as authoritative source material for study rather than as homilies. The English monk Bede added considerably to the body of available Latin commentary on Scripture by collecting extracts from the respected old sermons relating to each passage. Thus a trend began, a habit of conscientiously reading the Bible with and through the tested opinions of trusted authorities.

Bede and his older contemporary Benedict Biscop (c. 628-689/690) found themselves having to build a bridge from the old world to the new. Benedict Biscop made two journeys to Rome and also spent two years in the monastic community at Lérins near the French Mediterranean coast. There he became a monk and was fired with enthusiasm to found a monastery of his own at home in Northumbria. He founded the double monastery at Wearmouth and Jarrow in northeast England, in which Bede spent his life from childhood. Bede's family apparently gave him to the monastery to be a monk whether or not he turned out to have a vocation when he grew up, as was customary at the time.[1]

His European journeyings and meetings with Christians in Rome had taught Benedict Biscop that there was a literature of Christian writing and also a classical literature to be rediscovered. He set about acquiring copies for the library of his new monastery. Among the best collections to draw on, he found, was the library at Monte Cassino, the mother house of the Benedictine Order. This meant arranging for copies to be made, an expensive and slow business which took persistence to arrange.

It was, however, one thing to fill a library and another to know what to make of the contents of the books. The school system of late antiquity had broken down everywhere except in some parts of Italy. The old culture in which an educated man was above all a literary man, capable of making a

---

[1]On double houses see Katharine Sykes, "'Canonici Albi et Moniales': Perceptions of the Twelfth-Century Double House," *Journal of Ecclesiastical History* 60 (2009): 233-45.

fine and persuasive speech in politics or the law courts, no longer existed. The *cultured* man of ancient Rome was to turn into the *learned* man of the Middle Ages. The scholars of these centuries—most of them monastic, for that was the best way to find oneself with a library and the leisure for the work—had to find their way without guidance, except from the books themselves, to an understanding of the books available to them, including the Bible. This encouraged the growing reliance on books as authority, and the use of extracts from former commentaries on the books as authorities with which to understand them. Books were read with intent concentration word by word and sentence by sentence. A favorite image of the medieval monastic world described reading as a process of mastication, even chewing the cud in its thoroughness.

This method of study set a pattern which was to continue throughout the Middle Ages and into the sixteenth century. It applied to teaching, where the lecture was going to involve students reading the book bit by bit, with the lecturer making points about each passage drawn from earlier commentary. It even applied to preaching, though the robust exegetical series of the past became relatively rare. Sermons were often not preached regularly by early medieval parish priests, whose general level of education remained very modest as Europe recovered from the crash in educational standards that had come with the fall of Rome and the barbarian invasions. In monasteries at mealtimes, someone would often simply read aloud one of the old sermons. The future of preaching was bright, but not until the twelfth-century transformation of academic expectations.

That came as, after a generation or two of experiment, universities were invented at the end of the twelfth century.[2] They became something quite new and hugely important to the development of dissident opinions in the later Middle Ages. If challenges to the teaching of the ecclesiastical authorities were to be perceived as more than the cries of naughty children, they were going to need to be developed with theological expertise and a degree of sophistication and put into circulation in writings by educated people. Only when a statement of theological

---

[2] Though Bologna claimed an earlier origin and there had apparently been a school of notaries and lawyers there in the eleventh century.

opinion is condemned and burned can it be seen to be having an impact. Women had only a tiny part in this process of academic development because they were not accepted as students in the universities or cathedral schools, let alone as teachers. Such women as Hildegard of Bingen (1098-1179) and Gertrude the Great (1256-c. 1302) tended to make their names through their influence in the monastic world.

Sources of the idea of a university: The cathedral schools and the new canons. In the period after the end of the ancient world and at the beginning of the Middle Ages, the clergy attached to the cathedrals of Europe could find themselves doing pastoral work in the diocese, filling in when a parish lacked a priest. In order to ensure that they lived "regular" lives, they were expected to live under a rule which imposed a discipline on them, while allowing them to travel about the diocese as required. From the time of Charlemagne—who insisted on it—they were also expected to have sufficient learning to enable them to act as the diocese's local repositories of theological knowledge. Charlemagne was called Roman Emperor from 800-814, in an imperial tradition that remained a legacy of the ancient Roman Empire but in a new Europe, where the style of government and politics was predominantly feudal and power struggles were still almost tribal. Charlemagne liked to see himself as a latter-day Constantine, ruling in the tradition of the first Christian emperor of Rome.

It is possible to get a glimpse of the quality of the study in these cathedral schools from the letters of Fulbert of Chartres (c. 970-1028), who ran such a school about the year 1000. These are mostly full of practical problems in the diocese and pastoral advice for misbehaving or worried monks or clergy. But theological questions arose too. He wrote to one priest in or after 1008 with guidance about the celebration of the Lord's Supper. A priest should not say Mass alone, he thinks, because the Eucharist should be a celebration of the church as a community. Does the priest not say "the Lord be with you"? This means others ought to be present:

> I think it is safer for you to stop celebrating mass rather than to celebrate it without at least two or three of the faithful present. Your anxiety concerning those who are making the offerings can be solved like this: while

we are the ones who are sacrificing, those for whom we are doing it are offering the sacrifice of praise to God through our hands.[3]

During the twelfth century there were one or two experiments in founding new orders of "regular" canons, that is, canons who lived according to a rule but who were not attached to a cathedral with its school. A rule existed, probably older than the Benedictine one and attributed to Augustine that allowed people to dedicate themselves to the religious life with a special intensity while remaining active in the world, serving as ministers or preachers.[4] When Augustine became a Christian and returned to his native North Africa, only to find himself made bishop of Hippo, he had surrounded himself with a group of like-minded friends, and they chose to live a community life, with rules which may indeed be the origin of the Augustinian rule.

The Victorine canons, called after the abbey of St. Victor, had their house in Paris, where they ran a school that competed with the cathedral school at Notre Dame and with the experimental rival schools that were intermittently run at St. Geneviéve on the south bank of the Seine. From time to time a teacher, such as William of Champeaux (c. 1070-1121), formerly a canon of Laon and then from 1103 a teacher at Notre Dame, would retreat from the aggressive academic scene of Paris to the gentler school of the Victorines. There William took himself in 1108, after losing a public philosophical dispute with Peter Abelard (1079-1142/1143), his notoriously challenging former pupil.[5]

Hugh of St. Victor (see pp. 91-92) was an excellent practical pedagogue.[6] For example, he taught his pupils to use a color scheme of initials to help them memorize the opening lines of the Psalms. He wrote straightforward manuals such as the *Didascalion* to help students master the basics according to a few clear principles. These were perhaps modeled on the encyclopedia produced by Cassiodorus (c. 485/490-

---

[3]Fulbert of Chartres, *The Letters and Poems*, ed. and trans. Frederick Behrends (Oxford: Clarendon Press, 1976), pp. 36-37.
[4]George Lawless, *Augustine of Hippo and His Monastic Rule* (Oxford: Clarendon Press, 1987).
[5]John Marenbon, *The Philosophy of Peter Abelard* (Cambridge: Cambridge University Press, 1997); and David Luscombe, *The School of Peter Abelard* (Cambridge: Cambridge University Press, 1970).
[6]Boyd Taylor Coolman, *The Theology of Hugh of St. Victor: An Interpretation* (Cambridge: Cambridge University Press, 2010).

c. 580), when he rightly feared that the fall of Rome to the barbarians was going to end the ancient educational tradition and wanted to salvage what he could for future generations.[7]

The study of the Bible should involve a spiritual exercise, Hugh thought six centuries later. One should not separate the intellectual and the devotional when reading Scripture: "There are two things which anyone who wants to learn should concentrate on, that is reading and meditation, of which reading comes first for the learner."[8]

Being a great reader of Augustine, Hugh encouraged students to learn the seven liberal arts as well as to read the Bible. They will, he explains, need a knowledge of grammar, logic, rhetoric, arithmetic, music, geometry and astronomy to understand Scripture. That is simply the pursuit of wisdom and self-knowledge, which form essential foundations.[9]

In *On the Sacraments of the Christian Faith* (*De sacramentis Christianae fidei*), Hugh explains the whole of theology in two phases of God's work. The first was the "work of creation" (*opus creationis*), when God, whose nature the student has to learn about, made the world, and sinners damaged it. The second was the "work of restoration" (*opus restaurationis*), when God mended the world by sending his Son to die for humankind. Other Victorines became influential writers too. Richard of St. Victor (d. 1173) made his name as a mystical theologian, a writer on spirituality, although he was also an accomplished scholastic. Andrew of St. Victor (d. 1175) concentrated especially on scriptural commentary. He seems to have been one of the few mid-twelfth-century writers who had some knowledge of Hebrew, and he brought that interest to the writing of commentary on Old Testament books, though in a manner still heavily dependent on the work of Jerome.[10]

The Premonstratensians were an order of canons founded near Laon in 1120 by Norbert of Xanten (c. 1080-1134), who was later to become an

---

[7]James J. O'Donnell, *Cassiodorus* (Berkeley: University of California Press, 1979).
[8]This text of Hugh of St. Victor's *Didascalion* is taken from Charles Henry Buttimer, *Hugonis de Sancto Victore Didascalion de Studio Legendi: A Critical Text*, Studies in Medieval and Renaissance Latin 10 (Washington, D.C.: Catholic University Press, 1939), pref. and bk. 1.1, http://freespace .virgin.net/angus.graham/Hugh.htm (my translation).
[9]Ibid.
[10]Andrew of St. Victor, *Opera*, CCCM 53.

archbishop in Germany, at Magdeburg. His ideal was to ensure a greater strictness of life in communities of working priests. His small community of thirteen adopted the Augustinian rule but imposed extra requirements on themselves so as to make their life more rigorous. By 1126 the order had papal approval and had expanded to nine houses. It became a roaring success, with well over a thousand houses for men and several hundred for women in the fourteenth century. Much of its work was missionary, for Europe was still not fully Christianized and there was work to do in the east and the north converting peoples living in near the rivers Elbe and Oder, such as the Wends. It did not restrict its houses to particular styles of religious life beyond keeping the rule, and keeping it strictly. So it allowed the development of a variety of specialist preaching and pastoral skills.

Towards the university. There had been independent schools offering higher education in the twelfth century, often growing up close to the cathedral schools which had been flourishing since Carolingian times. These schools provided natural attractions for itinerant teachers, wandering scholars, particularly near the cathedrals of Paris, Chartres and Laon in northern France. For these new arrivals it was all very freeform and not yet institutionalized, so a school did not need buildings or organization or a syllabus. Would-be masters could simply set themselves up and lecture to students, so they needed to be in places where potential fee-paying students might be found. There was rivalry. Masters tried to capture one another's students, sometimes adding critical comments about one another's opinions in their lectures.

Who were these masters, and why had they suddenly appeared? They seem to have been motivated by the burgeoning of a new style of intellectual interests, and especially the realization of the possibilities of logic. But there also had to be a market, a body of students willing to pay for the latest tuition. Many of these were undoubtedly seeking the qualifications they needed to get posts in the growing civil service that both church and state found they now needed. An indicator of the emergence of this need was the appearance from the 1070s of manuals on how to write a business letter (the *Ars dictaminis*). A demand for notaries and civil servants to serve both church and state was multiplying the numbers of students in search of an appropriate education. A small proportion of these had ambitions to be not clerks but clergy, though a career path could easily lead from one to the other. John of Salisbury was a student at Paris before the schools there had evolved into a university, and he spent most of his career as a senior civil servant until his ambition was crowned at last by his elevation to the bishopric of Chartres. So the driving force which created universities was not pastoral but career-oriented and intellectual.

One of the most notorious of these wandering masters, Peter Abelard, describes in his *History of My Calamities* how he went to hear Anselm of Laon (d. 1117) lecture at the cathedral school at Laon, with the express purpose of capturing some of his students. Abelard had already made his name as a daring logician and now he wanted to move on to theology, an obvious career move because it was regarded as a more advanced and prestigious subject.[11]

He makes disparaging remarks about what he heard. Here was a famous teacher, but what should have been a tree covered in leaves of wisdom turned out to have dropped its leaves and to bear merely bare branches. So Abelard arrogantly announced that he would himself be lecturing the next day, on Ezekiel. Ezekiel was famed for being a particularly difficult book of the Bible, and Abelard was not a trained theologian. He had, however, skills in linguistic analysis from his knowledge of logic, and he began to apply these to the interpretation of the text of Scripture with disturbing results. Students loved this for its danger and novelty. They flocked to hear him. He was able to set up a school in Paris at St. Geneviève on the left bank of the Seine.

The pattern of his career illustrates a trend. The work of these new academics immediately caused fear in the minds of the ecclesiastical authorities. Arnold of Brescia (d. 1155), a controversial figure some pointed to as a heretic, spent some time in the early 1140s teaching in Paris, "but he had no listeners except poor students who publicly begged their bread from door to door to support themselves and their master." He was orthodox on points of doctrine, says John of Salisbury, but he caused of-

---

[11]Peter Abelard, *Historia Calamitatum*, ed. J. Monfrin (Paris: J. Vrin, 1967).

fense by criticizing the wealth and greed of bishops (*episcopis non parcebat ob avariciam et turpem questum*), because, he said, their very lives were "stained" (*propter maculam vite*). He was also found in Rome preaching to the people there and winning their respect and support—particularly that of "religious women"—by his austerity of life (*austeritas vite*).[12]

Whether or not they preached anti-establishment ideas, academics were potentially dangerous to the establishment. They spoke freely; they applied their minds and challenged what they believed did not stand up to rational analysis. They published books about what they thought. They influenced those who came to hear them lecture. And in the case of Abelard, the fact that he was doing this in Latin does not seem to have prevented his gaining fame as a popular purveyor of exciting and dangerous opinions. It was not long before he found himself on trial for his opinions, not once but twice.

Abelard's dangerous new teaching came from what on the face of it seems an unlikely source, the new and increasingly technical study of the arts of language in the area where grammar and logic overlap. Logicians like Abelard tried to apply Aristotle's rules to the fundamentals of Christian theology. How did they fit God himself? Nobody disputed that God is a divine "essence"; God *is* Godness or divinity. But whereas qualities such as goodness, mercy and justice are clearly changeable if they are attributed to you and me, in God they never change. God does not have off days. God's goodness can be regarded as substantive, part of his very self. Augustine and others had long ago recognized the importance of this unique substantiveness of the divine attributes.[13] So are there any "accidents" or variables in God? What about "relations"? If in the Trinity there are Father, Son and Spirit, and the Son is not the Father and the Father is not the Son, then what is the nature of their relationship as one divine essence?

Another leading thinker of the mid-twelfth century, nearly as notorious as Peter Abelard for giving theologically dangerous lectures, was Gilbert of Poitiers (d. 1154). He got into trouble and found himself on trial at the

---

[12]John of Salisbury, *Historia Pontificalis*, ed. and trans. Marjorie Chibnall (Oxford: Oxford University Press, 1986), pp. 63-5.
[13]See for example Augustine, *De Trinitate* XV.v.7-vi.9, CCSL 50A, p. 468.

Council of Reims in 1148 for trying to explain the relationship of the persons of the Godhead in an unfortunate way, by postulating that there was an abstract *divinitas* which was the essential basis of the Trinity of persons in their relations to one another. His opponents, shocked, claimed that he was in effect saying there were four distinct "things" in God—Father, Son, Spirit, and the divine essence itself—not three distinct persons who are nevertheless the same God.

It is a highly technical question, but the church wished to take no risk that he would lead his students astray. This may in reality have been unlikely, for he was known to be a lecturer of extreme opacity. One student observed that his lectures commenting on the philosophy and theology of Boethius (c. 480-c. 524) were more obscure than the text they were supposed to elucidate.[14] Nevertheless, the church assembled its big guns, led by Bernard of Clairvaux, and brought to the trial copies of the books from the cathedral library which might be needed to prove that they were right, marked ready for quoting in the debate.

John of Salisbury provides a vivid account of this trial, which took place while he was a papal civil servant, in his *Memoirs of Life at the Papal Court* (*Historia Pontificalis*), including the story of the behind-the-scenes plotting, which he witnessed, to ensure that Gilbert was found guilty.[15] Elsewhere he describes his own dozen years or so as a student in the schools of Paris in the first half of the twelfth century, lecture-tasting and comparing masters. He evaluates their efforts with great frankness (it seems that student criticism was already brisk). So on every front, from the very beginnings of a higher education movement in Europe the ecclesiastical authorities and their civil servants were alert to the potential danger of free-thinking inquirers with access to new generations of students and freedom to publish and disseminate their ideas.

The institutionalization of universities. The institutionalization of universities in their local (secular and ecclesiastical) political context, and the exploration of their relationship with the authorities seems to have begun

---

[14]Gilbert of Poitiers, *Commentaries on Boethius*, ed. N. M. Häring (Toronto: Pontifical Institute of Mediaeval Studies, 1969), p. 4 (PL185.609B)
[15]John of Salisbury, *Historia Pontificalis*, pp. 15-41.

in earnest in the thirteenth century, in Italy, France, England and Spain.[16]

The first *universitates* were called after the word for a trade guild, *universitas*. Legally, the academic *universitas* was by definition a guild just like any other guild of masters in the Middle Ages. Its masters together formed a "corporate person." Together they allowed admission to their membership, registering students, awarding the bachelor's degree, which was the equivalent of becoming a journeyman fishmonger or goldsmith in a craft guild, and finally examining the bachelor to judge whether he deserved the award of the master's degree or *gradus*, and admission as a full master. That admission, or inception, involved the counterpart of producing a masterpiece in a craft guild. The new master had to preside over a public disputation (*quodlibeta*) and thus display his wares, his knowledge, and his skills and his fitness to be a master in the university in question.

Philip II Augustus (1165-1223) issued a royal charter for the University of Paris in 1200. This required the chief holder of an office in the city on behalf of the king to take an oath in public in the presence of the scholars when he takes office as *prévôt*, as an active reminder that the university had the royal protection and a mechanism for ensuring that the relations and mutual obligations of town and gown were recognized. That did not prevent disputes arising. In 1229 the scholars wrote themselves a charter with twenty-one seals attached threatening to leave Paris in indignation at the behavior of the previous *prévôt*. Pope Gregory helped to resolve the problem with a bull *Parens scientiarum*. This gave the university a new status but also sought to determine its teaching.[17] Oxford came into being even earlier, sometime shortly before 1200; in 1209 some scholars left it in a huff after a town-gown fight, and set up what became the University of Cambridge in the East Anglian fens.

The medieval practice as it evolved was for the academic community in each university to determine what it should teach. Before the univer-

---

[16]Christoph Friedrich Weber, "Ces Grands Privileges: The Symbolic Use of Written Documents in the Foundation and Institutionalization Processes of Medieval Universities," *History of Universities* 19 (2004): 16.

[17]Ibid., pp. 17-19.

sities took charge, the early masters took what liberties they chose. John of Salisbury's descriptions of the teaching available in Paris may be found in his *Historia Pontificalis* and *Metalogicon*. Teaching could be very informal in the middle of the twelfth century. Masters still simply set up and taught any students they could get, and the students chose whose lectures to hear and what to learn. There was no formal syllabus, no examination and no degree at the end of one's studies. John described his own wandering from master to master for a dozen years.

Once an institutional framework began to evolve, a syllabus was laid down. This could be left to individual faculties or approved by the whole community of scholars. The curriculum might then be embodied in a statute and the approval of the city or prince sought, since in Italy and some other parts of Europe, the salaries of the lecturers were paid out of local taxes. But the content, set books and method of examination began to be regarded as an academic, not a political or administrative, concern. Local politicians and secular authorities did not always understand or wish to respect this. Protecting the distinction between academic and nonacademic regulation, and deciding where one ended and the other began, was to be of incalculable importance and continuing difficulty far into the future.

The basic syllabus everywhere consisted of the seven liberal arts, divided into a three (the *trivium* or three ways, comprising grammar, logic and rhetoric) and a four (the *quadrivium* or four ways, comprising arithmetic, music, geometry and astronomy). These were derived from subject areas recognized in the ancient world and relied heavily on textbooks from Greece and Rome. Grammar was the first subject. By now Latin, though still very much a live language, was no one's native language. It had to be learned to a level where students could hear lectures and read books and conduct disputations in it before study at a university could be possible at all. But the advantage of this universal requirement was that it provided a common language for scholars all over Europe and meant that ideas could quickly be spread and picked up everywhere. Students would probably arrive fairly well-equipped in Latin, but there grew up a fringe of specialist tutors who could help with this practical preliminary study.

Within the syllabus itself the study of grammar at university concentrated on the theory of linguistics and was based on the textbooks of the Roman grammarians Donatus (fl. mid-fourth century) and Priscian (fl. 500). The theory of linguistics overlapped at strategic points with elementary logic as Abelard and others had perceived. This second *trivium* subject depended by 1200 on Aristotle's six books on logic, some available in Latin translations by Boethius, some in more recent translations directly from Greek versions, some from Arabic translations of the Greek. The possibilities of logic for having fun and tripping up lecturers if they contradicted themselves proved enormous.

It also had its uses in the interpretation of Scripture, as Peter the Chanter (d. 1197) was quick to spot. His *De Tropis Loquendi* ("On Modes of Speaking"), apparently deriving from lectures given in Paris at the end of the twelfth century, made use of some of the principles of the theory of fallacy, ahead of the adoption of the *Sophistici Elenchi* of Aristotle, which offers a more sophisticated treatment of the topic. Fallacious arguments can be dangerously persuasive if the recipient is not aware of the ways in which games can be played with the propositions and the way the conclusion is drawn. The Chanter's concern was to use the theory constructively and find ways to show that the seeming contradictions in Scripture area apparent rather than real, for example by suggesting that reading one or both of two conflicting passages figuratively will avoid their confronting one another in a conflict of literal meanings.[18] Given the widespread recognition of the problem that the Bible must be true in every part and God could not have contradicted himself, this made the formal discipline of logic a tool of some importance and practical usefulness to theologians.

Lastly, there was rhetoric, taught for most of the Middle Ages from the Roman philosopher Cicero's (106-43 B.C.) *De inventione* (and the *Rhetorica ad Herennium*, which was also then believed to be his work). Rhetoric had been the leading subject in a citizen's education in antiquity, but by the Middle Ages it tended to be the least studied of the first three subjects. It was hugely important in the study of Scripture, how-

---

[18]Luisa Valente, *Phantasia contrarietatis: Contraddizioni scritturali, discorso teologico e arti, del linguaggio nel "De Tropis loquendi" di Pietro Cantore* (Florence: L. S. Olschki, 1997).

ever, because it provided a training in the way language was used figuratively as well as literally, persuasively as well as in plain narrative. It made the reader sensitive to the words of a text everyone believed to have been dictated directly by the Holy Spirit. The *quadrivium* subjects were less fully studied by most students. These, the quartet of arithmetic, geometry, music theory and astronomy, were regarded as mathematical. There arrived in the early thirteenth century an additional component of philosophy, derived from the newly arrived philosophical works of Aristotle. Offering this general syllabus entitled the institution to regard itself as a *studium generale*.

The fundamental subject matter of a course of lectures in the Middle Ages was normally a book—a textbook or set book—usually deriving from the classical world. New books could prove disturbing arrivals, even if they were by respected authors. There might be considerable reluctance to admit them to the syllabus. When the scientific and philosophical writings of Aristotle arrived in Western universities at the beginning of the thirteenth century in Latin translations mainly derived from Arabic versions of the original Greek, and accompanied by Arabic commentaries and analyses, they presented themselves as new books, despite their antiquity. Disturbing new answers to old questions raised in these books upset the universities, such as whether the world was eternal and not created by God at the beginning of time as Genesis says, and what was the origin and function of the soul. There were attempts to crack down and even to ban them from being discussed at all. Yet it was impossible in the end to refuse admission to a name as august as that of Aristotle. These books enlarged the syllabus, not at once, and not without controversy, but decisively. These battles illustrate the continuing centrality of the textbook to the expansion or modification of the syllabus.

They are also a reminder that arts faculties could get their students involved in theological debate almost by accident, once they tacked on to the old seven liberal arts a new philosophy component to enable study of the scientific works of Aristotle. For example, some of Aristotle's ideas about the soul were not the same as Christian ideas; students who were not sufficiently wary of aspects of his thought were liable to run away with dangerous notions.

A crisis. A crisis arose in the arts faculty in Paris in 1339-1340 that illustrates the tensions which began to be created by the clash of new regulation with the old freedoms of the twelfth century, which allowed lecturers to teach what they liked, how they liked. In September 1339 the arts faculty said it had the right to determine the list of books allowed to be lectured on. A statute was drafted (possibly two):

> We have sworn to observe a certain ordinance which was issued by our predecessors, who were not unreasonably concerned as to the books to be read publicly or privately among us; and because we ought not to read certain books not admitted by them or customarily read elsewhere.[19]

And since some have been holding secret meetings to read these banned books, it is decreed by the new statute:

> That henceforth no one shall presume to dogmatize the said doctrine by listening to it or lecturing on it publicly or in private, or by holding small meetings for disputing said doctrine, or by citing it in lecture or in disputations.[20]

Anyone breaching this new rule is to be suspended ("may not obtain any office or degree among us"). The second statute (or part two of the first), comments that "bachelors and others present at these disputations dare to argue on their own authority, showing little reverence toward the masters who are disputing, and making such a tumult that the truth of the conclusion being debated cannot be arrived at, so that the said disputations are not in any way fruitful for the listening scholars."[21]

Student life. Medieval students did not have to win a place at their chosen university. In most places they simply arrived, presented themselves to a master to be put on his register and found themselves lodgings in the town. Students made controversial lodgers then as now, and town and gown fights could get violent. Early in the history of universities students attended lectures as they chose, making sure they heard

---

[19]William J. Courtenay and Katherine H. Tachau, "Ockham, Ockhamists, and the English-German Nation at Paris, 1339-1341," *History of Universities* 2 (1982): 54-55.
[20]Ibid.
[21]Ibid.

fashionable and popular lectures as John of Salisbury says he did.[22] Later
a syllabus emerged. Lectures were *lectiones*, detailed readings of set
books, with, from the twelfth century, sessions set aside in the after-
noons for disputations, when the pros and cons of particular interpretations could be discussed.[23]

The atmosphere of academic life had its recognizable features among
students as well as among their elders. "Almost all the students at Paris,
foreigners and natives, did nothing but learn or hear something new,"
complains Jacques de Vitry (c. 1160/1170-1240). Some are driven by curiosity to study vanities. Some become students in pursuit of a good
income. They are not only constantly engaged in disputations about
academic matters; they are also full of enmity toward one another, the
student "nations" in particular.[24] In their slanging matches they call the
English students drunks, the French proud and effeminate, the Germans bad tempered, the Burgundians brutal and stupid, and so on. They
often come to blows.[25] Their studies turn logic into a trivial pursuit of
sophistries. As to the theologians, they are like sounding brass and tin-
kling cymbals; they too are full of mutual dislike and anxious only to
capture one another's students for themselves, providing they pay. Elsewhere de Vitry mentions some of the scholars of Bologna living together (*congregati*) so as to read the Bible, with one of them teaching, in
order to prepare themselves for responsible preaching.

The misbehavior of students and more senior scholars was troubling
enough for William Langland to mention it. Scholars are clerics. Like
the clergy, some clerics are only interested in money and take any remu-
nerative work:

> Some serve the king / and his silver count
> In Chequer and Chancery courts / making claim for his debts

Some enter the households of "lords and ladies" for remuneration.

[22]John of Salisbury, *Metalogicon* 2.10, ed. C. C. J. Webb (Oxford, 1929), pp. 77-83, and *Letters of John of Salisbury*, 1.xiii.
[23]For an example, see Simon of Tournai, *Disputationes*, ed. J. Warichez, 12 (Louvain: Spicilegium Sacrum Lovaniense, 1932).
[24]John of Salisbury, *Historia pontificalis*, pp. 63-64.
[25]Jacques de Vitry, *Historia Occidentalis*, Spicilegium Friburgense 17, ed. J. F. Hinnebusch (Fribourg: University Press, 1972), 28:142-43.

And the social leaders of the laity are also failing to live as their calling should require and as the good of the community demands. Public order and the common good are in the hands of rogues. The lawyers who ought to ensure respect for justice will not say a word "unless money were showed."

Bible Study and the Beginning of Academic Theology

Academic theologians and the beginning of theology as a degree subject. Peter Abelard could not have moved so airily from logic to theology if he had been teaching in Paris a century later. Theology had by then been identified as a subject for a higher degree. It was for graduate study, not undergraduate study. Relatively few students stayed on at the universities or returned after they had graduated as masters of arts to study a higher-degree subject leading to a doctorate. Three such subjects were available: law, medicine and theology. These were not research degrees in the modern sense. They were advanced degrees, prepared for in taught courses, and not all were offered in every university by a specialist faculty.

Of them all, the "queen" was theology. Those who studied theology were entering on a lengthy and demanding course which could take them well into middle age before they finished it and became doctors of theology. This course had to be invented. In the twelfth century the subject we now call theology was known as the *studium sacrae scripturae*, the study of Holy Scripture. That did not mean that it consisted solely in Bible study. It already included the content which was to grow into systematic theology, for the Bible is not a textbook which treats topics in a systematic order. Something was needed to assist the student to understand what he was reading when he studied Scripture, but the process of systematizing had to be worked out.

The queries prompted by the study of the text and by the comments on those questions by early Christian writers, especially Augustine, Gregory and Bede, formed a body of material for study in their own right. This had been drawn together in an orderly manner by Peter Lombard (c. 1100-1160) shortly before his death in 1160. The question for students and their teachers was how best to approach the task of mastering the content of a theology course, which would include both Bible study and theology. In his *Sentences* Lombard ordered the opinions (*sententiae*) of these authorities in a sequence that already approximated to the usual order of systematic theology. What sort of study is this? Is there a God? What is God like? How can God be both three and one? How did God create the world? What went wrong with this creation? What did God do about it? Where are we now? What will happen in the end? This text, which soon won out over biblical commentaries as the basic text for theological study, was the model for the even more elaborate *Summae* of the thirteenth century. These were consolidated attempts to put the great and growing body of theological questions into the best possible order, of which Thomas Aquinas's *Summa Theologiae* (incomplete at his death in 1274) is the best-known example.

Does the Bible always make sense? The underlying assumption throughout the medieval history of Bible study was that if a biblical text appears ungrammatical, contradictory or untrue, the fault lies with the reader not with Scripture, for Scripture is the Word of God and God does not make that kind of mistake. Within this frame of reference there could be little room to treat the Bible like any other book, beyond the respectful suggestions Augustine had made about possible minor emendations. The *studium sacrae scripturae* demanded special skills of interpretation which would respect the fact that it is the Word of God, who does not contradict himself. The puzzled reader has simply misunderstood, or he would not be puzzled. He must redouble his efforts to understand what God has said in his Word. He must if necessary learn the appropriate technical skills, which the student would have learned from his study of the liberal arts, especially grammar, logic and rhetoric.

Abelard's *Sic et Non* (*Yes and No*) addressed the problem of seeming contradictions, "since in such a multitude of words some even of the holy sayings seem to differ or even contradict one another."[26] He wrote it as a teaching aid for his own students. It consists of a challenging

---

[26]"*Cum in tanta verborum multitudine nonnulla etiam sanctorum dicta non solum ab invicem diversa verum etiam invicem adversa videantur.*" Peter Abelard, *Sic et Non*, PL 178.1339, ed. B. Bouer and R. McKeon (London: University of Chicago Press, 1976-1977), p. 89.

preface followed by lists of opinions, many from respected early Christian authors, who appear to disagree. The students were to consider these contradictions and work out what to think.

The problem was not new. It had been worrying students of the Bible for centuries. In the next generation of teachers in Paris, Peter the Chanter knew the literature on this problem and reminds his readers that Augustine had written a *Harmony of the Gospels* in which, he says, Augustine "resolved the contrarinesses of the Gospels and restored harmony."[27]

Augustine's approach was to claim that the Gospel writers should not be expected to repeat the very same events in the very same way. For example, Matthew undertook to give the lineage of Jesus and to concentrate on the things he said and did that "relate to present human life"; Mark seems to follow Matthew very closely and to provide a briefer but very similar account, adopting Matthew's actual words at times. Yet Luke has a different objective. He discusses the priesthood and priestly lineage of Christ.

Another solution was to suggest that words may be being used in different ways (*modi loquendi*) and are therefore not as contradictory as they seem. As discussed earlier, Peter the Chanter was also the author of the *De Tropis Loquendi*, which survives in long and short versions, a possible sign that it is the remains of a lecture course he gave in Paris on more than one occasion in the infant university there. This is not simply the familiar notion that sometimes the meaning is figurative as well as or instead of literal. It penetrates more deeply into the way language works. One of the most important ideas was that the meaning of a word or phrase or even a whole story may be transferred. The literal meaning may acquire figurative associations by *translatio*, and sometimes the figurative meaning may be the true one. In Jesus' parables the sower and the seed (Mt 13:18-23) must surely be the preacher and his listeners, the fictional characters more true than if they had been historical, if that is what Jesus meant when he told the story.

The subtlety of mind bred in those who studied these matters is visible

---

[27]"*Contrarietatem Evangeliorum soluit et ad concordiam redigit.*"Peter the Chanter, *Verbum Abbreviatum*, Prologue, ed. F. Guisberti (Naples, 1982), p. 105.

in the Arts Statute agreed in December 1340 at Paris.[28] This was drafted in an attempt to deal with the problem of what to do when it seemed that a lecturer was teaching error. No notion of academic freedom was in play. (Academic freedom as we understand it now is a surprisingly modern concept.) The question was whether the lecturer intended to mislead, which would be culpable, and that depended in its turn on whether he meant his words to be taken literally or figuratively.

Suppose, the Statute adumbrates, that the lecturer had said something which was false in its literal sense (*de virtute sermonis*), but there is reason to believe he understood it in a true sense. That must be permissible, because otherwise it would become necessary to condemn some of the things the Bible says. It is suggested that a word means what its user intends it to mean, and so intention is all when it comes to condemning or acquitting a lecturer for the apparent error of his remarks. Yet, the statute continues, if care is not taken to ensure that everyone is clear in what sense a statement is to be taken, the lecturer may mean one thing and his listeners hear another. Similarly, in disputations, if the primary subject matter is not kept in view, the words may be misleading and there may be confusion as to whether opponents are really on opposite sides at all.

These ideas proved durable because they were useful ways of dealing with practical problems of understanding that were bound to arise in every age. Expressions such as *de virtute sermonis* and *ad proprietatem sermonis*, conveying the idea that a word or expression has a certain force, remained in common use among humanists in the fifteenth and sixteenth centuries.

Peter the Chanter was especially interested in *aequivocationis fallacia*, "the fallacy of equivocation," which occurs when someone mistakenly understands a term that has more than one meaning.[29] Much of his discussion uses the conventional examples of the Boethian logic course.[30] But where he can he uses "theological examples" (*theologica exempla*) instead.

---

[28]Courtenay and Tachau, "Ockham, Ockhamists, and the English-German Nation," pp. 58-59.

[29]"*Aequivocatio est dissimilis eiusdem vocis acceptio. Fallacia aequivocationis est deceptio proveniens ex dissimili eiusdem vocis acceptione.*" Peter the Chanter, *Verbum Abbreviatum*, prologue. See J. Leclercq, "Un traité *De fallaciis in theologia*," *Revue du Moyen Age Latin* 1 (1945): 43-46.

[30]*Logica Modernorum*, ed. L. M. De Rijk, 2 vols. (Assen: Van Gorcum, 1967).

Luke 3:1, 19-20 speaks of the baptism of Jesus under Herod, while in Matthew 2:19, Herod is said to be dead. There is no contradiction, says Peter, so long as we understand that two different Herods are involved.[31]

These medieval strivings to ensure that the Bible is read with respect for the utmost intimacies of its language and its divine truth set a high and technically exacting standard for students. Unfortunately, they also led into abstruse byways of ever-greater technicality, and they added to the difficulty faced by ordinary Christians whose education did not equip them to enter into such discussions.

Gloss and commentary, springs and sources, and the question of textual authority. The Bible stood at the apex of textual authoritativeness, with approved Christian writers such as Augustine, Gregory the Great and Bede beneath it, and beneath them, selected secular authors of the classical period, especially Cicero and some of the Roman poets and historians who remained familiar because they were used by schoolboys to help them master the Latin language. Christian authors grew in number down the centuries. To the existing set of approved and set texts, Christian writings and certain Latin classics, the sixteenth-century West added texts now available to them of various Greek fathers.[32] The fathers were embraced even by reforming academics who disparaged Scholasticism, and the Greek patristic authors in particular were novel and exciting for many of the Reformers of the sixteenth and seventeenth centuries.

The question was not only who should be trusted but how the trusted texts should be used. From about the time of Bede it became customary to borrow extracts from Christian—and occasionally classical—authorities to support an interpretation or illustrate an argument when lecturing on the Bible as a set text. There developed an immense apparatus of gloss and commentary incorporating these extracted authorities. In the twelfth century this became the *Glossa Ordinaria*, but a gloss grew upon this gloss, until the late medieval Bibles had a small

[31]G. R. Evans, *"Ponendo theologica exempla*: Peter the Chanter's *De Tropis Loquendi," History of Universities* 2 (1982): p. 5ff.

[32]Irene Backus, *The Reception of the Church Fathers in the West: From the Carolingians to the Maurists* (Leiden: Brill, 1997).

square of Bible in the center of each page, and surrounding rectangles of commentary.

From the later fourteenth century there began to emerge a subtly different view of the role of the approved Christian writers. Antiquity was seen to carry its own authority. Earliest was best, nearest to the apostles and therefore to Jesus himself, closest to the "springs" or "sources": *ad fontes*. Within strict limits the early Christian authors could themselves be seen as springs from which authentic Christian teaching flowed, mingling with and augmenting the stream of Scripture itself and supporting its claims to a special authority because they brought with them a whiff of the very air of divine dictation.

All this affected the very notion of the "book" and its inherent authoritativeness. Academic pedagogy was heavily dependent from its beginnings on teaching from set books that formed the backbone of the syllabus. The lecture (*lectio*) was merely a reading of that book with comments. A whole apparatus of formal "introductions to the authors" (*accessus*) had been in use during the medieval centuries to position a new set book for students by telling them who had written it, what branch of study it belonged to and the purpose the author had had in mind in creating it. Confidence that *the* Book, the Bible, set the rules for its own interpretation was going to be shaken as well, not only by new attitudes to the book bred by Renaissance studies but also by the schism in the Western church brought about by the Reformation.

12

THE EVANGELICAL
URGE AND THE
WANDERING PREACHERS

PREACHING BECOMES POPULAR AGAIN

Well before the end of the Roman Empire bishops saw it as one of the
defining duties of their office, especially in the West, that they should
expound Scripture for the people by preaching, often in serial form on
a whole book at a time, in a lengthy series of substantial sermons. It was
in order to discharge this duty that the bishop had a *cathedra*, or preaching seat, in the principal church, or cathedral, of the diocese. Gregory
the Great particularly emphasized this aspect of the episcopal office in
his book on *Pastoral Rule* (*Regula Pastoralis*). Great preachers such as
Augustine of Hippo and Gregory himself left a legacy of sermons on
which subsequent generations relied, including several extended series
on books of the Bible in which exegesis and homiletic were combined.

A lengthy pause followed the collapse of the Roman Empire, before
the urge to preach emerged strongly again. For many centuries the missionary task was to bring the faith to Europe bit by bit, often by means
of "missions," which are hard to distinguish from invasions, involving
much political fixing and rather little instruction. The essential thing,
in Christianizing new lands, was to ensure that the ruler accepted the
faith. Bede's account of the conversion of the English by Augustine of
Canterbury (d. c. 604) at the end of the sixth century describes him be-

ginning with a diplomatic overture to King Ethelbert of Kent (d. 616), and a politically nicely judged address to the king and certain nobles.[1] Teaching the ordinary faithful came later, if at all. Boniface (c. 675-754) conducted his missions to the German tribes under safe conduct and a similar awareness of the need to be diplomatic with rulers. Some homiliaries survive from the period of the missions and after, but this was not an era when sermons attempted to compare with those of the patristic period in length and theological sophistication.

Then a new sort of preacher altogether emerged. The revival of an interest in preaching seems to have come, like so much else by way of change in pastoral provision, with the twelfth century. If people were to hear sermons, it was important that preachers knew what they were talking about and could be trusted not to mislead them. This necessity became apparent to the ecclesiastical authorities only gradually. One of the earliest to experiment with teaching by preaching at the end of the eleventh century was Anselm of Canterbury. Before he became archbishop of Canterbury he was a monk, and he continued to live with a community of monks about him when he was archbishop. He had to do a certain amount of traveling on behalf of the abbey of Bec, where he eventually became abbot, and later, as archbishop, he crossed Europe on his way to Rome to appeal to the pope over his difficulties with successive kings of England, first William II (c. 1056-1100) then Henry I (c. 1068/1069-1135).

He stayed in monastic houses and took the opportunity to address the community. He seems to have done this first with his own monks at Bec and then with the community with which he surrounded himself at Canterbury. Anselm would tell vivid stories in the form of analogies. If you live in a fortified castle to which enemies are laying siege, it is wise not to keep looking out of the windows or your enemies will hit you with their arrows. So it is with the Christian soul. The devil is always lying in wait to spot a vulnerable place to send his arrows. Do not give him the chance. These "similitudines" and "sayings" proved very popular, and they were collected and copied for other communities of monks to benefit from.[2]

---

[1]Bede, *Ecclesiastical History*, 1.25, pp. 72-75.
[2]Anselm of Canterbury, *Memorials of St. Anselm*, ed. R. W. Southern and F. S. Schmitt (London: Oxford University Press, 1969).

Their easy-to-understand and memorable character and the apparent demand for them did not distract Anselm from the serious business of teaching the study of the Bible and sound doctrine. At home with the monks at Bec, he ran what would now be seminars but were probably then thought of as colloquies of the kind John Cassian (c. 360-after 430) had held with his monks near Marseilles, or Gregory the Great at Constantinople exploring the book of Job with his confreres. These were sessions of purposeful discussion and exploration of the Christian faith and its application to daily life. They resulted in Anselm's first theological writings. In the *Monologion* he discusses the nature of God and the doctrine of the Trinity in terms he says he has used with his brothers, and they have pressed him to write it all down for them.

In the *Proslogion* he gives a single argument for the existence of God, the famous ontological argument, an argument which, he claims, can also show everything else we believe about God. In the same period he was writing other treatises, three of which he describes as "treatises pertaining to the study of Holy Scripture." These are remarkable works for their time. He takes a series of linked topics—truth, freedom of choice, the fall of Satan—and asks hard questions of a small number of key passages of Scripture. He was trying to make his monks apply the increasingly sophisticated tools of contemporary study of grammar and logic to this analysis, for the scholars of the day had become very interested in "signification" and how it works. For example, what does John's Gospel mean when it says that Satan did not "stand fast in the truth" (*non stetit in veritate* in the Vulgate [Jn 8:44])?

Bible study through preaching develops further. The most notable monastic preacher of the early twelfth century was Bernard of Clairvaux, whose eighty-six sermons on the Song of Songs survive as part of a considerable body of his sermons, many of them preached in the course of the liturgical year; others were encouraged by his example to preach in imitation of his style. Bernard's head was so full of Scripture that it seems he could scarcely compose a sentence without quoting it or referring to it. He was a great reader and admirer of Gregory the Great as well as of Augustine, and he automatically played with the interactive possibilities of the many shades of meaning in the text in some of the ways they had done.

At the beginning of the first sermon on the Song of Songs, he flatters his monks with the assurance that they were ready for something more than milk. His sermons were going to give them solid food. If he had been preaching to "people in the world," he would preach in a very different manner. But the monks are assiduous students of "divine teaching"; they have mortified their senses and disciplined themselves for hard work; they have meditated on God's law day and night. They are ready for the rigors of grown-up study.[3] Bernard's sermons were certainly meaty in length. On one occasion he says when only halfway through the sermon he eventually completed that he knows time is passing and he ought to end his remarks.

Bernard does not claim to be wiser than his listeners. The Word is the teacher, not Bernard himself. He explains his position in a series of scriptural echoes and citations. The bread he is offering them is the bread shared by the stranger who accompanied the disciples on the road to Emmaus after the resurrection, and who turned out to be the risen Lord himself (Lk 24:30). If they are going to be given bread, it is the Master of the house who will break it, the "Lord you must see in the breaking of the bread" (para. 4).

His approach to the commentary on the text closely resembles that of Augustine. He peers closely at the exact wording of the Latin. "Let him kiss me with the kiss of his mouth" (*osculetur me osculo oris sui*) is an abrupt beginning. Why does the Song of Songs start like that? It is as though we overheard a conversation in the middle, with no indication who is speaking to whom. And why "with his mouth"? How else can one kiss except with the mouth? And why "his" mouth? It is not possible to give a kiss with any mouth but one's own. This is all done to startle and interest and challenge readers, Bernard suggests, to make them think. And we are intended to read this closely for every fragment

[3]Bernard of Clairvaux, *In cantica canticorum*, Sermo 1.1.1, *Opera Omnia*, ed. J. Leclercq, H. Rochais and C. H. Talbot (Rome: Editiones Cistercienses, 1957), 1.3, www.pathsoflove.com/bernard/songofsongs/sermon01.html.

counts. Indeed, we are taught to gather up the fragments—every crumb of Scripture—just as the disciples were told to gather the bread after the feeding of the five thousand (Mt 14:20). Here is Bernard reverently coaxing every lesson he can out of the text and taking care to provide a scriptural reference and anchor for everything he says, confident that the monks will pick up the echoes of the Bible texts for themselves.

Bernard posed no problem for, and caused no worries to, the ecclesiastical authorities. Indeed he was often used as a diplomatic emissary in church affairs, and he was relied on to put the case against two academic "heretics" who were tried for their misleading teachings in his lifetime, Peter Abelard at the Council of Sens in 1141 and Gilbert of Poitiers at Reims in 1148.

Other preachers of a respectable sort left records of their preaching in the form of collections. William of Newburgh, Augustinian canon and historian (1136-c. 1198) is a twelfth century case in point.[4] But much of the corpus of medieval sermons as it survives does not tell us for sure whether these were the words as delivered or edited for publication. This is particularly tantalizing in the case of the sermons preached by the Cistercians against the Albigensian and Waldensian heretics, and other sermons preached to ordinary people who would not understand them in Latin. Vernacular shadows can be glimpsed behind the Latin and vernacular sermons which survive for the later Middle Ages.[5]

Dissident and heretical preachers. Other self-appointed preachers did cause concern in the twelfth century. There was a fashion for demagogy, especially among renegade monks. Henry the Monk (Henry of Lausanne, d. c. 1148) was preaching from about 1116 to 1148. His teaching is known only from the publications of the church's apologists, who sought to condemn him. Peter the Venerable (1092/1094-1156), the abbot of Cluny, wrote one "Against the Petrobrusians," whom he couples with the followers of Henry, but who were named after Peter de Bruys (d. c. 1130). The offense of the Petrobrusians was to claim that the church's authority

---

[4]William of Newburgh, *The Sermons of William of Newburgh*, ed. A. B. Kraebel (Toronto: Pontifical Institute of Medieval Studies, 2010).

[5]*A Repertorium of Middle English Prose Sermons*, ed. Veronica O'Mara and S. Paul (Turnhout: Brepols, 2007).

was redundant. Nor were its sacraments essential. Christians needed
only the gospel as they themselves interpreted it. Arnold of Brescia
preached apostolic poverty in a church already uncomfortably attached
to its wealth, and he was condemned and eventually burned for his opinions. Here were early examples of what were to be the key themes of the
dissidents of the later Middle Ages, and they were already seen as dangerous and threatening to the stability of the church and likely to mislead the faithful. The problem was that such preachers were often attractive, natural demagogues. The Roman Catholic Church began to apply
strict rules in the licensing of preachers.

There was an exception to this. When the Waldensians appeared on
the scene in the later twelfth century, a case was made for the idea that
the danger really lay in those who were not properly educated and officially approved pretending to teach doctrine. The teaching and preaching of matters of faith must remain for the church to supervise. Teaching the simple basics of good Christian living was, arguably, another
matter, and there was for a time a certain amount of permissiveness
about allowing unlicensed preachers to do that.

The Waldensians. Among the topics he touches on are indications that
Peter the Chanter was cautiously sympathetic to the Waldensian
preachers who were popular at the time with the people in the Lyons
area, and who were urging them to live good Christian lives.[6] Preaching
about good conduct might be acceptable. But it was becoming an important consideration that "amateurs" should not pretend to teach doctrine, and the development of the sophisticated new art of preaching
was above the heads of the laity and left them out.

The Waldensian preachers presented a problem here. Indignation
about clerical sleaze had been one of the prompters of the twelfth-century
Waldensian movement that arose in France. Waldes (or Waldo or Valdes)
led a movement whose members became known as the "Poor Men of
Lyons" and who formulated several of the central principles which are

[6]Katherine Chambers, "The Rich and Poor in Twelfth-Century Paris: The Social Thought of Peter
the Chanter," Ph.D. thesis, University of Cambridge, 2006; and see John W. Baldwin, "An Edition
of the Long Version of Peter the Chanter's *Verbum Abbreviatum*," *Journal of Ecclesiastical History*
57 (2006): 78-85; and Petri Cantoris Parisiensis, *Verbum adbreviatum: Textus conflatus*, ed. Monique Boutry, CCCM 196 (Turnhout: Brepols, 2004).

also to be found in later medieval movements, toward the extreme left of reforming activity. They wanted to return to the life they believed the apostles had led, which they said must surely be closest to what Jesus had intended for his followers. They embraced a life of poverty and disputed the need for clergy and even for the sacraments, disparaging all the complex apparatus of church life which had grown up in their own day. Believers could be Christians without all these aids, they said.

They took advice from friendly local clergy and began to try to read the Bible for themselves, making translations and learning quotations in support of their position. These were the new bourgeoisie, a burgeoning middle class of craftsmen and tradespeople, with sharp wits and independent views. They proved discomfitingly adept at quoting the Bible smartly back at preachers sent by the church to persuade them back into the fold.

Waldensians in bands traveled in small groups of missionaries, wearing sandals; they preached popular sermons encouraging ordinary people to join them. They did not set out to create a schism. They intended to preach only to encourage their listeners to live good Christian lives as the gospel taught. But the official church feared their influence and in particular the danger that they would mislead the faithful on points of doctrine. Only those licensed to do so were allowed to preach about the faith, and licenses were granted by the church only to those who had the appropriate education. But where did matters of conduct end and matters of faith begin?

Ejecting them from areas where they were becoming influential only ensured that their influence spread as they moved elsewhere. Dissidents and the dissatisfied and excluded of society were drawn to them. They allowed women to preach. Disaffected clergy and monks and nuns came to join them. They were widely persecuted, some were executed, and the movement thus gained the attraction martyrdom tends to bring. They reached the north of Italy, always a hotbed of heretical and radical movements, where they found other groups such as the Humiliati, with similar ideas and a similar calling to return to the living of the apostolic life.

However, the movement's ideas and its ideals persisted, forming a looming and fundamental challenge to the institutional church as others took them up. The Waldensians themselves had had their day a century before Langland wrote about the "fair field of folk," and the movement was beginning to fade, though groups lingered throughout much of continental Europe, ready to be reawakened in Moldavia and in Bohemia, where it discovered it agreed with John Hus and the Hussites. Waldensians were still seen as a sufficient threat in Piedmont in the seventeenth century to prompt the Duke of Savoy to arrange to have them massacred, though the Puritan leader Oliver Cromwell (1599-1658) wrote to beg him not to. John Milton (1608-1674) composed an agonized sonnet, "On the Late Massacre in Piedmont":

> Avenge O Lord thy slaughter'd Saints, whose bones
>> Lie scatter'd on the Alpine mountains cold,
>> Ev'n them who kept thy truth so pure of old
>> When all our Fathers worship't Stocks and Stones,
> Forget not: in thy book record their groanes
>> Who were thy Sheep and in their antient Fold
>> Slayn by the bloody Piemontese that roll'd
>> Mother with Infant down the Rocks. Their moans
> The Vales redoubl'd to the Hills, and they
>> To Heav'n. Their martyr'd blood and ashes sow
>> O're all th' Italian fields where still doth sway
> The triple Tyrant [the pope]: that from these may grow
>> A hunder'd-fold, who having learnt thy way,
>> Early may fly the Babylonian [woe].

THE FORMAL RHETORICAL ART OF PREACHING

Once universities began to appear (from the end of the twelfth century), and with them the higher study of theology, university sermons began. There were splendid learned sermons on passages of the Bible to be heard in universities for centuries afterward. This preaching typically took a text as its theme and drew in other passages for comparison and illustration.

In this context the art of preaching *(ars praedicandi)* was one of the three medieval rhetorical arts which the Middle Ages developed, the others being the art of letter-writing and the art of poetry. These consciously followed in the tradition of classical rhetoric. We have seen how Augustine brought to preaching the skills of a professional orator, for the standing of rhetoric in late antiquity had been very high. Educated men were above all to be good orators. They would need to be able to act as advocates in law courts, to make political speeches, occasionally to flatter an emperor with an *encomium*. These needs diminished sharply with the end of empire and as the schools system collapsed, including the finishing school period many young men spent in Athens learning philosophy.

The heritage of the medieval art of preaching manuals drew on classical rhetoric in a particular way. The branch of ancient oratory this involved was the training in putting together an argument. That involved logic or dialectic, which proved a case, but also the utilization of "topics." This is what Cicero, writing his *De inventione*, called "finding arguments" (*inventio*). The orator learned to collect illustrations, examples, quotations and useful materials he could include in a speech so as to make it more persuasive and interesting for the listeners. When these skills were adapted for the purposes of preaching, preachers were taught to use biblical materials (as well as historical and literary examples) to make their case in much the same way.

The ars praedicandi: *Alan of Lille.* The author of one of the first known manuals on the art of preaching in this style was Alan of Lille (d. 1203). He seems to have lived to a great age, and died, as did many other retired academics of the day, as a Cistercian monk. But when he was younger he had frequented the schools of Paris and taken part in the early evolution of the movement that was going to create the first universities about the time he died. His *Art of Preaching* has a preface in which Alan gives would-be preachers general guidance. He evidently sees the importance of rhetorical skills. For instance he tells the preacher to stop when the audience is seen to be weeping with emotion.

The text mainly consists of a set of compressed sermons ready to be expanded by the user. The collection of topics was an established feature of ancient rhetorical method. Strictly, these are closer to topical collections. Some are concerned with vices and virtues, and it is certainly possible that a preacher might have reason to take, say, "avarice" as his subject and need as many references as possible on the subject conveniently to hand. It is less likely that a preacher will face a congregation consisting entirely of widows or princes, but Alan provides collected material for use in these eventualities too.

Bible awareness quickly arrived. In the developed art of preaching manual, which came fully into its own about 1230, the preacher was taught to take a passage of Scripture as a theme and then to divide the points to be covered, and if necessary subdivide them further, so as to deal systematically with each. For this purpose the most important handbook was a directory of biblical terms. If the word *arm* occurred in the text to be preached on, perhaps with reference to the Lord reaching out his strong right arm (Ps 118:16), the preacher might want to refer to other passages in Scripture where arms are mentioned. Such dictionaries were already being created at the end of the twelfth century. Alan of Lille was the author of one of those too.

Peter the Chanter. Among the leaders of the art of preaching movement, Peter the Chanter was one of the most Bible conscious. His *Verbum abbreviatum* (*Little Word*) is a lively manual for preachers in which the way they were to use Scripture was paramount.

Peter was interested in many aspects of the social life of his times, which all seemed to him relevant to the preacher who wanted to encourage better behavior. Among the clusters of comment and topical material he offers the would-be preacher are chapters "against those who entertain suspicions and rush to judgement" (75, col. 220). This was topical because the late twelfth century saw the emergence of the concept of notoriety in legal practice. The idea was that a legal process could be shortened if it could be shown that the accused was known to have committed the alleged offense, and there had as a consequence been energetic sharing of gossip in order to show that it was common knowledge about "the bishop and the actress." Peter follows this chapter with another (76, col. 224) "against rumor-mongers," citing 2 Thessalonians 3 (remember: verses of the Bible did not yet have numbers) and another "against the changeable" (77, col. 225), because he believes tale-tellers are unreliable.

He also inveighs against the idle (81, col. 246); those who indulge in excess and are extravagant in taking an interest in fashionable dress (including soft garments and wanting too many of them), good food and fine houses (81-85, col. 250); those eager in their interest in secular pleasures (89, col. 261).

Thomas of Chobham. Meanwhile, the steady evolution of the art of preaching manuals was proceeding. Thomas of Chobham (c. 1160-1233/36), who certainly studied at Paris and may have been a pupil of Peter the Chanter, begins his *Art of Preaching* with a brief description of the four wheels of the chariot in which Scripture carries the soul to heaven. These are its historical, tropological, allegorical and anagogical senses. The four powers of the soul, sense, reason, understanding and wisdom, engage with these.[7] What then is preaching? "It is preaching of the divine Word to inform faith and explain how to live a good Christian life." The first preachers had to convert the people from idolatry and bring them to believe in the one God and the incarnation and death of his Son. The modern preacher's task is to bring those who already believe to good behavior (*in bonis moribus*). He must draw chiefly on Scripture in doing this, although it is true that moral philosophers of old had useful things to say and could arrive at some of the articles of faith by reason alone, and they may be used too.[8]

It is a nice irony that the only area where unlicensed preachers such as the Waldensians were permitted (reluctantly) to do some preaching was where they kept strictly to advice on the living of a good Christian life, and well away from anything overtly theological.

THE FRANCISCANS AND THE DOMINICANS

From canons to friars: The evangelical urge and the apostolic life. The *Libellus de diversis ordinibus* (*Little Book on the Different Orders*) is an anonymous work of the first half of the twelfth century which casts an anxious eye over all the monastic experiments of the time. Many of these did not last very long; they involved dubious characters such as rene-

---

[7]Thomas de Chobham, prologue, *Summa de arte praedicandi*, CCCM 82, ed. F. Morenzoni (1987), pp. 4-5.
[8]Ibid., p. 15.

gade monks who had taken to preaching and proved dangerously charismatic, as well as the sort of honest middle-aged seekers after a more
serious and devout way of life.

One of the foundation principles of Benedictine monasticism had
been the expectation that those who entered the religious life would be
"stable." This meant that they were expected to remain in the monastery
where they had been professed, that is, taken their vows. That did not
prevent their performing various social services, the care of the sick by
providing physicians and even running hospitals for the local people,
and giving shelter to pilgrims, hospitality to travelers and alms to the
destitute. There had always been exceptions to the expectation of stability in one place. The canons of a cathedral and the different kinds of
new-style canons regularly invented in the twelfth century were expected to lead active lives in the world by, for example, providing services as priests for parishes.

Events of the late twelfth and early thirteenth centuries transformed this scene of experimentation in the religious life and adapta-
tion of the ideal of enclosed, contemplative, stable monastic life to the
needs of those who wanted to take God seriously while working actively in the world.

The need for missionary preaching. The need for preachers for missionary purposes had grown in the late twelfth century, because of the expansion of heresy and dissidence in a long corridor running from southern France and northern Spain across north Italy and into the Balkans.
The Cistercians, reformed Benedictines, some of them talented preachers after the model of their great leader Bernard of Clairvaux, tried and
failed to convert the heretics by preaching.

There were two distinct categories of these heretics, though there
seems to have been some crossing over between them and possibly some
confusion and some hedging of bets among the ordinary faithful. (It was
said that many attended both the ordinary church services and also the
worship of heretical groups, just to be on the safe side.) The Waldensians
and the Albigensian dualists of southern France and northern Spain in
particular were perceived as a serious threat because of the hold they had
on the faithful and their disregard for the church's authority.

The Albigensians were adherents of opinions wholly incompatible with Christian faith. They were dualists. They held that there is not one God but two. The good god and the evil god are eternally at war, fighting for ultimate control of the cosmos. The faithful must therefore do everything they can to ensure that the evil god is defeated.

It was usual to identify evil with matter, the physical, the body with its lusts, and the good with the spiritual, and here there was a long heritage from the Gnostics and the Manichees of the early Christian centuries. (Augustine belonged to the Manichaean sect for nearly ten years before he became disillusioned with it.) Adherents of these Albigensian, Cathar and Bogomil sects were encouraged to fight for the good by living a spiritual life. It followed that those who wanted to be good must deny themselves fleshly pleasures, lead ascetic lives, fast and be celibate. Bodily pleasures and the enjoyments of the senses were regarded as tempting and seductive, and were to be resisted at all costs. It will be apparent that such attitudes chimed closely with those of the orthodox, with Christians like Guibert's mother.

There was another thread in the Gnostic-Manichee-Albigensian set of beliefs which was to remain important. This was the concept of the "elect," understood as a small number of adherents regarded as specially chosen by God and fit for salvation, even above other Christians. They were sometimes called the *perfecti*; lesser adherents could gain merit by serving them. Albigensian heretics therefore presented a danger which went far beyond that of a laity, like the Waldensians, which had decided to read the Bible for itself and appoint its own leaders and ministers but which was not fundamentally heretical.

So the church's preachers needed to be able to address whole local communities as they went about their work of converting people back to orthodox beliefs. The two movements, the antiestablishment Waldensian and the dualist Albigensian, had in common a fair amount of articulateness in their adherents. They would need to be persuaded back into the church. They were not estranged from it in their minds.

Dominic and the Dominicans. Faced with this need, the Spanish cathedral canon Dominic (c. 1174-1221) discovered a new kind of vocation. Jordan of Saxony (1190-1237) helped to bring together two strands of the developments of these crucial decades as one of the principal chroniclers of the early Dominicans and the person who followed Dominic as leader of the order. Jordan was also influential in ensuring that the Dominicans took a leading part in the development of the first universities. Jordan says that Diego, the bishop of Osma, was particularly careful to "to urge his canons, by frequent admonitions and salutary exhortations, to agree to observe a canonical religious life under the Rule of St. Augustine."[9] He was himself especially keen on missionary work, it seems.

Dominic had a good education, but, like other prospective saints of the period, he was said to have left off learning for the sake of the study of the Bible:

> In due time he was sent to Palencia for instruction in the liberal sciences, which flourished there in those days. When he was satisfied that he learned them sufficiently . . . he abandoned them for something on which he could more profitably spend his limited time here on earth and turned to the study of theology. Now he began to have a strong savor of the word of God as of something sweeter than honey to his mouth.

As well as becoming notable for his holiness and good works, he became conspicuous for the way he took the Bible seriously:

> To these sacred studies he devoted four years, during which he learned, with such continual eagerness, to drink from the streams of Sacred Scripture that, in his untiring desire to learn, he spent his nights with almost no sleep at all and the truth which he heard made its way into the deep recesses of his mind, where it was held fast by his memory.

As Jordan tells the story, Dominic was traveling through Toulouse in the retinue of his bishop when he became aware of the pervasiveness of the Albigensian heresy in the region. "When they reached Toulouse, they discovered that many of its people had for some time been heretics." As a cathedral canon he was already a priest and used to the expectation that the priests attached to a cathedral could be used by the diocese to meet pastoral needs as required:

---

[9]All quotations in this section on the Dominicans are from M. Aron and P. Mandonnet, *The Life of Blessed Jordan of Saxony* (London: Blackfriars, 1955).

Dominic's heart was moved to pity at the great number of souls being so wretchedly deluded. At the inn where they found shelter in Toulouse, Dominic spent the entire night fervently exhorting and zealously arguing with the heretical innkeeper, who, no longer able to resist the wisdom and the spirit that spoke, returned by God's grace to the true faith.

He began to form the idea of founding an order with a special mission to preach against the heretics in the region. This, his biographer Jordan claims (in a topos often used by hagiographers), had been foreseen by his mother in a vision

> that she would bear in her womb a dog who, with a burning torch in his mouth and leaping from her womb, seemed to set the whole earth on fire. This was to signify that her child would be an eminent preacher who, by "barking" sacred knowledge, would rouse to vigilance souls drowsy with sin.

The pope sent him and his former bishop to begin this work in support of the Cistercians. ("At the time the Lord Pope Innocent had directed twelve abbots of the Cistercian Order to take each a companion and preach the faith against the Albigensian heretics.") The Cistercians were not proving very effective; they had not been trained primarily as preachers. Dominic's former bishop had a very clear idea why they were not succeeding:

> Then he commented that the methods these heretics were using to convert souls of their perfidy by persuasion, preaching, and the example of their false holiness were in striking contrast to the stylish and expensive carriages and furnishing displayed by those who had been sent. "This is not the way, my brethren, this is not the way for you to proceed. I do not think it possible, by words alone, to lead back to the faith such men as are better attracted by example. Look at the heretics! While they make a pretense at piety, while they give counterfeit examples of evangelical poverty and austerity, they win the simple people to their ways. Therefore, if you come with less poverty and austerity, you will give hardly any edification, you will cause much harm, and You will fail utterly of your objective. Match steel with steel, rout false holiness with the true religion, because the arrogance of these false apostles must be overthrown by genuine humility. Was this not the way whereby Paul became unwise, namely, by enumerating his true virtues and recounting his austerities and dangers,

in order to burst the bubble of those who boasted about the merits of their holy lives?"

His idea was that there should be a wholehearted concentration on preaching and that the preachers should be conspicuously humble and Christlike. They were to go from house to house and beg for their meals and lodging as Christ had taught his disciples to do. At the same time they would have to be determined and able to sustain lengthy disputations with their adversaries. Jordan describes occasions when the leaders of heretics in a region would challenge the missionary preachers to debate, and all the people would watch, the contest sometimes going on for days. It was very important that the preachers should be able to use such occasions to win the watching populace to their side. There were even competitive book burnings in which the publications of the heretics and those of the church's preachers were thrown into the fire, and it was observed that the work of the preachers of the true faith leaped out again while those of the heretics were destroyed.

There are indications in Jordan's account of the growing importance of laypeople as active participants and even leaders in such debates:

> The basis [for the discussion] chosen by the heretics was that Arnold Othon said that the Roman Church, defended by the bishop of Osma, is not holy, nor [is it] the spouse of Christ, but the church of the devil, [holding] the doctrine of the demons, and that it is that Babylon which, in the Apocalypse, John calls the mother of fornications and abominations, drunk with the blood of the saints and the martyrs of Jesus Christ. Its institution is neither holy nor good, nor established by the Lord Jesus Christ; and neither Christ nor the Apostles established or Posited the order of the Mass as it is established today. The bishop offered himself to prove the contrary by the authoritative words of the New Testament. What a shame! [Even] among Christians the status of the Church and the Catholic faith had reached that point of dishonor where the judgment about such great outrages had to be entrusted to laymen! When, therefore, the writings were distributed among the aforementioned laymen, to whom both sides gave the authority for deciding [the truth], they refused to deliberate, went away, and left the business unfinished.

Some disputations were with Albigensians, some with the Waldensians, who were known to be particularly adroit in quoting Scripture. In some places the local nobility took sides, some with one group of heretics, some with another, sometimes within the same family. In the case of the Count of Foix, for example, according to Jordan, "his wife was publicly known to be a follower of the Waldensian sect and, of his two sisters, one professed the teachings of the Waldensians, while the other professed the heresies common to other apostates."

It was after the death of his former bishop that Dominic emerged as the leader and began to develop his new order. In 1208 one of the Cistercians was assassinated and an armed crusade was launched against the Albigensians, as the bishop had feared would eventually happen. Dominic did his best to moderate the effects of the violence and hold himself aloof from the fighting. He wanted to found "an order whose duty it would be to travel throughout the world preaching the Gospel by word and example and defending the catholic Faith against the heretics then rearing themselves." Others began to offer themselves as members:

> One was Brother Peter of Seila, later the prior at Limonges; the other was Brother Thomas, a very gracious and eloquent man. The former of these, Brother Peter, gave Brother Dominic and his companions the tall, stone houses he owned . . . near the village of Narbonne. And, so, for the first time, they began to live together at Toulouse in the same houses. From then on, all who were gathered there began to grow more and more in humility and to live according to the customs of religious.

At the Lateran Council of 1215, Dominic obtained papal approval of the new order "which would be called and would be an Order of Preachers":

> Now the future preachers chose the Rule of St. Augustine, who had been an outstanding preacher, and added to it some stricter details about food and fasts, as well as about bedding and clothing. They agreed, also, to hold no possessions, lest concern about temporal things be an obstacle to their office of preaching, but would remain content with their revenue.

The Friars Preachers got on with their work and organized themselves. They also had to make arrangements to ensure that their members would be adequately educated:

A certain priest noticed that Blessed Dominic and his friars dedicated themselves fervently in preaching without any concern about temporal rewards and busied themselves about spiritual matters to the exclusion of all else. So, in a spirit of pious emulation, he began to desire their manner of life, considering that he would be happy, if he could follow them and imitate them to some degree. Accordingly, he thought of completely abandoning all things and following in their footsteps, provided he could get a book of the New Testament, which he judged necessary for preaching. As he was turning these matters over in his mind, he beheld a young man carrying under his cloak a book he wanted to sell. When the priest looked to see what the book was, he found that it was the New Testament and gladly purchased it at once. But now that he had the book, he experienced a temptation and began to wonder whether he should carry out the resolution he had formed in his mind and whether God was truly pleased with it. As one thought followed another, it occurred to him to look to God for an answer in that book; so, after a prayer to God, he closed the book and, tracing the sign of the cross on it, he pronounced the name of God. Then he opened the book and cast his eyes conjecturally on the chapter that first offered itself upon his opening the book. He happened to open it to the Acts of the Apostles apropos of the messengers sent by the Holy Spirit from Cornelius to St. Peter. "Arise, therefore, get thee down and go with them, doubting nothing, for I have sent them" (Acts 10:20). Then, as though reassured by this divine message, he at once left the world and followed the brethren.

Francis of Assisi and the Franciscans. Meanwhile, in 1208 the young nobleman Francis of Assisi (1181/1182-1226) had heard a sermon on Matthew 10, which describes how Jesus sent out his disciples to tell the people about the kingdom of heaven, traveling humbly, without possessions or equipment. This call to the apostolic life, understood as the simple life, the life of dedication and service and missionary zeal, fired his imagination much as it fired that of Dominic. In his *Testament* he writes of the way he felt when he tended lepers, "and when I left them, that which had seemed to me bitter was changed for me into sweetness of body and soul."[10] (Those suffering from what would now be recog-

---

[10]On the dubiousness of *Testament* and 1221 and 1223 rules, see Malcolm D. Lambert, *Franciscan Poverty* (St. Bonaventure, N.Y.: Franciscan Institute, 1998), chap. 1, where he discusses the incon-

nized as a variety of skin diseases all tended to be called lepers in the Middle Ages.)

Francis emphasizes in the *Testament* that he had no wish to interfere with the regular pastoral work of the church. He "would not preach against their will in the parishes in which they live." This was an important point because wandering preachers, even if they had preaching licenses from the local bishop, were easily seen as a threat by parish priests. He says that those who were priests among the Franciscans said the divine office like other clergy and those who were laymen said the Lord's Prayer.

Francis saw himself as a missionary not only to God's people in Europe, where the task was to awaken a livelier faith in people who were already Christian, but also a missionary to unbelievers (*gentiles*). For example, he went to Egypt, where Jacques de Vitry describes how he was captured by the Saracens and simply said, "I am a Christian. Take me to your master." He spent several days with the sultan, unfolding the faith to him, and when he left the sultan asked for his prayers in order that he might understand the Christian faith.[11] Francis was aware that this was difficult work and he instructed: "Let all of the brothers who by divine inspiration desire to go amongst the Saracens or other infidels, ask leave therefore from their provincial ministers. But the ministers must give permission to go to none except to those whom they see are fitted to be sent."[12]

Like other charismatic leaders of new religious movements in the twelfth and thirteenth centuries, Francis soon found he had imitators and followers. Once he had companions, he was conscious from an early stage that they would need a rule or guide for their common life. "No one showed me what I ought to do," he explained, but God himself revealed to him that the way to go was to "live according to the form of the holy Gospel." So he wrote a brief and simple guide "and the Lord

---

clusiveness and difficulty of attempts to get back to Francis's authentic mind, before the general ideas of the movements of the time had been worked into original documents in the process of their transmission.

[11] *The Historia Occidentalis of Jacques de Vitry*, Spicilegium Friburgense 17, ed. J. F. Hinnebusch (Fribourg: University Press, 1972), 28:162.

[12] *The Writings of St. Francis of Assisi*, trans. Paschal Robinson (Philadelphia: Dolphin, 1906), www .lulu.com/items/volume_31/484000/484729/1/print/PaschalRobinsonWritingsofSt Francis.pdf.

Pope confirmed it for me." He had gone to Rome to seek the pope's approval for a new order of religious. Innocent III gave it to him, partly through the good offices of a sympathetic cardinal.

Those who joined Francis gave away all their property to the poor and "were content with one tunic." He and his brothers chose to call themselves "friars minor." They saw themselves as strangers and pilgrims. They worked with their hands to earn their livings or begged for alms.[13] This was the closest they could come, they felt, to living the apostolic life as Jesus had commanded his disciples to do.

Within two years, Clare of Assisi (1193/1194-1253) had been won to the new cause, and an order was established for women in 1212, called the Poor Clares. Francis encouraged them to be "espoused to the Holy Ghost," "choosing to live according to the perfection of the holy Gospel."[14] Why were people drawn to this life? These were evidently charismatic leaders, and such leaders repeatedly started enduring movements in the medieval centuries. But there were features of these mendicant orders which were new. They allowed those attracted to the religious life to embrace it without also having to undertake to live in an enclosed community for the rest of their lives. Poverty, chastity and obedience were still expected as they were for Benedictine monks, but friars could travel, could preach in towns, could be highly educated, indeed needed to be highly educated and had to work under strict regulations:

> The brothers must not preach in the diocese of any bishop when their doing so may be opposed by him. And let no one of the brothers dare to preach in any way to the people, unless he has been examined and approved by the minister general of this brotherhood, and the office of preaching conceded to him by the latter. I also warn and exhort the same brothers that in the preaching they do their words be fire-tried and pure, for the utility and edification of the people, announcing to them vices and virtues, punishment and glory, with brevity of speech because the Lord made His word short upon earth.[15]

---

[13]*Writings of St. Francis of Assisi*, www.lulu.com/items/volume_31/484000/484729/1/print/ PaschalRobinsonWritingsofStFrancis.pdf.
[14]Ibid.
[15]Ibid.

These instructions for Franciscan preachers from the head of their own order show the pervasiveness of the sense, not only among the church's authorities but also in the approved religious orders, that preaching must be licensed and controlled.

Gaining official approval and designing an education for mendicant preachers. Dominic and Francis were said to have met about the time of the Fourth Lateran Council in 1215. Were they rivals already? On the face of it the two orders had complementary preaching missions, Dominic against the heretics, Francis to the people and, in time, to unbelievers. But the seeds of competition were there in the need both orders were going to have for appropriately educated preachers and the consequent development of a higher education to fit them for the work. Within a quarter of a century the Franciscans had arranged that each convent was to have a lector who would see to the basic education of the friars and ensure that those who went to the universities were properly prepared. The provincial chapters made the final selection of these academic high flyers. The Franciscans had a school in Paris in 1219 and in Oxford as early as 1229. Dominican *studia* quickly appeared too, in most of the new university towns. They were in Paris before the Franciscans.

This success, particularly in the new world of the universities, began to make the friars enemies. It was possible for any prospective ordinary student to arrive in a university and attach himself to a master, who would keep a register of students of the university. The friar students did not need to do this, for they had their own lectures and teachers. But they admitted some of the secular students to join them, partly in the hope of winning them for the order in due course. This caused great resentment in the universities, for it took fees from the secular masters. By the middle of the thirteenth century, in 1254, the University of Paris was so annoyed that it sent out a circular letter complaining that the friars were monopolizing the faculty of theology, especially the Dominicans. Innocent IV (d. 1254) was sympathetic, but he died too soon to make a difference, and his successor took a different view.

The resentment was not confined to academe. The general council of 1274 at Lyons considered the status of the mendicant orders in the face of growing indignation from churchmen that they were taking over many of the pastoral functions of the church—such as burying the dead—and they were hearing confessions and granting absolution. The complainants wanted them banned from granting absolution or imposing penances, from preaching in churches except on special occasions, and from expanding their numbers any further. The politics of the time were not with the opposition, however, and although it was agreed that the lesser orders such as Austin friars and Carmelites should have their future reviewed, canon 23 of the council of Lyons allowed the Franciscans and Dominicans to carry on. The council of Lyons of 1274, criticizing the "presumptuous rashness" which had "produced an almost unlimited crowd of diverse orders, especially mendicant, which have not yet merited the beginnings of approval," decreed that this was to stop, for "insecure mendicancy usually provides a living through public begging," and uncontrolled tongues must not be let loose on "the office of preaching and hearing confessions and the right of burial." The new restrictions were not to apply to the Dominicans and Franciscans, who were deemed respectable by the Fourth Lateran Council.

Friars and preaching. The most serious education and preaching of Scripture available to the laity from the thirteenth century was the work of these friars. This was ironic since toward the end of the Middle Ages they became the focus of so much hatred on the part of the laity and the leaders of dissent both clerical and lay. It was the friars above all who created the literature of preaching aids, for their primary vocation was preaching. They also counted among their number many of the leading names of late medieval thought, especially Bonaventure, John Duns Scotus (1265/1266-1308) and William of Ockham (c. 1285-1347) for the Franciscans, and Albertus Magnus (Albert the Great, d. 1280) and Thomas Aquinas for the Dominicans.

Jordan of Saxony at Oxford. Jordan of Saxony followed Dominic, founder of the Dominicans, as head of the order. He was preaching in England, probably in 1229.[16] The first sermon he is known to have given seems to have been delivered in Oxford in November. A letter from theologian Robert Grosseteste (c. 1170-1253) suggests that this may have

---

[16]A. G. Little and Decima Douie, "Three Sermons of Friar Jordan of Saxony, the Successor of St. Dominic, preached in England, A.D. 1229," *English Historical Review* 54 (1939): 1-20.

been more than a brief visit and that he may have spent some time in the city. He asks Jordan to recall "with what familiarity, when you were in Oxford, your sweet good-nature afforded us frequent conversations."

Jordan's sermon is mainly a general exhortation to the clergy to preach to the people and win their ardent commitment to the faith, but he breaks off to make a special appeal to the Oxford scholars. It would not be right, he warns them, to aspire unworthily to high positions, or the status of master of arts. It is as though Satan were constantly whispering to those who have a duty to teach (*qui docendi habent officium*) to tempt them to teach, lecture, hold disputations for their own glory. Bringing together three texts (1 Kings 7:41, on the two columns of the temple; Is 22:23-24, on the nail fastened in a sure place from which all kinds of vessels hung; and Judith 8:21, "Ye are priests in the people of God, from you hangs their soul" [p. 8]), he reminds them that they are priests, and the souls of the people in all the parishes of England hang from the cord which they must hold secure. They should remind themselves how Jesus behaved when the devil took him up to a high mountain to tempt him (Mt 4:1-11).

13

RELIGIOUS EXPERIMENTS BY THE LAITY

WORKING PEOPLE, ACTIVE ORDERS

Beguines appeared in the Low Countries toward the end of the twelfth century. These associations of women lived in or at the edge of towns where they could work to help the poor. Their members sought to live a dedicated religious life without entering a traditional religious community and becoming nuns.

Individual women with this inventive new kind of vocation came together by a process it is now difficult to reconstruct. They made their own rules for a shared way of life, each group in its own way. It gave them an independence they could not have in ordinary family life and freed them from the patronage under which wealthy women who became conventional nuns might be placed as abbesses by their families regardless of vocation or aptitude. They varied considerably in the social mix they admitted. In some communities noblewomen and women of the servant classes lived companionably together, as in the huge Beguinage at Ghent with its eighteen houses and hundreds of members. They were an unwitting social experiment.

All this was potentially undesirable in the eyes of the ecclesiastical authorities. The large numbers and the lack of proper supervision were seen as a recipe for trouble, both in terms of allowing unorthodox beliefs to flourish and because such assemblages could lead to disorderly behavior. They often cultivated mysticism too, with its potential for unsupervised experience and religious emotion. In 1310 Marguerite Poreta, a French Beguine who was also a famous mystic, was burned at the stake for heresy and for being influenced by the fringe lay group, the Brethren of the Free Spirit. Her chief offense was, perhaps, that she had written a book. Books were often regarded as dangerous for their capacity to spread undesirable beliefs and practices. The following year the pope accused the whole movement of spreading heresy, and the Beguines were persecuted by successive popes.

Beghards, the male counterpart of Beguines, were in a way less remarkable than the women, who had made for themselves an independent way of life in a society which had no natural place for the professional or the independent woman. But as laymen engaged in an independent religious endeavor, the Beghards were still anomalous. They tended to be craftsmen or artisans—people such as the Beghard weavers of Brussels. Or in many cases they were retired practitioners of these trades, too old to work and needing what was in effect a retirement home. Just as elderly noblemen had retired to Benedictine life in the late eleventh century and elderly academics had often become Cistercians in the twelfth, so aging weavers could find a home in a Beghard house.

But as in the case of the Beguines, a combination of a lack of education and a lack of supervision was regarded as dangerous. It easily led some into heresy, and the Beghards, like the Beguines, were repeatedly condemned by the ecclesiastical authorities during the fourteenth century.

Another of these grassroots social experiments created the Humiliati. These were a "back to the apostolic life" movement too. Jacques de Vitry says that "there are in Italy and especially in Lombardy congregations of men and women living by a rule who call themselves 'humiliati.' In their poverty and simplicity of dress and gesture and in all they say and do, they are a great example of humility. They live in community and live mainly by their own manual labour." The much more modern notion of the dignity of labor is perhaps foreshadowed here. They include laypeople and clergy. "Most of them are literate." The Humiliati seem to have had papal permission to preach, not only within their communities but in public, and, with the permission of the local clergy, in churches.

They are reported as having an impressive effect in winning people to a more serious religious commitment.[1]

However, again there are dangers. They attract hangers-on. These pretend to associate with them, but they preach like demagogues and whip their hearers into a frenzy of excitement by claiming to be directly inspired by the Holy Spirit.[2] Another danger is the way the Patarenes claim to be associated with them. The Patarenes began as an eleventh-century movement of would-be church reformers, with anticlerical opinions not unlike those of the Waldensians and concentrated in Lombardy, but by the early thirteenth century they had moved toward Cathar opinions.[3]

The Brethren of the Common Life formed another movement of the same broad type in the Low Countries in the fourteenth century, and again it seems to have been associated with the urban life and with tradespeople and craftsmen, the new articulate and independently minded middle classes. This *devotio moderna*, as it was known, seems to have been the creation of Geert Groote (1340-1384). He was born into a wealthy merchant family, and in his early thirties he had a conversion experience. This led him to the decision to lead a simple life, a life of self-denial, and then, like Francis of Assisi, he began to preach about this modern mode of return to the apostolic life or "imitation of Christ." One of the features of this new life was the discounting of good works in favor of the developing of a close relationship with God through faith and a personal search for perfection.

The *Imitation of Christ* is usually attributed to Thomas à Kempis (c. 1380-1471). He joined the Brethren, chiefly drawn it seems by their tradition of mysticism, retirement and a non-intellectual approach to seeking God. "I would rather feel contrition than be able to define it," says the first chapter. The *Imitation of Christ* sought to awaken longing, to motivate the reader to seek Christ, first by the practice of humility. Curb your desire for knowledge, for it will distract you, calls the second

---

[1] *The Historia Occidentalis of Jacques de Vitry*, Spicilegium Friburgense 17, ed. J. F. Hinnebusch (Fribourg: University Press, 1972), XXVIII, pp. 144-46.
[2] Ibid.
[3] Ibid.

chapter. Knowledge will feed your vanity and make you want to appear wise. And the more knowledgeable you are, the more severely you will be judged if you do not live as you know you should. You should seek to let Truth himself teach you what he is in himself (chap. 3). A pure, humble, sincere and steadfast spirit will be best able to learn that, and such a person will also be efficient when he goes abroad in doing what he planned and not getting distracted. He will be able to make the best of the human condition, in which, in this life, all perfection is dimmed and diminished by imperfection.

But the tradition of the Brethren was far from being wholly unintellectual. They preached that it was important for laypeople to read the Bible, or at least hear it in their own language, and they therefore encouraged the making of translations. Houses of the Brethren were mainly filled with laymen, but they usually contained a cleric or two who could help with the education of the lay members in this way. Brethren often ran schools too. The educational level of what was offered could be high—both Erasmus and Luther got part of their education at such a school.

The movement spread, with new houses being set up across northern Europe as far east as Poland. Sisters of the Common Life emerged to found houses for women. And the movement pressed for reform.[4]

Beguinages were eventually mainly drawn into the mendicant movement, and some Beguines joined the Flagellants. The Flagellants represent one of the extremes to which popular religion could easily take its adherents. They began as pilgrims who sought to make their journey as meritorious as they could by inflicting suffering on themselves on the way, by lashing themselves as they walked. It was a vivid public sight and compelling to the imaginations of those inspired to imitate them. The Flagellants were seen in Perugia after a bad year of failed crops in the late 1250s.

The social impact of one of their processions could be electric. Several thousand sometimes joined in with singing and with banners. This was again the kind of thing both ecclesiastical and secular authorities feared,

---

[4]*Devotio Moderna: Basic Writings*, Classics of Western Spirituality, ed. John H. Van Engen (Mahwah, N.J.: Paulist Press, 1988).

especially since the participants were often apparently the same individuals as those who became involved in dissident movements. There
was cross-infection, some Flagellants claiming that taking part in one of
the processions was as effective in cleansing sin as confession, absolution and penance. There was also violence, with anticlerical lynch mobs
sometimes attacking priests and other, anti-Semitic, mobs attacking
Jews. The pope made an attempt to stop all this with a ban in 1261.

The Flagellants appeared in northern lands, including the Low
Countries in later episodes of popular public demonstration, and especially during the period when the pandemic Black Death was striking
fear into the population across Europe, cutting a swath of deaths in
every town and village. Sometimes they walked very long distances in
their conspicuous white robes, attracting attention across Europe. Some
groups claimed to have a letter brought to them by an angel endorsing
what they were doing, and this would be read out at the beginning of
the flagellation ritual. People would take home pieces of the resulting
blood-soaked cloth and keep them as relics, holy remains, full of spiritual power.

The claims made by the Flagellants grew bigger and bolder. Some
became millenarians, a notion connected with the claim in the book of
Revelation that Satan was to be bound for a thousand years and then
released (Rev 20:2-5). Since Constantine in the fourth century was the
first Christian emperor, naturally the fourteenth century felt nervous
about what might happen in their times. The end of the world might be
the beginning of a new world. It was claimed by one German group of
Flagellants that they could bring back the dead Holy Roman emperor
Frederick II (1194-1250) and inaugurate a New World Order. Their
leader was condemned by the Inquisition and burned in 1369.

EXEMPLARY INDIVIDUALS
AND BEING AN EXAMPLE TO OTHERS

These daring experiments showed that the call to make a special commitment as a Christian could be felt by anyone, not only the nobility
and gentry, who had something of a monopoly of membership of monastic orders by the later Middle Ages. One of the effects was to en-

courage in some individuals a heightened consciousness of the importance of developing a personal relationship with God. This did not
require a priest as intermediary, but the style in which it was envisaged
and attempted was quite different from the private spirituality of the
Reformation ideals. A few in the Middle Ages felt a vocation for the life
of a hermit, and they attracted respect and visitors much as their coun-
terparts had done in late antiquity.

Ailred of Rievaulx's (1109-1167) *De institutione inclusarum* was written
about 1160 for his sister, to provide a rule for the anchoritic life, "a forme
of lyuing according to thyn estat, inasmuche as thou art enclosed." It
was twice translated into Middle English in the later fourteenth and
the mid-fifteenth centuries.[5] Ailred presents the life as "moost fruitful
to helthe of soule." His sister has sought "fredom of spirit" and that is
why she has chosen to be "closed in an house out of alle mennes sight."
The danger most to be avoided is to become the sort of recluse who sits
all day at her window gossiping with those who come to see her, exchanging news, backbiting against her neighbors, being a "teller of tid-
ings of that monk, or of that clerke" or the wantonness of girls, so that
her mind is crowded with unclean thoughts and negative emotions. Si
lence is best. But a recluse ought not to be idle. She should say divine
service and work with her hands, and she should pray, breaking off to
read or work if her attention wanders. She should bewail her sins and
concentrate on feeling wretched because her sins are keeping her from
heaven and from bliss. She should commend her chastity into the hands
of God, for God loves the clean and the pure. She should go to bed early
so as to be ready to rise early to begin her matins.

The *Ancrene Wisse*, written in the early thirteenth century probably in
the English West Midlands, describes the anchorite's outward life in
the form of bookends at the beginning and end, with the inward and
spiritual life occupying the six central chapters. Middle English, French
and Latin early versions survive.[6] This text begins with the promise that

---

[5] Aelred of Riveaulx, *De institutione inclusarum*, ed. John Ayto and Alexandra Barratt, EETS 287 (Oxford: Oxford University Press, 1984), pp. 5-6.
[6] *The English Text of the Ancrene Riwle: The "Vernon Text,"* ed. Arne Zettersten and Bernhard Diensberg, EETS 310 (London: Oxford University Press, 2000).

those who live "aftur rule" live rightly. The writer has been asked again
and again to provide a rule for his sisters. There are many rules of life, he
explains, but two stand out. One rules the heart and makes it tranquil
(evene) and "smooth without spot." It is this the apostle describes when
he speaks *de corde puro et conscientia bona et fide non ficta.*[7]

What rule should the anchorite follow? She should certainly observe
that one first of all. As to bodily self-denials such as fasting and vigils,
"sum is strong. And sum is unstrong." The same rule will not do for all.
There must be flexibility and appropriateness and proportionality.[8]

Aelred's book was not the only one in use in a Middle English version to offer practical advice about good Christian living, especially for
women, and carrying the authority of the name of a famous Latin author. The *Manere of Good Lyving* is a translation of a Latin work attributed to Bernard of Clairvaux and allegedly written for his sister.[9]

Men were drawn to this extreme commitment too. Richard Rolle
(c. 1300-1349) was the son of a modest family which was able to send
him to a local school; eventually he went to Oxford with the support of
patron. He would have gone at an age where today he would have been
at a high school, not a university, and he did not take to the style of
teaching or the content. It did not engage with his interests or his feelings. He found the formal disputations and the complexity of the analysis frightening and unsympathetic. He left.

Then he decided to become a hermit. There were rules to be followed. In the case of a recluse, the local bishop's permission was
needed. The person who proposed to become a recluse had to have a
permanent place to live and a means of subsistence. If the bishop approved, he would enclose him in his cell and he (or she) could then
never leave it. The church's view was that the safest place for those
who believed themselves profoundly alone with God was to be shut
away from others. For—much as happened in the earliest Christian
centuries when the desert hermits proved such an attraction—people

[7]Ibid., p. 3. See 1 Tim 1:5.
[8]Ibid., p. 4.
[9]Anne Mouron, "*The Manere of Good Lyving:* The Manner of a Good Translator," *Medium Aevum*
78 (2009): 300-321.

would visit them for guidance or healing. Those who lived in seclusion could be widely influential.

In some ways hermits were under less strict restraints than those who belonged to communities, and they could pose problems for the ecclesiastical authorities because it made them unpredictable. Rolle felt quite free to move to another "permanent" dwelling if he felt the Spirit leading him; the head of a leading local family, having satisfied himself of the seriousness and merit of Richard's purpose, gave him a room in his own house for his "cell." This sort of household shelter had parallels elsewhere in Europe. Catherine of Siena (c. 1347-1380) lived the eremitical life in her father's kitchen as a young girl.

Rolle was only eighteen but he already had certain fixed ideas: to get to heaven he needed to give up the world and its pleasures, especially sexual enjoyment. He describes a lengthy battle with himself to put away the temptation to marry his girlfriend. Chastity he deemed essential to the holy life. He had as his objective a mystical union with God, and he describes his striving and its success in the *Incendium Amoris*.[10] His Latin was good enough for him to write in the learned language of the time and with some fluency, if little sense of orderly explanation. The *Fire of Love* is a spiritual autobiography. He begins by describing the turning of the soul to God and the burning of the heart he has experienced "not merely imaginary, but like a real fire" and so powerful that he was taken by surprise at its fierceness. When he understood that this "fire of love" was the Creator's gift, he melted with longing for a still greater and sweeter love. The way to it he finds is by despising the world and entering the Lord's service. He offers his book in the dedication "not to philosophers, not to the worldly wise, not to great theologians entangled in infinite questions," but to the "simple and unlearned" (*rudibus et indoctis*) who are trying to love God better. This is known not by argument but by action. And the first thing to do is to stop seeking worldly dignity and display and vainglory, and live in poverty with prayer. His teaching is that the higher life with God is only to be attained by self-denial and detachment from worldly and sensory

---

[10] *The Incendium Amoris of Richard Rolle of Hampole*, ed. Margaret Deanesley (Manchester: Manchester University Press, 1915), www.ccel.org/r/rolle/incendium/incendium.htm.

pleasures. These were very old ideas in Christianity. The adherent was to cultivate an extreme, considering everything which was not concerned with the love of God a sin and the hope of heaven the only objective worth any man's (or woman's) aspiration.

Where did he get these ideas? He had been long enough at Oxford to hear of them. But he seems to have developed them by self-examination and by making comparisons with his observations of the way members of the congregation behaved in church. There are the outwardly observant whose hearts are far from God. They attend services with distracted thoughts. They give to the poor but do not repent of their sins. He wants them to realize what they are doing. There are relatively good people whose love for God is lukewarm. His purpose in writing is to awaken in them the fire he has discovered in himself.

Mysticism. Mysticism is the cultivation of the sort of intense unmediated experience of the presence of God Rolle describes. But he was far from being the only English mystic of his time. Mysticism had had its fashions, though it was to be curiously unenticing to the Reformers of the sixteenth century. Two styles of mysticism are characteristic of the Middle Ages. The first had a long history and is exemplified in the brief moments of union with God in a rapture described by Bernard of Clairvaux and others. It never lasted long because it was believed to be something a sinful and corporeal human being could not sustain in this life. Mystics in this tradition worked hard for the experience. They shut themselves off from the world and spent long hours in meditation. The contemplative religious life, the life of prayer, was designed to foster such experiences.

The second form of later medieval mysticism is the paradoxical dark sense of the absence of God, of his unknowability. This derived from a strand of late antique Platonism, linked with a figure who was believed to be the first-century Dionysius, a member of the Areopagus converted by Paul (Acts 17:34), but was really a fifth- or sixth-century thinker now known as Pseudo-Dionysius. He wrote on the "celestial hierarchy" and on the "divine names." His idea was that God is so high, so remote from anything that we can understand, that even his names and attributes tell us much more what God is not than what he is. The only way of approaching him is to climb in imagination from that which we know and see until we reach the level of that which we cannot know and do not see, moving from the material to the spiritual, and then, in the ultimate darkness, we may "know" God through his (conceptual) absence. The Dominican Meister Eckhart (c. 1260-c. 1328) was one of the best known of the practitioners of this method, but his views were controversial and (for other reasons) he was accused of heresy.

Rolle's burning love seems to have been like that described by Bernard of Clairvaux in the twelfth century, an ardor ever seeking—and sometimes apparently granted—a momentary experience of union with God. Walter Hilton (c. 1343-1396), likely educated at Cambridge, wrote a practical guide for women in religious orders called the *Scale of Perfection*, in which he taught a ladder-climbing approach to growing in the love of God and progressing in the Christian life.

The author of another spiritual autobiography of the time was the restless middle class woman Margery Kempe (c. 1373-after 1438), daughter of a Mayor of Lynn, wife of a burgess and mother of a family. She ran two family businesses. She became serious about her religion after the birth of her first child. She said she had a vision of Jesus in which she was told to separate herself from worldly vanities. She found it difficult not to be caught up in what seems to have been a busy social life with many temptations to flirt. Deciding that she would have to try harder, she set about a process of what would now be called "discovering herself." She eventually persuaded her husband to agree that henceforth their marriage would be celibate. She went around Europe on pilgrimage, seeing the famous sights at Rome, Jerusalem, Santiago de Compostela and having adventures. Between 1413 and 1420 she made tours of the English pilgrimage sites too. She visited influential people and religious leaders, including the archbishop of Canterbury and also her fellow leading "religious woman" Julian of Norwich (c. 1342-after 1416). She writes of her sense of persecution by such people. Year after year she continued to report mystical conversations with Christ. She may have known of Rolle's work and drawn her understanding partly from him.

How did an uneducated woman exploring her faith for herself ensure that her belief was orthodox? She discussed this with the anchorite Julian of Norwich, and they agreed that the test was to examine the results, the conformity of a person's life with the guidance of the Holy Spirit.

She did not literally write her book herself. She had two scribes, the first of whom began his work during the 1420s and the second began when the first died with the work unfinished. This makes the composition doubly interesting since it introduces the possibility that this notorious woman may have been used as an example by her ghostwriters, who had lessons they wanted to draw from her life for their and her readers. The second scribe found the work of the first to be oddly written, and it may be that Margery's daughter-in-law, who was Swedish, was the actual writer.

Margery apparently had the *Revelations* of Birgitta of Sweden (c. 1303-1373) read to her on more than one occasion. Birgitta was a well-born woman, a wife and mother, who like Margery had led an energetic life of exemplary public holiness and had gone on pilgrimages which gave her the opportunity to travel and see the world. She became a moral crusader, calling for reform of behavior. She founded a religious order for women, the Brigittines, for which she obtained papal approval in 1370. Margery's own *Revelations* balanced this practical and outgoing religious fervor with an inward spirituality. She too claimed to have had visions, and she too depended on services of a ghostwriter to record them and, in her case, to translate them into Latin.

Margery's book couples accessibility with encouragement and inspiration. It is an offering she hopes will be "comfortabyl" for "wrecchys" like herself. All God's works in anyone are meant to teach us by example. "Alle the werkys of ower Saviowr ben for ower exampyl and instruccyon, and what grace that he werkyth in any creatur is ower profyth." She has, she explains "thorw steryng of the Holy Gost" striven for years in penance and fasting "to folwyn oure Savyour," through "gret behestys of fastyngys" and "many other dedys of penawns." But it was not until she encountered hardship and adversity that she was able to enter the way of perfection at last. Naturally, she feared that she might be being misled by the devil, but she took advice. "Than went sche be the byddyng of the Holy Gost to many." She consulted "clerkys, bothe archebysshopys and bysshoppys, doctowrs of dyvynyté and bachelers also." They were all impressed. Some were so sure she "was inspyred" by "the Holy Gost" that they begged her to write the present book "of hyr felyngys and hir revelacyons."[11]

The connection of these independent medieval vocations to cultivate a personal relationship with Christ with the way sixteenth-century Reformers saw the same imperative is not easy to trace. These lives were lived within a culture which bred particular expectations with a distinctively medieval flavor of self-denial.

GLIMPSES OF ORDINARY LIVES:
LEARNING WHAT TO BELIEVE AND HOW TO LIVE

Ordinary people took their religion seriously in the late Middle Ages, but not necessarily with much understanding of the technicalities of theology. This was not an age when people expressed doubts about the existence of God. Except for members of the small Jewish communities, everyone in Western Europe was baptized in infancy, and lives were measured in Christian events and stages, marked by the church's year and its ceremonies. Being a Christian was part of life, part of the good order of things, approved by the secular as well as the ecclesiastical authorities. A contented population, passive in its acceptance of what it was taught to believe and do, was the ideal of medieval governments because it made for peace.

The interested laity could, nevertheless, learn a good deal about the faith, even some serious theology, and some of the higher clergy were anxious that they should. The realization of earlier centuries that adults needed catechism classes just as much as children now became sharp once more. John Pecham (c. 1225-1292, archbishop of Canterbury from 1279) held a council at Lambeth in 1281. One of the resulting canons required the parish clergy to teach doctrine to their flocks at least four times each year. They were to do this through the medium of the texts which it was considered reasonable for the laity to know something

---

[11]Margery Kempe, *The Book of Margery Kempe*, bk. 1, pt. 1, ed. Lynn Staley (Kalamazoo, Mich.: Medieval Institute Publications, 1996).

about, including the creeds and the Ten Commandments; they were also to teach the people about the virtues and vices, and the sacraments. These "Lambeth Constitutions" set a standard and a requirement. They were promulgated in Latin, but they were rather successful, and demand for them grew. By the fifteenth century they had been made available in English.

John Thoresby (d. 1373), the archbishop of York, made a systematic effort to provide church-approved teaching for the laity in the north of England. The Black Death of 1348-1349 had affected priests as well as people, and the number of clergy in the northern province had dropped considerably. Some theologically dubious practices had begun as a result of the shortage of manpower. For instance, priests would sometimes ask laymen to do things only priests had authority to do, such as celebrating the Eucharist or hearing confessions. Those priests who remained were tempted to take up posts as private "chantry" priests, for there was a good living to be had in saying prayers for the dead in return for payments by grieving relatives. There had also been numerous deaths in the enclosed communities of the religious orders, where the plague could spread fast once it took hold. Thoresby sent round to find out how many had died. He ordained more priests. He tried to ensure that priests were resident in the diocese, and he set about banning incumbents from leaving their parishes to become chantry priests, for that denied the local people the pastoral care they needed.

The importance of instructing the laity was coupled in the minds of both Pecham and Thoresby with the equal importance of ensuring control over the content of the instruction:

> And for no creature might come to that ilk blisse
> Withouten knowing of god.[12]

The lamentable ignorance of ordinary people must be mended if they are to be saved. The archbishop wanted the people taught by those clergy responsible for the cure of souls, both by teaching and preaching

---

[12] *The Lay Folks' Catechism*, prologue, EETS 118, ed. T. F. Simmons and H. E. Nolloth (London: Oxford University Press, 1901), pp. 2, 5, 6.

in English every Sunday.[13] In 1357 Thoresby announced a scheme to improve the theological knowledge and religious instruction of the laity. He said they needed to be taught in their own language. He listed what they were to be taught, very much as Pecham had done: articles of faith or creeds, the Ten Commandments, the virtues and the deadly or mortal sins, the sacraments. Details of what is to be taught under each of these heads are given, so that the clergy shall be in no doubt what they are to teach, and at the same time a central control was maintained of the ideas to be sown in believers' minds. That at least was the plan.

Thoresby got a Benedictine monk, John Gaytryge from Mary's Abbey, York, a house guest of his in December 1356, to turn his instructions into English to make sure people would be able to understand the teaching. It was proposed by Thoresby that when people come to confess, as they are required to do once a year, they are to be tested on their religious knowledge. (This proposal too had originated with John Pecham.) Thoresby's manual designed for this purpose therefore has a penitential as well as a pedagogic purpose.

The Lord's Prayer is expounded as a series of petitions designed to draw attention to the underlying theological ideas. The same method is used for the creeds. The creeds, it is explained, are three: the "creed of the apostles; the creed of the Church [the Nicene Creed] and the creed of Athanasius 'that was a gret doctour.'" The Apostles' Creed is taken for purposes of explanation because it is the shortest and "more comyn." The exposition does not dwell on the question which apostles were responsible for which clauses (a topic of much interest to scholars of the time). "For oure beleve techis vs that god ordenyned hyt all."[14] And if "prelatys" fail to teach the faith, Christ said the stones would cry out.

The points raised in the discussion of the creeds are familiar enough in medieval theology, but the choice of what to include sometimes suggests a lack of foresight. Intellectually curious laypeople might begin to think about what they were being told and ask to know more. In that way the type of catechism that is designed simply to be learned, with

---

[13]Ibid.
[14]Ibid., p. 14.

the person being instructed repeating stock answers to stock questions, could turn into something closer to Augustine's struggles in "catechising the unlearned" of the fourth and fifth centuries—who were curious beginners with further questions. For example, the Creed speaks of God the Father Almighty, Maker of heaven and earth. The commentary emphasizes that omnipotence is not an attribute of the Father only; the Son and the Holy Spirit, being true God together with the Father, are also almighty.[15] Similarly in expositions of the vices and virtues, it was tempting to elaborate. (How many kinds of lechery are there?) Exploring such subjects, however, could lead the Christian adventurer into trouble.

Mystery plays as popular drama. There is plentiful evidence of the vigor of the curiosity and interest and the wish to know more about the faith among ordinary people in the later Middle Ages. In late medieval towns mystery plays were performed by members of the craft guilds. They were called "mystery" plays not because they were intended to be mysterious, but after the mysteries (special skills) of the various crafts.

The Coventry Play begins by filling in behind Genesis the story of the creation and fall of the angels. Its opening proclamation sets out the story in outline, from the Fall of Adam to Cain and Abel, Noah, Abraham and Isaac, Moses and the tablets of the law, Jesse and the prophecy of the Virgin birth, the annunciation, the nativity with shepherds and kings.[16] This must have provided a memorable moving picture of the story that was easy for the audience to remember.

Those mystery plays which were probably performed in Wakefield from the fourteenth century to the sixteenth survive in a fifteenth-century manuscript. They reveal a conscientious care on the part of the writers to stay close to the basics of Christian orthodoxy, but once more it is easy to see how curiosity could be aroused and interest piqued. The creation play begins with God announcing in Latin that he is Alpha and Omega. God then speaks of his omnipotence:

---

[15]Ibid., p. 15.
[16]*Ludus Coventriae*, EETS, ed. K. S. Block (Oxford: Oxford University Press, 1922).

Agans my grete might
May [no]thing stand then be.[17]

He explains that he is "a thowsandfold / Brighter then is the son [sun]."

But Lucifer claims that he is bright too. Should he not have a place "in seyte of Trinité"? "I trow me seme as well as hym." Some of his fellow angels egg him on, and Lucifer tries to fly up to what he says is his rightful place. Suddenly the fallen angels are anxiously discussing what happened. Why did he fall. Why are all his supporters, who were so beautiful and who sat so high in the firmament, now "waxen blak as any coyll" and ugly. "Alas!" they cry that they ever had prideful thoughts and sinned.

Thus the play deals dramatically and urgently with the angelic creation and what befell it before describing the creation as it is set out in Genesis. God speedily makes "erthly bestys tha[t] may crepe and go" and then man in his "liknes" to be their "keeper" and lord. He makes Eve. He gives Adam and Eve their instructions about not eating the fruit of "the tre of life." The pace then slows as Adam suggests to his wife that he should make a tour of the garden to see what is growing there, and Eve, left alone, becomes the victim of Lucifer bent on revenge. Again there is a combination of high drama and memorable pedagogy.

The Church Fosters the Mixed Life

We have seen how some felt the attractions of living a life apart, and how their very apartness could be an attraction to local people who wanted to learn from them. Recluses were not under proper control by the ecclesiastical authorities, so their ideas might be dangerous. That meant they could be dangerous in giving rise to unorthodox opinions among the laity.

As a result the ecclesiastical authorities might be as anxious to talk to notorious individualists to discover their views, as the individualists were to seek their advice. Thomas Arundel, bishop of Ely and arch-

---

[17] *The Towneley Plays*, EETS, ed. Martin Stevens and A. C. Cawley (Oxford: Oxford University Press, 1994), p. 5ff.

bishop of York and Canterbury, developed concerns about the effect of
lay piety and its concomitant growing literacy and growing popular
awareness of religious ideas.[18] If laypeople read in the vernacular the
writings of recluses and others writing for a general readership, they
were bound to pick up ideas. Arundel met Margery Kempe at Lambeth
Palace and walked her round the garden while he listened to her descriptions of her mystical experiences.

Yet these fringe figures and ecclesiastical dignitaries were not necessarily a class apart when it came to the sharing of attitudes and concerns.
Arundel was for a time a patron and employer of Walter Hilton, who
was no autodidact, but a Cambridge man and a canon lawyer. Hilton
and others in Arundel's circle and household read Richard Rolle's work
with interest and admiration, and felt the tug of a life which took them
away from administrative responsibilities and let them be. Arundel was
drawn to the idea and even joined a fraternity (Mount Grace) in 1409.

The solution seemed to be to encourage the laity to live a "mixed life,"
a life not involving a permanent commitment as a member of a religious
order, but where life in the world could be combined with contemplation.

Appeals to religious emotion. The popular demand for spiritual comfort
often focused on the saints, figures who seemed easier to reach, closer to
the ordinary person than the divine as well as human person of Christ.
From the twelfth century, when Bernard of Clairvaux's sermons placed
Jesus' mother Mary in a new and more intimate light,[19] she became a
natural bridge between the human and domestic and the unimaginably
remote. Something of its flavor is to be found in "The Lament of the
Virgin Mary," a verse dialogue between Mary and her son recorded by
Pierre de Langtoft (d. c. 1307), an Augustinian friar and the author of a
history in Norman French verse:

> Those who were in grief, he comforted them;
> Those who were dead, he restored them to life;

---

[18]A useful overall study of medieval literacy is Charles F. Briggs, "Literacy, Reading, and Writing
in the Medieval West," *Journal of Medieval History* 26 (2000): 397-420.

[19]Bernard of Clairvaux, *In laudibus Virginis Matris, Opera Omnia*, ed. J. Leclercq, H. Rochais, C. H.
Talbot (Rome: Editiones Cisterciensis, 1966), 4:14ff.; Anselm, *Orationes*, 5, 6, 7, *Opera Omnia*,
3:13ff.

> And now you render him evil in return for good. . . .
> Let me pass away with my so gentle son. . . .
> For the joy which I had when you were born,
> Suffer not now that I be so cruelly tormented.
> No one knows the joy which I conceived in my heart,
> When I received your godship in my body.

Jesus answers her

> It is my will to die for man. . . .
> There is no other who can pay off the debt
> Of that forfeit with which God charges man.
> And if it be not paid, goodness will never have place,
> That man be received into the joy of heaven,
> But they will all depart into that dark place
> Where I shall not come nor God be seen. . . .
> Therefore, fair mother, be not distressed.

She reports now that

> The third day after my son rose again,
> And has appeared alive to me and comforted me.[20]

The imagery used by some of the woman mystics in their writings could have its impact on visual representation by contemporary artists. Birgitta of Sweden described a blond Virgin Mary gazing on a shining infant Jesus lying on the ground. This was not an original version. It is found before she wrote her description. But she helped to give it currency. Pictures and illustrations representing the nativity in this way as an Adoration of the Child, with Joseph and the angels about the Virgin and sharing in her amazed worship, began to be popular.

Julian of Norwich wrote her *Showings* (also known as *Revelations of Divine Love*) in the form of conventional enough episodes in the life and work of Christ, applied to "show" the lessons to be drawn. But the flavoring of an overheated emotional spirituality is characteristic, for example "the Fourth Showing is the scourging of his tender Body with plenteous shedding of his precious blood." Birgitta of

---

[20]Pierre de Langtoft, *Chronicle*, Rolls Series, ed. T. Wright (London: Longman, Green, Reader & Dyer, 1868), 2:445-47.

Sweden helped to launch this popular devotional practice of showing honor to Christ for the blows he suffered in the Passion. She had been told in a vision that these numbered 5,475, and she was instructed to recite fifteen "Our Fathers" and "Hail Marys" and fifteen prayers or "ejaculations," each beginning with "O" (*O Jesu, O Rex* and so on).

Whether or not Birgitta was the originator of this practice of repeating prayers, it became established in parts of England where popular aspirations to mysticism and dedication to the religious life were stimulated by the influence of Rolle or the pious women mystics. The prayers encouraged meditation on the suffering of Christ on the cross, and they were sufficiently popular to be a natural choice for an early printed book by William Caxton (c. 1422-1491). One reason for their popularity may be the assurance that if they were used regularly during the year, a member of the faithful who had been assiduous in this way could expect an indulgence for fifteen relatives. Such lists of prayers to be repeated as a meritorious action, with the promise of indulgences, began to appear in Books of Hours, the devotional aids for well-born women whose husbands could afford to provide them with such beautiful prompters to prayer.[21]

---

[21]In certain circles of the gentry and would-be gentry, the patronage of literature was an established socially prestigious activity. See for example Anthony Bale, "A Norfolk Gentlewoman and Lydgatean Patronage," *Medium Aevum* 78 (2009): 261-80.

14

REBELS, REPRESSION AND THE STIRRINGS OF REFORM

SOCIAL COMMENT AND
THE DEBATE ABOUT POVERTY

The church's wealth, says the Lutheran *Treatise on the Power and Primacy of the Pope* of 1537, should not be used by senior clergy as though it were their personal property. It is entrusted to them to use for alms.[1] This remark distills the essence of a long discussion about the place of wealth in the church, expressing the disgust of dissidents who could see for themselves the links between wealth and corruption, and the unedifying picture presented by rich and decadent bishops.

The original vision of the Franciscans had been of a return to an apostolic life of poverty and simplicity. Francis of Assisi was not a scholar. His instructions to his followers were simple and practical. Those who chose his way of life were to be poor:

> The brothers shall appropriate nothing to themselves, neither a house nor place nor anything. And as pilgrims and strangers in this world, serving the Lord in poverty and humility, let them go confidently in quest of alms, nor ought they to be ashamed, because the Lord made Himself poor for us in this world. This, my dearest brothers, is the height of the most sublime poverty which has made you heirs and kings of the king-

---

[1] *The Book of Concord: The Confessions of the Evangelical Lutheran Church*, ed. Theodore G. Tappert (Philadelphia: Fortress Press, 1959), http://bookofconcord.org/treatise.php.

dom of heaven: poor in goods, but exalted in virtue.[2]

They were to behave lovingly to one another as brothers:

> And wheresoever the brothers are and may find themselves, let them
> mutually show among themselves that they are of one household. And
> let one make known his needs with confidence to the other, for, if a
> mother nourishes and loves her carnal son, how much more earnestly
> ought one to love and nourish his spiritual brother! And if any of them
> should fall into illness, the other brothers must serve him as they would
> wish to be served themselves.[3]

What went wrong? Why did these high-principled people who so
passionately shared the Christian objectives of living the apostolic life
as Jesus taught and spreading the faith become the objects of derision
and hostility? One reason we have already glimpsed in the narrative of
Guibert of Nogent. Thieves and conmen were quick to perceive that
they could make money by pretending to be friars and "begging for
alms." Whereas earlier medieval monasticism had been mainly a rural
activity, with houses of monks being built in quiet country places, these
orders were active in the towns. They needed to be if they were to assemble audiences for preaching. So the population of pickpockets and
petty criminals found where there is a concentration of people was ready
to take advantage of new opportunities.

The friars also built up influential contacts through acting as personal
confessors (similar to life-coaches) to the rich and powerful. John of St.
Giles (d. 1259/1260), for example, entered royal service in 1235 in the
entourage of Isabella (1214-1241), sister of the king of England, when she
married Frederick II. When she became pregnant with her first child,
John was apparently the messenger who brought the good news to
Henry III (1207-1272) and thereafter he found himself called into service by the royal household on a number of occasions. This meant that
some friar confessors to the great came to be perceived as having a liking for luxurious living and as having drifted a long way from the origi-

---

[2] *The Writings of St. Francis of Assisi*, trans. Paschal Robinson (Philadelphia: Dophin Press, 1906),
www.lulu.com/items/volume_31/484000/484729/1/print/PaschalRobinsonWritingsofSt
Francis.pdf.
[3] Ibid.

nal ideal of simplicity of life. But these manifestations were not fully apparent when the debate about poverty began.

Above all Francis seems to have feared that his followers would allow themselves to accept money and become corrupted in that way:

> I strictly enjoin on all the brothers that in no wise they receive coins or money, either themselves or through an interposed person. Nevertheless, for the necessities of the sick and for clothing the other brothers, let the ministers and custodes alone take watchful care through spiritual friends, according to places and times and cold climates, as they shall see expedient in the necessity, saving always, that, as has been said, they shall not receive coins or money.[4]

On the death of Francis, Franciscan poverty became contentious. There is always a crisis in a religious movement with a charismatic leader when the leader dies and the movement has to find an institutional structure to enable it to carry on. Some balance has to be struck between the original vision and the practical long-term realities. In the case of the Franciscans this caused a split between the adherents that wanted to move in this direction and a faction who were insistent that they would rather take the original vision to a further extreme than retreat from it.

There was already a literature of discussion on key New Testament passages that seemed to provide guidance on the difficult practical question how a group of disciples could organize their common life without money. Judas carried a bag (Jn 12:6), and it seems it contained money because Jesus told him to buy provisions for a meal. Those who opposed the Franciscan assertion that poverty mattered should therefore show that apparently the disciples and Jesus held "goods" in common. There were strong vested interests, of course. The church had a lot of property; it did not want to be told that it should give it away.

Moreover, the friars themselves were acquiring property in the form of the houses in which the friars lived and studied. Franciscans argue dthat their property really belonged to the pope. He had ownership and control (or jurisdiction). All they did was use it, which did

---

[4]Ibid. On the Franciscan controversy, see especially William of Ockham, *A Letter to the Friars Minor and Other Writings*, ed. Arthur Stephen McGrade and John Kilcullen, trans. John Kilcullen (Cambridge: Cambridge University Press, 1995).

not compromise their duty to live in poverty. This idea had been endorsed early in the thirteenth century by Pope Innocent III and then by Gregory IX (c. 1148-1241). In his *Apologia Pauperum* of 1269, the Franciscan Bonaventure argued that this was the right approach. Control and both individual and shared ownership were bad; "use" was not. Franciscan poverty permitted the exercise of a stewardship of property but no more. This adroit adjustment of the strict requirements of Francis himself, or something like it, was forced on the order during the thirteenth century by the unavoidable practicalities of organizing and running a large order. Money had to be raised for building work, and that meant selling indulgences and putting collection boxes in churches.[5]

John Pecham, another Franciscan, saw this clearly. Christ is Lord; from him come all rights of ownership and control and use of property. A king derives his power from Christ and so does the church. The Dominicans rather tended to separate *dominium*, ownership, from control, or jurisdiction. A ruler could exercise jurisdiction without owning that which he controlled. The Dominicans entered the debate not because the matter was proving divisive in their communities as dangerously as it was among the Franciscans, but because it was increasingly apparent that the ramifications went far beyond the internal organization of a novel order of friars. These were themes that especially interested John Wyclif, especially that of "dominion."

At any rate, the poor simply were not getting the help they needed. There is a natural tendency to resent the privileged, especially where it is perceived that they do not deserve their advantages. Anticlericalism seems to have been rife from its eleventh and twelfth century beginnings, especially among the emerging "middle class," who were beginning to run businesses in the developing towns of Europe. Yet rebellious talk on the late medieval scale criticizing those higher in the social hierarchy for behavior inappropriate to their position challenged social stability as well as clerical sleaze. These were assertions of popular independence and self-reliance under God. They included

---

[5]Malcolm D. Lambert, *Franciscan Poverty* (New York: Franciscan Institute Publications, 1998).

a call for a move "back to Scripture," but mainly as a reaction against acceptance of the church's authority and because in independent reading of Scripture could be found ammunition with which to attack the church's claims.

Challenging the powerful and institutional control of souls. "How may I save my soul?" is the question put to the church in Piers Plowman's Dream.[6] Medieval interest in religion seems to have been driven at its deepest level by the importance of finding the most certain way to heaven. By the late Middle Ages, the belief that there is no salvation outside the (Roman) church was well established. The laity were taught that they must obediently act as the institutional church told and taught them to do or they risked an eternity of hell. Karl Marx's observation that religion had a social effect and helped to keep order because it was the "opiate of the masses" was to that extent true.

Rebels had only one way to challenge the institutional church, and that was to claim that it was no longer the true church at all. That freed its critics to live as they believed was right without fear of eternal consequences. So for the church's authorities that challenge amounted to a threat to order and authority, to the church's very being, and the secular authorities saw it as a threat to order and authority in state as well as church. Statutes made at Leicester in 1414 against the "heretics called Lollards" identified them as a threat to public order ("congregations" and "insurrections"), and the magistrates are to assist the church authorities in extirpating and punishing them.

The unfolding of the challenge and the response of the authorities became clear in the story to be told in the following sections, of John Wyclif's life and condemnation and that of John Hus, with the emergence of groups inspired by their examples, who invented a cause which was not yet to flow seamlessly into Reformation, but which established ideas and principles that were taken up anew in the sixteenth century.[7]

---

[6]Derek Pearsall, "The Idea of Universal Salvation in Piers Plowman B and C," *Journal of Medieval and Early Modern Studies* 39 (2009): passus 1.

[7]On this see Anne Hudson, *The Premature Reformation* (Oxford: Oxford University Press, 1988).

JOHN WYCLIF

John Wyclif has had both more credit and more opprobrium attached to his name than he probably deserves. He was an Oxford academic, who left England only once on an abortive embassy to Bruges, concerned with England's duty to pay papal taxes. Unlike most of his academic contemporaries, he did not study in any of the other universities of Europe.

Lecturing on the Bible was a routine obligation for those who went on to take higher degrees in theology in any university in Europe in the Middle Ages. The usual choice was to practice on the Psalms for the Old Testament and on Paul's epistles for the New. Wyclif became involved in a quarrel with a fellow student over the nature of truth in Scripture.[8] The debate was really about technicalities of logic and language in the interpretation of Scripture, a debate intensely medieval and largely unrelated to the Reformation claim of *sola scriptura*.

As an academic Wyclif took part in disputations, some of which were very lively and contentious. Soon, perhaps annoyed that his performance with the ambassador team had not won him an invitation to come again, he began to write dangerous attacks against the powerful—attacks perhaps more dangerous to himself than to his victims. Those which got him into most trouble argued against the legitimacy of the exercise of dominion or power by authorities lay as well as ecclesiastical. He claimed that clergy whose behavior was unworthy of their calling could have no legitimate authority (and no right to hold property either). Lay authority might in some circumstances trump that of the clergy, he ventured. But misbehaving lay authorities could lose their right to dominion too. These lines of thought took him by a short track to traducing the pope (as antichrist), religious orders as a work of antichrist, and members of religious orders as false claimants to special respect as Christians. He became associated with a series of such contentious opinions. Powerful individuals in both church and state were naturally upset.

---

[8]John Wyclif, *De veritate sacrae scripturae*, ed. R. Buddensieg, 3 vols. (London: Wyclif Society, 1905). It should be noted that this treatise is presented by its nineteenth-century editor and the Wyclif Society which published it through the lens of strong Reformation sympathies.

When Oxford finally rejected him, John Wyclif retired to spend his last years in his parish at Lutterworth.[9] John Purvey (c. 1354-c. 1421) is said to have gone to live with him and to support him in disseminating his opinions. Purvey was listed with others of known sympathies with Wycliffite opinions in a document issued by the bishop of Worcester in 1387 in an attempt to ban them from preaching. His name appears again in instructions issued in 1388-1389 to seek out "heretical books," including those of Wyclif. In 1401 Purvey was the subject of an investigation by the archbishop of Canterbury.

There were seven main accusations of unorthodox belief.[10] Purvey was accused of heresy over the Eucharist. (He denied the doctrine of transubstantiation and claimed that the pope as antichrist was putting this forward as an innovation and calling it an article of faith.) He was said to have questioned the powers of priests to absolve sinners (another alleged "papal antichrist innovation," designed to give priests power to oppress the faithful); to have insisted that it was the duty of the clergy to be preachers; to have claimed that excommunication had no effect; to have spoken of the impotence of the pope to make laws which were not in accordance with the Scriptures; and of the priesthood of all believers. Purvey was feared to be writing as well as preaching, and a number of texts were attributed to him, although nothing of what survives can definitely be said to be his. Purvey gave in. He made a public recantation in London at Paul's Cross in 1401. After that he was less visible for some years though there are hints that he kept company with heretics and the rebels associated with the Lollard Sir John Oldcastle (c. 1378-1417).

The ecclesiastical authorities could be extremely purposeful in pursuing those they thought might be dangerous ringleaders. John Wyclif was now identified as one of these and his followers were rounded up. Among those who became prominent during his time in Oxford were Nicholas of Hereford (d. c. 1420), Philip Repyngdon (c. 1345-1424) and John Aston (fl. 1382). Repyngdon dropped out of the movement under

---

[9]*Knighton's Chronicle, 1337-1396*, ed. and trans. G. H. Martin (London: Oxford University Press, 1995).

[10]See the *Fasciculi Zizaniorum Magistri Johannis Wyclif,* ascribed to Thomas Netter, ed. Walter W. Shirley (London: Longman, Brown, Green, Longmans, and Roberts, 1858), pp. 383-407.

pressure, and became a respectable cleric pursuing a normal career. Aston was less prominent, but despite officially recanting along with Repyngdon, he seems to have gone on preaching in the Wycliffite cause until he died.

Hereford remained a rebel for the best part of a decade and then changed sides and began to pursue the Lollards. As a preacher of Wycliffite doctrine, he was a popular preacher as well as an author. In 1382 his writings were investigated and in 1388 a commission was set up to search out and confiscate his writings as well as Wyclif's. In the same year an injunction appeared against his English writings as well as those in Latin and included his compilations of unsavory opinions as well as his original works. During Wyclif's time in Oxford, Hereford and Repyngdon were active in spreading his ideas. In a foreshadowing of Luther's ninety-five theses, they were said to have nailed up a list of theses on the door of St. Paul's Cathedral in London in 1382. It was the natural thing to do in a world where public disputations were popular. They also used another contemporary means of dissemination by putting out broadsheets to get the message out to Londoners.

This sort of activity had the effect of ensuring that Wycliffite ideas were spread beyond Oxford and beyond the academic community. One or two of the nobility, such as Sir John Montagu (c. 1350-1400) and Sir William Neville (c. 1341-1391), apparently had sympathies for these theological rebels, so lay interest extended beyond the lower classes. These sympathies may not have been entirely theological. A preacher such as Hereford, who wanted to see the church disendowed and forced back into the apostolic poverty he had called for in his sermons, was bound to attract support from nobles with vested interests in land and property. The archbishop of Canterbury succeeded in achieving some condemnations of high-born sympathizers, notably that of Oldcastle.

The authorities were bent on extirpating heresy not only by burning alleged heretics or persuading them to recant, but also by destroying dangerous writings. There was a bonfire of books in Oxford in 1410, at Carfax (Quatervois), where the four main streets of the town intersected. The site was no doubt chosen to make sure as many townspeople as possible saw and learned the lesson.

At the Council of Constance (1414-1418; see pp. 99-102), Wyclif was posthumously accused, unsurprisingly enough, of the same sorts of theological errors as Purvey, along with his inflammatory views on ecclesial authority. The counterblast was fierce. Constance dismissed his ideas as having been duly challenged and refuted by "Masters and doctors of the universities and houses of study at Oxford and Prague." The pope ordered his books publicly to be "burnt," "strictly forbidding anyone called a Christian to dare to read, expound, hold or make any use of any one or more of the said books." The Council pronounced Wyclif a heretic, and since it could not execute him it ordered his bones to be exhumed "if they can be identified among the corpses of the faithful, and to be scattered far from a burial place of the church, in accordance with canonical and lawful sanctions."[11]

Lollard defiance. The authorities, however, were themselves slower to learn. Earlier attempts to suppress challenging opinions by force tended to encourage opposition, and to attract attention to the very ideas the authorities wanted to extirpate. People naturally wanted to be told what it was they were not supposed to see or hear.

Oxford was seen as an especially dangerous center of heretical opinion for some time after Wyclif's death. One of Wyclif's last works, the *Trialogus*, had been intended for popular consumption, and the orthodox William Woodford (d. c. 1397) was asked during the 1390s to explain eighteen passages from the work so as to show up their flaws. Archbishop Arundel and his allies did not concentrate their heresy hunting solely on Oxford. They went to Cambridge too. Arundel had already made an Episcopal Visitation of King's Hall in Cambridge in 1383 when he was still bishop of Ely. Arundel told the meeting of the Convocation of Canterbury in 1401 that its most urgent business was to address the rise of heresy among the clergy as well as among the laity. One priest, William Sawtre (d. 1401) was brought before Convocation for examination to explain his views on transubstantiation, and he was condemned. A statute requiring the burning of heretics (*De haeretico comburendo*) came onto the books in 1401, and Sawtre was promptly executed. The

---

[11]"Council of Contance," pt. 2, in *Decrees of the Ecumenical Councils,* pp. 414-15, www.daily catholic.org/history/16ecume2.htm.

new law required all writings that did not comply with the official faith
of the church to be surrendered to the local diocesan bishop, and if
heretics would not recant they were to be given to the secular authorities to be tried. This crossing of the line between the jurisdiction of the
church and that of the state was necessary because church courts could
not impose the death penalty. But it was also an indication that the
state saw heretics as a threat to good order every bit as much as the
church did.

The movement spreads. William Taylor (d. 1423) gave a famous and
disturbing sermon in Oxford in 1406, as is recorded by the St. Albans
Chronicle.[12] He took "bread" as his theme, the bread of John 6:5, which
describes how Jesus saw the growing hungry multitude that had come
to hear him and asked Philip where bread could be bought to feed
them (*unde ememus panes ut manducent hii*), and he spoke about Wyclif's teaching.

The sermon has the formal structure of an "art of preaching" sermon.
The first task was to divide the text or theme. Taylor explains that *bread*
in Scripture has several meanings. The first is "doctryne of the word of
God." The second is "breed of Cristis body." The third is "breed of almes."
For each he gives a biblical example.[13]

> Now then for the process in this sermon you shall understand that for
> the people of God should not perish by the hunger of bread and of the
> word of God, Christ when he should go up to heaven diligently com-
> manded his disciples, and in them all disciples of office that were to
> coming after that time, to break this bread to be the people of God.

Jesus also told his people to go and "preach the gospel to every crea-
ture." "This therefore is a work of great charge and of passing merit if it
be well performed" and to neglect to perform it deserves "damnation."[14]
Taylor quotes Augustine as a supporting authority for this view. But, he
regrets, "through malice of the Devil" it now comes about "that priests
are thus drawn from ghostly living and priestly occupation and are en-

---

[12]"The Sermon of William Taylor, 1406," *Two Wycliffite Texts*, ed. Anne Hudson, EETS 301 (Oxford: Oxford University Press, 1993), p. xiii.
[13]Matthew 4 (man lives not only by bread, etc.), John 6 and Isaiah 58.
[14]"Sermon of William Taylor, 1406," p. 4.

cumbered in worldly needs." He adds a supporting quotation from Revelation 12:1-17 (the passage about the serpent). He encourages priests to break the bread of teaching before the people as it is their duty to do.

The *Testimony* of William Thorpe (1381-1407), dated 1407, is an unusual account of an exchange between an alleged heretic and the ecclesiastical authorities.[15] Thorpe was another of the Oxford circle whose names were linked with that of Wyclif, though of a younger generation. He seems to have been preaching rather too successfully in the north of England, and had been arrested and released. So he was not formally on trial in 1407. Indeed it is not easy to be sure what the purpose of the meeting was intended to be. What he describes sounds almost like an exploratory conversation between himself and Arundel in which he gets the best of it and the archbishop the worst.

He explains his motives for writing in his prologue. His friends, knowing that he was to be transferred from prison in Shrewsbury to the archbishop's prison in Canterbury, urged him, if he had the opportunity, to write them an account of his examination before the archbishop. Second, friends who have visited him in Canterbury since the event have begged him to do the same thing. Third, it is his desire "that all men and women faithfully occupy all their wits in knowing and keeping of God's behests." Fourth, believers should be ready to give reasons for their faith, and his "sudden and unwarned apposing and answering" has taught him the value of being ready.[16]

Arundel was still concerned about Oxford in 1407, and designed a set of constitutions to keep control of opinion in the university. These were later sent to all the bishops and included instructions that no one was to preach without a license from the local bishop; the authorities in Oxford were to investigate what the scholars were teaching (every month); nothing was to be taught or allowed to be read unless it was orthodox. Richard Courtenay (d. 1415), under suspicion himself, was removed from the chancellorship of the university.

Dangerous associations. Heresy was tackled vigorously by the authori-

---

[15]"The Testimony of William Thorpe, 1407," *Two Wycliffite Texts*, ed. Anne Hudson, EETS 301 (London: Oxford University Press, 1993).
[16]Ibid., pp. 25-27.

ties partly because of its connection with the formation of dangerous groups and associations. An isolated malcontent was one thing, popular movements quite another, and there was much suspicion when heretics were thought to be in communication with one another. Records survive of heresy trials in Norwich in 1428. One of those accused, John Wardon, was said to have "often had familiarity and conversation with different heretics," some of whom are named and some of whom are said to have met to conduct "schools" (*scolas*) in places where they systematically taught their doctrine and preached.[17]

What were they all saying? The persecutors of heretics seem to have looked for much the same opinions everywhere. Wardon was accused of a number of specific heretical beliefs. He denied transubstantiation, maintaining that after the words of consecration had been said by a priest celebrating the Eucharist, the bread remained bread and the wine remained wine.[18] He denied that extreme unction had any effect, and insisted that no one was under a duty to fast on fast days, and no one need pay tithes.[19] He also said there was no merit in the celibacy of monks and priests, no one ought to pray to saints, and no one ought to venerate images. Oath taking and other characteristics of dissent are mentioned.[20]

A set of Lollard trial records survives from Coventry, covering the period 1486-1522.[21] Eight named individuals were accused of heresy or of conduct "at least savouring of heresy." John Blumston had been saying that the power Jesus gave to Peter did not pass to his successors. The pope is not possessed of this Petrine power. He had said that there is no point in praying for the dead because when someone dies he or she goes straight to heaven. There is no purgatory. There is no need to go to church to pray. One can pray just as well at home. Nothing is to be gained by going on pilgrimages or venerating images.[22] Robert Crowther

[17]*Norwich Heresy Trials*, Camden Fourth Series, ed. Norman Tanner (London: Royal Historical Society, 1977), p. 32.
[18]Ibid., p. 33.
[19]Ibid.
[20]Ibid., p. 34.
[21]*Lollards of Coventry*, 1485-1522, ed. and trans. Shannon McSheffrey and Norman Tanner, Camden Fifth Series (London: Royal Historical Society, 2003).
[22]Ibid., pp. 64-65.

had unsavory views on transubstantiation and penance and pilgrimages.[23] Richard Hegham was accused of offensive opinions, mainly involving the veneration of images.[24] Roger Browne would not venerate the consecrated bread, ate meat in Lent ("and was caught doing so"), did not believe in purgatory and said God "would remit all sins without confession and satisfaction."[25]

As in the cases of Hereford, Repyngdon and Aston discussed above, the accused in heresy trials were frequently intimidated into abjuring their unorthodox beliefs. This could be required to ensure that as many people as possible were aware of it and an example was made of the recanting offender. Thomas Wade, for example, a tailor, who repented publicly in a ceremonial procession on three Sundays so that others could see that he had admitted that he had been wrong.[26]

Hawise Moone and the treatment of woman dissidents. Women could find themselves in trouble too. Hawise Moone, wife of Thomas Moone, admitted having been associated with suspect groups where she had learned many errors and heresies, all of which at trial she forswore.[27]

Hawise admitted to several errors. Her first was that the sacrament of baptism "is but a trifle." Christ's people are sufficiently baptized in his blood and do not need any other baptism.[28] Confirmation is unnecessary too, because when a child thus baptized comes to years of discretion it is "sufficiently confermed [by] the Holy Gost."[29] She regrets that she had rejected the doctrine of transubstantiation by asserting that the consecrated elements remain simply bread and wine.[30]

The lack of priestly powers reappears as a theme in her other admissions. The Christian does not need a priest; confession should simply be made to God. Priests have no power "to remitte synne."[31] She recants

[23]Ibid., pp. 66-67.
[24]Ibid., pp. 65-66.
[25]Ibid., pp. 68-69.
[26]Ibid., p. 35.
[27]Hawise Moone, *Norwich Heresy Trials*, ed. Norman Tanner, Camden Fourth Series (London: Royal Historical Society, 1977), p. 140.
[28]Ibid.
[29]Ibid.
[30]Ibid.
[31]Ibid.

the opinion that no one needs to do penance at the instruction of priests, who in general, she had said, are lecherous and covetous, and only want to take money from people.[32] She regrets that she has called the pope antichrist and asserted that he has no more powers than any common man, cannot make priests or bishops, and is an extortioner and a deceiver of the people. It followed, according to her previous opinion, that it was lawful to withhold tithes and offerings, and even to take all possessions and temporal goods from men of the church, bishops and priests.[33] It is no sin, she used to think, to disobey the precepts of the church.[34] She no longer holds that it is unlawful to swear oaths.[35] She disavows her previous rejection of fasting, pilgrimage, "the worship [and] reverence" of images.

Reginald Pecock. Reginald Pecock (c. 1395-c. 1460) led an equivocal life as campaigner against the Lollards, for he was himself eventually accused as a heretic. He was at Oxford at the beginning of the fifteenth century, probably while Thomas Arundel was doing his best as archbishop of Canterbury to ensure that theological debate in Oxford kept to orthodox positions in the wake of the Wycliffite controversy. He spent much of his early career in London, teaching theology at Whittington College (where he was Master from 1431 until he became bishop of St. Asaph in 1444). At St. Asaph he set a bad example as an absentee bishop and thus exposed himself to criticism, since neglect of episcopal duties of this sort was a frequent anticlerical point among dissidents. In 1450 he became bishop of Chichester.

He engaged in the dangerous activity of studying what Lollards believed, the better to alert others to the dangers. In Pecock's view the best way to combat heresy was to *discuss* Lollard teachings. He says in a late work, *The Book of Faith*, that he had himself held debates with Lollards, and the Lollards had (they said) in return read his writings. Arundel of course had taken a different line, attempting to suppress all such discussion. Suppressing debate in universities

---

[32]Ibid., p. 141.
[33]Ibid.
[34]Ibid.
[35]Ibid., p. 142.

had never worked since it was first tried in Paris in 1210.

Pecock's confidence that debate could do only good rested on his conviction that people would be convinced by reasonable argument. His *Book of Faith* in English (about 1456)[36] and his *Repressor of Overmuch Blaming of the Clergy*[37] both attempt to pitch camp between holding it necessary to rely on the ecclesiastical authorities, "right or wrong," and what he understood to be the extreme Lollard position that the faithful had no need of institutional and sacramental support at all. He knows and acknowledges that the clergy have faults. But in the *Repressor* he defends practices and beliefs Lollards were challenging—ministry in the church, papal authority, the religious orders; extravagance by the ecclesiastical authorities and the pursuit of high living by the higher clergy; the sacraments, especially the Eucharist; the invocation of the saints, the use of images and pilgrimages. He considers critically the Lollard claim that all Christians should read the Bible for themselves and their belief that only a good man will understand it aright.

In book 1.14 he discusses the unreliability of "mannys resoun" which "often failith" as "experience ofte schewith." The senses too can mislead. However, he has confidence in the reliability of "a formal complete argument clepid a sillogisme in resoun, whos bothe premissis ben sureli or likely knowen for trewe." Such "probable" arguments complement the teaching of Scripture, especially in the "moral service of God" where Scriptue is "not the reule" but "a witnesser and a rehercer."[38]

But his habit of hobnobbing with dissidents proved dangerous. One convicted heretic (an Oxford man) told the abbot of Abingdon that he had learned all he knew about heresy from the bishop, so that Pecock's friends had to rally round and tell the king he was sound in his opinions after all. By 1457 Pecock was in serious trouble. Orders were given that his writings should be examined (both the Latin and the English ones). Pecock cleverly tried to dismiss responsibility for his earlier work, and

---

[36]Reginald Pecock, *The Book of Faith* (Cambridge: Trinity College, MS B.14.45), ed. J. L. Morison, *Reginald Pecock's Book of Faith* (Glasgow, 1909).

[37]Reginald Pecock, *Repressor of Overmuch Blaming of the Clergy*, ed. Churchill Babington, Rolls Society (London: Longman, Green, Longman & Roberts, 1860), http://lollardsociety.org/pdfs/Pecock_Repressor_vol2.pdf.

[38]Ibid., pp. 73-75.

he asked to be examined only on his mature and considered recent writings. These he hastily revised. The masters of Oxford asked to be allowed to examine Pecock's works. There was unrest in the province of Canterbury. In the end Pecock recanted and threw his own books into the fire. Details are uncertain, but there seem to have been unusual elements to them, including the notion that the church could err in matters of faith and a general council could be wrong, and also that it was not necessary to believe in everything the Apostles' Creed said. There were demands that Pecock should be removed from the bishopric of Chichester and that searches should be made for his books to ensure they were thoroughly destroyed.

Lollard preaching. Surviving Lollard sermons on Gospel readings for the liturgical year tell a story somewhat at odds with the idea that the Lollards were ahead of their times and thought just like the Reformers of a century later. Despite their reforming tendencies, the Lollards thought of themselves as straightforward members of the church, listening to sermons through the year in the ordinary way.

One such collection may have been designed as a manual from which would-be preachers could learn how to preach, rather than a published collection of sermons actually delivered. It seems to have been provided by someone with sufficient theological education to know of some traditional principal sources on Matthew's Gospel (Augustine, Gregory the Great and Chrysostom) and who was familiar with the conventions of the *ars praedicandi*, with its formal divisions and subdivisions of themes. A degree of Latin learning hovers behind the English words. Quotations are given in Latin and then explained.[39] There are surviving pieces of extra advice, to enable a would-be preacher to develop a point. For example, for sermon 11 there are suggestions of a sort found in late twelfth- and thirteenth-century "arts of preaching," which would enable a preacher to enlarge upon the virtues and vices with scriptural and other references. But there are also topical observations. "How many men nowadays are apostates, breaking through their foul and horrible pride the fair fellowship of holy Church."[40]

---

[39]*Lollard Sermons*, EETS 294, ed. Gloria Cigman (Oxford: Oxford University Press, 1989), p. xlvii.
[40]Ibid., p. 137.

Whatever the idea behind the collection, would-be Lollard preachers had here a practical guide and a body of detailed material on which to base their own sermons. Orderly scriptural exposition shapes the texts and is clearly intended to shape the preaching. Figurative or "spiritual" interpretations are accepted; Christian people are encouraged to imitate Christ, live good Christian lives and by the inspiration of the Holy Spirit break out into meritorious deeds, guided by the Word of God and supported by the sacraments.

John Hus

The seriousness with which Wycliffite opinions were being taken decades after the death of Wyclif in 1384 also owed a good deal to the perceived excesses of the Hussites and the University of Prague, which had equipped itself with copies of many of his writings. John (or Jan) Hus, an academic at the University of Prague, was excommunicated in 1411 and then condemned along with Wycliff by the Council of Constance.

He had offended by writing on the doctrine of the church in his *De Ecclesia* of 1413, a far more well-articulated book than Wyclif had produced, but strongly in sympathy with many of Wyclif's positions. Copies of Wyclif's works had been brought to Prague in some numbers by sympathizers. He also anticipated Luther's condemnation of indulgences and all they meant to the pastoral life of the church. Some ordinary people who said they agreed with Hus on the subject were beheaded for their opinions. Hus himself was arrested at the instigation of the clergy of Prague and brought to the archbishop, with the intention that he should be tried for heresy. Hus said the only judge he recognized was Jesus Christ.

The articles for which Hus was condemned, and about which he protested that he had in some cases been misunderstood, concerned a number of topics that cropped up again once the Reformation began. One was his interpretation of the theory of the church to be found in Augustine's *City of God* (see pp. 72-74). He was said to hold that "there is only one holy universal Church, which is the total number of those predestined to salvation" and that "those foreknown as damned are not parts of the church, for no part of the church can finally fall away from it, since the predestinating love that binds the Church together does not fail." That allowed him to say that there was indeed no salvation outside the church, but only if the church was understood to be not the visible, institutional structure, but "the convocation of those predestined to salvation, whether or not it be in a state of grace according to present justice."[41] Hus was on controversial ground here; Augustine's doctrine of the church was not acceptable to all medieval theologians, at least not in its entirety. It was to be embraced by the Reformers of the sixteenth century with varying emphasis and a variety of reservations.

Hus was also accused, in a list of condemned articles, of challenging papal primacy by saying that "Peter neither was nor is the head of the holy catholic church" (7) and that the powers of the pope came from the state and not from God for "the papal dignity originated with the emperor, and the primacy and institution of the pope emanated from imperial power" (9). On unworthy ministers he took a position not far from that of Wyclif, claiming that they "pollute the power of the priesthood" (8), even if it does not follow that they lose the power to administer the sacraments. This includes the pope. "Nobody holds the place of Christ or of Peter unless he follows his way of life, since there is no other discipleship that is more appropriate nor is there another way to receive delegated power from God, since there is required for this office of vicar a similar way of life as well as the authority of the one instituting." He also claimed that secular power could not lawfully be exercised by those in mortal sin (30).

A cluster of other articles suggest a flavor of the Reformation to the modern reader. One (15) is the claim that the Bible does not authorize "ecclesiastical obedience." Another (18) is that priests have a duty to preach to the people. Still another (19) is that excommunication is being overused, and improperly so, as an instrument of oppression.

The Council's sentence against John Hus identifies him as a "noxious son" of Wyclif and lists "articles" alleged to be his teaching, "some of

---

[41]For this and the articles in the following two paragraphs, see "Council of Constance," pt. 4, in *Decrees of the Ecumenical Councils*, pp. 430-31; www.dailycatholic.org/history/16ecume4.htm.

them . . . notoriously heretical and . . . long ago been rejected and condemned by holy fathers and by general councils." "Trustworthy" witnesses before the council have testified that "the said John has taught many evil, scandalous and seditious things, and dangerous heresies, and has publicly preached them during many years." His books are to be burned like Wyclif's. He himself is to be executed as a heretic.[42]

Hus chose to stand his ground and refuse to recant to spare himself the execution which followed on July 6. Hus's final statement was written as he faced imminent execution:

> I, Jan Hus, in hope a priest of Jesus Christ, fearing to offend God, and fearing to fall into perjury, do hereby profess my unwillingness to abjure all or any of the articles produced against me by false witnesses. For God is my witness that I neither preached, affirmed, nor defended them, though they say that I did. Moreover, concerning the articles that they have extracted from my books, I say that I detest any false interpretation which any of them bears. But inasmuch as I fear to offend against the truth, or to gainsay the opinion of the doctors of the Church, I cannot abjure any one of them. And if it were possible that my voice could now reach the whole world, as at the Day of Judgment every lie and every sin that I have committed will be made manifest, then would I gladly abjure before all the world every falsehood and error which I either had thought of saying or actually said!
>
> I say I write this of my own free will and choice.
>
> Written with my own hand, on the first day of July.[43]

Hus suffered treatment of which other medieval dissidents had also complained. Statements had been attributed to him, misunderstood and then condemned, he claimed.[44] The execution was public; he was tied to a stake with straw and wood piled round it and then burned.

Two main branches of Hus's followers set off along pathways leading toward the Reformation. An influence which may have been of some

---

[42]"Council of Constance," pt. 3, in *Decrees of the Ecumenical Councils*, pp. 428-29, www.dailycatholic .org/history/16ecume3.htm.

[43]John Hus, *The Letters of John Hus*, ed. Herbert B. Workman and R. Martin Pope (London: Hodder & Stoughton, 1904), pp. 275-76, www.fordham.edu/halsall/mod/1415janhus.html.

[44]Herbert B. Workman and R. Martin Pope, eds., *The Letters of John Hus* (London: Hodder & Stoughton, 1904), pp. 275-76.

importance for each was the presence in eastern Europe of Christians of the Orthodox tradition, for whom it was uncontroversial that the congregation should receive the Eucharist in both kinds and that clergy should be allowed to marry. A firm indicator of some Orthodox influence is that these heirs of Hus adopted a version of the creed without the *filioque* clause. The more radical of Hus's heirs were the militant and separatist Taborites, who insisted on a strict biblical basis for their faith and life, and were already of an extreme *sola scriptura* persuasion. The moderate Hussites pursued reforms within the existing structures and institutions of the church. Shortly before the Reformation, those moderates who were most committed to Hus's theology founded the Bohemian Brethren. The Bohemian Brethren found they had much in common with Martin Luther, and their heirs—including the Moravians—were often significant participants in the social and ecclesial life of the following centuries.

PART THREE

CONTINUITY AND CHANGE FROM THE REFORMATION

15

RENAISSANCE

THE REDISCOVERY OF THE
GREEK AND HEBREW SCRIPTURES

Printing. From the late fifteenth century, the invention of printing in
the West began to transform the ways in which challenging ideas could
spread and the necessary supporting knowledge be disseminated for reference. It came slowly at first, but by the first generation of the
sixteenth-century's Reformers it was possible to engage in pamphlet
warfare, with an avid readership for the latest salvo in a dispute over
(usually) a theological controversy.[1]

The sixteenth century reinvented the educated man (more rarely the
educated woman) who was not a professional member of the clergy, or
a clerically trained civil servant, or a "religious" (that is, a member of a
religious order). For the first time in the West since the fall of Rome and
the end of the ancient world, there was opportunity for intellectual inquiry driven by sheer curiosity, the exchange of ideas in letters among
friends, and the cultivation of a self-conscious stylishness, an elegance of
thought and expression. There had been glimpses of that sort of thing in
the twelfth century, but society's structures did not encourage it then,
especially in feudal northern Europe; the invention of the universities
soon took up the slack by drawing in the young and ambitious who had

---

[1]Elizabeth Eisenstein, *The Printing Press as an Agent of Change: Communications and Cultural
Transformations in Early Modern Europe* (Cambridge: Cambridge University Press, 1979); and
Elizabeth Eisenstein, *The Printing Revolution in Early Modern Europe* (Cambridge: Cambridge
University Press, 1993).

intellectual interests and correctly perceived in higher education a route to upward social mobility. For some centuries most intellectual life had been carried on under the auspices of the universities and by professional scholars and clerics. The intellectual secular and religious adventurers of the Renaissance and Reformation conducted their inquiries independently and within and alongside the universities of Europe.

The Reformation prompted intense and widespread interest. It was a people's movement as well as an academic one. When there was a public theological debate, the crowds were there to take sides; though there was sometimes a popular hostility toward scholars, who were accused of obfuscating religious teaching and making it unnecessarily complicated, popular interest was strong. The Renaissance was slower to percolate into the popular imagination, but it brought with it "humanism," a new attitude to the study of the classics and the place of human beings in the world, which also began to bring about social change.

The Renaissance and the Reformation began for different reasons, but eventually the two movements shared much common ground. Both eventually transformed the attitudes of people who had no contact with universities, yet both found many of their significant leaders in academe. This transmutation of intellectually sophisticated concerns into matters of world-changing religious and cultural significance is one of the most signal achievements of the period.

New approaches to Bible study. Nowhere were the changes of the Renaissance and the way they affected popular interest more important than in the revolution they brought about in the study of the Bible. The change began in the fifteenth century. The Venetian aristocrat Contarini (1483-1542) said he found secular studies an amusement but not a challenge, whereas the reading of Scripture made him uncomfortable and uneasy, and consequently made him think much harder.[2] The reading of Scripture was about to make a great many other people uncomfortable and uneasy too. Since the fifth century the standard version in use in the West had been Jerome's Vulgate translation. As mentioned previously (see pp. 51-52), he said himself that he was not inspired when he made it, but that had

---

[2]Constance M. Furey, *Erasmus, Contarini, and the Religious Republic of Letters* (Cambridge: Cambridge University Press, 2006), pp. 91-93.

not prevented preachers and commentators weighing his every word with as much meticulous care as if God himself had dictated it to him in Latin. To begin to read the Bible in any other language or any other version was a huge step, and it was never going to be uncontroversial.

Greek was the language in which the New Testament had originally been accepted by the early church as the authentic Word of God. It is also the language of the Septuagint, the oldest of the ancient translation of the Hebrew Scriptures, made in Alexandria in the third and second centuries B.C. With the revival of the study of Greek and Hebrew by a few scholars in the West at the end of the Middle Ages came the dawning realization that Latin was after all not Scripture's native language. Its "sources" (*fontes*) lay in the Greek and Hebrew textual record. *Ad fontes!* "Back to the sources!" became the cry.

On the face of it, the idea of studying Greek and Hebrew in order to understand the Bible better came surprisingly late to the medieval scene. It was partly that the efforts of commentators had been traditionally spent on comparing and summarizing the views of earlier commentators i order to better understand Scripture. It was also partly a matter of the language barrier. It should not be forgotten that even before the Roman Empire finally collapsed, the expectation that educated Roman citizens would know Greek as well as Latin was becoming harder to maintain. The two halves of the empire, Latin West and Greek East, were drifting apart linguistically. For nearly a thousand years until the fifteenth century, few in the West could speak or read Greek. There were Hebrew speakers in the small Jewish enclaves throughout Europe, but Latin scholars do not often seem to have asked them to provide Hebrew teachers, though it will be remembered that several noteworthy scholars such as Peter Abelard and Andrew of St. Victor had inquired of them as early as the twelfth century concerning the Hebrew word for a particularly puzzling term in Jerome's Latin.[3]

Alonso the "Toast" asks questions about the Bible. Alonso Fernández de Madrigal (c. 1400-1455), nicknamed Tostado ("the toast"), was one of Spain's early humanist thinkers, a bishop as well as an academic. He was

---

[3]Andrew of St. Victor, *Opera*, CCCM 53.

present at the Council of Florence, which he attended among the conciliarists who were hoping to limit papal monarchical power. He was a prolific author (whose collected works ran to fifteen volumes when they were printed between 1507 and 1530) and an important biblical commentator of his day as well as the author of books on politics, philosophy and other subjects.

This was a radical scholar with a well-furnished mind, writing a clear and challenging account of matters that were to become central to the Reformation debates on the study of the Bible. He made a significant contribution to the history of the study of the Bible in Spain. Alonso is quite frank in his preface to his commentary on Mark's Gospel that he has tried to do something new.[4]

Alonso begins by reviewing the medieval debate in the medieval academic way, a series of questions (*quaestiones*) on topics which were currently prompting disagreement. For example, he raises the old question of the number of books there are in the Bible. Canonicity is important, he argues, for the church is sure that the authors of the canonical books were inspired (*inspirati*). "The whole authority" of the canonical books comes from the church's certainty that their human authors wrote only what the Spirit told them to and did not include anything of their own authorship. The church does not require the faithful to accept other books in the same way, even if the church may make use of them in its teaching. "And so we take the Prophets more seriously [*strictius*] than Jerome." Alonso discusses differences of opinion about the Apocrypha of the Old Testament and whether they form part of the canon. Further questions ask what language the Evangelists actually wrote in; why their narratives do not exactly coincide; why Jesus himself wrote nothing; and other familiar queries of the later Middle Ages.

Alonso also includes new questions that struck him because he was one of the fifteenth-century scholars who had mastered Greek and Hebrew. He asks if the Latin text has become corrupted, and whether it is proper for it to be corrected from the text in the original languages.

---

[4]Alonso Fernández de Madrigal, *Introduccion al Evangelio segun San Mateo*, ed. José Manuel Sanchez Caro, Rosa Maria Herrera García and Inmaculadadelgado Jara (Avila-Salamanca: University of Salamanca, 2008).

Latin speakers meet Greek speakers again: The Council of Florence. Where could Western intellectuals meet educated Greeks in the West and discuss abstruse intellectual questions with them? The Council of Florence afforded an unprecedented opportunity in the mid-fifteenth century for scholarly exchange as well when it addressed itself to the problem of mending the East-West schism of 1054.

For the council the Roman Church brought in academics from universities as consultants. This was a bold but not unprecedented move, and it required a certain sophistication in the separation of functions and roles in the deliberations of the council.[5] Pierre d'Ailly (c. 1350-1420) had earlier discussed the respective roles of theologians and bishops in defining doctrine in his *Treatise on Behalf of the Faith Against a Certain Dominican Friar Giovanni di Montesono* (written c. 1388). He thought that theologians should be free to come to independent views, which might not accord with those of the bishops. Bishops have an authority from God when they make decisions about the faith; but theologians are still the experts, and bishops should respect their insight.

There were no universities of the Western sort in Byzantium. The flavor of intellectual life had matured differently in the Greek-speaking world after the collapse of the Roman Empire, with a notable philosphical leaning toward late Platonism rather than the Aristotelianism which had won favor in the West. Agreeing to a common methodology and corpus of texts to rely on was a problem area, for the West knew few of the writings of the Greek fathers and the Greeks did not in general read those of the West, with the exception of some works of Augustine. The occasion sharpened awareness in the West that there was a larger body of early Christian authors than they had previously been able to read.

The Greeks brought their scholars too:

> With the Greek emperor came a great many men, highly distinguished in both intellect and learning. Amongst these were Nicholas of Euboea, very learned in both Greek and Latin, and the famous Gemistos Plethon, called by Marsilio a second Plato, and acclaimed equally for his eloquence and his scholarship. When Cosimo heard him frequently

---

[5]Nelson H. Minnich, "The Voice of Theologians in General Councils from Pisa to Trent," *Theological Studies* 59 (1998).

discoursing before the scholars and winning their highest applause and admiration, it is said that he was set ablaze with an extraordinary desire to recall to Italy as soon as possible the philosophy of Plato, as of ancient right.[6]

Some of the Western academics involved in the Council had had a taste of Greek if not of Hebrew. There were new accessions to the potential academic booklist in the form of newly rediscovered works of Plato, which now begged to be read in Greek. The Italian humanist Petrarch (1304-1374) famously owned a manuscript containing sixteen writings of Plato.[7] The advent of a fashion for the study of Greek and Hebrew altered the balance and emphasis in the range of what was available to be learned by university students. There were respected pioneers in such studies. Nicholas of Cusa had studied at the University of Heidelberg in 1416 and then at Padua, graduating as a doctor of canon law in 1423. He learned Greek and Hebrew (and it was said also Arabic). In 1425 he was studying theology at Cologne. He had already entered public life at the Council of Basel in 1421, where Cesarini, formerly his teacher but now a cardinal, was prominent. He made himself useful enough to be sent to Constantinople by Pope Eugenius IV in 1437 to win support from senior Greek clerics for the the proposed Council of Florence.

The rediscovery of Plato had a profound effect. Its emergence and dissemination coincided with the sixteenth-century rejection by many leading intellectuals of the Aristotelian emphasis that had encouraged the dominance of the study of logic in the medieval universities. It began to foster a new style of intellectual life.

The West makes its rediscovery of Greek fathers. When Westerners debated with the Greeks, it had to be faced that the Western traditional list of reputable Christian authors would not do. The Greeks did not regard them as authoritative in the same way as their own Greek authorities, such as Origen and the Cappadocian fathers (whose views on Genesis so impressed Augustine when he heard Ambrose, bishop of Milan, preach about them in the late fourth century)—Basil, Gregory

---

[6]Giovani Corso, *Life of Ficino* (1506).
[7]Aubrey Diller, "Petrarch's Greek Codex of Plato," *Classical Philology* 59, no. 4 (1964): 270-72.

of Nyssa and Gregory Nazianzen. Jerome's catalog "Of Notable Figures" (*De viris illustribus*) belongs to a genre of lists of received or accepted writers and their writings, works which may safely be read by Christians, but it, and its medieval updates, concentrated on the Latins.[8] Isidore of Seville had provided a sixth-century revision.[9] The Greeks knew few of these authors and could not regard them as authoritative. In the Greek tradition the mindset was quite different. The importance of the early period of the ecumenical councils was such that any departure from their explicit conclusions was likely to be regarded as heresy solely because it was something new.

The shakeup of assumptions about the range of available authorities on Christian faith and life and their nature prompted by the encounter at Florence gradually effected academic change. By the sixteenth century the expression "the fathers" had come into use in a new way in the West, after some hard thinking about what should be included in a corpus of authentic patristic texts.[10] The universities were brought to alter their perspectives here rather than leading the alteration, in an example of the two-way pull of the forces of intellectual change, where sometimes academic and sometimes other needs were the drivers. The revival of Western awareness of the Greek fathers continued into the sixteenth and seventeenth centuries, as we shall see, and these writers came to be useful among the Reformers in putting forth their arguments.

Marsilio Ficino, the study of Greek and the revival of Platonism. Meanwhile, the renewed interest in the study of Greek, partly stimulated by the encounter at Florence and certainly by the availability of Greek texts new to the West, took on a life of its own. Marsilio Ficino (1433-1499) became something of a hero to the humanists in the generations

---

[8]See, for example, the introduction to my *Fifty Key Medieval Thinkers* (London: Routledge, 2002).

[9]See *El "De viris illustribus" de Isidoro de Sevilla*, ed. Carmen Codoñer Merino (Salamanca: Colegio Trilingüe de la Universidad, 1964), which includes thirty-three figures. The series of lists of approved authors was further revised and added to century by century in the West, with occasional self-indulgences such as that of Sigebert of Gembloux, who at the end of the eleventh century or the beginning of the twelfth, added himself to the end of his own list and included extensive details about what he had himself written.

[10]V. Phidas, "Hermeneutique et patristique au concile de Florence," *Christian Unity: The Council of Ferrara-Florence, 1438/9-1989*, ed. G. Alberigo (Louvain: Louvain University Press, 1991), pp. 303-25. See too *Studien zum 15. Jahrhundert*, ed. J. Helmrath (München: R. Oldenbourg, 1994).

that followed. That was perhaps partly because the *Life* of Ficino published in 1506 by Giovani Corso was designed to paint an idealized picture of what he achieved. He was presented as a great man, a ground-
breaker, fearless, visionary:

> When I considered writing about the life and character of Marsilio Fi-
> cino, who as guide penetrated the innermost sanctuary of the divine
> Plato, sealed for so many centuries, and thoroughly explored the whole of
> his Academy, the first noteworthy thing which came to mind and en-
> couraged me to write about this man was that he himself not only inves-
> tigated its precepts and mysteries but also penetrated, laid open, and then
> expounded them to others. This was something which no one else for the
> previous thousand years so much as attempted, let alone accomplished.
> . . . He had the highest regard for the study of fine literature, almost ex-
> tinct at the time, which he did his utmost to revive.[11]

Ficino was said by his biographer to have got the idea at the Council
of Florence and to have carried it through by making extensive collections of Platonist texts:

> Ficino gathered extracts from a wide selection of Latin authors; in short,
> he left nothing undone which he believed would be beneficial to the
> work undertaken. On this account he always had to hand all the Latin
> Platonists, namely Cicero, Macrobius, Apuleius, Boethius, St. Augustine,
> Calcidius, and other like-minded writers, about whom at that time he
> wrote a great deal which has never been published. Soon afterwards he
> left these writings in the care of Filippo Valori, a nobleman and one of his
> foremost pupils. . . .
>
> A little later, at Cosimo's instigation, he translated into Latin the book
> of Hermes Trismegistus *On Divine Wisdom and the Creation of the World.*

This work did not have a natural home in a university at this date. It
was supported—in a way which was to grow more common as the fifteenth century merged into the sixteenth—by aristocratic patronage of
the individual scholar:

---

[11]This and the following quotes are excerpted from *The Letters of Marsilio Ficino*, translated by the
Language Department of the School of Economic Science, vol. 3 (London: Shepheard-Walwyn,
1981).

For this purpose he was endowed by Cosimo with the most generous gift of a family estate at Careggi near the outskirts of the town, as well as with a house in town, and even with beautifully written Greek books of Plato and Plotinus which were very costly, especially in those times.

Lorenzo Valla criticizes the Vulgate. Valla had a checkered career. He was a humanist and a would-be controversialist who really wanted to be a senior civil servant in the papal curia but had to spend his early career wandering the universities of Europe lecturing here and there. Eventually he found a patron and employer in Alfonso of Aragon. He made and continued to make powerful enemies because he was outspoken about the stylistic deficiencies of contemporary writers and asked radical and uncomfortable questions. (No author enjoys being accused of bad writing.) It was Valla who exposed the Donation of Constantine as a fake. He thus overturned the assumptions of many centuries about the respective powers of church and state deriving from what had been believed to be the Emperor Constantine's concession of supremacy to the church in the fourth century. Eventually he achieved his ambition and got a post in the curia, but not until near the end of his life.

In typically challenging mode, and anxious to make use of his knowledge of Greek, he asked whether the Vulgate was really to be relied upon. He set out to make a critical comparison between the Vulgate and the Greek New Testament by comparing manuscripts. He used at least four Latin ones and four Greek (in discussing one passage he mentions five manuscripts). He completed a first version of this collation (*Collatio*) in 1442.[12]

Valla did not set out to re-edit the Greek or the Latin text from first principles. Theories of scholarly editing were still at the earliest stage of evolution. So he could not feel free to suggest a familiar text needed amending when that text was the Bible. Classical texts might be a different matter. He pointed out that there was a great deal of variation in the copies of the New Testament he had seen. It was a thousand years since Jerome's day, and he suggests that it is scarcely surprising if the stream has become muddy.[13]

---

[12] Valla, *Collatio Novi Testamenti*, ed. A. Perosa (Florence: Sansoni, 1970).
[13] Valla, *Collatio*, pref. 2, in *Opera Omnia*, ed. E. Garin (Turin: Bottega d'Erasmo, 1962), pp. 6-9.

Less controversially, the Spanish humanist Elio Antonio de Nebrija (1441-1522) wrote that in the case of the New Testament the Greek should be used in determining which of the variant Latin readings was correct. In the case of the Old Testament the Hebrew should be regarded as the source of both the Greek and the Latin versions.[14] Jerome had long ago suggested that under certain conditions Latin manuscripts would be better than Greek, and Greek better than Hebrew, when it came to restoring the text: *Et emendatiora sunt exemplaria Latina quam Graeca, Graeca quam Hebraea. Verum haec contra invidos.*[15] The manuscript situation had deteriorated since his day, and it is not at all certain that the cry *Ad fontes* was not leading scholars back to less accurate Byzantine Greek versions, which were the great majority of manuscripts then available to them.

Valla did not aspire to create a complete new text in either language; nor does he seem to have been willing to be so bold with the Bible as he was prepared to be with the classics, where he was proposing conjectural emendations.[16] He did not think such informed guesswork was appropriate in the case of the sacred text. Many of his notes are grammatical, bearing on differences between the norms of Latin and Greek, and showing a sensitivity to the innate deep structural differences between the two languages. Some of the notes are concerned with the choices a translator has to make when faced with this such differences. On Matthew 24, for example, he remarks, "I would have translated it . . . ," explaining his reasons for departing from Jerome.[17] He shows an awareness too of the way words in one language rarely translate exactly into their counterpart words in another, discussing the interchangeability of *extasis* and *excedere* (*"sive enim mente excedimus"*) in 2 Corinthians 5:13.[18] This *Collatio* was subsequently discussed in 1505 by Desiderius Erasmus (1466/1469-1536), who had come across a copy while studying in Louvain, which gained it longer-term influence.

---

[14]Elio Antonio de Nebrija, *Apologia* (1516), fol.a iir.

[15]*Patrologia Latina*, 28, col. 152.

[16]Lodi Nauta, *In Defense of Common Sense: Lorenzo Valla's Humanist Critique of Scholastic Philosophy* (Cambridge, Mass.: Harvard University Press, 2009).

[17]Valla, *In Novum Testamentum annotationes* (Basel, 1527), p. 58.

[18]Ibid., p. 256.

This was not necessarily the way these developments were seen by contemporaries. "The knowledge of Greek was lost," commented Philipp Melanchthon (1497-1560) a couple of generations later, trying to reconstruct the process by which the study of the Bible had reached its late medieval state and exploring the justification for modifying the university syllabus now.[19] In justification of change, Melanchthon gave a historically insecure account of the changes that had taken place at the end of the ancient world. He set out a conspiracy theory of the decline of the knowledge of Greek in the West. Greek had been forgotten, he claimed, because of the machinations of such figures as "Thomas, Scotus, Durandus," who preferred "a crippled Aristotle" and their own "bold way of commentating and philosophizing." They held sway, he says, for three hundred years. "Until that time philosophy had been altogether Greek, and only Cyprian, Hilary, Ambrose, Jerome, and Augustine had excelled in Latin. Greek had been in the West virtually the language of religion."[20] That sort of deliberate manipulation would justify departing from their example in the present.

The arrival of Hebrew. The advent of Hebrew consciousness was rather different. The study of Hebrew did not come with the enticement that it provided a key to a whole new classical literature. But Greek was naturally going to be linked with Hebrew where students of the Bible were keen to read it in the original languages and to go back to the sources. Hebrew would be frequently referred to by Robert Boyle (1627-1691) as *the* "Holy Tongue," on the authority of earlier opinion.[21] He quotes the famous saying of Giovanni Pico della Mirandola (1463-1494): "*Hebraei bibunt fontem, Graeci rivos, Latini paludes*" ("the Hebrews drank from the spring, the Greeks from a river, the Latins from a swamp").[22] The image of drawing upon a source of living water seems to have caught the scholarly imagination. Philipp Melanchthon used it too:

---

[19]Philip Melanchthon, *De corrigendis adulescentiae studiis*, CR 11, p. 15ff., trans. *The Reformation in Its Own Words*, ed. Hans J. Hillebrand (London: SCM Press, 1964), pp. 58-59.
[20]Ibid., p. 59.
[21]Robert Boyle, *The Style of the Scriptures*, *Works*, ed. Michael Hunter and Edward B. Davis (London: Pickering & Chatto, 1999), 2:396.
[22]Ibid., p. 450.

Led by the Holy Spirit, but accompanied by humanist studies, one should proceed to theology . . . but since the Bible is written in part in Hebrew and in part in Greek—as Latinists we drink from the stream of both—we must learn these languages, unless we want to be "silent persons."[23]

The rediscovery of Hebrew as a branch of Christian scholarship by Pico della Mirandola in the fifteenth century, and by Melanchthon's great-uncle Johannes Reuchlin (1455-1522), appears to have been the starting point of the Renaissance and Reformation revival of the Christian study of Hebrew. He had his early education in the Dominican *studium* to which his father was attached as an official, and he studied briefly at the University of Freiberg. Appointed to a post in a noble household because of his fine singing voice, he found himself sent to Paris to accompany the son of the household as a student there. He took the opportunity to study himself, learning Greek, and moved to Basle to the new university there in 1474, where he became a lecturer and fostered the new learning. He became increasingly interested in Hebrew, and eventually hit upon the idea of publishing a Hebrew grammar to assist others who wanted to learn the language. His ground-breaking *De rudimentis Hebraicis* of 1506 was the result.

So the rise of interest in the biblical languages had origins distinct from those which prompted the Reformers, closely though the two processes of change quickly became entwined. This entanglement of the two came largely from the adoption of the study of these languages in the universities, which had previously worked in Latin and confined themselves mainly to lecturing on Latin texts or texts translated into Latin for the purpose of academic study.

THE BIBLICAL LANGUAGES
AND THE UNIVERSITIES

Complutum, Louvain and the trilingual experiment. The study of Greek and Hebrew in universities benefited especially from a practical initiative. This was the idea of setting up specialist universities in which they could be studied alongside Latin. In 1498 the archbishop of Toledo

---

[23]Melanchthon, *Reformation in Its Own Words*, p. 59.

founded a new kind of *studium* at Complutum at Alcalá, near Madrid in Spain, dedicated to the study of the three sacred languages (Latin, Greek and Hebrew, in which the title "King of the Jews" was written over the head of Jesus as he hung on the cross accoring to Jn 19:20). This became the Complutensian University in 1508.[24]

The second significant location for the study of Hebrew to emerge at the beginning of the sixteenth century was to be the Trilingual University in Louvain. The University of Louvain had begun as a result of a petition by the Duke of Burgundy to the pope asking him to establish a *studium generale*, though until 1431 there was no faculty of theology at Louvain. Martin V issued a bull in 1425, conceding to the prince the right to grant privileges to the university. Rectors were elected for three months and then later for six, in rotation, by delegates of the faculties, which each took turns. The new university was well-supported by endowments from the family of the dukes of Burgundy. It benefited from the rise of the Hapsburg dynasty. There were other important patrons, such as Adrian Floris, tutor of Charles V, later cardinal of Utrecht, and finally pope under the name of Adrian VI (elected 1522). In 1517 a College of the Three Languages was founded at Louvain by Busleiden, to provide a house of study for those interested in acquiring Greek and Hebrew.[25]

Bishop of Rochester John Fisher (1469-1535) sought to emulate Louvain at the innovative St. John's College, Cambridge, founded in 1511. Oxford did not lag behind Cambridge in its eagerness to introduce the study of Greek and Hebrew. There were exchanges between Oxford and the Louvain *collegium trilinguale*. On July 20, 1536, Thomas Goldwell, an Oxford graduate of 1528, who took his master of arts degree in 1531 and his graduate degree in theology in 1534, matriculated at Louvain.

Later in the sixteenth century and into the seventeenth, Louvain became a place of resort for those who could not accommodate themselves to the changes of religious allegiance required of them if they remained in England. But at the beginning of the sixteenth century it was simply a good place to go to get a grounding in the new "learned languages."

---

[24]Benoît Pellistrandi, "The University of Alcalá de Henares from 1568-1618: Students and Graduates," *History of Universities* 9 (1990): 119-65.
[25]Félix Nève, *La Renaissance des lettres en Belgique* (Louvain, 1890).

Gabriel Dunne (c. 1490-1558), a monk of Buckfast, was sent to the Order's college of St. Bernard in Oxford (later to become St. John's College). On March 28, 1530, he matriculated at the University of Louvain. In June 1535 he left Louvain to return to England, where Henry VIII's chief minister Thomas Cromwell (c. 1485-1540) intended him to have the abbacy at Buckfast. He handed over the abbey to the King in 1535 and was granted a substantial pension in return. Dunne moved to London, where he found he had a promising future as a canon of St. Paul's. He remained in such high esteem at court that in 1549, when Edmund Bonner was deprived of his bishopric, Thomas Cranmer (1489-1556), then archbishop of Canterbury, appointed him to take care of the spiritual needs of the diocese of London as "keeper of the spiritualities."

Louvain remained theologically conservative, and this gave some of Oxford's Renaissance scholars a means of advancing their studies in this area while not simultaneously also becoming Reformation scholars. For example, it became a place of refuge for English scholars such as Thomas More (1478-1535),[26] who were uncomfortable with reforming ideas in their own countries.[27]

Louvain also remained competitive, with students from outside the Netherlands preferring to study there rather than in the Protestant universities to be found in Germany once the Reformation was under way. For a time, Louvain was allowed to enjoy a monopoly of higher education in its region.[28]

An affiliated university was set up at Douai, however, by Philip II of Spain (1527-1598), and this began to outshine Louvain. Additional institutions began to cluster around Douai—eventually as many as forty colleges. Spain already had its university tradition. In the fourteenth century the kings of Castile, Léon and Aragon had founded universities, notably at Salamanca and Valladolid. But higher education in Spain was to see a vast expansion under the Hapsburgs to as many as thirty-four institutions.[29]

---

[26]J. A. Guy, *Thomas More* (London: Arnold, 2000).

[27]Georges Minchamp, *Le Cartésianisme en Belgique* (1886). The same is true of the system of Copernicus and the trials of Galileo (G. Minchamp, "Galilée et la Belgique" [Brussels, 1892]).

[28]At one time Belgian students had to study there and were not allowed to study abroad.

[29]R. W. J. Evans, "German Universities After the Thirty Years War," *History of Universities* 1 (1981): 170.

Institutionalizing the study of Greek and Hebrew in Europe's universities. The independent efforts of individuals who had become interested in the study of Greek and Hebrew now had to be channeled into the institutional teaching the universities could provide. Melanchthon was one of those who proposed teaching Greek in universities and planning to edit "sacred writings" in Greek as well as Hebrew and Latin, with commentaries.[30] "Only if we have clearly understood the language will we clearly understand the content,"he maintained.[31] But the launch into syllabus revision would be risky. By the end of the fifteenth century, universities had existed in Europe for three hundred years, and the older ones had become set in their ways, with a standard syllabus and a more or less standard way of teaching. The old syllabus might be defective, but it had been well-tested and was well-established, and any suggestion of change was likely to encounter resistance. Designing a new one was going to be a challenging task, but these changes were going to be fundamental to the new approach to the study of the Bible that the Reformers encouraged.

The northern European areas where the Reformation was chiefly going to take root were also the locations of some of the new experiments in university education. Early modern German universities were comparatively numerous.[32] Vanity prompted the foundation of several of them as much as intellectual curiosity. Some others owed their origins to princely ambitions and enjoyed the subsequent protection and control of princes (or "magistrates," as Lutheranism described them in their bid to transfer jurisdiction away from the ecclesiastical to the secular authorities). The University of Tübingen had been founded in 1477 by Count Eberhard V, who had traveled in Italy and encountered Re-

---

[30]Philipp Melanchthon, Letter of September 24, 1518, *Corpus Reformatorum* 1, ed. Karl Gottlieb Bretschneider (Halle, 1834), p. 48.

[31]Philipp Melanchthon, *De corrigendis adulescentiae studiis, Corpus Reformatorum* 11, ed. Bretschneider (Halle, 1843), 15ff., as translated in *The Reformation in Its Own Words*, ed. Hans J. Hillebrand (London: SCM Press, 1964), p. 60.

[32]John M. Fletcher, "Chance and Resistance to Change: A Consideration of the Development of English and German Universities During the Sixteenth Century," *History of Universities* 1 (1981): 1-36; and Notker Hammerstein, "The University of Heidelberg in the Early Modern Period: Aspects of Its History as a Contribution to its Sextenary," *History of Universities* 6 (1986-1987): 105-33.

naissance learning and wished to start a school in Germany where it could be pursued. Frankfurt-an-der-Oder was founded in 1506.

The University at Wittenberg, where Martin Luther and his friend Melanchthon were to become leading Reformation figures, was founded by the local German prince, Frederick the Wise (1463-1525), in 1502. It had its links with the church too, especially financially. Funding for the salaries of professors came from an increase in the number of benefices at the collegiate chapter of All Saints, which was liked to the castle church. The university's professors were to be the canons who held these benefices (eighty in all). Four faculties were created, of which the most important became theology, where Luther was to become a lecturer (though he lectured first in philosophy). Wittenberg promulgated its first set of statutes in 1504,[33] basing them on those of Tübingen.[34] The German universities thus came under the direct control of what the Lutherans were to describe as the "Christian Magistrate"—the local prince, who might not behave as the church's local leader in any way which involved sacramental activities but who seemed to them to provide a very satisfactory substitute for the pope as head of the local church.

The Reformed would come to have their impact on higher education too, in Switzerland and France, and later in Scotland. John Calvin founded an academy at Geneva in 1559, which eventually became the University of Geneva. At the outset it taught theology and law, though its curriculum expanded during the eighteenth century.[35]

France's universities, like Oxford and Cambridge in England, benefited from having active links with scholars working elsewhere in Europe, some of them Protestant and some Roman Catholic. For example, the Dutchman Jan Standonck (1454-1504) was involved in the reform movement in the fifteenth-century French church, which included an

---

[33]It redesigned its syllabus on modern principles so decisively that it became somewhat fixed in the new ways, did not keep up with the times, and its reputation had decayed by the eighteenth century. It was closed in 1815, and what remained of it was merged with the University of Halle in 1817.

[34]Thus embodying the two *viae*. Fletcher, "Chance and Resistance to Change," p. 4.

[35]See Karin Maag, *Seminary or University? The Genevan Academy and Reformed Higher Education, 1560-1620* (Aldershot: Ashgate, 1995).

attempt to improve clerical education. Erasmus was one of his students, though not always an uncritical one. Standonck founded several colleges that insisted on a high sense of vocation, commitment and strict discipline. These included the Collège de Montaigu, which became part of the University of Paris.

In Switzerland, the University of Basel had been founded in the fifteenth century (1432/1460). Erasmus expressed a wish in his will that a study foundation should be established, and it began as the *Erasmusstiftung* in 1538 in Basel. This had welfare as well as educational objectives; it set out to help the aged in need, pilgrims, young men who wanted to learn a trade, even indigent young women.[36] Erasmus thus either intended to create a hybrid of existing types of provision or envisaged something quite new. Perhaps this was not intended to be a university. His idea was already set out in the first version of his will in 1527, and in the final version of 1536 he bestowed his entire estate for the poor. In any case, he could see in the three-languages *Collegium* of Louvain a useful earlier experiment in doing good through such a higher education bequest, coupled in his case with the aim of also doing general social good.

The law professor Bonifacius Amerbach (1495-1562), who was Erasmus's friend and who carried out his wishes, arranged for the foundation to award five scholarships a year to university students, conditional upon hard work and good behavior.[37] One of Erasmus's principles was that grants should not be limited to local students. It has been calculated that in the period 1538-1600 about 20 percent went to Germans, 7 percent to Swiss, 4-5 percent to Italians and French, with about 2 percent to the Low Countries and 1 percent to Bohemia.[38] The same spirit of internationalism in the provision of financial support for students seems to have affected other local grant-giving bodies, such as the academy, which was funded by the state; on the other hand, the Academy of Basel may have recognized its need of new blood from across Europe if

---

[36]Lucia Felici, 'The Erasmusstiftung and Europe: The Institution, Organization, and Activity of the Foundation of Erasmus of Rotterdam from 1538-1600," *History of Universities* 12 (1993): 25.
[37]Ibid., p. 31.
[38]Ibid., p. 32.

it was to raise its academic standing. Academic exiles (often for religious reasons) feature in the lists.[39]

These experimental variations explored by Erasmus are of interest because they tested the boundaries of the idea of a university in a period when it was meeting its first general challenge. The persistence of institutions through the often-threatening changes brought about by the Reformation is striking evidence of their powers of endurance. Some of these changes were internal, some external. Key internal changes were those to the syllabus reflecting not only Reformation but Renaissance ideas.

HUMANISM OR SCHOLASTICISM:
THE TWO WAYS

In these late medieval German foundations, some universities offered a choice of two *viae* to students, the old way or syllabus, and the new; in some cases a university specialized in one or the other. The traditional medieval university syllabus at the time contained a very great deal of advanced logic. *Scholastic*, describing the "school" mode of study, with its emphasis on the by now highly technical arts of argument, became a pejorative term for many among the new humanists. By the "Schoolmen" or "scholastics" the early modern world meant those authors who lived and wrote in the thousand years between the end of the ancient world and the beginning of the modern period. The fashionable often tried to appear as unscholastic as possible.

It is extraordinarily difficult to define what the terminology used to label such alternative curricula really implied. Alongside syllabuses that could be categorized as a "school of a named individual" and some that lumped such schools together under a particular name (such as "Ockhamist") which generalized them, there were some which have been variously described as "terminist" or "nominalist" on the one hand and "realist" on the other.[40] Part of the problem was that some of the concerns about the need for reform or for conservatism related to

---

[39]Ibid., pp. 36-43.
[40]Ibid., p. 25.

theological opinion and some to the humbler machinery of the way students were taught to think things through, using language and logic in particular ways and with particular assumptions about their relation to metaphysics.

Already by the time of Valla the observer could point in broad terms to opposing factions, the *antiqui* and the *moderni;* the moderns disparaging the work of the ancients. Valla, in the preface to the fourth book of his *Elegantiae,* suggests that the ancients are like bees, a real food source, while the moderns are like ants who merely steal.[41] There was little room in these old-style courses for a humanist approach, let alone the study of the Greek or Hebrew of the Bible's original texts, without major change. So choices would have to be made. The choice of syllabus and approach was always contentious.

Cologne (1388) was said to favor the *via antiqua* and Erfurt (1392) the *via moderna.*[42] Tübingen offered both from its inception in 1477. In some instances a *via* was associated with a particular famous scholar, as in Heidelberg's *Via Marsiliana* (1388, after Marsilius of Inghen, c. 1340-1396), and at Wittenberg in 1508 three *viae* were offered, the Thomist, the Scotist and the Gregorist (with the *Via Gregorii* named after Gregory of Rimini, d. 1358).[43]

In 1535 there was a royal visitation of both Oxford and Cambridge in which considerable pressure was applied to encourage a departure from the study of the scholastic authors. This appears to have extended to the destruction of copies of their works, so that the quadrangle at New College was reported to have leaves of Duns Scotus blowing about.[44] Cambridge was put under similar injunctions in 1535 at the instigation of its visitor Thomas Cromwell, when study of the "frivolous questions

[41]Valla, *Opera Omnia* 1, pp. 117-18.

[42]See Heiko K. Oberman, "Luther and the *Via Moderna*: The Philosophical Backdrop of the Reformation Breakthrough," *Journal of Ecclesiastical History* 54 (2003): 641-70.

[43]Heiko A. Oberman, "Via Antiqua and Via Moderna: Late Medieval Prolegomena to Early Reformation Thought," *Journal of the History of Ideas* 48, no. 1 (1987): 24; see www.jstor.org/pss/2709610. Alister McGrath disagrees with Oberman about the *Via Gregorii*, arguing that it was merely a synonym for the *Via Moderna*; McGrath, *Reformation Thought: An Introduction* (Oxford: Blackwell, 1994), pp. 80-81.

[44]*History of the University of Oxford,* ed. James McConica (New York: Oxford University Press, 1986), 3:127-28.

and obscure glosses of Scotus, Burley, Anthonius Trombetta, Bricot, Bruliferius, etc" was forbidden.[45] There had come to be quite a mythology about the characters in this revisionist drama. John Donne links the "Schools" and the "Casuists."[46] Donne explains that "this hath divided the School into that great opposition,"[47] and these are the "well known families of the School, whom we call, Thomists and Scotists."[48]

In a biography of 1688, John Dryden (1631-1700) describes how Francis Xavier (1506-1552) was sent to the University of Paris at the age of eighteen and had a hard struggle at first with logic, though he battled manfully to master it: "Whatsoever his Inclinations were towards a knowledge so crabbed and so subtle, he tugg'd at it with incessant pains."[49] The system of study and knowledge Dryden describes as "crabbed" and "subtle" was frequently caricatured in this way as universities shook themselves free of the medieval syllabus and moved into what they saw as a modern and more enlightened world.

A new taste for the literary. Among the humanists antiquity now seemed to come to life again. Under the stimulus of the rediscovering of Greek and its literature from the fifteenth century came a change of flavor in the study of the classics, their elevation from mere practice texts whose main use was to enable a boy to learn Latin to a subject of literary study in their own right. A Cambridge statute of 1488 said that during a student's first two years there had to be lectures in humane letters (including Terence, who was not going to be read primarily for his content).

The idea of the "humane" and the "humanities" has become hard to define, but one of its main early characteristics was certainly the idea that the secular classics had important things to teach about people and how to live a good life. Latin classics were always studied in the learning of the language, even if only as practice texts. Cicero, Virgil

---

[45]D. R. Leader, *A History of the University of Cambridge* (Cambridge: University of Cambridge, 1988), 1:332, citing *Statuta academiae Cantabrigiensis*, pp. 134-41.

[46]Donne, Sermon 4, *The Sermons of John Donne*, ed. G. R. Potter and Evelyn M. Simpson (Berkeley: University of California Press, 1953), 1:224.

[47]Donne, Sermon 9, *Sermons of John Donne*, 1:310.

[48]Donne, Sermon 6, *Sermons of John Donne*, 4:168.

[49]John Dryden, *The Life of St. Francis Xavier* (1688), *The Works of John Dryden*, ed. Alan Roper and H. T. Swedenberg (Berkeley: University of California Press, 1979), 19:14.

and Caesar could be held up as good examples for Christians up to a point. But this could never be a kind of writing ordinary people would know about or become familiar with.

Erasmus, a humanist from his youth, had the idea of writing *Against the Barbarians* (*Antibarbari*) before he was twenty. His barbarians are those who are hostile to the study of the classics. He describes the Middle Ages as a period of decline in the study of the classics, so this was an assault on the old formal patterns of study, particularly in the universities, though some *secula*, secular writings, were studied still, he concedes.[50] Erasmus wrote and rewrote this work, and his refusal to allow an earlier version to be printed indicates the seriousness with which he took it and his determination to get it right for its eventual publication after some three decades, in 1519-1520.

The form he ultimately chose is that of a Ciceronian philosophical conversation among friends who happen to meet the Mayor of Bergen (William Conrad) on a recreational country walk.[51] The question they discuss is why the study of classical literature is in decline and whether this is attributable to the influence of Christianity. The inclusion of the local Mayor and of James Batt, secretary to the city of Bergen, enables them to ask whether this has anything to do with current public policy. Batt describes his efforts to bring local educational provision up to scratch after he had been at the University of Paris and understood how unsatisfactory local teaching was.[52]

Erasmus conceived the idea of writing *How to Study* (*De ratione studii*) in 1511 in correspondence with John Colet (1467-1519).[53] Its full title became *On the Method of Study and Intepretation of Texts* (*De ratione studii ac legendi interpretandique auctores*). Erasmus, from whose pen the word *ludus*, "game," is rarely far away, approved of the idea that students do best if they enjoy learning. There should be wit and witticisms, and they should learn to handle language confidently enough to

---

[50]Erasmus, *Antibarbarorum liber*, ed. K. Kumaniecki, *Erasmi Opera Omnia*, 1-1 (Amsterdam: North Holland Publishing, 1969), p. 129, but *verum ut rariores, ita inferiores.*

[51]The chief model seems to have been the *De Oratore.*

[52]Erasmus, *Antibarbarorum liber*, pp. 1-138.

[53]Erasmus, *De ratione studii*, ed. J. Margolin, *Erasmi Opera Omnia*, 1-2 (Amsterdam: North Holland Publishing, 1971), p. 83.

play games with it, employing jests and figures of speech (*per lusum iocumque literarum figuris*). Basic learning should be coupled with and move immediately to the study of "modes of speaking" (*ad usum loquendi*), as a means of ensuring that they never develop barbarous habits in their Latin or their Greek.[54]

The other element in the longer title refers to teaching students how to read and interpret authors. Here too he was calling for a revolution, though Augustine's *On Christian Doctrine* was a much earlier attempt to set out ground rules on much the same fundamentals, how Christians were to use secular authors and the skills of secular rhetoric, and how they were to approach the reading and interpretation of the Bible. Erasmus was also convinced that this is the way to form good citizens: *How to Give Children a Rapid and Liberal Grounding* appeared in 1529.[55] Why, asks Erasmus, should we consider that age which is appropriate for learning good behavior to be inappropriate for the study of literature?[56]

Philipp Melanchthon and the experience of a new style of higher education. Melanchthon, a pioneer of the Renaissance study of Hebrew, was not left without a firm steer in that direction by his great-uncle. Reuchlin encouraged Melanchthon to become a humanist. It was he who suggested to Philipp that he might like to substitute the Greek for the German form of his surname (Schwarzerd, which meant "black earth"). Melanchthon became something of an early John Stuart Mill, in that he was intensively home educated. He was first taught by a private tutor then sent to Pforzheim to live with his grandmother. He was taught the Greek and Latin poets by the local rector, and Reuchlin took a strong continuing personal interest in his education. Melanchthon entered the University of Heidelberg at twelve, when humanism had already been partly established by the lectures of Rudolph Agricola (1442/1443-1485), who had taught there briefly from 1482 and was another Hebrew student. Young—but not much younger than many boys who became students at the time—he was able to study Greek alongside the usual lib-

[54]Ibid., p. 125.
[55]Erasmus, *De pueris statim ac liberaliter instituendis*, ed. J. Margolin, *Erasmi Opera Omnia*, 1-2 (Amsterdam: North Holland Publishing, 1971), p. 23.
[56]Ibid., p. 55.

eral arts, but although he had passed the examinations he was thought still too young in 1512 to be given his master's degree.

He gained his bachelor of arts degree in 1511, and went on to Tübingen, another of the advanced new modern universities of Germany where humanistic study was allowed, to continue his studies. He continued to study, trying his hand at the old higher degree subjects, particularly law. He got his M.A. in 1514 and began to teach in the university, first Roman poetry, then rhetoric. In 1516 he published an edition of Terence, and in 1518 a Greek grammar. He dipped into theology as well, reading the fathers and the Greek New Testament.

Melanchthon became an agitator for change in the university syllabus as he came to be known as a leading humanist reformer. Tübingen became an uncomfortable place for him to stay as a teacher because of the fierceness of the warfare between the old-fashioned scholastic teachers and the innovative humanist ones, so, at Martin Luther's invitation and with Reuchlin's recommendation, he moved again, to teach at Wittenberg in 1518. There he and Luther became friends and allies, with Melanchthon often providing a steadying mind, always reliable, useful for drafting texts the hyperbolic Luther may not have written so calmly or astutely.

Melanchthon the Reformer was clearly still a dedicated teacher. He kept a Latin school in his house for a decade, in which he taught boys their grammar in preparation for their university studies. In 1526 he started another experimental school, in Nuremberg, at a slightly more advanced pre-university level. This did not last, and Melanchthon was in any case turning his attention to the reform of the conventional university syllabus. His idea was to strengthen the study of the literary classics, as an end in itself and as a means of beginning a training in rhetoric. There was to be study of Greek and Hebrew. The study of logic, which had bulked enormously large in the late medieval course, was to shrink and be simplified. Philosophy had been a course mainly in the Aristotelian texts that had become available in Latin translations at the beginning of the thirteenth century, such as *On the Soul*, which raised questions at the borderline between physics and metaphysics. (The subject would eventually mutate into modern science, but not yet.) Melanchthon was most interested in bringing about an improvement in the way Scripture was studied, by considering the text in its original languages.[57]

Something of the flavor of Melanchthon's teaching is still to be tasted in his surviving Declamations, such as the *Musarum trium ludus* ("The game of the three muses," on the *trivium*).[58] *De Artibus Liberalibus* was given at Tübingen in 1517.[59] His policy statement *De corrigendis adolescentiae studiis*, given at Wittenberg on August 29, 1518, begins with a modest disclaimer of his unworthiness to address this assembly of masters and doctors and the Rector. He wants to discuss the way "the youth of Germany" are introduced to *hoc foelix certamen literarum*.[60] He rehearses the history of schools since the time of Charlemagne.[61] He describes the medieval norms, including mention of the place of the higher degree subjects of medicine and law as well as theology. This *ratio studiorum*, he explains, "held sway for about three centuries in Anglia, in Galliis, in Germania." The question now is whether some of these studies are redundant and others might take their place, particularly the study of Greek. What do the students learn now? Too much logic. *Logicum vim omnem ac discrimina sermonis tractat*.[62] How do you avoid their getting bored (*fastigia studiorum*)?[63] The best plan is to get the student to read Greek writings as well as Latin in a range of genres, such as works of philosophers, theologians, historians, orators, poets. The study of natural science is included in the study of Greek. Melanchthon complains (in an echo of Erasmus) that the "barbarians" demand "the titles and rights of learned teachers," in which category he himself would prefer to place individuals with cultivated minds and more modern tastes.[64] This address caused a certain furor, as contemporary correspondence shows.

Also like Erasmus, Melanchthon favored the study of rhetoric. This

---

[57]Sachiko Kusukawa, "Law and Gospel: The Importance of Philosophy at Reformation Wittenberg," *History of Universities* 11 (1992): 59-74.

[58]Melanchthon, *De corrigendis*, 11:10.

[59]Ibid., p. 5ff.

[60]Ibid., p. 15ff.

[61]Ibid., p. 15ff., col. 17.

[62]Ibid., col. 18.

[63]Ibid., col. 22.

[64]Melanchthon, *De corrigendis*, 11:15, as translated in *The Reformation in Its Own Words*, pp. 58-59.

had been the leading area of study in the late antique world, where skill in public speaking was highly valued, especially in politics and in the courts. In the Middle Ages the study of rhetoric had decayed, partly because there were few available classical textbooks, and partly because no comparably sophisticated political life requiring such skills awaited the educated man. The Middle Ages had invented three new arts of rhetoric: the art of formal letter-writing for the secular and ecclesiastical civil service, the art of poetry and the art of preaching, each involving formalized use of elements of ancient rhetoric. There was also study of "topics," which in ancient rhetoric had been the skill of collecting ready-made packets of material in the memory, both arguments and illustrations, so that the orator could speak fluently without a script.

In his *Encomium eloquentiae* Melanchthon argues for the return to something closer to the ancient uses of rhetoric. Every human society requires successful communication, he explains.[65] The benefits to the trained mind of the study of rhetoric include encouraging the students to compare themselves with the best models not only of style but of conduct, thus learning wisdom in their own dealings.[66] When it comes to the specific areas of rhetorical study, Melanchthon displays a strong consciousness of letter-writing as a literary genre. The eloquent approach to writing applies to letters too. He seems to have sought a conscious revival of the Ciceronian letter (as against the formats of the *ars dictaminis*). And he did not confine himself to Latin; sometimes he chose to write a letter to Reuchlin in German, and sometimes letter exchanges with other trained humanists were in Greek.

Melanchthon tried his academic reforming theories out at Tübingen and at Wittenberg—a university at which it was natural to attempt this, since he had Luther's backing—as well as Frankfurt, Leipzig, Rostock and Heidelberg.[67] Melanchthon designed a set of regulations for the arts faculty at Wittenberg in 1545. There were to be ten lecturers to teach languages and philosophy. Greek texts were specified as well as scientific texts of the ancient world such as Pliny's *Natural History*, and also moral

---

[65]Melanchthon, *De corrigendis*, 11, col. 52.
[66]Ibid., cols. 55-56.
[67]Where in 1557 he took part in the deliberations concerning the university statutes.

teaching.[68] Newer universities founded at Marburg (1527), Konigsberg (1544) and Jena (1558) also relied on his advice, and his former pupils helped to disseminate his ideas.[69]

Circles of friends. One of the results of this shift of educational thinking was to create a new social climate for humane studies. Eager "intellectuals" began to model themselves and their exchanges on the world of Roman antiquity in which a Cicero or a Seneca would send drafts of his writings to his friends, or read them aloud, and ask for comments.[70] This new style of activity of the mind also had some kinship with the late-Roman world of Augustine, who shared Cicero's ambition to retire from public life and spend his time in conversation with cultivated friends, discussing the world as it wagged politically, and higher questions about the cosmos. Augustine had done that for a time at Cassiciacum on Lake Como shortly after his conversion to Christianity in 386 and while he was preparing for baptism. Erasmus too made plans, which he did not live to realize, to enter with one or two like-minded friends into a reclusive house inside the walls of a Carthusian monastery and talk philosophy. To John Colet and Erasmus and many others of their day, this seemed an ideal life, serious, self-denying, intent upon what really mattered.

This ideal went on being attractive throughout the sixteenth century. John Astley writes to Roger Ascham (c. 1515-1568), tutor to the young Queen Elizabeth I of England, recollecting "our friendly fellowship together . . . our pleasant studies in reading together Aristotle's Rhetoric, Cicero and Livy." Here was a "commonwealth of learning," a "republic of letters." It seemed natural to Thomas Bodley (1545-1613) to have the latter phrase inscribed over the door of his new library in Oxford. This

---

[68] *Urkundenbuch det Universitat Wittenberg*, I, 1502-1611, ed. W. Friedensburg (Magdeburg: Selbstverlag der historischen Kommission für die Provinz Sachsen und für Anhalt, 1926), p. 267ff. See too Sachiko Kusukawa, "Law and Gospel: The Importance of Philosophy at Reformation Wittenberg," *History of Universities* 11 (1992): 33-57; "To the School of Wittenberg," 1546, *Corpus Reformatorum* 6, ed. Bretschneider (Halle, 1839), col. 58.

[69] *Supplementa Melanchthoniana* (1510-1528), ed. O. Clemen, vol. 1 (Leipzig: M. Heinsius, 1926).

[70] The rise of intellectuals as a distinctive class has been put in the sixteenth century (though the noun *intellectual* gained currency with this modern meaning only in the nineteenth century). It has been suggested that intellectuals were typically "alienated" (Constance M. Furey, *Erasmus, Contarini, and the Religious Republic of Letters* [Cambridge: Cambridge University Press, 2006], p. 165).

was one of the ways in which educated people who were not intending to be clergy or professional clerks of any sort began to enter into theological and intellectual controversies of the day. It was a huge change, revolutionizing the universities.

The invention of printing changes the student experience. The book needs of medieval university students, primarily for copies of the set texts, were much narrower than those of the early modern world. The scholastic method depended on the presumption that such books should be studied very closely in lectures (literally *lectiones*, "readings"), and in a particular way, line by line, even word by word. So medieval students needed books, but they did not necessarily need academic libraries of the more recent sort. The set books were sometimes made available in convenient pamphlet form or in "gatherings" by university booksellers, who could thus hire portions to students as they progressed through the lecture course. So study did not depend on everyone having a personal copy. In some lectures of which records survive it is apparent that the lecturer read a brief portion of the text out, pausing while the students wrote it down, before expounding it for them. Commentaries mainly took the form of extracts from respected earlier commentators, linked to the passages they illuminated. This approach continued, with modifications, after the invention of printing. Claude Mignault was a working lecturer in a college of the University of Paris in the 1570s. Pamphlet editions of the texts used by his students are still in existence, in which students' lecture notes survive.[71] This was a practice of immense importance in the way it had conventionally influenced the study of the Bible, as we shall see.

Nevertheless, it began to be perceived that a university ought to have its own collection of books. Encouragement of donations to Oxford in the fifteenth century went on till the chests where the books were kept were bursting and the pressure demand from readers and students was causing problems; corporate ownership was established. Restricting access and finding a permanent place to keep the books, attaching them to the furniture by chains to ensure they were not sto-

---

[71] Anthony Grafton, "Teacher, Text and Pupil in the Renaissance Class-Room: A Case Study from a Parisian College," *History of Universities* 1 (1981): 37-70.

len, all helped, as did the provision of reading desks.[72]

With the invention of printing came the transformation of attitudes to the book and to the ways in which it could be studied, and the emergence of a new concept of the library needs of universities. It had not yet arrived at the insight that even the paper detritus of daily life might be something a library of this sort ought to keep for posterity, but it was closer to that position than to the concepts of the first centuries of universities' existence. The substantive shift was from the concentration on an authoritative set book for each course to the notion that more extensive background reading was appropriate. This was in some respects a return to the classical idea of a library; that is the way the ancient world thought of it. The "vanished libraries of classical antiquity, included the considerable private libraries of such figures as Cicero and Varro (116-27 B.C.), running sometimes to thousands of rolls."[73] The same urge to form a collection for private reading and personal edification created monastic libraries in the Middle Ages in the West.

In either case, they were reference collections rather than reading collections. Many of the surviving copies of the philosophical set books introduced into the syllabus early in the thirteenth century with the arrival of the Latin Aristotle seem to have been made not by professional scribes but by the students themselves, constructing their own copies.[74] Students who were friars might be able to borrow the Order's copy of an expensive textbook for use during their course.

Two late-sixteenth-century (1572) students at Toulouse, one of whom died and the other dropped out, each left belongings including printed books.[75] The student who died, whose name was Lagarde, seems to have had 150 books, a writing desk, a candlestick, stationery and ink-holders and a stove, as well as a sword, a gun, a chess set, two lutes and some music to play them from, as well as a set of toilet articles, but nothing else is known about him so it is difficult to place this collection in his

---

[72]*History of the University of Oxford*, 2:476-77.

[73]Michael Lapidge, *The Anglo-Saxon Library* (Oxford: Oxford University Press, 2006), chap. 1.

[74]*The Cambridge History of the Book in Britain*, ed. Nigel Morgan and Rodney Thomson (Cambridge: Cambridge University Press, 2008), p. 455.

[75]Joan Davies, "Student Libraries in Sixteenth Century Toulouse," *History of Universities* 3 (1983): 62-86.

family or in his life. The books were course books, some recent Toulouse editions, including thirty law books.[76]

The student would usually still need to take notes to provide himself with a record of the lectures and the portions of the set texts they referred to. The old student habit of *reportatio* died hard. Jean Cécile Frey, who taught philosophy and medicine in Paris colleges between 1607 and 1631, had a student who published six bodies of notes as *Opuscula varia nusquam edita* in Paris (1646) after his death.[77]

Axioms, articles, commonplaces and conclusions. One thing did not change in these altered and innovative universities, even where it was the fashion to reject scholasticism. A fondness for disputation persisted, and that meant formal disputation, conducted according to established rules, like an intellectual jousting match. University disputations had begun in the twelfth century as a convenient way of dealing with questions arising from lectures. Students practiced answering such questions by assembling arguments for and against, with the presiding master determining (deciding) which side had won. The same method was used for examining students to see whether they had achieved the necessary standard to be awarded a degree and graduate. A third use of the disputation was to provide a more or less public forum for debate when a controversy arose. And a fourth use of one element in the method was the listing of propositions or "articles," statements of the sort which could form questions or conclusions.

The medieval enthusiasm for the Euclidean method of argument from which this was derived is startling to modern eyes. Its great attraction was that it offered something much more certain than the probable arguments of ordinary syllogisms. Those depended on the highly variable force of the propositions from which the conclusion was drawn. In geometry, Euclid began from self-evident truths (translated into Latin in the twelfth century by the phrase *communis animi conceptiones*), statements whose truth all rational persons should accept

---

[76]Ann Blair, "Ovidius Methodizatus: The Metamorphoses of Ovid in a Sixteenth Century Paris College," *History of Universities* 9 (1990): 73-118.

[77]Ann Blair, "The Teaching of Natural Philosophy in Early Seventeenth Century Paris: The Case of Jean Cécile Frey," *History of Universities* 12 (1993): 95-158.

as soon as they hear them. It adds some postulates and some defini-
tions. It then employs formal reasoning to get from these to various
conclusions, which can be taken to be so solidly established that they
too should be taken to be proven, and further arguments can be built
with these new bricks. So it proceeded from the recognition that to
begin from necessary propositions is to arrive at necessary conclusions.
It was known as "demonstrative" because it explicitly demonstrates its
procedures and conclusions.

There was a particularly strong motivation among some to achieve
this in the study of theology, for nothing could be more desirable than
certainly in that area. But the only subject in which it could be asserted
with any confidence that self-evident truths led to inescapable conclusions seemed to be Euclidean geometry. Experiments were made in
compiling lists of *regulae,* or axioms, for theology, for example by Alan
of Lille (d. 1202/1203) in the late twelfth century and by Nicholas of
Amiens (1147–c. 1200) in his *De arte catholicae fidei,* probably in the early
thirteenth. Alan tried to create a linear sequence in which one axiom
was derived from another. He found that the further he moved from his
starting point, the very first and most absolute self-evident truth, that
God is a Monad, the less certain subsequent axioms looked. Nicholas
was more ambitious and attempted Euclidean demonstrations rather
than a line of axioms each derived from the one before. But he too
found that he could not demonstrate the whole of Christian doctrine in
that way so as to establish it all as incontrovertible knowledge.[78]

This challenge ran on century by century, alongside the adversarial
disputation in which one probable argument was tested against another
and a winner declared. Scholars developed a liking for the short pithy
statement which had the look of a self-evident or at least a decisively
established truth. It might be called a *conclusio* or a *thesis* or an *articulus,*
or a *locus communis* ("commonplace," after the "topic" of ancient rhetoric). It became a favorite academic activity to find and list such axioms,
and a cat's cradle of interconnected *axiomata* was created by the very
process of adversarial disputation, as axioms or theses became *quaestio-*

---

[78]G. R. Evans, *Alan of Lille: The Frontiers of Theology in the Later Twelfth Century* (Cambridge: Cambridge University Press, 1983).

nes for the purposes of having a debate about them, and the opinions of rival masters were cited alongside the old *auctoritates*.

These "portions of knowledge" hoping to be seen as *certain* knowledge became fashionable in a new way in the sixteenth century as they were used in the compilation of lists of confessional statements. *Loci Communes* was a favorite title for such collections.

Martin Chemnitz (1522-1586), for example, published his *Loci Communes*, including some prefatory epigrams and an oration on the study of the fathers, and including an approving discussion of Melanchthon's work. He stresses the continuity of approach such *loci* represent. They are asserted to be a means the church has always used to set out points of doctrine so that they are pithy and clear and their interrelationship (ordering) is apparent (*breviter, ordine, proprie, et perspicue explicata*). He believes the *locus* was in use even before the time of Peter Lombard.[79] Richard Smith (1500-1563), by contrast, stood against Melanchthon in his *Refutatio locorum communium theologicorum Philippi Melanchtonis* (1563)—but he did not challenge the use of the method, merely the assertions made in the *loci*.

"Articles" remained a favored genre in academe, on both sides of the Reformation debates. *Articles by the Theological Faculty of Paris. The Dean and Faculty of Theology of Paris to All the Faithful in Christ* prompted Calvin to publish an "antidote" to each.[80] There is a heavy irony in such sentences asserting the reliability of such nuggets of "certain knowledge"—"it has seemed proper to set down briefly, in the following order, what, in reference to the Articles generally controverted, Doctors and Preachers ought to teach, and the rest of the faithful, with the whole Church, believe"—if this is to be taken as reliable, settled, not to be questioned, because it is a corporate decision of the Masters. "This being a magisterial definition, it is to be observed, that proofs are not added, because to do so were to derogate from the ancient privileges of the School of Paris." And, it is teasingly added, such a joint decision ought to have more force than the view of a single individual. "Since in the

---

[79]Martin Chemnitz, *Locorum theologicorum . . . quibus et Loci Communes P. Melanchthonis explicantur* (1599), p. 21.
[80]John Calvin, *Works, Tracts and Treatises on the Reformation*, 1:71.

school of Pythagoras the authority of one man prevailed to such a degree that his *ipse dixit* sufficed for proof, how much more ought that which so many of our masters have together, and with one voice pronounced, to suffice?"

Along with an increasing output of *Loci Communes*, articles of faith were commonly used in confessional documents of the sixteenth century, as in the Lutheran Augsburg Confession and the Thirty-Nine Articles of the Church of England. So these aspects of scholasticism was far from moribund. Scholasticism as an academic undertaking had a lively future among the Reformers and their heirs.

16

Luther and His Heirs

The Moderate Reformers

The Conversion of Martin Luther and Its Consequences

In 1505 Martin Luther was riding from his home back to university in a thunderstorm when lightning struck the ground close by. He took this as a divine prompting it would be unwise to resist, and decided to become an Augustinian Friar.[1]

Luther had been born into a bourgeois German family. He was the eldest son and his ambitious father wanted him to be a lawyer. He was sent to a series of schools, including one run by the Brethren of the Common Life. Then he went to University at Erfurt, and it was in the house of the Brethren of the Common Life at Erfurt that he decided to live his new life. He later described his student days at Erfurt disparagingly as consisting mainly of drinking and sex, so he was now seeking the strongest possible contrast. He applied himself to what was expected of him, trying desperately hard to meet the new demands.

Experienced senior figures in the order, including Johann von Staupitz (c. 1460-1524), to whom Luther confessed his sins at immense length, had seen this kind of thing before and knew that it led to breakdown, so

---

[1]On the reforming movements taken as a whole, see Diarmaid MacCulloch, *Reformation: Europe's House Divided, 1490-1700* (London: Allen Lane, 2004); and Euan Cameron, *The European Reformation* (Oxford: Oxford University Press, 1991).

Luther was instructed to begin an academic career to take his mind off this obsessive preoccupation with his inner life. It was a commonplace of the spiritual life from the patristic period to experience fear of hell, terror of conscience, spiritual despair. Here is an example of a decision often faced by medieval academics who belonged to religious orders, that is, whether to concentrate on the spiritual or the intellectual life. Staupitz hoped perhaps to cure Luther, to relieve him of suffering, as well as to prevent a more serious collapse.[2]

It had become apparent in the thirteenth century, almost in the first generation when universities were invented and the cleverer recruits to the orders of the friars were sent to study in houses of their orders where they could get a higher education in the local university, that this was going to set up some uncomfortable tensions. Franciscans such as Bonaventure sought to keep an appropriate place for the spiritual life and the kind of writing which helped people to live a consciously spiritual life. His *Journey of the Soul to God* (*Itinerarium Mentis ad Deum*) offered a thinking man's spiritual journey. Others, Dominicans among them, concentrated on a densely packed course of study with the emphasis on the cultivation of powers of reasoning.

Von Staupitz, a doctor of theology and head of the theology faculty at Wittenberg from its foundation in 1502, had himself found that scholarly work could be a helpful distraction from inner turmoil. The medieval higher degrees (which always offered the same choice of theology, medicine or law, though not all of them could be studied everywhere) still followed the traditional syllabus and required years of study. So Luther's formal theological knowledge became detailed and extensive. In 1507, he was ordained a priest, and by 1508 he was lecturing in theology at the University of Wittenberg as a bachelor of theology. He got his doctorate in 1512.

Indulgences and the ninety-five theses. In the year 1516-1517 Johann Tetzel, one of the Dominicans who were busy touring Europe selling indulgences to raise money to build the great basilica which is now St. Peter's in Rome, arrived in Germany. Luther wrote to the archbishop of

---

[2]See Martin Brecht, *Martin Luther: His Road to Reformation, 1483-1531* (Philadelphia: Fortress Press, 1985-1993), p. 81.

Mainz and Magdeburg to protest, enclosing a list of academic conclusions challenging the doctrine of indulgences.

These were, in essence, only a list of the sort of conclusions or questions that had routinely been used in disputations in medieval universities for centuries. When Luther (or his students) posted his ninety-five theses on a door at Wittenberg in 1517, he was just putting out a traditional challenge to debate:

> Out of love for the truth and the desire to bring it to light, the following propositions will be discussed at Wittenberg, under the presidency of the Reverend Father Martin Luther, Master of Arts and of Sacred Theology, and Lecturer in Ordinary on the same at that place. Wherefore he requests that those who are unable to be present and debate orally with us, may do so by letter.[3]

The topics of the theses are untidily arranged, but they cluster around certain concerns. The first concern is the management of sin. Luther is impatient with the formal penitential process, making confession and performing penitential acts of satisfaction, administered by the priests who declare absolution. He thinks grappling with sin and its consequences ought to be regarded as the lifelong task of the soul and to be part of a process of forming a relationship with God. The church's role (or specifically, as Luther came to see it, that of the pope) is almost incidental to this real inward process. Penances can be imposed by the church and it can remit the ones it has imposed. The church can declare God's forgiveness, but it cannot of its own authority remit sin. It cannot reserve penances to be discharged in purgatory, for death brings an end to the penitential process. This was an important assertion, because the system of indulgences rested on the presumption that when a person died there were likely to be undischarged penances (and that purgatory existed to allow them to be discharged).

Luther was concerned here to ease the "terrified conscience," the conscience so frightened by the teachings of the church about the threat of punishment after death that it experiences despair, not hope and love.

---

[3] *Disputation of Doctor Martin Luther on the Power and Efficacy of Indulgences, Works of Martin Luther,* ed. and trans. Adolph Spaeth, L. D. Reed and Henry Eyster Jacobs (Philadelphia: A. J. Holman, 1915), 1:29-38, www.iclnet.org/pub/resources/text/wittenberg/luther/web/ninetyfive.html.

He cries out, just as Wyclif had done, against "human impositions" on the faithful, and argues that it is positively misleading to tell people they must focus on the penitential process to be saved. On the contrary, they must concentrate on faith and repentance. Similarly, he claims, the church ought not to be marketing the alleged advantages of paying for private masses. The church has no true "treasury of merits" with which to pay for the release of souls from purgatory but only possesses "the Most Holy Gospel of the glory and the grace of God," which is there for all, and not under the control of the church's hierarchy.

The theses seem to have caught the popular imagination and they were translated into German and printed within weeks, with copies reaching readers beyond Germany. This essentially academic challenge was proving to have a popular appeal, once it had got past the language barrier and into the vernacular.

Luther did not have the satisfaction of having his challenge taken up straightaway in a public disputation in front of a live crowd. The archbishop, who had a conflict of interest because he had personal need of the revenue from the sale of indulgences, played safe and sent the theses to Rome for examination. The Vatican took its time to formulate a formal response; it sent emissaries to contest Luther's teaching, who irritated him and contributed toward his becoming more staunchly "antipapalist." The emperor was alerted too, and he suggested that Luther should be brought to answer for the views expressed in his theses at the Diet of Augsburg in 1518. (The German emperor held such diets or parliaments at intervals and the occasion was not exceptional in itself.) He offered to guarantee Luther's safe conduct.

Luther was in no mood for compromise. He heightened the tone of his challenges to the church magisterium and the pope. In Rome, noisy public slanging matches with academics were thought to be unhelpful, so in early 1519 the papal nuncio was looking for an irenic solution. Dogged Luther agreed to stop saying such things if his enemies stopped denying them.

This precarious plan for peaceful compromise was capsized by the theologian Johann Maier von Eck (1486-1543). He was tall and broad and impressive, an excellent orator and a doughty combatant, and he could pull in the crowds to a public disputation every bit as well as Luther. He had been educated at the universities of Heidelberg and Tübingen, and had continued as a university teacher. He knew Luther personally; they had even been friends. In 1517 there had been quite a merry exchange of "Obelisks" and "Asterisks." Eck's *Obelisks* argued against Luther's ninety-five theses and called Luther a Hussite, and Luther argued back in the *Asterisks* and called Eck names in return.[4]

It began to seem that Luther might get his public debate after all. The combatants threw down challenges, including setting special conditions, just as though they were knights agreeing to joust in a tournament. Eck said he would debate with Andreas Bodenstein von Karlstadt (1486-1541), one of Luther's supporters, although this was a ruse to get to Luther. Luther was unable to keep out of it, and when at the end of 1518 Eck published the twelve theses he proposed to defend against Karlstadt, Luther offered to join the fray as well.

The debate took place at Leipzig in 1519, dealing with the currently contentious topic of the way human free will works. A stock topic of the university lecture room, and one which had been of interest ever since Augustine wrote about it a thousand years earlier, was whether a sinful human being could do any good thing of his own free will. Some said the human will was so broken by sin that only with God's help (grace) could anyone choose to do good. Some said that even then the good thing done was not to the credit of the person who did it because it was by God's enabling mercy. It was easy to see that that could undermine the whole theology of the benefit of doing good works as a way of pleasing God. Karlstadt was easily vanquished among the technicalities, but not so easily Luther, who stepped into the ring next after him. Arguing backward and forward, Eck and Luther tackled the papacy, the penitential system and purgatory, taking up twenty-three days of July in argument. The result was a draw, for the judges could not decide who had won (though on the whole it was thought that Eck had).

It cannot be overemphasized how conventional an academic passage of arms this was. No one seems to have paused to consider whether a

---

[4]Erwin Iserloh, *Johannes Eck (1486-1543): Scholastiker Humanist Kontroverstheologe* (Münster: Verlag Aschendorff, 1981).

change of heart or a change of conviction could actually result from such efforts. It was chiefly a display of academic bravura and knowledge of the standard arguments, answers and authorities.

Yet Eck attempted to follow up his "victory" by getting the Elector of Saxony to burn Luther's writings in public; he tried to get German universities to condemn Luther; he went to Rome and came back with the papal bull *Exsurge Domine*, condemning forty-one of Luther's alleged arguments.

This was a mistake, politically speaking. Germany, especially the universities, which have always defended their autonomy, responded angrily to this interference. An indignant Eck demanded that the state should join its forces with those of the church, and urged the emperor to move against Luther and his supporters. Charles V responded cooperatively, ordering that Luther be brought to answer before the Diet of Worms. This was now politics and a power struggle in which there would need to be face-saving to achieve any resolution short of disaster for Luther. And it was to lead to a new set of rules and assumptions about the respective roles of church and state in the control of ecclesiastical affairs in a given political territory.

Johann van der Ecken, chancellor of the Archbishop of Trier, employed a method of allegation which had been used before at ecclesiastical trials of alleged heretics; it involved confronting the accused with his alleged published views, usually selected or modified so as to appear damning, and ask him to say whether he still believed these things or would recant. Eck put copies of Luther's writings before him and asked him to confirm that he had written them and that these were indeed his opinions. Luther had the wit to ask for time to consider before he answered the second question, for the trap yawned largely before him. His reply was that he would rely on Scripture for evidence not popes or councils.

There was then much secret plotting and meeting behind the scenes in order to decide how to act against Luther and win influential support—just as there had been in analogous exercises in earlier centuries like the occasions when Peter Abelard and Gilbert of Poitiers had been put on trial by the church in the twelfth century. Charles V issued the

Edict of Worms, which turned Luther into an outlaw and forbade the emperor's subjects from associating with him, possessing his writings or adopting his ideas. However, the politicians acted adroitly to avoid confrontation and violence from Luther's supporters. Arrangements were made to ensure Luther was able to leave Worms safely, and the Elector of Saxony hid him in Wartburg Castle at Eisenach, where Luther did some hard thinking and got on with some work.

Luther's change of heart and the discovery of justification by faith. While all this had been going on, Luther had experienced the most transformative experience of his spiritual and intellectual life. Lecturing on the Bible had been a staple of medieval theology courses since before the beginning of the universities. For new lecturers learning how to lecture, particular prominence was traditionally given to the Psalms for the Old Testament and the Pauline epistles for the New. Luther was no exception. But for him these required lectures were more than routine practice exercises. In 1519, he says, he gave a fresh course of lectures on the Psalms. He felt more confident about this than he had previously because he had now gained experience in lecturing on Romans, Galatians and Hebrews.

He had found himself trying unsuccessfully to understand the meaning of the phrase *iustitia Dei* in the Vulgate Latin version of Romans 1:17. His theological training had taught him to understand this to mean the justice that is a divine attribute and according to which God punishes sinners. He did not find this a comfortable understanding. It left him feeling that he could never be sure that he had satisfied this just God, and he found it impossible to love such a demanding and threatening God. "I pestered St. Paul about what he had meant," he says. At last, after many sleepless nights, he realized that the phrase must be understood in its context, where it says that "the just [person] lives by faith." What if what fundamentally mattered to God was that he, Luther, should have faith, trusting only in God's grace demonstrated in the work of Christ on his behalf? Once he grasped this idea, he says, the struggle ended, the burden fell away, and he felt as though he had been born again and had entered paradise. This new insight cast all the Scriptures in a different light. Excitedly, he recalled other passages, seeing that they too should be interpreted so as to understand that this God in whom we trust sees us as we are in Christ and makes us like him. God's work is the work he does in us. God's power is what makes us powerful. God's wisdom makes us wise. God's strength makes us strong. God's salvation saves us, and so on.[5]

Scholar as he was, he did his research. He read Augustine's *On the Spirit and the Letter* and found that, as far as he could see, Augustine seemed to have reached a similar conclusion. He began to formulate his doctrine of justification by faith alone. Luther's argument that only faith grasps the mercy of God began by removing any possibility that God is moved to forgive and bless by anything a sinner does. He argues that because of original sin, the default state of all human beings is sinful. Only God can alter that by a free act of grace.

For Luther this was not to be a straightforward matter of thinking things through all at once. He was going to have to unfold the implications in the course of a high profile and dangerous battle. He often conducted it in extreme and acrimonious language. And in so doing Luther exemplifies a pattern of behavior that became characteristic of the polemic of the times. The subject matter of grace, forgiveness and good works notwithstanding, disputants regularly treated one another with strong personal animosity, scattering expletives.

What did Luther mean by sola scriptura? Meanwhile, the contest begun by the posting of the ninety-five theses had gone on. After 1517 there was high tension in the air. As he settled into the role of rebel against the church authorities, Luther went on writing fiercely against indulgences and those who countenanced their sale for profit. His range of doctrinal areas needing review was expanding as he thought things through, and by 1521 he was beginning to crystallize his objections to various teachings of the church—for example, that the Mass is a sacrifice, that the pope has a right to require confessions.

He also further developed his position on the Bible while he worked on his translation of the New Testament into German. In a passage published as part of his *Table Talk* he claimed that when he

---

[5] *Preface to the Complete Edition of Luther's Latin Works* (1545), trans. Andrew Thornton (Berlin: de Gruyter, 1967), www.iclnet.org/pub/resources/text/wittenberg/luther/tower.txt.

was young, he "read the Bible over and over and over again, and was so perfectly acquainted with it, that [he] could, in an instant, have pointed to any verse that might have been mentioned." This, he said, was a better use of study than reading commentaries. He had tried that, but he had soon cast them aside. "I found therein many things my conscience could not approve, as being contrary to the sacred text. 'Tis always better to see with one's own eyes than with those of other people.'"[6]

For Protestants of the Reformation, the Bible as the Word of God was the sole and sufficient normative authority for Christian faith and life. No gloss or commentary could add to it's intrinsic authority or meaning in any way. As Zwingli was to put it in the fifth of his sixty-seven *Conclusions*, "All who consider other teachings equal to or higher than the Gospel err, and do not know what the Gospel is."

This does not mean the magisterial Reformers rejected the significance of the church or its tradition. The driving force of this attitude was a wish to prevent what the Reformers perceived as an intruding institutional magisterium from seeking to claim to be the Bible's only official interpreter. Still, this tended to put the Reformers in one of two positions, each of which had its own difficulties. They could insist the Bible is in some sense its own interpreter; or they could say that the Holy Spirit is the direct guide of the individual private reader.

Meanwhile, the Reformers themselves were always keen to interpret the Bible for others in their sermons, and they were far from reluctant to engage the old commentators (and to write their own commentaries). For example, when Calvin addresses the issue of the Gospel of Matthew claiming that Christ being called "a Nazarene" is a fulfillment of biblical prophecy (though no explicit prophecy of this exists in the Old Testament), he says:

> But it remains to be seen, in what part of Scripture the prophets have stated that this name would be given to Christ. Chrysostom, finding himself unable to loose the knot, cuts it by saying, that many books of the prophets have perished. But this answer has no probability: for, though

---

[6]"On God's Word," *Table Talk* 33.

the Lord, in order to punish the indifference of his ancient people, deprived them of some part of Scripture, or left out what was less necessary, yet, since the coming of Christ, no part of it has been lost. In support of that view, a strange blunder has been made, by quoting a passage of Josephus, in which he states that Ezekiel left two books: for Ezekiel's prophecy of a new temple and kingdom is manifestly distinct from his other predictions, and may be said to form a new work. But if all the books of Scripture which were extant in the time of Matthew, remain entire to the present day, we must find somewhere the passage quoted from the prophets.[7]

Moreover, and for the same reasons, the Protestant instinct was to treat the Scriptures as given. It was as hard for Protestants to admit that God could have allowed errors and imperfections to appear there as it was for the Roman Catholic Church at the Council of Trent to accept the implications of the mistakes which had recently been found littered throughout the Vulgate. It was a careful balancing act, therefore, to uphold *sola scriptura* by appealling to the Spirit speaking through the Scriptures in the midst of a complex history of revelation and a variegated tradition of interpretation.

1530s: Luther's German Bible. Luther began his translation of the Bible during his imprisonment in Wartburg Castle in 1521-1522. He was not the first to attempt a German Bible, but he became the most successful of the day. His ambition was to make the Bible available to the German nation, indeed all the people of the Holy Roman Empire. He went to some trouble to find familiar colloquialisms to make the result reader-friendly, listening—when he was free to move about again—to the talk of ordinary people in the street. But he was also, like other translators into the European vernaculars at the time, tempted to ensure that the meaning reflected the reforming theology they were embracing. For example, Luther added *allein* to Romans 3:28, so that it was absolutely clear that Paul was advocating justification by faith "alone." When he was challenged, he said it was his translation and his business. He wanted his translation to make doctrinal points, to speak

---

[7]Calvin, *Commentary on Matthew 2.23*, available online at http://calvin.biblecommenter.com/matthew/2.htm

to the people of Germany not only in their own language but in language that conveyed a faithful (Lutheran) interpretation.[8] This was a similar instinct to the one which made Miles Coverdale and other contemporary English translators sensitive to the implications of choosing one English word rather than another to represent God's own Word. *Priest* and *church,* for example, were English terms with strong political and theological associations.

Luther began with the New Testament and used the Greek text Erasmus had prepared, which had come out in a second edition in 1519. Here were conjoined both Renaissance and Reformation strands of the changes which were taking place. Luther could also be critical of the value or the very canonicity of whole books. In the case of the New Testament, these were the epistle to the Hebrews, the epistle of James and that of Jude, and especially the book of Revelation. He changed the accepted order of the books and put these last in token of his view that they had a lesser claim to be the evangelical Word of God. His version was published in 1522, a few months after he had been able to go back to Wittenberg.

Understandably, the Old Testament took a good deal longer. With the aid of a group of collaborators, including Philipp Melanchthon, Luther was ready in 1534 to add a translation of the Old Testament to his 1522 New Testament (he continued to amend the text over the course of his career). The Apocrypha, the books whose canonicity most Reformers denied, he left to Melanchthon and Justus Jonas to translate. Even in the canonical Old Testaments Scriptures, however, Luther had his doubts about Esther.

The trouble he took to make his translation readable by ordinary people, coupled with his own notoriety and the success of the Lutheran movement, had a significant effect on the evolution of a German language that had become fragmented into dialects whose speakers could be almost unintelligible to one another. The German people who sympathized with his views took the translation to their bosoms, carried it about, learned passages by heart, quoted it in debate. In English there

---

[8]Heinz Siegfried Bluhm, *Martin Luther: Creative Translator* (St. Louis: Concordia Publishing, 1965).

was as yet no single dominant version which could have quite the same effect. The King James Version was still more than half a century away when Luther died.

MELANCHTHON, MODERATION AND
BUILDING A BRIDGE BETWEEN
THE ACADEMIC AND THE POPULAR

While Luther was at work in hiding, the University of Wittenberg was beginning a program of reform of its own and—as an academic—Philipp Melanchthon was coming under a variety of pressures from students and colleagues.[9] Melanchthon began to think and write in defense of Luther with his customary calmness (and a restraint that led some to think him diffident). He also saw the advantage of creating a full, clear statement of the Lutheran position, amounting to a Lutheran theology, so that Luther's ideas would not look like mere reactions and scattergun responses to polemical challenges.

Melanchthon published a first version of his *Commonplaces on Theological Themes* or *Loci Communes Rerum Theologicarum* in 1521. It went through several iterations, the final version coming in 1555. Being systematic was always important to Melanchthon. He always tried to bring order, restraint and reason to Luther's energetically expressed views. This seems to have been done with no intention of self-aggrandizement, no rivalry with Luther, no ambition to create a "Melanchthonism." His idea was to set out a series of statements in the highly respected style of the demonstrative method, with discussions accompanying each to provide proof and support. For example, Melanchthon begins the 1555 version of his *Commonplaces* with a first locus thus: "In earnest invocation of God it is necessary to consider what one wants to address, what God is, how he is known, where and how he has revealed himself, and both if and why he hears our pleas and cries."[10]

Melanchthon's students probably started him on this project. It seems that the first version was an attempt to publish a correction to an

---

[9]Robert Stupperich, *Melanchthon*, trans. Robert H. Fischer (London: Lutterworth, 1966).
[10]Philipp Melanchthon, *On Christian Doctrine: Loci Communes*, trans. and ed. Clyde L. Manschreck (New York: Oxford University Press, 1965), p. 3.

unauthorized printing of his own lectures on Paul's epistle to the Romans by some of his students.[11] This sort of thing had been the standard practice of the later medieval centuries, when students created a *reportatio* of lectures (with the master's permission), but in getting them printed they were adopting the new technology of the day and giving them a wider reach than could have been possible in the days of hand-copied manuscripts. In this way, the printing press was the Facebook or Twitter of its time.

The dissemination of the *Loci*, once Melanchthon published them on his own account, was energetic, with eighteen Latin editions and several German translations published within a few years. So the *Loci Communes* were direct products of the academic environment of Wittenberg in a new age, a deliberate polarization for the educated non-specialist reader.

The townspeople become involved. The discussion going on in the university and with the prince and the court was affecting ordinary people too. The heated atmosphere in Wittenberg also produced riots involving the townspeople, with images being smashed in the churches. The intensity of this was a phenomenon of a new era. Medieval dissidents had sometimes seemed to threaten civil unrest, but not on this scale. The Zwickau prophets, for example, who were millenarian extremists on the Anabaptist wing of the reforming movement, appeared in that city calling for adult baptism to replace infant baptism, announcing that the end of the world was at hand and Christ was about to return—and most dangerous of all to the secular authorities, preaching radical social equality.

The alarmed town council called Luther back to help them restore order, and he returned to Wittenberg in March 1522. He preached a series of sermons, reminding the congregation of Christ's teaching about charity and patience, and calling on them to avoid violence. This did a good deal to restore public order, and for a time there was a following wind for Luther's attempts to work with the civic authorities to establish a new church order and exclude radical and revolutionary reformers. This was an important period in the forming of Lutheranism because it helped to place Luther and the great majority of his sympathizers—de-

---

[11] Ibid., p. xxiii.

spite the violence of his own language—among the moderate Reformers and to separate them from certain kinds of extremists. Luther and
Melanchthon remained a worry to the authorities but not to the extent
these "prophets" were.

Liberating the religious. Mistrust of the religious orders had been
rumbling since at least the time of Wyclif. It will not have been forgotten that they caused popular offense by the wealth of some of their
houses, and in the case of the mendicants, by their skill in inserting
themselves into the corridors of power as confessors to important people. The medieval dissidents fixed on the outrageousness of any claim to
be able to rise higher before God by taking vows. Wyclif was particularly fierce on the subject of such second "baptisms."

Luther had of course himself been an Augustinian friar, and as such
was under obedience within his order. Rome wrote to Staupitz as vicar-
general of the order in 1520, demanding that he bring Luther under control. By 1522 discontent among local Augustinians had many leaving.
Some became uncomfortable about saying private masses, and students
broke up the altar at the Franciscan house. This was the beginning of the
wholesale breakdown of the system of religious orders across northern
Europe. Nuns became restless too, and Luther became personally involved with their bid for change and liberation when he helped a dozen
nuns escape from their Cistercian monastery in herring barrels in 1523.

One of these, Katharina von Bora, became Luther's wife in 1525, and
this much-noticed event initiated a departure from the clerical celibacy
the church had succeeded in imposing universally in the eleventh century. Melanchthon was surprised and concerned; he thought Luther
had gotten carried away and had rushed into this marriage. (It was not
long since he had been telling his friends he thought he would never
marry, and he had grown used to living in a certain comfortable bachelor squalor.) Nevertheless, leader after leader of the reform began mar-
rying as the sixteenth century wore on. It almost came to be expected as
a gesture or a statement of commitment to overturning a previous ide-
alization of monasticism.

The women who married those former priests and monks who became
reformers and were emboldened to break their vows of celibacy do not on

the whole stand out as reformers in their own right. Although some reforming communities allowed women to preach, they were not generally encouraged to serve as ministers or leaders. The times did not easily favor it, although the Lollards had had some women preachers in the fifteenth century, and they appeared again among the Methodists of the eighteenth.

Forming a church. Things had now reached a stage in the German Reformation where Luther and Melanchthon and their supporters needed to think hard about what makes a reformed church still truly the church. To reject papal authority was to reject much of the structure and rationale of the existing institutional church, with its pyramidal power structure and its claim to be led by the successor of Peter, with all the spiritual (and temporal) authority that was taken to entail. If that was not right, questions were going to arise, much like those of the early centuries, about the ways in which new or different ecclesiastical communities or gathered congregations could be or become churches, and their relationship to *the* church. One answer, favored by many Reformers, was to say like Augustine that though there are myriad true churches, the one, holy, catholic church—of which they are little outposts—is invisible.

Luther had thought at first that it would be possible to allow each congregation to choose its minister. Some reforming communities—the predecessors of the Congregationalists—were doing so, but with the arrival of the Zwickau prophets it quickly became clear that that could lead to a number of undesirable results. Demagogues of extreme views could take over congregations where there was no higher or broader authority to ensure that ministers had an adequate education, that their teachings were not heretical and that they could be held to account when necessary.

So in the second half of the 1520s Luther seems to have come to the conclusion that there would have to be a supervisory structure. There would also need to be requirements about the form of service, for it was not in dispute that a liturgy embodies a theology and that regular use of approved forms of words in worship can help to ensure that the congregation holds an orthodox faith.[12] In other words, worship mat-

---

[12]In response to demands for a German liturgy, Luther wrote a *German Mass*, which he published in early 1526.

ters to the spiritual health and growth of Christians.

Luther's direct influence in making these constructive practical proposals was chiefly in the territories of the Elector of Saxony, and he accepted the ancient presumption that the church ought to be organized locally in a way that matched the territorial arrangements for secular government. Congregations further afield sought his advice and followed his example.

Luther and the popular touch. Academic or political writing was not going to win a popular following without some ingredients which would give it popular appeal. Luther was a great talker at the dinner table, with a forthright manner. Even if he monopolized the discourse, he would not fail to entertain and to move his listeners.

> The devil is like a fowler; of the birds he catches, he wrings most of their necks, but keeps a few alive, to allure other birds to his snare, by singing the song he will have in a cage. I hope he will not get me into his cage.

> When I die I want to be a ghost and pester the bishops, priests, and godless monks so that they have more trouble with a dead Luther than they could have had before with a thousand living ones.[13]

It is easy to see how a figure such as Luther could become a hero to his followers, as great pastors still do. Luther's *Table Talk* was published in 1566, partly at the instigation of Johannes Aurifaber (John Goldsmith, c. 1519-1575). He had heard Luther's lectures as a student at the University of Wittenberg and became both a Lutheran and a controversialist in his own right (with detrimental effects on his career). He was involved in the publication of the whole corpus of Luther's works, but the *Table Talk*, like the *Letters*, became rather a special project with him. This was an age when the modern biography was unknown and the only familiar model was the hagiography of the Middle Ages, with its stylized depictions of idealized figures and aim of achieving canonization. Aurifaber had to devise his own literary route to the celebration of his spiritual (and political) hero.

Aurifaber's preface to the *Table Talk* was addressed, in an attempt to ensure the widest possible recognition and circulation, "To the Honorable and Right Worshipful the Head Governors, the Mayors and Aldermen of

---

[13] Luther, *Table Talk* 616, 1442.

the Imperial Cities, Strasburg, Augsburg, Ulm, Nuremberg, Lubeck, Hamburg, Brunswick, Frankfurt-on-the-Maine, etc." He offered them Luther the champion who had rescued Christian magistrates from subjection to the pope: "For although many learned men, universities, popes, cardinals, bishops, friars, and priests, and after them emperors, kings, and princes, raised their strong battery against this one man, Luther, and his doctrine, intending quite to suppress it, yet, notwithstanding, all their labor was in vain." He gave them Luther the fearless rescuer of Scripture: "God, through Luther, brought forth the Bible, or the Holy Scripture, which formerly lay, as it were, under the table; translated by Luther *ex ipsis fontibus*, out of the Hebrew into the German tongue." Now,

> it may easily be read and understood by young and old, rich and poor, clergy and laity, so that now, a father or master may daily read the Holy Scriptures to his wife, to his children, and servants, and may instruct them in the doctrines of grace, and direct them in the truth and in the true service of God.

Again he blames the papacy for hiding this treasure away: "Whereas, before, in Popedom, the Bible was known to none; nay, the doctors in divinity themselves read not therein; for Luther often affirmed in my hearing, that Dr. Andrew Carlstadt was a doctor in divinity eight years before he began to read in the Bible."

Luther's activities in seeking to bring the faith to the uneducated took various forms. One was the writing of hymns.

> A safe stronghold our God is still,
> A trusty shield and weapon;
> He'll help us clear from all the ill
> That hath us now o'ertaken.
> The ancient prince of hell
> Hath risen with purpose fell;
> Strong mail of craft and power
> He weareth in this hour;
> On earth is not his fellow.[14]

Luther wrote hymns because he understood their power as spiritual

---

[14]Martin Luther, "A Mighty Fortress Is Our God" [*Ein' feste Burg ist unser Gott*].

aids. Luther's hymns became something more than liturgical extras, included in worship so as to provide variety and a greater element of participation for the congregation. His hymns were theology in verse, set to music. In 1524 he turned the Creed into a hymn, and in 1539 he produced a hymn version of the Lord's Prayer. This approach had the effect of largely sparing Lutheranism the battles about removing music from worship, which occurred in a number of reforming communities.

Luther taught that it was important to instruct children in the faith. In his *Table Talk* he recognized that children do not understand sermons and have to be taught in a different way, tedious for the teacher but essential if they are to learn: "Sermons very little edify children, who learn little thereby; it is more needful they be taught and well instructed in schools, and at home, and that they be heard and examined what they have learned; this way profits much; 'tis very wearisome, but very necessary."[15] He seems to have had no difficulty with the idea that these simple instructions are derived from God himself:

> In the catechism, we have a very exact, direct, and short way to the whole Christian religion. For God himself gave the ten commandments, Christ himself penned and taught the Lord's Prayer, the Holy Ghost brought together the articles of faith. These three pieces are set down so excellently, that never could any thing have been better; but they are slighted and condemned by us as things of small value, because the little children daily say them.
>
> The catechism, I insist, is the right Bible of the laity, wherein is contained the whole sum of Christian doctrine necessary to be known by every Christian for salvation.[16]

Luther himself accordingly composed a shorter and a longer catechism to buttress the faith of the Lutheran congregations. The Large Catechism contained fuller instruction for the use of parish priests and teachers, and the Small Catechism was intended for the congregation to commit to memory. The basic needs in making the faithful familiar with key texts had not changed. The subject matter covered is much like

---

[15]Luther, *Table Talk* 266.
[16]Ibid.

that proposed by Archbishop Pecham in England centuries before: the Ten Commandments, the Creeds, the Lord's Prayer and explanations of the sacraments and their meaning.

Fighting talk at table. But not all Luther's talk at the table was concerned with such matters. He used the opportunity to talk fighting talk. The adherents of some of the sects come in for castigation. "The Antinomians, Swenckfelders, Enthusians, co-agents, were also very diligent to eclipse again the true doctrines which Luther had cleared up, and brought again to light."[17]

In his Preface, Aurifaber provides Christian magistrates with a convenient summary of the way things used to be (that is, in need of reform) and what has been achieved by Luther and his followers, at some risk to themselves: "But others, who, like true and constant teachers, fought against those enemies of God, were reviled and held as rebels, boisterous and stiff-necked, that would raise needless strifes and divisions, and were accordingly persecuted and plagued."[18] Aurifaber lists the Commandments and explains how the pope broke them all to put human impositions in their place. In "Popedom" these new rules of Christian living were invented and multiplied. The pope, he says, claimed to be lord of the world, above councils and princes, empowered to make new articles of faith and incapable of error.

Aurifaber then lists the principal doctrinal bones of contention between Rome and the Reformers, which Luther had helped to make prominent. The pope, he claimed, had failed to comfort the "distressed sorrowful consciences" of ordinary people by explaining what Christ had done for them. Christ was portrayed as "a severe and an angry judge, who would not be reconciled with us, except we had other advocates and intercessors besides himself." The result was that people took "refuge in dead saints to help and deliver them, and made them their gods . . . and they placed the Virgin Mary, instead of her Son Christ, for a mediatrix on the throne of grace." That led to the encouragement of pilgrimages and all the rest of the apparatus by which "people were

---

[17]Ibid., xxii.
[18]Ibid.

taught, that they must purchase heaven by their own good works, austerities, fastings, and so on."[19]

Prayer, which ought to be "the highest comfort of a Christian," the
pope turned into "a tedious babbling without spirit and truth," and in a
language, Latin, which the people did not understand but they were
told this "should merit pardons and remissions of sins for the space of
many thousand years."[20]

Baptism was not understood by the people and "Popedom" constituted "monkery as a second baptism, of equal value and operation." "The
Lord's Supper, in Popedom, also was dishonored, corrupted, turned into
idolatry, and wickedly abused; for they used the same not in remembrance of Christ, but as the offering of some wicked priest." These "eucharistic sacrifices were then sold for money, to be imparted to the souls
in purgatory, thereby to redeem them; so that out of the Lord's Supper
they made a mere market." Denying the faithful the wine led to the
consecrated bread, the corpus Christi, being turned into an object of
worship, "and therewith they wrought fearful idolatry."[21]

Confession was distorted by the penitential system, with absolution
granted only in return for good works. "Instead of true keys," the pope
"made false, thievish picklocks, which he used in all his wicked proceedings." And the pope, it is claimed,

> then, at last, . . . proceeded to tread under foot the divine state and orders in
> the world; and of the pulpit and church government, made a temporal rule,
> wherein he sat as head and monarch, and under him, in order, the cardinals,
> archbishops, bishops, prelates, abbots, friars, nuns, priests, and innumerable
> other orders; the poor laity being altogether made a scorned tool of.[22]

CREATING A LUTHERAN DOCTRINAL SYSTEM

The Augsburg Confession. At Wittenberg, Melanchthon's career had become enmeshed with that of Luther. His quieter mind, his capacity

---

[19]Ibid., xx.
[20]Ibid., xxi.
[21]Ibid.
[22]Ibid., xxii.

for standing back and taking an overview, were to prove invaluable in the work of formulating the Lutheran confessions of faith. These were not an attempt to replace the ancient creeds with modern matter, though they sometimes enlarged upon what the creeds said. They represented attempts by reforming groups to state doctrinal principles they believed to be right. These confessions were going to be heavily influenced in their basic form by this contemporary liking for axioms and commonplaces.

Melanchthon was the natural choice to design a confession of faith for the Lutherans that could be acceptable to the secular authorities in Germany, those Christian magistrates whose role as replacement overseers of the church was becoming more and more obviously important in Luther's eyes.

The Augsburg Confession was so called because it was put to the Diet of Augsburg in 1530. Luther complained that it was too quiet and obliging, but this moderate approach was going to help to ensure the long-term impact and continuing usefulness of the work. It is probably also the case that the juxtaposition and involvement of Melanchthon and the university context at Wittenberg helped to turn Luther's views into a Lutheranism which would claim and keep adherents who were not extremists or polemicists.

Melanchthon had approached its composition with what can only be called "ecumenical intentions." He asked

> that in this matter of religion the opinions and judgments of the parties might be heard in each other's presence; and considered and weighed among ourselves in mutual charity, leniency, and kindness, in order that, after the removal and correction of such things as have been treated and understood in a different manner in the writings on either side, these matters may be settled and brought back to one simple truth and Christian concord, that for the future one pure and true religion may be embraced and maintained by us, that as we all are under one Christ and do battle under Him, so we may be able also to live in unity and concord in the one Christian Church. (preface, Augsburg Confession)

If this succeeded, the intention was to extend the process to "the other Electors, Princes, and Estates of the Empire" so that they may all "confer amicably" "in order that we may come together, as far as this may be honorably done, and, the matter between us on both sides being peacefully discussed without offensive strife, the dissension, by God's help, may be done."

The articles are in many respects—like Aquinas's *Summa Contra Gentiles*—an attempt to explain to those of differing opinions why they should return to orthodoxy. They form two sections. The first few articles suggest that Melanchthon thought it best for the Lutherans to set out a comprehensive theological statement and not merely to make their own position statements on currently controversial points. He did not resist the temptation to include a number of points of fine-tuning; he took the opportunity to distinguish the Lutheran position from that of other Reformers, particularly the Anabaptists with whom they were at that time especially anxious not to be confused.

The substantive "currently controversial" points came next in a second section. Pastorally, as Luther knew, this is difficult material for believers of limited theological education to understand:

> For the blind children of the world the articles of faith are too high. That three persons are one only God; that the true Son of God was made man; that in Christ are two natures, divine and human, etc., all this offends them, as fiction and fable. For just as unlikely as it is to say, a man and a stone are one person, so it is unlikely to human sense and reason that God was made man, or that divine and human natures, united in Christ, are one person. St. Paul showed his understanding of this matter, though he took not hold of all, in Colossians: "In Christ dwelleth all the fullness of the Godhead bodily." Also: "In him lies hid all treasure of wisdom and knowledge."[23]

That did not stop him jesting about such matters at the table, the kind of humorous seriousness that he found made best sense to non-specialists. Someone asked him, "Where God was before heaven was created?" He knew Augustine's answer. "He was in himself." But Luther had been asked this question too. "I said: He was building hell for such idle, presumptuous, fluttering and inquisitive spirits as you."

---

[23]Luther, *Table Talk* 65.

After he had created all things, he was everywhere, and yet he was nowhere, for I cannot take hold of him without the Word. But he will be
found there where he has engaged to be. The Jews found him at Jerusalem by the throne of grace (Exod. xxv.). We find him in the Word and
faith, in baptism and the sacraments; but in his majesty, he is nowhere to
be found.[24]

He also used lively imagery: "Dr. Jonas, inviting Luther to dinner,
caused a bunch of ripe cherries to be hung over the table where they
dined, in remembrance of the creation, and as a suggestion to his guests
to praise God for creating such fruits." Discussing creation over dinner,
Luther suggested that children are a better reminder of God's power
than a bowl of cherries:

In the married state we find that the conception of children depends not
on our will and pleasure; we never know whether we will be fruitful or no,
or whether God will give us a son or a daughter. All this goes on without
our counsel. My father and mother did not imagine they should have
brought a spiritual overseer into the world. 'Tis God's work only, and this
we cannot enter into. I believe that, in the life to come, we shall have nothing to do, but to meditate on and marvel at our Creator and his creatures.
"Why not rather remember this in one's children, that are the fruit of
one's body?"
For these are far more excelling creatures of God than all the fruits of
trees. In them we see God's power, wisdom and art, who made them all
out of nothing, gave them life and limbs, exquisitely constructed, and will
maintain and preserve them. Yet how little do we regard this. When
people have children, all the effect is to make them grasping—raking
together all they can to leave behind them. They do not know, that before
a child comes into the world, it has its lot assigned already, and that it is
ordained and determined what and how much it shall have.[25]

Meanwhile Melanchthon was patiently persevering in the background with his task of systematizing, not in a polemical tone. "Nor has
anything been here said or adduced to the reproach of any one." He
began the articles of the Augsburg Confession with matters the church

[24]Ibid., 67.
[25]Ibid., 259.

had long deemed fundamental and which he suggests need not now be
regarded as controversial. Article 1 contains a reassurance that "Our
Churches, with common consent, do teach that the decree of the Council of Nicaea concerning the Unity of the Divine Essence and concerning the Three Persons, is true. . . . They condemn all heresies which have
sprung up against this article."[26] Article 2 affirms the doctrine of original sin against "the Pelagians and others who deny that original deprav-
ity is sin." The third article, which deals with the incarnation, directly
echoes the creeds but with additional provisos reflecting the concerns of
the day, especially those of the Lutherans:

> The Word, that is, the Son of God, did assume the human nature in the
> womb of the blessed Virgin Mary, so that there are two natures, the divine
> and the human, inseparably enjoined in one Person, one Christ, true God
> and true man, who was born of the Virgin Mary, truly suffered, was cruci-
> fied, dead, and buried, that He might reconcile the Father unto us, and be
> a sacrifice, not only for original guilt, but also for all actual sins of men.

So Melanchthon is emphasizing a point of central importance to
Luther and his followers, and that is the sufficiency of Christ's sacrifice;
its sufficiency means that there is no need for additional or supplemen-
tary sacrifices such as had been claimed to take place in celebrations of
the Eucharist.

Again the creed can be heard in an amplified form in:

> He also descended into hell, and truly rose again the third day; afterward
> He ascended into heaven that He might sit on the right hand of the
> Father, and forever reign and have dominion over all creatures, and sanc-
> tify them that believe in Him, by sending the Holy Ghost into their
> hearts, to rule, comfort, and quicken them, and to defend them against
> the devil and the power of sin.

And once more in: "The same Christ shall openly come again to judge
the quick and the dead, etc., according to the Apostles' Creed."

---

[26]"As the Manichaeans, who assumed two principles, one Good and the other Evil—also the Val-
entinians, Arians, Eunomians, Mohammedans, and all such. They condemn also the Samosatenes,
old and new, who, contending that there is but one Person, sophistically and impiously argue that
the Word and the Holy Ghost are not distinct Persons, but that 'Word' signifies a spoken word,
and 'Spirit' signifies motion created in things" (ibid., 23).

With the fourth article, and the subject of justification, Melanchthon moves once more to a distinctively Lutheran emphasis:

> Also they teach that men cannot be justified before God by their own strength, merits, or works, but are freely justified for Christ's sake, through faith, when they believe that they are received into favor, and that their sins are forgiven for Christ's sake, who, by His death, has made satisfaction for our sins. This faith God imputes for righteousness in His sight.

The centrality of justifying faith does not mean, says Melanchthon, that works have no place, but good works are fruits of the Christian life, not prerequisites of salvation (art. 6).

Lutheranism never rejected the need for an institutional church with a ministry of the sacraments, as well as a ministry of the gospel, as Melanchthon explains in article 5: "That we may obtain this faith, the Ministry of Teaching the Gospel and administering the Sacraments was instituted" because through these "instruments," "the Holy Ghost is given, who works faith." This ministry does not have to take the same form everywhere. There may be variation of rites, for these are mere "human traditions" (art. 7). Article 8 sets out Augustine's view that the visible church is composed of wheat and tares growing together until harvest, and only God knows who are his own. It also states the settled doctrine that God can still work by grace even through the unworthy minister.

Proper institutional calling is essential for Lutheran ministers. Article 14, "Of Ecclesiastical Order," teaches that "no one should publicly teach in the Church or administer the Sacraments unless he be regularly called." Melanchthon takes the opportunity to distance Lutherans from the extremists, "the Anabaptists and others," who "think that the Holy Ghost comes to men without the external Word, through their own preparations and works" (art. 5).

Lutheran ministers will be ministering the sacrament of baptism. The Anabaptists are rejected again at article 9, which accepts baptism as "necessary to salvation" and also approves infant baptism, which the Anabaptists do not allow. Lutheran ministers will be celebrating the Eucharist on certain understandings. Lutherans accepted the "real pres-

ence" of the body and blood of Christ at the Eucharist (art. 10). Article
11 provides for private absolution of penitents by Lutheran ministers.
"Confession in the churches is not abolished among us; for it is not usual
to give the body of the Lord, except to them that have been previously
examined and absolved" (art. 25):

> Of Repentance they teach that for those who have fallen after Baptism
> there is remission of sins whenever they are converted and that the
> Church ought to impart absolution to those thus returning to repentance.
> Now, repentance consists properly of these two parts: One is contrition,
> that is, terrors smiting the conscience through the knowledge of sin; the
> other is faith, which is born of the Gospel, or of absolution, and believes
> that for Christ's sake, sins are forgiven, comforts the conscience, and
> delivers it from terrors. Then good works are bound to follow, which are
> the fruits of repentance. (art. 12)

Lutherans have, however, a distinctive position when it comes to easing the "terrified conscience." Article 20 stresses that good works cannot
reconcile the sinner with God. "We obtain this only by faith when we
believe that we are received into favor for Christ's sake, who alone has
been set forth the Mediator and Propitiation, 1 Tim. 2, 6, in order that
the Father may be reconciled through Him."

Lutheran standpoints are also set out on abuses that have been corrected: the invocation of the saints (art. 21), not allowing Communion
in both kinds (art. 22), not allowing marriage of priests (art. 23); beliefs
about the Mass (art. 24), confession (art. 25), fasting (art. 26) and monastic vows (art. 27), all of which are identified as human impositions and
invention. As article 26 claims:

> These traditions have obscured the commandments of God, because tra-
> ditions were placed far above the commandments of God. Christianity
> was thought to consist wholly in the observance of certain holy-days,
> rites, fasts, and vestures. These observances had won for themselves the
> exalted title of being the spiritual life and the perfect life.

There are also

> complaints concerning indulgences, pilgrimages, and the abuse of ex-
> communications. The parishes have been vexed in many ways by the

dealers in indulgences. There were endless contentions between the pastors and the monks concerning the parochial right, confessions, burials, sermons on extraordinary occasions, and innumerable other things. Issues of this sort we have passed over so that the chief points in this matter, having been briefly set forth, might be the more readily understood.

1540s: Melanchthon the mediator: The Peace of Augsburg, 1555. Melanchthon was again involved in a colloquy at Worms in 1540. There was a further colloquy at Regensburg in 1541. Germany—and leaders of religious opinion more widely—were now trying to find common ground between Roman Catholics and Protestants among the various attempts at setting out the reforming faith in lists of key points or "articles." The Augsburg Interim of 1548, a declaration of the emperor, proposed a compromise which would allow some concessions on either side. There was vigorous opposition, so another attempt was made in the same year in the Leipzig Interim, brokered by the Elector Maurice of Saxony, in which Melanchthon sought to allow as many Roman Catholic usages as possible to be deemed *adiaphora*, "things indifferent," which the believer could hold or not as he or she chose, so that they need not be church dividing. That too failed.

More attempts followed. The Colloquy of Worms was held in October 1557 as a follow-up to the Diet of Augsburg in 1555 and a meeting at Regensburg in 1556. These ecumenical meetings between Roman Catholic and reforming scholars intended to take key topics for resolution. But they were easily wrecked. At Worms the claim from the Roman side that the Reformers themselves were not united in all points on the central subject of justification led to the end of the debate.

The battles over transubstantiation and a new doctrine of the Eucharist. Consolidated controversies involving several groups began to emerge, especially on topics of general interest and where fine differences of opinion could be crucial. Among these the Eucharist was particularly important. There had come to be clustered about it, and especially about the doctrine of transubstantiation, many of the concerns of the Reformers about alleged abuse of power in the late medieval church. This largely depended on the interpretation that had come to be placed on the doctrine of transubstantiation as involving a power in the priest to "make

Christ" and even in some way to repeat or present again his sacrifice on the cross by celebrating the Lord's Supper.

Luther had struck a moderating position, accepting that there is a "real presence" of Christ in the consecrated bread and wine, but rejecting the doctrine of transubstantiation in its technical medieval form. One of Luther's fellow academics at Wittenberg published three pamphlets on the Eucharist rejecting the doctrine of transubstantiation. Zwingli approved, and began to publish on the subject himself, claiming that the important *copula* or linking verb *is*, in "this is my body" (1 Cor 11:23-26), merely indicates that the bread signifies or refers to the crucified body of Christ. Luther disagreed. The celebration of the Eucharist is more than a "memorial" of that sacrifice. But it is not a reenactment.

A public disputation was held in 1526, involving Eck, Thomas Murner and Johannes Oecolampadius (1482-1531). Eck was deemed to have won and that emboldened the would-be persecutors of Zwingli. Martin Bucer attempted to make peace. The Landgrave of Hesse called a colloquy at Marburg in 1529 to try to arrive at a joint position among the Reformers on a number of subjects, including the Eucharist, and it was the Eucharist which proved the stumbling block. Again, Zwingli, Melanchthon, Bucer and Oecolampadius could not agree what happens when a minister repeated Jesus' words, "This is my body."

The debate was still going strong in 1531, after Martin Bucer proposed a concord, which he sent to Wittenberg. Melanchthon, supported by the Landgrave of Hesse, began discussions with Bucer which took Melanchthon some distance from Luther's doctrine and caused some bad feeling between him and Luther.

The passions provoked by differences about the Eucharist were long-lasting and could be dramatically divisive in the sixteenth century, as the furor in Oxford in 1548-1550 amply demonstrated. In the reign of Edward VI (see pp. 334-35), and at the instigation of reform-minded figures in the government of the day, Italian Reformed theologian Peter Martyr Vermigli (1499-1562) was invited to England to become Regius Professor of Divinity in Oxford. He gave a series of lectures, on topics known to be inflammatory, and was brought to agree to holding a public disputation on the Eucharist in the presence of the Visitors, who were inspecting the university on behalf of the Crown. In Oxford conservative views prevailed and Peter Martyr thought it would be safer to go to London for a time. His enemies set up a debate solely on transubstantiation which they sought to fix so as to ensure that he looked foolish.

A number of reforming principles began to emerge, all tending to diminish the powers of the minister, which had been so strongly enhanced by the development of the doctrine of transubstantiation. The first, prevalent among the more radical reformers, was that the Eucharist was not a sacrifice but a memorial or commemoration. The second, more redolent of Calvin's view, was that Christ was really present in the consecrated bread and wine, but it was by the Holy Spirit and not a literal physical presence. The third, shared by all the reformers, was that the Eucharist ought to be a celebration of the worshiping community as a whole.

The Book of Concord. The end result of several decades of striving for an accepted Lutheran statement alongside honest efforts to reconcile differing views and achieve unity among Christians was the German-language Book of Concord (1580). In it Martin Chemnitz and Jakob Andreae (1528-1590) brought together the texts of the Nicene, Apostles' and Athanasian Creeds to emphasize the continuity of the Lutheran beliefs with those of the early church; the Augsburg Confession (the original or *Invariata*); Melanchthon's *Apology*, which is an explanation and defense of the Confession; Luther's Small and Large Catechisms and his Smalcald Articles; Melanchthon's *Treatise on the Power and Primacy of the Pope*; and the *Formula of Concord.* The Book of Concord, however, was not simply a profession of Lutheran solidarity with Christian orthodoxy. It was in most respects a victory for the self-proclaimed "genuine (Gnesio-)" followers of Luther over the more irenic Philippists. The Gnesio-Lutherans had disapproved of doctrinal developments from Melanchthon and others that seemed to bring Lutheran theology closer to a Roman Catholic account of free will, and a Reformed theology of the sacraments—the latter particularly evident in Melanchthon's more Calvinistic description of Christ's presence in the Supper in the revised version of the Augsburg Confession (the 1540

Variata), which was officially overruled in favor of the *Invariata* for inclusion in the Book of Concord.[27]

The idea of a formal confession was by now as important a feature of many Protestant communities as the listing of articles of faith. Both went with the development of a confessional identity, a sense of belonging to a particular ecclesial community attempting to hold faithfully to Christian truth in light of deep disagreement about much of what that truth entails.

[27]See *The Book of Concord: The Confessions of the Evangelical Lutheran Church,* ed. Robert Kolb, Timothy J. Wengert and Charles P. Arand (Minneapolis: Augsburg Fortress, 2000), pp. 481-84; Martin Chemnitz, *The Lord's Supper,* trans. J.A.O. Preuss (St. Loius, Mo.: Concordia, 1979).

17

HENRY VIII AND THE ENGLISH REFORMATION

THOMAS BILNEY (C. 1495-1531) WAS CONVERTED as a young scholar at Cambridge, when he read Erasmus's new Latin version of the New Testament and came across 1 Timothy 1:15, "It is a true saying and worthy of all men to be believed that Christ Jesus came into the world to save sinners." He at once experienced the classic symptoms of conversion, that sense which has been so often described of all anxieties falling away and a feeling of clean and beautiful newness.[1]

His conversion led him to embrace reforming opinions. He became a popular preacher, especially in the diocese of Ely, where Cambridge lies, and where he was licensed to preach by the bishop from 1525. He went about denouncing images and the popular practice of going on pilgrimage to the shrine at nearby Walsingham. He delivered sermons in London too, inciting the congregation to violent destruction of images.

Such objections to the "worship" of images of Christ and Mary, to the reliance on relics of the saints for cures, and going on pilgrimages to the shrines of saints and the invocation of the saints in general, seem to have traveled as a cluster throughout the reforming decades of the sixteenth century. The central objection seems to have been that this looked very much like idolatry. But there was an additional current of unease about

---

[1]On the beginning of English reforming activity, see Alec Ryrie and Peter Marshall, *The Beginnings of English Protestantism* (Cambridge: Cambridge University Press, 2002); and Alec Ryrie, *The Gospel and Henry VIII: Evangelicals in the Early English Reformation* (Cambridge: Cambridge University Press, 2003).

294 THE ROOTS OF THE REFORMATION

the idea that holiness could somehow lodge itself in objects, joined with a further concern not to encourage the belief that Christ's sacrifice on the cross had left unfinished business—a merit gap that had to be filled by the merits of the saints, accessed through their holy leavings (relics) or depictions of their holy selves. There was also a cry from the social conscience wing of protest, with its resentment of wealth and privilege, that money spent on gilding statues should be spent on relieving the poor.

The attack on popular veneration of images was worrying to the ecclesiastical authorities, and in November 1527 Bilney was summoned to explain himself before Cardinal Thomas Wolsey (c. 1471-1530) and a panel of bishops. It turned out that the church was chiefly worried that he might be a Lutheran. This he denied, and indeed he called Luther a heretic. Wolsey then left him to be dealt with by the bishop of London.

Bilney does not seem to have been very brave in holding to his opinions when confronted. He was willing to go so far as to say that there might be a place for showing respect for images insofar as they were a teaching aid, "books for laymen" (*cum sint libri laicorum, adorare oportet*).[2] Witnesses were brought, who claimed that they had heard him preach in much more extreme terms. He claimed he could not remember the exact words of his sermons. Faced with execution, he recanted and his sentence was commuted to one of imprisonment.

The authorities' handling of Bilney illustrates the tensions created by dissent in a violent age and the difficulty of being sure whether it was indeed dissent. Some topics that had been burning issues in their time caused few disagreements in the sixteenth century. The controversies of the early centuries had chiefly concerned Trinity and Christology. These were not the hot topics of the mainstream sixteenth-century Reformation, although debates about various implications of these doctrines for salvation held a prominent place. The ease with which the dissenters came to see themselves as standing for a matter of spiritual life and death is the more striking because so much was in the melting pot, and it was so hard to be sure what might be a matter of indifference and what might be serious enough to be church-dividing or deserving of hellfire.

---

[2]"When they are the books of laymen, it is proper to revere them" (John Foxe, *Acts and Monuments* [1563], 4.625-26).

Bilney's conscience tormented him after he recanted, and shortly after his release from prison he set off to preach in the open air in a manner bound to challenge the authorities and bring him the punishment he had avoided by his earlier cowardice. Bilney won his martyrdom in the end, in London in 1531, where he was executed in "the Lollard's Pit" before a large and interested crowd of supporters. The authorities of both church and state were to learn that in creating martyrs they ran the danger of creating more sympathizers. In this case, violent iconoclasm became rife in East Anglia.[3] And paradoxically the objection to images and all that went with them came to be accepted by moderates. During the 1530s, Thomas Cranmer was preaching a version of the things Bilney had been saying.

King Henry changes sides. Henry VIII, King of England from 1509-1547, ruled throughout the early years of the Reformation. He was an able man, interested in the new ideas Protestant sympathizers were quick to bring to England, but inclined to treat their proponents as terrorists with the intention of undermining social order. The king, interested in the questions the reformers were raising, even wrote a book himself, the *Defense of the Seven Sacraments.* He began it in 1518, as soon as news of Luther's claims began to spread as far as England, and he may have had assistance from Thomas More, whom Wolsey arranged to have chosen as Speaker of the House of Commons in 1523.

During the period when Luther came to prominence as a perceived threat, Wolsey was Lord Chancellor (1514-1529). Wolsey, a merchant's son, was sent to Oxford by his father, but he remained a practical politician rather than an intellectual.[4] He had been made a cardinal in 1515, and papal legate in England from 1518, and he had mighty ambitions for himself and his monarch, including a chance at the papacy for himself and imperial powers for Henry. So naturally the first response of the English government was to ally itself with Rome in condemning Luther's teachings. Wolsey was present at a public burning of Lutheran writings in London at St. Paul's in 1521. In 1526 there was a raid, arranged by Wolsey, on the

---

[3]Hugh Latimer became associated with Bilney over this; see Margaret Aston, *England's Iconoclasts* (Oxford: Oxford University Press, 1988), pp. 169-70.
[4]Peter Gwyn, *The King's Cardinal: The Rise and Fall of Thomas Wolsey* (London: Pimlico, 1992).

warehouses of books which were being imported from Germany by the merchants of the Hanseatic League, and again the Lutheran books among them were burned. Wolsey too began to take up the theological aspects of the conflict. He had ambitious plans for a new college at Oxford, which was to be called Cardinal College, though after his fall it eventually became Christ Church. His first idea was that it was to be set up as a center for antiheretical studies.

These moves were really as much political as theological. The royal attitude—and with it the policy—changed when Henry VIII decided that he no longer wished to be married to his Spanish queen, Catherine of Aragon. She had borne him a sickly daughter, Mary, but no son. He wanted an heir. He persuaded himself that the lack of an heir was a divine punishment for a marriage he should not have entered into. Catherine had first been the wife of Henry's older brother Arthur, who had died before he came to the throne. In order to obtain a divorce Henry needed to show that the marriage had been null and void from the beginning, or else that there were grounds for a divorce. While the Mosaic law states that it is unlawful for a man to have sex with his brother's wife (Lev 18:16), less conveniently for Henry it also legislates that if one's brother dies then it is the family duty of a remaining brother to marry his widow and bear his dead brother an heir (Deut 25:5-10; compare Gen 38:8).

Opinions on the weight to be placed on the scriptural testimonies were commissioned from the leading theologians of Oxford and Cambridge. Thomas Cranmer was one of these. Cranmer studied at Cambridge as an adolescent and remained there as a fellow of Jesus College until Wolsey's eye fell on him in his search, not only as a contributor to the formation of advice but also as a suitable diplomat to be sent with an embassy to Spain in 1527. On his return from this mission Cranmer began to enter the king's service as a trusted insider.

Representations were made to Rome. But Wolsey was not able to get a speedy divorce arranged; the pope would not oblige. Wolsey fell from royal favor with dramatic suddenness in 1529; he lost his office and his property was confiscated, but he was allowed to remain archbishop of York. He died the next year while traveling to London to answer charges of treason.

Henry's theological interests now changed tack. He began to feel that there was much to be said for the Lutherans' ideas, especially the view that the pope was antichrist, a usurper, and that the proper head of a local church was the Christian magistrate, in fact just such a magistrate as himself. This Lutheran notion that a secular magistracy could provide headship for the church was to have important implications for the evolving church in England (although Luther himself never advocated the permanent estabishment of political authority over the church's affairs).

If the king was authoritative head of the church in England, he could of course make sure that his own divorce was approved. Thomas Cromwell, of humble origins but businesslike and efficient and an appointee of Wolsey in his days of power, had risen to be the king's right-hand man and a power in the land from at least 1532. He advocated a break with Rome, and saw the resultant Act of Supremacy through Parliament in 1534.

But the new English Church with its royal head would need to define its doctrine. England had no Luther to take a lead here, but it did have Thomas Cranmer. Cranmer had made good use of the opportunities for consultation and travel which had come his way since Wolsey took him up. In 1529, during one of the frequent episodes of plague which sent people out of Cambridge, Cranmer was able to hold discussions with Stephen Gardiner (c. 1497-1555) and Edward Foxe (c. 1496-1538) about the great question of the annulment of the king's marriage. Cranmer's preference was to seek the views of leading theologians throughout Europe and try to build a consensus. This plan took him to Rome, with another official English embassy, and Foxe put together the opinions gathered in a "very copious collection" (*collectanea satis copiosa*), together with a document containing resolutions of the conflicting views (*determinationes*) made in the traditional academic manner in which a master would resolve the question addressed in a disputation. The resolution was in favor of the view that the king had supreme jurisdiction in England.

Cranmer was also able to meet and talk with Reformers from the continent who had direct knowledge and experience of the debates going on there. Simon Grynaeus (1493-1541) came from Basel in 1531 to offer advice to the king on behalf of reforming theologians in Europe, such as Oecolampadius and Zwingli. He seems to have taken to Cranmer and later mentioned him in correspondence with Martin Bucer. This initiated a growing familiarity between Cranmer and the Swiss Reformers, which was going to take him in due course in a Reformed rather than a Lutheran direction in his own Protestantism. In 1532 Cranmer was sent as resident ambassador to Charles V, at the imperial court. The imperial court traveled, and in the emperor's retinue Cranmer found himself in various German cities and coming into contact with active Lutheranism as well.

Then the archbishop of Canterbury died, and thanks to the influence of Anne Boleyn's (c. 1501-1536) family—though much to everyone's surprise—the still little-known Cranmer was chosen to replace him. From 1533 he was archbishop of Canterbury and in a position to conduct the process of the divorce and to declare the king's new marriage to Anne to be valid, and then to crown her Queen.[5]

His position remained uncomfortable for some time. Some local bishops strongly disapproved of his appointment and his support of the king's position. Anne bore a daughter, Elizabeth, who was to become Elizabeth I (1533-1603). But the legitimacy of what had been done grew more contentious when in 1536 Anne miscarried the son Henry had longed for, and he began to murmur that he had been badly advised and should not have married her. Now he thought he would like to marry Jane Seymour (c. 1508-1537), and Cranmer found that he was expected to countenance the removal of Anne to the Tower of London on charges of treason. He had his reservations, but nonetheless heard the queen's confession, and declared that this marriage too was null and void, before her speedy execution. He was left to negotiate the process by which Henry now took Jane, the future mother of Edward VI, as his queen. Between 1535 and 1538 Cromwell claimed jurisdiction in ecclesiastical matters as vicegerent after the Act of Supremacy, and Cranmer's powers and position remained partly unclear. Nevertheless, Cranmer was also to outlast Cromwell, who also fell out

---

[5]Jasper Ridley, *Thomas Cranmer* (Oxford: Clarendon Press, 1962).

of favor with the king and met his death in 1540.

Cranmer was more comfortable as a theologian than he ever was as a politician. He was to be chief architect of the Articles of the Church of England and its liturgy. The Convocation of the Province of Canterbury sat in the mid-1530s to discuss its theological position. Cranmer continued to benefit from the help and support of his old Cambridge ally Foxe. In 1536 Foxe, now bishop of Hereford, came back to report on a visit he had made to Saxony to discuss matters with the Lutheran magistrates there.

Diplomat enough to survive the fall of his old patron Wolsey, Foxe now put forward ten points which seemed to him appropriately Lutheran, essentially Wittenberg articles he thought the Church of England could properly adopt, and got them accepted by convocation in 1536. They spoke of justification and faith, and said that only three sacraments were necessary for salvation: baptism, eucharist and penance. They were unsure about purgatory and sought to set limits to the veneration of images of the saints and the celebration of saints days.

These proved to be steps along a path. *The Institution of a Christian Man*, which emerged in 1537-1538, was immediately known as "the Bishops' Book." This was the product of a synod under the leadership of Cromwell as vicegerent, but theologically speaking it was run by Cranmer and Foxe. The king was too busy to read it, and it lacked formal royal approval. Much still remained to be settled in any case about the boundaries between the ecclesiastical jurisdiction of a lay monarch and the sacramental functions of the church.[6] A party of Lutherans from the Smalcaldic League arrived in May 1538, by invitation, to help with the drafting of a new confessional statement by the English Church.

The Bible in the vernacular. It was now decided that all parish churches should have copies of the Bible in Latin and English. The idea that this was desirable had been developing for some time. Miles Coverdale (1488-1568), an Augustinian friar, was a Cambridge graduate, but not one of those who had been assiduously studying Greek or Hebrew as

---

[6]Henry eventually made his own corrections to the Bishops' Book, to which Cranmer formally replied; see *Miscellaneous Writings and Letters of Thomas Cranmer*, ed. John Cox (Cambridge: Cambridge University Press, 1846), 83-114.

essential equipment for the modern student of the Bible.[7] Nevertheless, he helped to initiate a process which eventually led to an approved English translation of the Bible being placed in every parish church.

The idea was being mooted officially, however, in 1530. This was the end of a decade during which England had begun to feel its way uncertainly toward adopting ideas that were making their way from the Continent. William Warham (c. 1450-1532), then archbishop of Canterbury, issued a statement on behalf of an assembly of leading churchmen and theologians who had been called together by Henry VIII to discuss the matter. The statement said that a translation was unnecessary and warned that it could be dangerous to allow ordinary people to read or hear the Bible read in the vernacular. Nevertheless, the king undertook to make provision to ensure that an English translation was prepared, at least for the New Testament, with approved translators who could ensure that the translation did not contain anything heretical.[8]

This plan came to nothing until a few years later, as the king moved further toward his Reformation stance, when Thomas Cranmer tried to put it into effect by selecting scholars and the more learned bishops of safe opinions and apportioning the text among them. One of the more conservative, Stephen Gardiner (c. 1483-1555), now bishop of Winchester, took a corrective pen indignantly to the drafts of Luke's and John's Gospels.

The enterprise of producing a reliable English translation was complicated by the tangled ambitions of Coverdale himself, William Tyndale (c. 1494-1536), whose own New Testament had appeared in English in 1526, John Rogers (c. 1500-1555), George Joye (1495-1553) and others, in a Europe where individuals could and did publish rival translations. The book trade was still expanding in this new world of paper and print. New skills were needed, quite different from those of the scribes who had made copies of manuscripts. Coverdale, who certainly spent time in Antwerp in the mid-1530s, may have worked for a time as a proofreader for Merten de Keyser (d. 1536) at Antwerp, a task to which he would have

---

[7]Henry Guppy, *Miles Coverdale and the English Bible, 1488-1568* (Manchester: Manchester University Press, 1935).
[8]David Wilkins, *Concilia magnae Britanniae et Hiberniae* (1737) 3:728-37.

brought the valuable asset of being a native English speaker. An English translation of Campensis's 1532 paraphrase of the Psalms was published in Antwerp in 1534. This may have been the work of Coverdale, but in any case he had got the taste for making translations and was now at work on a project to translate the whole Bible in English. Coverdale was the first to finish and publish, in October 1535 in Antwerp, and it was not long before a reprint was available from an English printer.

The rules of "modern" scholarship were still in process of initial formation throughout Europe. It was not yet inconceivable that a translator should knowingly rely on a defective or less reliable text. The pioneering translators were not necessarily Greek or Hebrew scholars themselves. Coverdale explained on the title page that he had not worked from the Hebrew for the Old Testament. Others' work was used, sometimes with acknowledgment, sometimes not. Tyndale had produced a version of the Pentateuch from the Hebrew in 1530, which Coverdale used. He also borrowed from Tyndale's work on the New Testament.

The great thing to these busy translators was to get the translation done and published so that it could be used, and if others had done useful work, they borrowed it. That did not mean that there was never any ill feeling on the part of those who felt their work had been stolen. George Joye was asked to revise Tyndale's New Testament, and when his version appeared in 1534 it was clear that his main contribution was to supply alternative words where Tyndale's choices were likely to be controversial. (Though he had in some cases introduced the possibility of other, different controversies.)

In his *Apology* of 1535 "to satisfy, if it may be, W. Tindale," Joye explains and defends himself against "Tindals uncharitable and unsober pystle" accusing him of theft of his work.[9] Tyndale had accused that Joye "had not used ye office of an honest man/seinge he knew yat I was in correctynge it my selfe."[10] He points crossly to various changes of wording, such as "Resurreccion" to "ye lyfe after this lyfe."

The politic choice of wording was important. Coverdale's most origi-

[9]George Joye, *An Apology Made by George Joye, to Satisfy, If It May Be, W. Tindale* (Birmingham, 1882). This was in reply to Tyndale's condemnation of Joye's edition of Tyndale's New Testament.
[10]This immediately became a banned book.

nal contributions lay in his selection of English words that did not carry
theologically controversial "baggage." Like Tyndale he used *congregation*
for local church community and *elder* to avoid becoming trapped in
controversy about priesthood and ministry. Imitating Swiss and German Bible translators, Coverdale was inventive with the English language in search of the right word or phrase to convey most faithfully the
meaning of Scripture.

Tyndale was in Antwerp in the mid-1530s too, and so was John Rogers, who went to Antwerp in 1534 to be chaplain to the English members of the Company of Merchant Adventurers trading there. The two
met in the small expatriate community, and Rogers was won to the
reforming cause. Tyndale was soon to face martyrdom for his opinions.
He was burned at the stake as a heretic in 1536, and Rogers seems to
have moved smartly to rescue manuscripts of his work in progress.
Rogers pressed on after Tyndale's death and completed a whole Bible
translation with a greater reliance on the texts in the original languages
than anyone had achieved before. This was a hybrid, made up of parts
of Tyndale's incomplete work on Joshua and the books of Chronicles,
with the later part of the Old Testament in Coverdale's version and the
New Testament a reprint of the revision Tyndale and made in 1534. It
was published in 1537 as "Thomas Matthew's Bible" because it was realized that an association with the name of Tyndale was likely to be
damaging to its prospects. At first it was published in Antwerp and in
Paris, but a royal license was obtained to allow it to be published in
England on the same basis as Coverdale's version, which was granted a
royal license in the same year.

The principle that a satisfactory English translation must begin from
the Greek and Hebrew texts was still not yet fully established, but it was
well on its way. Scholars seeking to move away from the Vulgate, with
its obvious faults, could do so from the Latin. George Joye translated
the Psalms from Martin Bucer's Latin version in 1529 and then revised
it for publication in 1534, this time using Zwingli's Latin text.

The official approval of the Matthew's Bible proved insecure. Cranmer sent a copy to Thomas Cromwell when he received it from the
English publisher, Grafton, in 1537. Again, Cromwell had already insti-

tuted a process which was intended to ensure that there was a copy of the Bible in English in every parish church. The king licensed the Matthew's Bible for the purpose. It soon turned out that not enough copies had been printed. There was a shortfall of about seven thousand; yet it was feared that reprinting the Matthew's Bible would be too controversial. Coverdale's version of 1535 should not be used as a substitute, it was decided, because it had not been made from Greek and Hebrew. A revision of the Matthew's Bible was commissioned, to be carried out by Coverdale in Paris.

Coverdale now revised the Matthew's Bible, but he did so partly by going back to the Vulgate, partly by turning to Erasmus's 1516 Latin version of the New Testament and using new Latin versions available in Europe, such as that of the German Hebrew scholar Sebastian Münster (1488-1552). The result was the Great Bible of 1539, though Coverdale went on revising during the next year.

As archbishop of Canterbury, Cranmer provided a Preface to the revised 1540 edition of the Great Bible.[11] He argued (relying heavily on Chrysostom throughout, as he acknowledges) first from custom and precedent. It is understandable that people should be slow to welcome change, but if they persist, they are not only "foolish, froward and obstinate, but also peevish, perverse, and indurate." He also claims as ancient precedent Bede, perhaps Aldhelm, first Bishop of Sherborne (d. 709), and Wyclif. The Bible was once read in

> the Saxons' tongue, which at that time was our mother tongue, whereof there remain yet divers copies found lately in old abbeys, of such antique manner of writing and speaking, that few men now be able to read and understand them. And when this language waxed old and out of common usage, because folk should not lack the fruit of reading, it was again translated into the newer language, whereof yet also many copies remain and be daily found.

He also argues that there are clear benefits to the spiritual life of the nation if its Christian people form the habit of daily Bible reading be-

---

[11]The citations in the following three paragraphs are from Harold R. Willoughby, *The First Authorized English Bible: And the Cranmer Preface* (Chicago: University of Chicago Press, 1942), www.bible-researcher.com/cranmer.html.

tween the hearing of sermons, to prepare and furnish their minds for the better reception of preaching. He reproves not only those who "refuse to read or to hear read the scripture in the vulgar tongue" but also those who go to the opposite extreme and "by their inordinate reading, indiscrete speaking, contentious disputing, or otherwise by their licentious living, slander and hinder the word of God most of all other, whereof they would seem to be greatest furtherers." The first category are like people who "after tillage of corn was first found, many delighted more to feed of mast and acorns wherewith they had ben accustomed, than to eat bread made of good corn."

If people object that they are busy and have a living to earn (Bible reading is for the professionals), Cranmer answers that it is precisely those whose lives bring them into conflict with the world and who experience its knocks who need to know their Bibles so as to have "remedies and medicines at hand": "For as mallets, hammers, saws, chisels, axes, and hatchets, be the tools of their occupation; so be the books of the prophets, and Apostles, and all holy writers inspired by the holy ghost, the instruments of our salvation." Cranmer was now presenting the move to vernacular translation as progress in religion.

By the reign of Elizabeth the acceptance by church and state that there should be a widely available authorized translation of the Bible in English was no longer politically or theologically controversial in England. Moreover, it was now accepted that such a version must be based on the Greek and Hebrew texts and not on any Latin version. The version known as the Bishops' Bible appeared in 1568, with a revision in 1572. Matthew Parker (1504-1575) organized this project, allowing the bishops responsible for particular books to include their initials at the end. But he did not arrange for an overarching editor to ensure consistency or a good standard throughout. The text, in its further revision of 1602, became the official basis of the work to be done by the committees set up to create what became the "King James Version" (the Authorized Version).

The dissolution of the monasteries. Among the major changes of the 1530s, especially 1536 (the First Suppression Act) and 1539 (the Second Suppression Act) was the dissolution of the monasteries. This was partly a response to the movement of rejection of the religious orders and the fraternities which was part of the tide of the reforming times. The preamble to the Act of 1536 says:

> FORASMUCH as manifest sin, vicious, carnal and abominable living is daily used and committed among the little and small abbeys, priories, and other religious houses of monks, canons, and nuns, where the congregation of such religious persons is under the number of twelve persons, whereby the governors of such religious houses, and their convent, spoil, destroy, consume, and utterly waste, as well their churches, monasteries, priories, principal houses, farms, granges, lands, tenements, and hereditaments, as the ornaments of their churches, and their goods and chattels, to the high displeasure of Almighty God, slander of good religion, and to the great infamy of the king's highness and the realm, if redress should not be had thereof. And albeit that many continual visitations hath been heretofore had, by the space of two hundred years and more, for an honest and charitable reformation of such unthrifty, carnal, and abominable living, yet nevertheless little or none amendment is hitherto had, but their vicious living shamelessly increases and augments, and by a cursed custom so rooted and infected, that a great multitude of the religious persons in such small houses do rather choose to rove abroad in apostasy, than to conform themselves to the observation of good religion; so that without such small houses be utterly suppressed, and the religious persons therein committed to great and honorable monasteries of religion in this realm, where they may be compelled to live religiously, for reformation of their lives, there can else be no redress nor reformation in that behalf.[12]

But the dissolution was also potentially highly profitable to the king, for he simply appropriated the lands and property of the religious houses, with "all their rights, profits, jurisdictions, and commodities." He took the opportunity to reward loyal servants with lands, and thus to create the English gentry of the next few centuries.

On the other hand, England was left suddenly without a number of social provisions for which the monasteries had become responsible. The friars and pardoners, banned by the Reformation parliaments in

---

[12]The full text of the Act is available at www.tudorplace.com.ar/Documents/act_dissolution1.htm.

England, sometimes became vagrants. The Elizabethan Poor Laws placed great emphasis on supporting only local people who were needy precisely because these wanderers could not be vouched for as genuine and honest poor, rather than mendicant beggars or religious outlaws.[13]

---

[13]A. V. Judges, *The Elizabethan Underworld* (London: Routledge, 1930).

18

PEACEFUL EXTREMISTS?

The Anabaptist Heirs of the Medieval Sects

HULDREICH ZWINGLI AND
THE BATTLE WITH THE ANABAPTISTS

Zwingli was one of the Reformers who had met and been influenced by Erasmus at the University of Basel between 1514 and 1516.[1] He had learned Greek and also Hebrew, so he was able to read the Old Testament in that language.[2] From 1519 he was serving as a pastor in Zurich, where he became noted for his preaching.

From the beginning of his time in Zurich he decided to go back to the practice of some of the famous preachers of the early church, such as Augustine and Gregory; he would preach his way through a book of the Bible at a time, beginning with Matthew's Gospel. This in effect meant combining preaching with lecturing. During the medieval centuries the two had become formally distinct, with university students hearing lectures and occasional sermons separately. But now the need was recognized for preaching to congregations of ordinary people in their own language. These were not university students, but they were hungry for teaching.

Zwingli's frankly expressed opinions marked him straight away as a Reformer, and a bold one. He shared Luther's indignation about the

---

[1]G. R. Potter, *Zwingli* (Cambridge: Cambridge University Press, 1976).
[2]Heinrich Bullinger, *Reformationsgeschichte*, 1.30, trans. *The Reformation in Its Own Words*, ed. Hans J. Hillebrand (London: SCM Press, 1964), p. 120.

church's teaching on indulgences. The "pardoners," whose job was to raise money for the building of St. Peter's in Rome by selling portions of time off from a sentence to be served in purgatory while undischarged penances were complete, came to Zurich too. Zwingli's flock asked him what he thought. He told them in no uncertain terms.

He also spoke out on favorite themes of the Reformers, against the veneration of saints and fasting in Lent (openly sponsoring the handing out of sausages as a provocative gesture on a fast day in March 1522). He married in secret and publicly claimed that there was no need for priestly celibacy. He denied that children who died unbaptized automatically went to hell. He campaigned against the friars, claiming among other things that they were at fault on social policy grounds, and that their wealth and their buildings should be applied to the needs of the poor, for example in the running of hospitals.

The authorities became uneasy. The question was whether the threat Zwingli posed was merely spiritual or a challenge to the good order of the city. The answer to that question was wrapped up with whether he should be examined by the city council or the ecclesiastical authorities. Zwingli was called to account before the council, expecting a public disputation, but he was not allowed to conduct one. The church's representatives argued that theological questions ought not to be discussed in front of laypeople. On this occasion the city council did not force the matter to a condemnation.

In 1523 a further concern led to the calling of another meeting of the city council. There were those who wanted to take their condemnation of images further and destroy statues and pictures in churches. This was leading to vandalism and violence. Several hundred people are said to have come to this meeting, and it was not possible for the church authorities to say it was none of their business this time. The bishop simply absented himself.

Extremists took the chance to make their own demands. Many of the repeating patterns of social and theological complaint which run through the discontent of medieval dissidents became mainstream concerns of the Reformers. Some became the special anxieties of extreme wings of reforming activity, such as the Anabaptists, and were decisively rejected by other groups.

The Anabaptists were already causing concern early in the Reformation. The Augsburg Confession of 1530, presented by Luther's supporters to the diet which met at Augsburg in April of that year, contains a series of disclaimers rejecting Anabaptist opinions, which neatly flags the areas of left-wing opinion that caused the moderate Reformers most concern. This tended to polarize the would-be Reformers and encourage the fragmentation we have already seen in the debates on key issues in which Lutherans and others engaged.

The Anabaptists with whom Zwingli had to deal wanted immediate and radical change in Christian society, a program which often coalesced around a rejection of infant baptism. They also sometimes wanted to overthrow the civil government so that the truly righteous might rule. Zwingli took the side of good order. He worked with the authorities to maintain the rule that infants must be baptized and anyone who refused to baptize their babies must leave Zurich. The Anabaptists took no notice and began the practice of adult baptism, denying that the infant baptism they had themselves experienced had been baptism at all. The dispute deteriorated into slanging matches, with the two sides shouting at one another. In 1526 the city council ordered that rebaptism should carry the death penalty.

In the end, however, the city council compromised. It agreed to the removal of images but undertook to arrange for them to be taken out in an orderly manner. Zwingli's party won the council's consent to a number of other modest but significant changes of custom and practice.

The fierceness of feeling on the subject of baptism had its counterpart in the strong divisions of opinion about the Eucharist we have already glimpsed among the Lutherans and their challengers. By 1525 Zwingli was replacing the old liturgy for the Eucharist with a new one of his own devising, which would emphasize its primary character as a memorial meal and an act of thanksgiving. Instead of silver vessels there were to be wooden cups and plates, and the congregation was to sit at tables, as it would for its meals at home. The central moment in the service was the sermon, not the consecration and distribution of the bread and wine.

The marks of other changes were apparent to everyone in the absence of music in church services. Also missing among Zwingli's followers were the ancient and familiar celebrations of the church year. No feast was held at Candlemas in February and there was no Palm Sunday procession.

One of the serious drawbacks to the replacing of ecclesiastical with secular authorities (as in Lutheran Christian lands), which these Swiss Reformers were now tempted to do, was this unavoidable entanglement of church affairs with politics. The thirteen Swiss cantons became divided into Reformed and their Roman Catholic opponents, and they went to war in 1529. Zwingli himself was killed in battle in 1531, and his disappearance from the scene so early may be one reason for the comparatively minor role his approach played in subsequent events.

LUTHERAN "GOOD CITIZENS" AND ANABAPTIST "ANARCHY"

The need to distance themselves from the radicals probably helped to push the Lutherans into a conventional respectability.[3] One of the most important features of the claims of the Waldensians and the Lollards had been that the faithful could be saved without a ministry of the Word and sacraments offered in and through the institutional church by properly approved ministers. It may well be that the driving motivation was resentment of clerical privilege and perceived clerical corruption, but the effect was to mount a radical challenge to the doctrine of ordained ministry. The Lutherans (Augsburg Confession, art. 5) said that "the Ministry of teaching the Gospel and administering the Sacraments was instituted" as the chosen means through which the Holy Spirit works by grace to justify those who believe. "[We] condemn the Anabaptists and others who think that the Holy Ghost comes to men without the external Word, through their own preparations and works."

The sacrament of baptism was particularly important to the traditional view, for those who held that through baptism the Spirit confers membership in the church and union with Christ, so that baptism is a

---

[3] Hans-Jürgen Goertz, *The Anabaptists* (London: Routledge, 1996).

necessary means of salvation. In article 9 of the Augsburg Confession the Lutherans therefore "condemn the Anabaptists, who reject the baptism of children, and say that children are saved without Baptism."

The further cluster of Anabaptist opinions from which the Lutherans wished formally to dissociate themselves concerned participation as good citizens in the affairs of this world. The Lutherans were keen to be good citizens.

> [We] teach that lawful civil ordinances are good works of God, and that it is right for Christians to bear civil office, to sit as judges, to judge matters by the Imperial and other existing laws, to award just punishments, to engage in just wars, to serve as soldiers, to make legal contracts, to hold property, to make oath when required by the magistrates, to marry a wife, to be given in marriage. (art. 16)

Anabaptists are condemned because they "forbid these civil offices to Christians." The background to this radical difference of opinion was a series of events of the early 1520s. The extremists had a revolutionary social agenda. The Zwickau Prophets called for a new world order in which peasants would be the equals of their social superiors and nearly all traditional family and civil institutional structures would be rendered obsolete.

Thomas Münzer. Münzer (c. 1488-1525) had a university education at Leipzig and Frankfurt and therefore belongs to the group of academic activists who were theologically informed but also capable of rabble-rousing. He was a political radical and came into conflict with Luther over his conviction that if there was to be reform it should be social reform as well as reform of the church. He became a pastor at Zwickau in 1520 and began to meet opposition from the church authorities, especially when he began to preach against infant baptism. By 1524 he had made himself a leader of a "peasants' war," which had among its objectives the creation of a communal society where all goods were held in common. He pitched his claims in a way which better reflected the disillusions of townspeople and failed to rouse up the peasantry as he had hoped, and in the end he was defeated and executed, and his severed head publicly displayed as a warning to others.

It was not that Luther had no time for a call for social justice, but he disliked the destructiveness of the movement and the plundering and looting by the mob. He sided with the authorities, and the position he took in these early and formative years contributed to the development of the Lutheran approach of working closely with Christian magistrates.

The Zwickau prophets under the leadership of Nicholas Storch (d. 1525) had been particularly alarming on this front because they believed the end of the world was at hand and the Holy Spirit was leading them to create a spiritual kingdom on earth. Because of their apocalypticism, Anabaptists were considered eccentric on the theology of the last things as well as on the theology of present things.

Anabaptist beliefs. The shape of a body of beliefs may be seen both negatively, through the points condemned by others, and positively, through the confessional statements now commonly being formulated by each community who shared a particular set of opinions. The Schleitheim Confession of the Swiss Brethren, 1527, provides a useful example of a typical Anabaptist view of what was important to their position: "The articles . . . in which we have been united, are these: baptism, ban [excommunication], the breaking of bread, separation from abomination, shepherds in the congregation, the sword, the oath."[4]

The rejection of infant baptism tended to be fundamental among Anabaptists, and with it the insistence that baptism in the mainstream church was not baptism at all. The Anabaptists did not consider that they were rebaptizing believers. They were baptizing them for the first time. Only the properly baptized could take part in the Eucharist and be full-fledged members of the community. (Schleitheim Confession 3).

Excommunication, exclusion from the sacraments of the church, had become controversial in the medieval world because it was used as a weapon by the papacy to bring secular rulers to order. It was bad enough for the excommunicated monarch, since a person who died in a state of excommunication was deemed to be bound for hell. There was "no salvation outside the church," and such a person was put outside by the "ban." This also affected the subjects of an excommunicated ruler. The

---

[4] *The Schleitheim Text, Brotherly Union of a Number of Children of God Concerning Seven Articles,* trans. and ed. John Howard Yoder, www.anabaptists.org/history/the-schleitheim-confession.html.

church also taught that if a king or emperor was excommunicated, the sacraments could not be properly celebrated in his realm.

The Anabaptists were strict in insisting on personal and communal separation from evil. This was another characteristic feature of the extremist Reformers, and it had several faces. A dimension of some of the groups which belong in the Anabaptist range of reforming opinion was the conviction that they were the only remnant of the true church and must keep themselves pure. These preached separation from the world and an exclusivist attitude. There must be no fellowship with the wicked (Schleitheim Confession 4). They threw out those of their own members who broke ranks or acted in such a way as to deserve to be disciplined, though the usual course was to warn those who repeatedly slipped, and to keep the ban as a final and exceptional recourse.

Ministers are simply to be pastors (Schleitheim Confession 5), men of good repute, chosen and appointed by their congregations, whose work is to "read and exhort and teach, warn, admonish, or ban in the congregation" and to lead or "preside." They are not ordained in the traditional sense in which the medieval church understood the term, as conferring an indelible character or stamp by the action of the Holy Spirit, a stamp which made them priests forever.

With some exceptions, the Anabaptists set their faces against violence and also against the taking of oaths, because they believed Jesus had forbidden it. The words of Christ are especially clear and say what they mean. An example is Jesus' very call to make "yes" "yes" and "no" "no," and to avoid extreme language (Mt 5:33-37; cf. Jas 5:12). The ban on swearing had been taken extremely seriously by dissidents from the late Middle Ages, who included the taking of any form of oath as well as swearing in the sense of "taking the name of God in vain" or the use of profane language in general.

This resistance to oath-taking was of course one of the most typical features of medieval dissidence and often used as the main test by medieval inquisitors and their later heirs. The same feature was important as late as the English Quaker Act of 1662, which required the taking of an oath of loyalty to the monarch. It was known that the Quakers refused to swear, and this was felt to be dangerous to national security.

Anabaptists argued that the Bible is its own interpreter, in the sense that it can be taken to mean simply what it says in its immediate context.[5] The New Testament takes precedence over the Old, but the Holy Spirit present here and now can be trusted to guide the reader through any difficulty. This was found to lead to some problems of conflicting interpretation among members of the local congregation, which the Anabaptists tried to resolve through a mutual process of congregational exegesis.

---

[5]Stuart Murray, "Biblical Interpretation Among the Anabaptist Reformers," *A History of Biblical Interpretation*, ed. Alan J. Hauser and Duane F. Watson (Grand Rapids: Eerdmans, 2009), p. 408ff.

19

CALVIN AND HIS HEIRS

The Reformed Churches

JOHN CALVIN

Calvin became a Reformer in the generation after Luther. Much had changed in that generation. Whereas Luther had an essentially medieval university education as a young man, Calvin's was much more strongly flavored not only with Renaissance learning but also with new expectations about the balance of different sorts of knowledge to be expected, and he grew up in a climate where reforming ideas were in the air, even in Roman Catholic France.

He studied at the Collège de la Marche and then the Collège de Montaigu in Paris. Plans to study law took him on to Orléans, but he experienced a conversion and his plans for his life were transformed. He describes this moment in his preface to his *Commentary on the Psalms* as an experience of being abruptly shaken out of his previous convictions: "God by a sudden conversion subdued and brought my mind to a teachable frame, which was more hardened in such matters than might have been expected from one at my early period of life."[1]

He became, with the zeal of the convert, eager to pursue the truths he had newly glimpsed and reluctant to spend time on other activities. He found that he was drawn to Protestant reform. Within a year others joined themselves to him, seeing him as their natural leader and seeking

---

[1]John Calvin, *Commentary on Psalms* 1, preface, www.ccel.org/ccel/calvin/calcom08.vi.html.

him out, although he was, in his own estimation, shy and unpolished
and a mere beginner. By this new way of life and his power to attract
followers, he made himself dangerously unpopular in his native France.
He says he fled to Germany partly to get away from these hangers-on,
with the purpose of leading a more retired life so that he could explore
his new thoughts about God, but once more his retreats became like
public "schools." He moved on again, arrived in Switzerland and settled
in Basel, where his presence was known to only a few people at first.

But his determination to live a retired life did not cut him off for long
from the news about what was going on elsewhere. While he was in
Basel he heard about the burning of "faithful and holy persons" in France.
This caused such a flurry of popular indignation that briefings were cir-
culated by the authorities responsible, claiming that only dangerous
Anabaptists were being punished in this way. Calvin found himself out-
raged by this spin, defending the reformers with passion and coming to
public prominence again.

It was this episode which seems to have prompted him to write his
Institutes of the Christian Religion, first published in 1536. He wanted to
set the record straight and cleanse the reputations of these martyrs to
ensure that others could learn not only the truth *about* what they believed but also what he considered to be the truth *of* their beliefs. From
the beginning Calvin's *Institutes* sold very well, and he was soon preparing a second edition, which involved considerable revision, while
he rethought how best to make it serve its purpose as a compendium
for Christians seeking to learn about their faith and understand the
contemporary reforms in a systematic way. He sought to do this anon-
ymously and left Basel to go once more into hiding if he could, this
time at Strasbourg.

William Farel (1489-1565) had been a pupil of Jacques Lefèvre
d'Étaples (c. 1455-1536). Faber Stapulensis, as the latter was also known,
had been Erasmus's rival in the venture of making new Latin Bible
translations. Farel became a French Reformer and a stirring preacher
who had also felt obliged to move to Switzerland to do the work to
which he believed he was called. As a man of his generation, he naturally began his reforming life as a disciple of Luther. Farel had already

spent time in Zurich, which was a major center of Swiss reforming activity, and there he met Zwingli. He had been at Strasbourg too, where he was able to talk to Bucer. By 1536 he was in Geneva; upon learning that Calvin was passing through on his way to Strasbourg, Farel put it to him with the passion of a prophet that God needed him to work openly for reform, and he must give up his wish to live a retired life of scholarship. He urged Calvin to help him lead reform in Geneva.

Here we may observe the effect of the way the Swiss arranged their civic life. Switzerland was a confederacy of cantons or areas, six of which were rural and seven were cities. Each canton was autonomous and their governance varied. The "land" cantons tended to be democratically run, while the cities, though nominally democracies, tended to be controlled by their leading families and were consequently more like oligarchies. But in any case, the division into relatively small political units in a small area meant that a few individuals could have a powerful influence or pose a forceful challenge.

Geneva was far from quiet. Calvin tried at first to refuse to accept any ecclesiastical office there, but the Anabaptists and other factions were openly squabbling in the city and he found he could not remain behind the scenes. He accepted a modest ministerial status as a "reader," which allowed him to teach and preach, if not to exercise a full pastoral ministry. Settled at Geneva, Calvin became an assiduous preacher—twice on Sunday, three times in the week—and a dedicated reformer. His plans included fundamental change to the liturgy, with the congregation joining in the singing and a requirement that those who wished to be members of their community should accept a simple reformed confession of faith.

Geneva was not very receptive to Farel and Calvin's reforms. The city council objected that few had subscribed to this confession of faith, and it was not appropriate to make it a requirement. The councilors wanted the reformers to comply with certain liturgical practices in Bern, a neighboring city whose political support Geneva needed. Besides, there were negotiations occurring with France, and it would not be helpful for Geneva to be sheltering two high-profile renegade Frenchmen. Geneva expelled them both in 1538. For a time (1538-1541) Calvin finally got his chance to go to Strasbourg, where Bucer had invited him.

Geneva was obliged to think again about its reforming stance when it received a letter from Cardinal Sadoleto urging it to return to its allegiance to the Roman Catholic Church. Calvin was asked to write a reply by some who were favorably disposed to his views, and he robustly defended the reforms at Geneva. A grateful city invited the somewhat reluctant Calvin back, in 1541. Geneva was now much more receptive to his ideas. City ordinances were passed in November 1541 defining the four essential ministerial tasks: the administration of the sacraments, the teaching of the faith, the maintenance of good order and discipline, care for the poor. The intention was that specialist ministers should carry responsibility for each of these. Calvin remained in Geneva for the rest of his career, doing much to shape the Reformed faith which was to color the religious life of much of northern Europe for centuries.

Nevertheless, Calvin did not often find Geneva a comfortable place to exercise his ministry. He felt that some of those he had influenced and encouraged in the assurance that they enjoyed freedom through grace considered that they no longer had a duty to obey any law, of church or state. These "libertines" came from a cluster of Geneva's important and powerful families, the families which really ran the place. Though he attacked their morality, the rivalry was primarily political—and Calvin was never quite forgiven for being a Frenchman.

Serious trouble arrived in the person of the Spaniard Michael Servetus (c. 1511-1553). He had been corresponding with an increasingly irritated Calvin, attacking parts of the *Institutes*. He had long disputed the doctrine of the Trinity and had been engaged for some years in public debates, including one as early as 1530 in Basel. In 1553, the Inquisition had convicted him of heresy and the city of Vienne had sentenced him to death, though he narrowly escaped. He came to Geneva on his way to Italy and went to hear one of Calvin's sermons. Calvin spotted him, and Servetus was arrested and brought to answer a list of allegations in court in Geneva. Calvin was the trial's chief prosecutor and expert witness. Servetus was condemned by the city authorities, and though Calvin attempted to get his sentence commuted to beheading, the Spaniard was burned as a heretic along with his books on the outskirts of Geneva.

By 1555 more French exiles had Genevan citizenship, and Calvin's supporters formed an elected majority. The "libertines" were sidelined and some driven out. An ecclesiastical polity on Calvinist lines was given relatively free reign. This was an important moment for the European Reformation.

These events all prompted fresh consideration of the doctrine of ministry the Reformers were to adopt. Whereas the Lutherans had tended to see no reason to depart from the traditional hierarchy headed by an episcopate, those who were to become known as the Calvinists or the Reformed (with a capital R) saw things differently. Calvin wrote a letter to Olevianus summarizing his position. He explains that in his church would-be ministers have to demonstrate their knowledge and understanding of Scripture and be examined on their grasp of doctrine. They have to preach a specimen sermon. A senate or appointing committee then decides whether they are qualified, and if they are approved their names are published for the people to see. If anyone knows anything against them, there should be an opportunity to object. But the process has a secular input and secular controls, and it amounts to ministerial appointment rather than sacramental ordination.

Order is maintained in the congregations by observance of certain principles. Infants are to be baptized in the presence of the congregation and not privately. Only those who have demonstrated some mastery of the faith and have passed an examination are admitted to the Eucharist. This includes newcomers to the community who may be experienced believers but must still demonstrate their good standing.

There is also an inspection of the peace and good order maintained domestically by families who worship with the congregation. A committee of twelve elders supervises morals and conduct, failure to attend church regularly, blaspheming, drunkenness, fornication, dancing and other misbehaviors. Minor offenders are gently reproved. The more serious offenses, including doctrinal error, may be punished with excommunication.[2]

Consolidating a Reformed theology. Calvin was not universally regarded

---

[2]John Calvin, Letter 26 (to Olevianus), November 1560.

as safe in his theological views. For examle, he was accused of Arianism in 1537 by a truculant minister in Lausanne, Pierre Caroli. He felt obliged to put the record straight in a reply in *Confession on the Trinity* (*Confessio de Trinitate*). Despite such challenges, Calvin's catechetical work, of which the *Institutes* formed the bedrock, continued with the drafting of catechisms for the church of Geneva (published in 1537 and 1542). Calvin was not setting out to create an alternative reforming strand from that which Luther had woven, any more than he wanted to start a new church. Still, through his work along with that of many others a set of Reformed confessional positions was now becoming clear, though not in the same way as had happened in the evolution of Lutheranism, with formal public statements.

The last and largest edition of the *Institutes* appeared in 1559. The six chapters of 1536 had become eighty, in four books, with new topics modeled on Melanchthon's *Loci Communes* and engaging the debates of the intervening years in which Calvin had become involved. The basic systematic structure depended on the sequence of the Creed.

How are we saved? Calvin turns, in book 3 of the *Institutes*, to the practical question how God saves and how the believer receives this accomplished and offered salvation. Calvin begins his discussion of the working of grace, with the warning that Christ's death is not automatically beneficial.

> As long as Christ remains outside of us, and we are separated from him, all that he has suffered and done for the salvation of the human race remains useless and of no value to us. Therefore, to share with us what he has received from the Father, he had to become ours and to dwell within us. . . . Hence [the Spirit] is called the "Spirit of sanctification" . . . because he not only quickens and nourishes us by a general power that is visible both in the human race and in the rest of the living creatures, but he is also the root and seed of heavenly life in us.[3]

Faith in Christ is then the gift of the Spirit (3.1.4).

Predestination. This process of the self-giving and indwelling of the Holy Spirit takes place in those God has already chosen and redeemed

---

[3]Calvin, *Institutes*, 3.1.1-2.

in Christ from all eternity, the elect. Calvin's strong Augustinian doctrine of predestination—with its concurrent doctrine of reprobation, God's eternal decision to permit much of humanity to remain "outside" Christ's redemptive work, and to judge them justly for their sins—was predictably controversial, as had commonly happened when doctrines of predestination were propounded in earlier centuries. It is famously difficult to reconcile a strong belief in predestination with confidence in the operation of human free will. It can easily look as though God is making the sinner sin. Jérôme-Hermès Bolsec (d. c. 1584), a medical practitioner in Geneva, accused Calvin of preaching exactly that in 1551. Geneva banished him, but he remained resentful in exile and wrote attacks on Calvin's character. Calvin's *On the Eternal Predestination of God* (*De Aeterna Praedestinatione Dei*) was published in 1552 in Geneva in an attempt to put the record straight.

He was prompted to write the book both by this episode and by one of the academic squabbles of the day. Albertus Pighius (c. 1490-1542) had studied at Louvain and Cologne. He became an ecclesiastical diplomat in the papal service and a polemicist in the debates on key themes of the day at issue between Reformers and the church. In *De Libero Hominis Arbitrio et Divina Gratia Libri X* (Cologne, 1542) he argued against Calvin's teaching (and also Luther's). Calvin identifies "such of Pighius' objections as have any plausibility."[4] The ensuing summary is heavily fleshed with quotations from Scripture, those on which Pighius relies and Calvin's counter-quotations. Pighius had claimed that "the whole question turns on this: To what end was man created?" Pighius says God did not need human beings to glorify him. He created them as beings who would be capable of receiving his goodness. No, says Calvin, the Bible says that to glorify God is "the chief and ultimate end of man's salvation." Pighius says God gave human beings free will because this was essential to the potential of human beings to enjoy his goodness. So predestination becomes a logical impossibility. Each person is in control of his own destiny. "Therefore God, as if blind, awaited the outcome in doubt and suspense," says Calvin, mockingly paraphrasing Pighius. And Pighius argues that

---

[4]Calvin, *Concerning the Eternal Predestination of God* 6, trans. J. K. S. Reid (London: James Clarke, 1961), p. 96.

salvation is offered to all, and not to a select and elect few.[5] Throughout
this account Calvin throws in insults to Pighius's sanity and calls him
"rabid and petulant," and illiterate ("he pours out words without sense
and in contempt of grammar").[6]

The heart of the matter, if it is suggested that God predestines the
condemned to hell as well as the elect to heaven, is whether this makes
God seem the author of evil; that must be impossible if he is wholly good.
This had been a point of major controversy in Carolingian times. Calvin's
key passage on reprobation (the divine predestination of the condemnation of the damned) is to be found in *De Aeterna Praedestinatione Dei* (5.5).
He relies heavily on the passage in Isaiah 6:9 where the prophet is sent out
to preach to a people who will not understand, but later implies that a
chosen few will hear and receive. Calvin discusses the implication that
this seems to make God the author of evil, by addressing the argument
that "if all things are done by the will of God, and men contrive nothing
except by his will and ordination, then God is the author of all evils"
(10.14). His explanation is that God's actions are all good, but they may,
through the responsible actions of sinful humanity, lead to evil consequences. That does not make God the cause of the evil.[7]

Is this fair? Calvin could regard divine reprobation as perfectly fair,
provided it was properly understood how thoroughly everyone deserves
to spend eternity in hell. He felt, much as Augustine had, that the rescue of anyone is an act of unimaginable mercy and generosity by God.
Condemnation is in this case the height of fairness, and mercy the opposite of what is deserved: "Those justly perish who are by nature children of wrath. Thus no one has cause to complain of the too great severity of God, seeing that all carry in themselves inclusive liability."[8] This
was very much Augustine's view.

A special Calvinist development of the doctrine of predestination
was the belief that the elect can certainly know they are such and enjoy
assurance on the point. This was to have potential pastoral disadvan-

---

[5]Ibid., pp. 96-99.
[6]Ibid., pp. 110-11.
[7]Ibid., 10.14.5, p. 179ff.
[8]Ibid., 8.5, p. 121.

tages if handled badly, in that it followed for some that however badly behaved and sinful the elect were, nothing could lose them heaven. But Calvin would say that good behavior could not win heaven either; it is simply the true fruit of election to faith and incorporation into Christ.

Eucharist. Calvin wrote from Geneva on October 7, 1543, to advise the people of the church of Montbelliard, who had asked him questions about the Eucharist.[9] He set out principles of good practice for them. Those who wish to receive the bread and wine should present themselves to the minister beforehand. The aim of this requirement is to ensure that they are worthy, and it was intended to replace the medieval expectation (reinforced by the Fourth Lateran Council of 1215) that the faithful should go to confession and receive absolution before receiving Holy Communion. With the removal of this requirement, new rules had to be designed in order to protect what Calvin describes as the "purity" and the "discipline" of the church. He recommends that the interview with the minister should be a private examination and that the minister should use the occasion as an opportunity to advise and encourage.

One of the most important changes reformers wished to see was the return to the understanding that the Eucharist is a communion, an act of worship of the community together, and not a solitary or private act of the minister as it had sometimes been in the later Middle Ages. Private Masses for the dead, paid for by anxious relatives, carried several theological assumptions the Reformers now questioned. The idea that the priest celebrating such a Mass was making a separate sacrifice somehow additional to the sacrifice of Christ on the cross was now being challenged, and the conceptions about the personal powers of priests which went with it.

Yet the Mass should remain a special event, Calvin insisted. Do not indulge in indiscriminate private use of it, he advises, allowing it to be confused with an ordinary supper. It is not right to treat all your meals as though they were Eucharists. Nonetheless, Calvin desired that the Eucharist should be celebrated frequently, whenever the church came together to hear the preaching of the Word. It is a real communion with

---

[9]John Calvin, Letter 9, to members of the church of Montbelliard, abridged, www.godrules.net/library/calvin/143calvin14.htm.

the body and blood of Christ, though with faith by the Spirit more than
the lips and the teeth. Calvin pressed for weekly celebration, but the
Genevan authorities would not sanction it any more frequently than
every quarter.

In Calvin's work as in Luther's, the mingling of advanced theology
and an attempt to meet the needs expressed by popular demand shaped
the system like a pair of hands modeling a clay vessel, countering one
another harmoniously to form the whole.

FRANCE, HUGUENOTS AND
SOME NOTABLE WOMEN

Women too became fired with reforming zeal, but the opportunities
for them to make their mark depended on class and opportunity as
much as on enthusiasm or ability. For those who had a role in public
life through birth or marriage, there were routes by which they could
exert an influence. That did not make it possible for them to become
recognized intellectual leaders, though some were very able. Mary
Queen of Scots (1542-1587) spoke several European languages and had
a reputation for cleverness. Elizabeth I could hold her own with her
bishops and archbishops when it came to discussing the content of
the Elizabethan Settlement of 1559 and after, which has underpinned
the Church of England ever since. But the old route to intellectual
recognition which had been open to abbesses such as Hildegard of
Bingen and Gertrude the Great was closed with the decisive rejection
of the monastic life by almost all strands of the reforming movement
and with the closing of religious houses in some parts of Europe. Although Elizabeth was feted by the University of Oxford, which offered her cerebrally challenging entertainments such as Latin orations
and academic disputations when she visited it in 1592, apparently well
aware that she was capable of appreciating them, women could not
become university graduates or recognized scholarly authorities. They
might write pious works of a conventional kind, even become saints,
but not enter the lists in scholarly disputation with male theologians.

However, some of the female French aristocracy found themselves in positions where they could make a significant mark on events. In 1531, Marguerite of Navarre (1492-1549) wrote a controversial *Mirror of the Sinful Soul* (*Miroir de l'âme Pécheresse*), which was condemned by the academic theologians of the Sorbonne as a heretical work. One monk was said to have proposed that she should be put into a sack and thrown into the river Seine. She was rescued.

More commonly, able women who supported Protestant ideals had their say as the consorts of influential men. This is particularly noticeable in France and the Netherlands. Marguerite was married (for the second time) to Henry II of Navarre (1503-1555). She gained a reputation for diplomacy. She became a patron of the arts. She encouraged leading writers to frequent her social gatherings at court. She favored reform in the Roman Catholic Church. When John Calvin's ideas spread in France and his influence began to be felt, she was interested. Though she did not choose to leave the Roman Catholic Church and join the Calvinists, she acted in a diplomatic capacity to assist attempts at discussion between Calvin and the church authorities. And she did what she could, again using her well-developed diplomatic skills, to ensure that Francis I of France (king from 1515-1547), a Renaissance but not a reforming monarch, did not oppress the Reformers unduly.

Marguerite's daughter Jeanne d'Albret (1528-1572) and her husband succeeded Henry II after his death. The French Wars of Religion began in 1562, prompted as much by secular politics and the rivalries of the great noble houses as by religious commitment. Jeanne's husband died fighting for the Catholic side in 1562, in one of the early battles in these wars.

As a widow, Jeanne ruled Navarre in her own person until 1572, as the mother of the minor heir, Henry IV of France (see p. 120). She was said to be slight but fiercely intelligent and combative. As early as Christmas 1560 she publicly acknowledged her own reforming views, and from 1568 she came to be recognized as a leader of the Huguenot (Calvinist) cause both politically and in terms of the beliefs it supported. There were dangers to her life in this, and she had to take refuge in the Huguenot city of La Rochelle.

She adopted an essentially Erastian (see pp. 383-84) or state-dominated approach to imposing reform in her own territories. She called a conference of reforming ministers. She declared the Reformed faith the official religion of her realm. Catholic churches were destroyed, priests, monks and nuns banished, and the practice of Catholic worship banned. A vernacular translation of the New Testament was commissioned. But in France at large she sought peace and took an active part in the negotiation of the settlements that temporarily ended the war. The pause was not for long.

The St. Bartholomew's Day Massacre. On August 24, 1572, a mass assassination of the Protestants was planned, and it led to further mob violence. Another woman of great influence, the Queen Mother Catherine de' Medici (1519-1589), was rumored to be behind it. The massacre had its effect, because it removed many of the leading figures of the Protestant movement and sent many Huguenots into exile in more sympathetic lands, and it may have contributed in that way to the eventual triumph of Roman Catholicism in France.

An eyewitness account of the way the massacre was initiated survives, in the massive *History of His Times* of Jacques Auguste de Thou (1553-1617), a politician and historian.

> The duke of Guise, who was put in full command of the enterprise, summoned by night several captains of the Catholic Swiss mercenaries from the five little cantons, and some commanders of French companies, and told them that it was the will of the king that, according to God's will, they should take vengeance on the band of rebels. . . . Victory was easy and the booty great and to be obtained without danger. The signal to commence the massacre should be given by the bell of the palace, and the marks by which they should recognize each other in the darkness were a bit of white linen tied around the left arm and a white cross on the hat.[10]

The assassinations were a bloody business, characterized by the kind of behavior also described in accounts of medieval episodes of mob brutality. At the death of Huguenot leader Gaspard de Coligny (1519-1572),

> After his body had been treated to all sorts of insults, they threw it into a neighbouring stable, and finally cut off his head, which they sent to Rome. They also shamefully mutilated him, and dragged his body through the

---

[10]Jacques Auguste de Thou, *Histoire des Choses Arrivees de Son Temps* (Paris, 1659), p. 658ff., in J. H. Robinson, 2 vols. (Boston: Ginn, 1906), 2:180-83, www.fordham.edu/halsall/mod/1572 stbarts.html.

streets to the bank of the Seine, a thing which he had formerly almost prophesied, although he did not think of anything like this. As some children were in the act of throwing the body into the river, it was dragged out and placed upon the gibbet of Montfaucon, where it hung by the feet in chains of iron; and then they built a fire beneath, by which he was burned without being consumed; so that he was, so to speak, tortured with all the elements, since he was killed upon the earth, thrown into the water, placed upon the fire, and finally put to hang in the air.[11]

Catherine's precise part in all this and her intentions remain a vexed question, but her influence seems indisputable.

In the Netherlands too, women's names appear in the power plays of the process by which Protestants or Roman Catholics eventually determined the religious norms of the region. Charlotte of Bourbon (1546-1582) had been brought up in a convent with the intention that she should become a nun. In 1572, she escaped, fled the country and became a high-profile Reformed convert. In 1575 she became the third wife of William the Silent (1533-1584), the prince of Orange, who led the Dutch in their attempts to resist Spanish domination. His fourth wife (from 1583) was Louise de Coligny (1555-1620), whose first husband had died with her father in the massacre of St. Bartholomew's Day.

JOHN KNOX AND SCOTLAND

That the Reformed faith took hold so strongly in Scotland was largely the work of John Knox (c. 1513-1572).[12] He had served as a chaplain to Edward VI and had some influence on the framing of the Book of Common Prayer in its early form before he was drawn into the Reformed camp. For example, he objected to the requirement to kneel at Holy Communion, because he said it would encourage worshipers to look on the consecrated bread and wine in an idolatrous manner. That could indeed have been the case in the past; the faithful who believed—according to the doctrine of transubstantiation—that the bread was really transformed into the body of Christ occasionally reported that

---

[11]Ibid.

[12]Alec Ryrie, *The Origins of the Scottish Reformation* (Manchester: Manchester University Press, 2006).

they saw a complete miniature Jesus when the host was elevated. Knox was not the only one to see difficulties in the practice of kneeling. Cranmer was persuaded to add a clear statement to the rubric to stress that the kneeling does not connote adoration of the sacramental elements themselves.

Going into exile in Geneva when Mary became queen, Knox met Calvin in person. He asked him for guidance as to whether a woman could be a legitimate ruler, and if not, what Christian citizens were to do. Perhaps seeing a gleam of impassioned feeling in his eye, Calvin advised him cautiously and sent him off to talk to Bullinger in Zurich. Knox's hostility to Mary Queen of Scots—and also to "Bloody Mary" Tudor's (1516-1558) occupation of the throne of England—derived from their staunch Roman Catholicism. Having taken advice, he presented it as an attack of "the monstrous regiment [rule] of women" in his *First Blast of the Trumpet*, which was published in 1558 while he was still in Geneva.

Bullinger was a successor of Zwingli and influenced by the ideas of Waldensian communities which survived in continental Europe. Where there was controversy his name was liable to appear. He had been involved in the debates on the Eucharist with both Luther and Calvin. By 1548-1549 Bullinger was helping Calvin draft the document that was to become the Consensus Tigurinus (1549), whose aim was agreement on the Eucharist between Calvinian and Zwinglian Reformed accounts. Bullinger also wrote the Second Helvetic Confession (1562-1564), an originally private attempt to provide a unifying statement of Reformed faith for the Swiss churches which was longer and a bit less Lutheran than the First Helvetic Confession of 1536 (Bullinger had been involved in the drafting of that too). This new version was highly successful, eventually adopted not only in Switzerland but in Scotland, Hungary, France and Poland. It became for much of the Reformed community the counterpart of the Lutheran Book of Concord.

From Calvin and his colleagues, Knox learned a new way of looking at the question of governance in the church and the old disputes about bishops. The Reformed taught him the advantages of a presbyterian form of ministry. In due course John Knox came to be regarded as a leader by many of the English community that settled at Geneva during

Mary's reign, with some dozens of new admissions of church members each year. The community ran itself as a presbyterian congregation, the only group of exiles at the time to do so. Knox designed an order of service, derived from that of Calvin, and which, with revisions and new editions, was to form the basis of the Book of Our Common Order until 1645 when it was replaced by the Westminster Directory.

When Elizabeth succeeded her sister as queen of England in 1558, Knox returned from exile, but to Scotland not to England. In Scotland he set about creating a presbyterian polity for the church. In Scotland politics were in a turmoil of their own, and as in England the question of the future national religion was at the forefront of the matters that urgently needed to be resolved. Mary returned to Scotland in 1560 on the death of her husband. In 1567 she was to be imprisoned in Loch Leven Castle after an uprising and forced to abdicate in favor of her infant son James, who became James VI of Scotland (1566-1625) and eventually, on Elizabeth's death in 1603, James I of England. Mary sought Elizabeth's help and support, but as a Roman Catholic she was dangerous to the Protestant Queen, and only too natural a focus of recusant discontent.

In 1560 Knox was commissioned with a group of others to create a confession of faith for the Scottish Church. They did it at speed. It was achieved in four days, by the expedient of relying heavily upon Reformed doctrine and presbterian church governance. The Scottish Parliament declared itself happy with it, though naturally as a Roman Catholic Mary Queen of Scots would not accept the confession, and its approval was delayed until her imprisonment and enforced abdication in 1567. But in 1560 Parliament continued with its reforming sweep and passed three Acts: to abolish the jurisdiction of the pope in Scotland; to condemn all but Reformed teaching; and to forbid the celebration of the Mass in Scotland.

The Confession begins with a preface heartily condemning those who have plotted against Scotland and the truth. "We do not suppose that such malice can be cured merely by our Confession, for we know that the sweet savour of the Gospel is, and shall be, death to the sons of perdition."[13]

---

[13]See "The Scottish Confession of Faith, 1560," in Reformed Confessions of the Sixteenth Century, ed. Arthur C. Cochrane (Louisville, Ky.: Westminster John Knox, 2003), ch. 10.

The confession of faith forms a comprehensive overview of the chief topics of Christian faith and practice with a distinctive Reformed flavor. It is asserted that Christ's people are elected (chosen) by the Father before the world began (art. 8 [Eph 1:11; Mt 25:34]); that we can do no good works of our own volition but only those which the Holy Spirit working in us to sanctify us "brings forth." The elect, in whom the Spirit dwells, turn from their sinful ways and learn, though not without struggle, to hate the bad behavior they formerly enjoyed (art. 13). Signs of this change are a new self-discipline and restraint: "to keep our bodies clean and holy, to live in soberness and temperance." Though such good works cannot earn merit with God, they are "pleasing and acceptable" to him and he freely rewards them (art. 14).

The doctrine of the church (Kirk) is set out in article 16 according to the marks or notes in the Creed. The Kirk is eternal, "one company and multitude of men chosen by God." It is universal "because it contains the chosen of all ages, of all realms, nations, and tongues, be they of the Jews or be they of the Gentiles." It is "called the communion, not of profane persons, but of saints."

The Kirk is, echoing Augustine and his reforming heirs, nonetheless invisible, for only God "knows whom he has chosen." The church is visible only as a local worshiping community. That does not necessarily ensure that all those who worship there are among the elect, but Calvin's teaching that those who are saved enjoy an assurance that God has chosen them provides comfort on that point.

In the Kirk are further notes by which it may be known which is the true church. In additional to the creedal notes of an earlier age, these reflect a more polarized view of things after the Reformation:

> The notes, signs, and assured tokens whereby the spotless bride of Christ is known from the horrible harlot, the false Kirk, we state, are neither antiquity, usurped title, lineal succession, appointed place, nor the numbers of men approving an error. . . . The notes of the true Kirk are . . . first, the true preaching of the Word of God . . . secondly, the right administration of the sacraments of Christ Jesus, with which must be associated the Word and promise of God to seal and confirm them in our hearts; and lastly, ecclesiastical discipline uprightly minis-

tered, as God's Word prescribes, whereby vice is repressed and virtue nourished. (art. 18)

There is also provision to ensure that the church is able to determine what is true doctrine. True doctrine "is contained in the written Word of God," and "the interpretation of Scripture . . . does not belong to any private or public person, nor yet to any Kirk for preeminence or precedence, personal or local . . . but appertains to the Spirit of God by whom the Scriptures were written." When there is controversy it should be resolved not by looking merely at "what men have said or done before us" but to "what the Holy Ghost uniformly speaks within the body of the Scriptures and what Christ Jesus himself did and commanded" (art. 18). Scripture is the supreme authority and it is "sufficient to instruct and make perfect the man of God" (art. 19).

General councils of the church have their place, according to article 20, but they can err, and possess no authority to "forge for us new articles of faith." They are useful "to refute heresies, and to give public confession of their faith to the generations following," and for maintaining discipline.

The confession of faith acknowledges only two sacraments, as directly instituted by Christ himself, baptism and the Lord's Supper or Table (art. 21). Echoing Calvin, the sacraments are not to be dismissed as "nothing else than naked and bare signs."

> No, we assuredly believe that by Baptism we are engrafted into Christ Jesus, to be made partakers of his righteousness, by which our sins are covered and remitted and also that in the Supper rightly used, Christ Jesus is so joined with us that he becomes the very nourishment and food of our souls.

This is not to accept the doctrine of transubstantiation, of course, which is firmly rejected:

> Not that we imagine any transubstantiation of bread into Christ's body, and of wine into his natural blood, as the Romanists have perniciously taught and wrongly believed; but this union and conjunction which we have with the body and blood of Christ Jesus in the right use of the sacra-

ments is wrought by means of the Holy Ghost, who by true faith carries us above all things that are visible, carnal, and earthly, and makes us feed upon the body and blood of Christ Jesus, once broken and shed for us but now is in heaven, and appearing for us in the presence of his Father.

The sacraments must be administered by lawfully appointed ministers, and in the ways which God has appointed (art. 22). This is taken to outlaw the "pretend" sacraments of the Church of Rome. Article 23 rejects the Anabaptist practice of denying baptism to infants.

The Book of Discipline. Scottish Presbyterianism also displayed an interest in deep moral and social transformation—which came to be known more generally as puritanism—associated with Reformed influence everywhere. In the first Book of Discipline (1560), lists of ministers were approved for the "ministrie of the word and sacraments of God." A high level of good behavior was demanded, with heavy sanctions for those who failed to meet the standard. Provision was made

> for eschewing of the wrath and judgement of the eternall God and removeing of the plagues threatned in his law, that sharp punishment may be made upon the persons underwriten, and uthers idolaters and mantainers thereof, in contempt of God his true religioun and acts of Parliament, whilk sayes and causes messe to be said and are present thereat within the places following.

Provision was also made "for suppressing of idolatrie throughout the whole realme, and punishing the users thereof, maintainers of the samein, haunters and frequenters therto."[14]

The Westminster Confession of 1646 and its Catechisms ultimately became the key documents for Scottish Reformed faith and practice. It was created by the Westminster Assembly of leading reforming theologians of their day, set up by the Long Parliament during the English Civil War (1642-1651), as an assembly of "learned, godly and judicious divines" to consider the future of the Church of England.[15] England

---

[14]Maitland Club, *The Proceedings and Legislation of the Church of Scotland in the First Decades After the Reformation*, 3 vols. (London: Institute of Historical Research, 1839-1845), www.british-history.ac.uk/source.aspx?pubid=595.

[15]S. W. Carruthers, *The Westminster Assembly: What It Was and What It Did* (Manchester: Manchester University Press, 1943).

too was confronted with a choice between a presbyterian and an episcopal future for its church government.

THE ENGLISH REFORMATION
TURNS REFORMED

Calvin's heirs. In his *Laws of Ecclesiastical Polity*, Richard Hooker praised Calvin and his formative influence in Reformed doctrine and polity:

> I think [Calvin was] incomparably the wisest man that ever the french [*sic*] Church did enjoy. . . . Divine knowledge he gathered, not by hearing or reading so much, as by teaching others. . . . At the comming of Calvin [to Geneva] the forme of their civill regiment was popular, as it continueth to this day: neither King, nor Duke, nor noble man of any authorities or power over them, but officers chosen by the people yercly out of themselves, to order all things with publique consent. For spiritual government, they had no lawes at all agreed upon, but did what the pastors of their soules by persuasion could win them unto.

Hooker says Calvin could see "how dangerous it was that the whole estate of that Church should hang still on so slender a thred, as the liking of an ignorant multitude is, if it have power to change whatsoever it selfe listeth." He encouraged the Genevan congregation to introduce a form of "ecclesiaticall government." He observed, says Hooker, that not to do so led to "marvelous great dissimilitudes, and by reason thereof, jealousies, hartburnings, jarres and discords amongst them."[16]

Hooker's assessment was made at the end of the sixteenth century, a period when the direct influence of Calvin on English religious affairs was (for good and ill) very plain. This influence grew partly because at a crucial period for the formation of the Church of England many of the Protestants who had begun to flourish under Henry VIII and Edward VI (1537-1553) fled during the reign of Mary Tudor and settled in the Swiss Reformed cities where Calvin's teaching was becoming firmly established. There they met and talked to him and other leaders of Reformed thought and opinion.

Edward VI and Thomas Cranmer. Edward VI came to the throne as a

---

[16]Richard Hooker, *Laws*, 1:3-4.

small boy when his father Henry VIII died in 1547. Naturally enough, there clustered about his clever childish head a group of powerful men anxious to gain control of the kingdom. Henry had made provision in his will for sixteen executors, who were to form a Regency Council to govern while Edward grew to manhood. There was a certain amount of horse-trading, which removed some of the more conservative, so that in the end the power lay with the would-be reformers of the church.

It had been Henry's intention that the council should make joint decisions, but on Edward's accession Edward Seymour (c. 1500-1552), his uncle, was allowed by the Council to become Lord Protector of the new king, to make himself Earl of Somerset and to acquire immense personal power. Seymour was brother to Jane (c. 1508-1537), Henry VIII's third wife and the mother of little Edward. He had become a favorite of the old king and remained in the inner circle in the last years of Henry's reign. The Lord Protector eventually fell out of favor in the Council, was stripped of his power, arrested and executed.

Meanwhile, Thomas Cranmer continued as archbishop of Canterbury, in a climate which, however turbulent politically, was relatively benign toward the promotion of a Protestant Reformation in the Church of England. The pious young king was brought up in Protestant opinions under Cranmer's guidance, and Cranmer took the opportunity to begin to create the Book of Common Prayer, which was to reach its settled form in Elizabeth's reign. While it owed much to older traditions, it was designed in a strong awareness that a liturgy carries a theology.

Cranmer also published books of homilies to ensure that ill-educated parish clergy—not all of whom, it was quite certain, would have been keeping up with the trends—could preach sound reforming doctrine to their flocks. The emphasis of the *Homilies* was on practical Christianity and the living of a good Christian life, following the new assumptions about what that meant.

Cranmer ensured that his *Homilies* had royal approval, in the form of a preface by Edward. Anxiety to ensure that an agreed form of service is required as a civil as well as a spiritual duty was already manifesting itself in Edward VI's preface to the *Homilies*. Cranmer's compilation of a *Book of Homilies* was speedy enough to ensure that the homilies were published for use under Edward VI. The preface bewails "the manifold enormities which heretofore have crept into His Grace's realm through the false usurped power of the Bishop of Rome and the ungodly doctrine of his adherents," so Edward wants his subjects "to be truly and faithfully instructed" so the clergy with "spiritual cure" are instructed to read one of these sermons in order to their flocks every Sunday at Communion "when the people be most gathered together."[17]

Mary Tudor turns England Roman Catholic again. These were times of the utmost importance to the future development of the Church of England, but they were interrupted. Edward was always sickly, and he died still an adolescent. After a brief struggle among the powerful of the realm, his eldest sister, Mary, daughter of Henry's first wife, Catherine of Aragon, and a zealous Roman Catholic, succeeded to the throne and set about bringing England back to the old religion during her five-year reign (1553-1558). She did it ruthlessly. There were to be many martyrs, including Cranmer himself.[18]

Matthew Parker, who would organize the Bishops' Bible, had been influenced by reforming ideas at Cambridge and became chaplain to Anne Boleyn. He seems to have been close to Martin Bucer during his time lecturing at Cambridge. He did not go into exile during Mary's reign, and that caused some resentment among those who had, for he had not been martyred either, and that smelled of a failure to stand up for Protestant truths. Parker was to become archbishop of Canterbury on Elizabeth's accession and remained in office until his death.

The exiles learn the Reformed faith. The heritage of the development of the Protestant Church of England to this point had been still in many respects unique, an episcopal church under the headship of the monarch, neither strictly Lutheran or Reformed. But letters were already going back and forth across Europe, and Reformed doctrine and polity were increasingly in the air. Protestant English theologians fled the country and spent some years of exile on the continent of Europe, in the cities of Europe where there were sympathetic friends, particularly in the Re-

---

[17]Thomas Cranmer, *Homilies*, pp. 3-5.
[18]See Eamon Duffy, *Catholic England Under Mary Tudor* (New Haven, Conn.: Yale University Press, 2009).

formed heartlands of Strasbourg, Basel and Zurich. They took refuge
with leading Reformers there. Leaders of the continental Reformation
welcomed the exiles and made practical arrangements for their temporary accommodation and support.

This was not an exodus of representatives of all classes. The majority
of these several hundred exiles were clergy or scholars or gentry. Few
have been identified as artisans or servants. That immediately distinguishes them and their age from the dissident movements of the Middle Ages, when the ringleaders and most of their followers were apparently peasants or ordinary townspeople. One reason was the recent
extension of higher education to a class of the well-born who were not
bound for professional life as clerics.

They learned a great deal about the cutting-edge European Protestant ideas, especially those of Calvin, but their faces were set—with
longing toward the possibility of return. It was possible for the exiles to
continue to worship according to the liturgy established under Edward
VI, as happened at Strasbourg. They had the Book of Common Prayer
of 1552. They were waiting anxiously to come home, sometimes vexed in
their consciences because they had run away and not stayed to face possible martyrdom. Correspondence continued and enabled them to keep
up to date with events and developments in England.

So the reign of Elizabeth, which began on Mary's death in 1558,
brought back many leading figures (some of whom became bishops
themselves) who had spent the reign of her elder sister in exile with continental Reformers. The exiles who were to become important in the
forming of the Church of England on their return included Miles
Coverdale, at Strasbourg; Edmund Grindal (c. 1519-1583), who was to
become archbishop of York and then of Canterbury; Edwin Sandys (c.
1516-1588), another future archbishop of York; and John Jewel (1522-1571).

Continental influences. Continental influences remained strong when
Elizabeth succeeded her sister, for the exiles and other interested Eng-
lishmen continued to correspond with their friends and allies abroad
long after their return.[19] Sir Anthony Cook wrote to Bullinger on

---

[19]See the *Zurich Letters*, ed. Hastings Robinson, published by the Parker Society in 2 vols.
(Cambridge: Cambridge University Press, 1842-1845).

December 8, 1558, "There is however great hope, especially if the reports from Antwerp are to be depended upon, that the spirits of the papists are entirely cast down, and that they will not offer to attack us, unless our own discord should afford them an opportunity."[20] Another leading figure in the affairs of the continental Reformation with whom Elizabeth's reforming clergy remained in active touch was Peter Martyr.

New ideas of order. When Elizabeth came to the throne there was considerable anxiety to ensure that order was restored, both a quiet orderliness and regularity in the life of the church, and a security and regularity in secular government. In her own preface to a new edition of the *Homilies,* Elizabeth wrote of her subjects' "duty towards God, their Prince, and their neighbours."[21] The documents of the Elizabethan Church of England add to Jesus' summary of the commandments, with its duty to love God and neighbor, a good citizen's duty to honor the monarch and keep the law.

The Thirty-Nine Articles include at article 37 a distinctly Erastian assertion that the monarch is civil magistrate and "hath the chief power in this Realm of England, and other his Dominions, unto whom the chief Government of all Estates of this Realm, whether they be Ecclesiastical or Civil, in all causes doth appertain, and is not, nor ought to be, subject to any foreign jurisdiction." The principal point here is to establish that secular headship of the Church of England replaces that of the pope ("the Bishop of *Rome* hath no jurisdiction in this Realm of *England*"), but with careful provisos that this authority shall not extend into sacramental actions:

> We give not to our Princes the ministering either of God's Word, or of the Sacraments, the which thing the Injunctions also lately set forth by Elizabeth our Queen do most plainly testify; but that only prerogative, which we see to have been given always to all godly Princes in Holy Scriptures by God himself; that is, that they should rule all estates and degrees committed to their charge by God, whether they be Ecclesiastical or Temporal, and restrain with the civil sword the stubborn and evildoers.

---

[20]*The Zurich Letters,* Second Series (1558-1602), letter 1, ed. Hastings Robinson (Cambridge: Cambridge University Press, 1845), p. 1.

[21]Cranmer, *Homilies,* pp. 3-4.

That contemporary thinking on this point still adopted this imagery indebted to the motif of the two swords is an indication of the immense staying power of this way of seeing things.

Shall we keep bishops? Among the subjects which preoccupied the returning exiles was the way the Anglican Church should be run, and prominent in that cluster of questions was the matter of bishops. In 1569 Thomas Cartwright (1534/1535-1603), a Cambridge graduate, proposed the introduction of a presbyterian ecclesiology in England. The exiles who came home to England with the accession of Elizabeth included many who were sympathetic with the Reformed styles of church government they experienced in Geneva, Zurich and elsewhere.[22] Yet through it all Anglicanism retained an episcopal system of government. Why? The ultimate answer unfolded only as Elizabeth's reign progressed, and it remained uncertain even when Scotland's James VI succeeded her as James I, for many Scots continued to be keen Presbyterians.

The continental Reformers observed the situation at the beginning of Elizabeth's reign with some concern. Influential Zurich pastor Rudolph Gualter (1519-1586) sent a letter to Queen Elizabeth on January 16, 1559, containing what he believed to be good advice. Bullinger and Gualter wrote to Calvin's successor in Geneva, Theodore Beza (1519-1605) on August 3, 1567, still deploring the way positions have become polarized in England between the bishops and those who wanted to get rid of them:

> The fault seems to have arisen at first from too much rigour on their part, and . . . in course of times the contest increased, and grew warm, as is always the case when people quarrel; and that feelings have been so exasperated on both sides, that each party is now to blame.

The presbyterians seemed to speak of the bishops only "what is painted in the blackest colours, and savours of the most perfect hatred."[23]

Beza likewise wrote to Bullinger in 1566 about "the English affair" in

---

[22]William Haller, *The Rise of Puritanism* (New York: Columbia University Press, 1938), pp. 8, 172.

[23]Theodore Beza to Henry Bullinger, July 29, 1567, letter 60, *Zurich Letters*, Second Series, p. 153.

some exasperation at the behavior and attitudes of English polemicists:

> Some of them, I admit, are rather hard to please, but in so much affliction
> it is difficult to keep within bounds. . . . I once thought that the matter
> was only about caps and I know not what other externals, but I after-
> wards understood that the controversy was of a far different character;
> and I now plainly perceive it to be so, not without the utmost distress of
> mind. . . . First, since an outward call (after due examination as to doc-
> trine and moral character), not by any single individual but at least by a
> congregation of the brethren, is as it were the basis and foundation of an
> ecclesiastical ministry, what can be more abominable, what more extra-
> vagant, than that assumed power of the bishops, by which they admit at
> their pleasure parties not so called, but who enter the ministry of their
> own accord; and immediately, without assigning them any cure, approve
> them as qualified either to serve . . . or to teach.[24]

Bullinger wrote more sympathetically to Grindal on March 10, 1574,
to say that he understands

> that the contests among you had been revived by certain disorderly young
> men, who are endeavouring to do away with the whole ecclesiastical sys-
> tem, arranged with so much labour by most excellent men, and to intro-
> duce a new one formed at their own pleasure. . . . We are plagued also
> throughout Germany by characters of this kind. . . .
>
> There are persons in Germany who pride themselves upon being
> Lutherans, but who are in reality most shameless brawlers, railers, and
> calumniators.[25]

"What good can be expected in England, while things remain as
they are?" wrote Beza to Bullinger in 1567.[26] After the choppings and
changings of the Tudor monarchy, the ecclesiastical authorities were
keen on establishing and upholding good order not only in the Church
but also in society. They took upon themselves the supervision of a
number of aspects of public order. The flavor of expectations is nicely

---

[24]Theodore Beza to Henry Bullinger, September 3, 1566, letter 53, *Zurich Letters*, Second
Series, pp. 127-29.

[25]Heinrich Bullinger to Edmund Grindal, March, 10, 1574, letter 99, *Zurich Letters*, Second
Series, pp. 244-46.

[26]Heinrich Bullinger and Rudolph Gualter to Beza, August 3, 1567, letter 61, *Zurich Letters*,
Second Series, pp. 154-55.

caught in the inquiry in his diocese made by the bishop of Exeter written as late as 1625:

> Whether you know, or have heard, that any person or persons bee entertained or admitted into any taverne, or into the house of any . . . alewife, to eate, drinke, or play at dice, cards, or tables, in the time of common prayer, or sermon, on the Sundayes or holydayes? Or whether any peddler, butcher, taylor, shoomaker, miller, tucker, barber, or other person, by using huis manuall trade or craft, have violated and prophaned the sabboth or any holy-day.[27]

Similar enquiries went out in other dioceses.

It was not all a matter of integrity and conviction. Fashionable religious attitudes could change with government policy. In the universities there was comment—running long beyond this period—on the readiness of those who wished to be safe and popular and to be candidates for promotion, to adapt to political expectations. Wood noted the speed with which "the junior scholars trained up in the presbyterian discipline" changed their habits when presbyterianism and its puritan habits ceased to be popular:[28]

> Those that hated a taverne or alehouse formerly, now frequent them. . . . Another party would strip them of their puritanicall cut and forthwith put on a cassock reaching to their heeles tied close with a sanctified circingle. . . . That party of the juniors that were preachers and educated in the said discipline of the Presbyterians, . . . left nothing undone so that they might seem episcopall. At their coming into the pulpit they knelt downe and used some privat ejaculations, which was so far from being done in the late times that it was ridiculous so to do. They left off their long extemporarie prayers and conformed to a short prayer. . . . They quoted also in their sermons the fathers and Schoolmen, and framed their sermons (which before were verie practical and commonly full of dire) to a polite quaint discourse.[29]

---

[27]*Visitation Articles and Injunctions of the Early Stuart Church*, ed. Kenneth Fincham, Church of England Record Society 5 (Woodbridge: Boydell Press, 1998), 2:5.

[28]Anthony à Wood, *The Life and Times of Anthony à Wood*, ed. A. Clark (Oxford: Oxford University Press, 1961), pp. 366-67.

[29]*The Life and Times of Anthony Wood*, ed. Andrew Clark (1891), pp. 366-67.

Calvin's Institutes *in England.* Calvin's *Institutes* was being read in England in these formative early Elizabethan years. It was translated into English in 1561 by Thomas Norton (1532-1584), a Cambridge graduate in the service of the Protector Somerset, who became an increasingly enthusiastic Calvinist. The fourth edition of this translation appeared in 1581 with a preface that recognizes the way in which Calvin's original brief *Institutes* had grown with successive revisings, as he realized the importance of new topics. He describes the difficulty in which he found himself as a translator. He could see that Calvin had "purposely labored" to write "exactly, and to pack great plenty of matter in small room of words"; he was conscious of "the peculiar terms of arts and figures, and the difficulty of the matters themselves, being throughout interlaced with the school men's controversies." This is not an easy book and it is peculiarly hard to translate either literally or so as to make it readable:

> If I should follow the words, I saw that of necessity the hardness in the translation must needs be greater than was in the tongue wherein it was originally written. If I should leave the course of words, and grant myself liberty after the natural manner of my own tongue, to say that in English which I conceived to be his meaning in Latin, I plainly perceived how hardly I might escape error, and on the other side, in this matter of faith and religion, how perilous it was to err.

He decided to aim for the literal as far as possible but to try to not to make the translation longer than the Latin (a requirement which would in any case lead to some abbreviation since English often takes longer to say what Latin says more briefly). He sees the *Institutes* as a contribution to the "books of common-places of our religion" written by leading reforming theologians in recent years, and in his view the best. "[The Holy Scriptures excepted] this is one of the most profitable books for all students of Christian divinity."

The creation of an English liturgy: The Book of Common Prayer and the Thirty-Nine Articles. The Articles of the Church of England had been evolving since the reign of Henry VIII, with different numbers of articles (beginning with a mere ten in 1536) and in different versions reflecting the changing beliefs and allegiences of the time. In 1563 they had settled in number at thirty-nine. These Articles, like the liturgy of the Book of Common Prayer, became obligatory, with parish priests required to assent to them before entering into office, and students at Oxford and Cambridge were also required to assent before they could be admitted to either university.

The first few of the Articles deal with what in the sixteenth century were the relatively uncontentious themes of the creeds, which are separately approved as consonant with Scripture in article 8. Others settle the Church of England's official position on a number of the key questions of the time. Article 6 claims the primacy of Scripture: "Holy Scripture containeth all things necessary to salvation: so that whatsoever is not read therein, nor may be proved thereby, is not to be required of any man, that it should be. believed as an article of the Faith, or be thought requisite or necessary to salvation." Justification by faith is the subject of article 11 ("Of the Justification of Adam"):

> We are accounted righteous before God, only for the merit of our Lord and Saviour Jesus Christ by Faith, and not for our own works or deservings: Wherefore, that we are justified by Faith only is a most wholesome Doctrine, and very full of comfort, as more largely is expressed in the Homily of Justification.

Articles 9 and 10 assert the Augustinian doctrine of the damage to the exercise of free will which followed Adam's sin. Good works are seen as a natural outflow of justification, but before justification works are not only not good but positively wicked, and "have the nature of sin" (art. 13). Sin after baptism may be forgiven if the sinner repents (art. 16). Article 17 approves a moderate Calvinist doctrine of predestination (not mentioning reprobation), for "the godly consideration of Predestination, and our Election in Christ, is full of sweet, pleasant, and unspeakable comfort to godly persons, and such as feel in themselves the working of the Spirit of Christ."

The Articles set out a doctrine of the church focusing on its identity as a visible institution, "a congregation of faithful men, in the which the pure Word of God is preached, and the Sacraments be duly-ministered according to Christ's ordinance" (art. 19). To the church thus constituted is credited "power to decree Rites or Ceremonies, and authority in Controversies of Faith" (art. 20), but with the restrictions that it may not "ordain any thing that is contrary to God's Word written" or seek to add anything to Scripture and claim it is essential to salvation.

The Articles set out a doctrine of ministry (art. 23) which outlaws the self-appointed. Ministers must be "called" and "sent":

> It is not lawful for any man to take upon him the office of publick preaching, or ministering the Sacraments in the Congregation, before he be lawfully called, and sent to execute the same. And those we ought to judge lawfully called and sent, which be chosen and called to this work by men who have publick authority given unto them in the Congregation, to call and send Ministers into the Lord's vineyard.

The use of the vernacular in worship is insisted on (art. 24). "It is a thing plainly repugnant to the Word of God, and the custom of the Primitive Church, to have publick Prayer in the Church, or to minister the Sacraments in a tongue not understanded of the people."

The sacraments are described (art. 25) as "effectual signs" not mere "badges or tokens," so that they are means by which God "doth work invisibly in us." Only two sacraments are recognized, baptism and the Eucharist, and the rest are rejected as not clearly "ordained of God." The habit of carrying the consecrated host "about" is outlawed. The "effect or operation" is felt "in such only as worthily receive the same." Infant baptism is approved. Baptism is a sign of regeneration (art. 26): "They that receive Baptism rightly are grafted into the Church; the promises of forgiveness of sin, and of our adoption to be sons of God by the Holy Ghost, are visibly signed and sealed."

The Eucharist is a sacrament of "our redemption by Christ's death" (art. 27). But it is not (art. 31) a sacrificial offering which can add to the "offering of Christ once made" on the cross, for that is the "perfect redemption, propitiation, and satisfaction, for all the sins of the whole world." The doctrine of transubstantiation is rejected in favor of the view that "the Body of Christ is given, taken and eaten in the Supper, only after an heavenly and spiritual manner" through faith. Therefore (art. 29) the wicked do not partake of Christ when they eat the conse-crated bread. Communion is to be received in both kinds (bread and wine) by all (art. 30).

The effect of the sacraments is not diminished by the unworthiness of the minister (art. 26). But there should be disciplinary investigation if a minister is alleged to be evil, and he should if "finally being found guilty, by just judgement, be deposed."

Marriage of the clergy is to be allowed (art. 32). The excommunicated are to be "avoided" (art. 33) until reconciled with the Church. The Arti-cles (art. 21) approve of general councils and they take the stance that only princes may call them. They assert that councils may err.

The Articles also deal sensibly—and repressively or approvingly—with a number of the topics that recur in reforming circles. Purgatory is deemed "repugnant to the Word of God" (art. 22). Swearing oaths is acceptable in some circumstances but not in others (art. 39). Goods are not to be held in common, but those who have worldly goods should give alms (art. 38).

Drastic reform or good order? Richard Hooker remained of the opin-ion that public worship according to a proper and approved liturgy, "dulie ordered," is a unifying strength to the nation as well as benefi-cial to the souls of its people.[30] In much of Europe, churches in con-junction with their local civil authorities enjoyed a certain autonomy. Since England differed from much of Protestant northern Europe in that its Christian magistrate was its monarch, the situation in Eng-land was far from mirroring the pattern of potential variation among the Swiss cantons and in areas where the popular vote or a town or city council could make independent (and sometimes vacillating) de-cisions about the theology or liturgy they wished to adopt.

Hooker looked beyond the national good as well. A well-designed liturgy, he thought, is also an appropriate way of ensuring that the peo-ple have a sense of joining with the whole Christian community, celes-tial as well as earthly, when they worship. "The howse of prayer is a court bewtified with the presence of coelestiall powers," so that we pray and

---

[30]Hooker, *Laws*, 5.25.1.

sing "havinge his Angels intermingle as our associates."[31]

Such dignified worship during which the minister "standeth and speaketh in the presence of God for them" because "God hath so farre received him into favor, as to impose upon him by the handes of men that office of blessinge the people in his name and makinge intercession to him in theires," had all sorts of lessons to teach. It is a marker of good order and also a reminder that the minister is a bridge between the people and heaven, in the spirit of the *pontifex* (literally, "bridge-maker") of the Middle Ages.[32]

In Elizabeth's preface to the *Homilies* the emphasis has shifted away from overt hostility to Rome to the positive requirement to combine sound religion with good citizenship:

> The word of God . . . should at all convenient times be preached unto the people, that thereby they may both learn their duty towards God, their Prince, and their neighbours, according to the mind of the Holy Ghost expressed in the Scriptures, and also to avoid the manifold enormities which heretofore by false doctrine have crept into the Church of God.[33]

In response to any accusation that the Church of England's liturgy was too like that of Rome, Hooker replied, "Where Rome keepeth that which is ancienter and better; others whome we much more affect leaving it for newer and changing it for worse, we had rather followe the perfections of them whome we like not, than in defectes resemble them whome we love."[34]

Conforming worship. The English Church had to make its decisions about its mode of worship. Was it to be fairly extemporaneous, as some continental Reformers favored? Or was it to be a modernized and Reformed version of the ancient and medieval liturgies involving mostly set readings, responses and prayers? The choice in the end was for the latter.

A liturgy carries a theology within it, but especially one whose wording is thought through. An underlying principle for the reforming Church of England—as expressed in the *Homily on Reading and Knowl-*

[31]Hooker, *Laws*, 5.25.2.
[32]Hooker, *Laws*, 5.25.3.
[33]Cranmer, *Homilies*, pp. 3-4.
[34]Hooker, *Laws*, 5.28.1.

edge of Holy Scripture—is the sufficiency and primacy of Scripture, that
"there is no truth nor doctrine necessary for our justification and ever-
lasting salvation but that is or may be drawn out of that fountain and
well of truth," Holy Scripture.[35] The liturgy was designed to immerse the
worshipping community in Scripture. The Book of Common Prayer's
preface explains that the liturgy of the early church provided that "all
the whole Bible, or the greatest part thereof, should be read over once in
the year." This had lapsed: "these many years past this godly and decent
order of the ancient fathers hath been so altered, broken and neglected
by planting in uncertain storied, legends, responds, verses, vain
repetitions."[36] Hooker reiterated that the Church of England professes
that Holy Scripture contains "all things necessary to salvation." "It see-
meth to us that naturall light, teaching morall virtues, teacheth things
necessarie to salvation, whiche yet is not perfect without that which is
supernaturall knowledge in holy Scripture reveileth."[37]

Putting Scripture first is not the same as saying that Scripture alone
is all the Church or the faithful need; as we have just seen, the Articles
were busy taking positions on the key issues in this area where a reforming church must position itself with care and exactitude to avoid confusion. This was not yet an era in which Anglicanism could be expected to
frame its identity in the broad and inclusive terms which it later
stretched to accommodate.

Under Elizabeth, with her concern for the maintenance of good
order, there was a strong concern to ensure that the prescribed liturgy
was followed exactly and the prescribed homilies read. The main liturgical document seeking to ensure uniformity in worship was the Book of
Common Prayer, again Cranmer's creation, first published in 1549 and
revised in 1552. It was reissued with minor amendments with Elizabeth's
approval in 1559. The Act of Uniformity which passed the same year
binds all ministers in the realm to "say and use" the form of liturgical
prayer laid down, and only that form, and if they refuse or "preach, de-

---

[35]Cranmer, *Homilies*, p. 7.
[36]The Book of Common Prayer, 1559, ed. John E. Booty (Charlottesville: University Press of
   Virginia, 1976), pp. 14-15.
[37]Hooker, "A Christian Letter" (3), *Laws* 4, p. 11.

clare or speak anything in the derogation or depraving of the said book," he shall be fined the income from his benefice and imprisoned for six months. If laypeople sneer at it or interrupt worship they shall be fined and fined again for a second offense, and for a third offense imprisoned for life.[38]

The perceived danger was that individuals with dissenting opinions might alter patterns of worship if they had parishes and the cure of souls, and that they might preach doctrines that could lead their congregations astray if they were allowed to make up sermons as they chose. The Anglican minister was not assumed to be able to compose his own sermons. As the Elizabethan preface to the *Homilies* puts it, "all they which are appointed ministers have not the gift of preaching sufficiently to instruct the people which is committed unto them"—so here were ready-made sermons.[39] The Thirty-Nine Articles (art. 35) confirmed that these were appropriate "to be read in Churches by the Ministers, diligently and distinctly, that they may be understanded *of* the people."

The antivestiarian controversy. Among many of the most adventurous adherents who were keen to preach, the continental liturgical style and Reformed ecclesiology continued be attractive, and posed the threat of nonconformity well into Elizabeth's reign and beyond.[40] As had sometimes happened elsewhere during the Reformation, some began to see the use of music or visual art in churches as idolatrous; there was destruction of statues and pictures and stained glass. There was even controversy about the use of crosses as symbols in churches, and certainly about the making of the sign of the cross by believers. Many rejected the wearing of surplices and other ceremonial ministerial garments, which became an extremely contentious matter in Oxford and Cambridge at the end of the sixteenth century. It was the norm for the Fellows of colleges to wear surplices in chapel; when they did not, the gesture constituted an obvious challenge to the ecclesial (and political) status quo. The presumption was that academics, though naturally rather dangerous, were at least capable of understanding the theology they were preaching, but that

---

[38]The Book of Common Prayer, pp. 6-7.
[39]Cranmer, *Homilies*, pp. 3-4.
[40]W. Fraser Mitchell, *English Pulpit Oratory from Andrewes to Tillotson* (London: SPCK, 1932).

did not prevent their becoming dangerous as well.

Thomas Cartwright became a leading "Puritan" in the antivestiarian disputes of the mid-1560s at Cambridge. At the time Cartright was making his name as a notable preacher to packed congregations in Cambridge, and in 1569 he was given the Lady Margaret Chair of Divinity. His inaugural lectures, on Acts, gave him an opportunity to expand his view on the practice of the primitive church and the desirability of a return to it throught a much more thorough purifying of the Church from its remaining unreformed practices. The students found this exciting. Their elders found it dangerous. John Whitgift (c. 1530-1604) deprived him of his office in 1570, after he became vice chancellor.

Cartwright also insisted that the Church of England could not be right, could not accord with the governance of the primitive church, unless it adopted a presbyterian form of government. Cartwright was expelled from the university, although he continued to be a fellow of Trinity. He retreated to Switzerland, where he went on teaching Puritan ideas in Geneva with Beza. He was not forgotten in Cambridge, and there were many keen to have him back, especially when the Admonition Controversy broke out after Beza wrote to Grindal in 1566 arguing that the presbyterian system was best. His letter was published in 1572 with an *Admonition to Parliament* on the subject by fellow Puritan clergy Thomas Wilcox (c. 1549-1608) and John Field (1545-1588).

The pressure for change to presbyterian church government became entangled with a drive for a purified standard of dress and behavior in the universities. Cartwright had renewed hostile exchanges with Whitgift, in which he sought to get him to agree that vestments truly mattered.

The Marprelate tracts and the attack on episcopacy. By Elizabeth's time the political importance of the bishops in ensuring the security of the monarchy was considerable enough to make it unlikely that the Church would be open to the suggestion of governing itself in any other way than through an episcopate, "the Estate of the Prelacie, being one of the three auncient estates of this Realme under her Highnesse."[41] On the contrary, any such suggestion attracted a fierce reaction from the estab-

---

[41]Royal proclamation of February 13, 1588-1589, *An Introductory Sketch to the Martin Marprelate Controversy*, English Scholar's Library 8, ed. Edward Arber (London, 1880), p. 110.

lishment of both church and state. Moreover, John Whitgift became archbishop of Canterbury in 1583, and one of his chief objectives was to eradicate presbyterianism in England.[42]

The "Marprelate" tracts were anonymous, highly inflammatory publications circulating in 1588 and 1589 with the purpose of trying to work up resistance to bishops among the more zealously reform-minded in England. Marprelate's *The Epistle to the Terrible Priests of the Convocation House*, for example, advances the argument that no one can be a true pastor unless he can actually shepherd his flock in person:

> Whosoever therefore clayme unto themselues pastorall authoritie over those Christians with whome they cannot possiblie at any time altogether in the same congregation sanctifie the Sabboth: they are vsurping prelates Popes and pettie Antichrists.[43]

This of course includes all bishops, for their flocks are too widely dispersed throughout the diocese for them to be true pastors to them in person every Sunday.

The tracts were extreme (painting bishops as antichrist). From 1586, they were also illegal. In that year a Star Chamber "censorship" edict gave the archbishop of Canterbury authority to license printing so unlicensed printing was as unlawful as unlicensed preaching. It became a matter of treason to create or disseminate these materials. A royal proclamation of 13 February 1588/1589 identified their purpose as seditious:

> Containing in them doctrine very erroneous, and . . . slaunderous to the State, and against the godly reformation of Religion and Gouvernement Ecclesiastically established by Lawe, and so quietly of long time continued, and also against the persons of the Bishoppes, and others placed in authoritie Ecclesiasticall under her Highnesse by her authoritie.[44]

Undeterred, secret printing presses produced and distributed the Marprelate tracts, and a number of depositions survive in which evidence was taken in an attempt to root those responsible out from their hiding places.[45]

---

[42]Ibid.
[43]Marprelate, *The Epistle to the Terrible Priests of the Convocation House*, ed. Edward Arber (London, 1880), p. 9.
[44]Ibid., p. 109.
[45]Ibid., pp. 81-104, 112-17.

Polemical preaching. Henry Smith (1560-1591) was a popular London preacher unable to reconcile himself with the liturgical requirements of the Church of England. He was rumored to have spoken out against the Book of Common Prayer and refused to subscribe to the Thirty-Nine Articles. In 1587 he was "elected" by the congregation of St. Clement Danes without Temple Bar to be their "lecturer" (reader), but because he did not have a license from the bishop of London he was forbidden to preach.[46] William Cecil (1521-1598), Lord Burghley, one of the principal advisers to the queen, was known to support the view that the Church of England already had the marks of the true "reformed" church in its doctrine and worship, and he was not to be drawn into public support for Puritan positions (whatever his private sympathies may have been). Smith, politically more naive perhaps, tried to get Burghley's support, claiming that it was not true that he did not subscribe to the Articles. Burghley and the loyal congregation spoke up for him, and his sermons when published were dedicated to Burghley. Smith's natural gifts of oratory were probably improved by his knowledge of classical rhetoric. His sermons, clear and forceful, were enormously popular, and persons of high birth were said to be prepared to stand in the aisles to hear him when the pews were full.[47]

Thomas Adams (1583-1652) was another highly regarded preacher with Puritan leanings, and another stylist. He let fly against Rome, the pope and the Jesuits as well as against self-indulgence and worldliness in his congregations. He was not, however, an extremist at all points. He did not think it unacceptable or papist to kneel when receiving Communion. Nor was he actively against the retention of bishops. John White (1570-1615), vigorous and colorful, also gained a reputation for his polemic against the Church of Rome. He felt his writings were pastoral endeavors to "help the seduced out of their [Catholic] errors and confirm Protestants in the truth."[48]

---

[46]*The Sermons of Master Henrie Smith, Gathered into One Volume*, first published in 1591; three further editions had followed by the end of 1594, and several more afterward. They were reprinted, with an introduction and a précis of Smith's life, by Thomas Fuller in 1657 and again in 1675.

[47]Ronald A. Rebholz, *The Life of Fulke Greville* (Oxford: Clarendon Press, 1971), p. 26.

[48]*The Way to the True Church: An Answer to a Popish Discourse, Concerning Marks of the Church* [A

Some, however, like the statesman Fulke Greville (1554-1628), spoke up for compromise. He thought it wise not to make even metaphorical martyrs of the remaining English Roman Catholics, but he also thought it sensible to unite the policy and framework of church and state as far as possible.[49]

How important was this question about bishops? Francis Bacon put into private circulation in 1589 "An Advertisement Touching the Controversies of the Church of England," in which he tried to put the current controversies in perspective:

> For they are not touching the high Mysteries of Faith such as detained the Churches for many years after their first peace, what time the heretics moved curious questions and made strange anatomies of the Natures and Person of CHRIST, and the catholic fathers were compelled to follow them with all subtilty of decisions and determinations.[50] . . .
>
> "We contend about Ceremonies and Things Indifferent, about the Extern polity and Government of the Church."[51]

This was, in the end, the pragmatic view taken of this debate in the Church of England. It kept its bishops. But the Presbyterian question did not go away. It was to loom again in the seventeenth century during the reign of King James's son, Charles (1600-1649), who would lose his head to the Puritan rebels led by Oliver Cromwell.

The Bishops' Bible and the Authorized Version.

Puritans Leave for the New World

A new world. In 1493 the pope wrote to Ferdinand of Castile and his wife to praise them for the recent success of Spanish Christian rulers in driving the Arabs out of Spain after many centuries. They had, he said, recovered "the kingdom of Granada from the tyranny of the Saracens in these our days." But this triumphant Spain was looking to further hori-

<hr>

Treatise of Faith by J. Percy] (printed by R. Field for John Bill and William Barrett, 1608), preface *3.
[49]Rebholz, *The Life of Fulke Greville*, p. 27.
[50]Francis Bacon, "An Advertisement Touching the Controversies of the Church of England," in *Introductory Sketch*, p. 146ff.; and *The Works of Francis Bacon*, ed. J. Spedding (1861), 8:74ff.
[51]Bacon, "An Advertisement," p. 146ff.

zons. The pope knew of their determination "to seek and find certain islands and firm lands far remote and unknown (and not heretofore found by any other) to the intent to bring the inhabitants of the same to honor our Redeemer and to profess the Catholic faith." They had sent Christopher Columbus, and he had been successful in his exploration and made discoveries. The peoples he had found were not Christians yet, but the pope was informed that "The nations inhabiting the foresaid lands and islands believe that there is one God, Creator in heaven, and seem apt to be brought to the embracing of the Catholic faith and to be imbued with good manners."[52]

In the course of the sixteenth century there were many more voyages across the Atlantic as English and French settlers took over northern areas of the Americas while the Spanish concentrated in what is now Latin America. An agreement was brokered to encourage the Portuguese to look East while the Spanish looked West of a line fixed between their prospective areas of conquest. For the most part the Portuguese therefore sailed toward India, but as it turned out the part of South America which became Brazil jutted out far enough to the West to fall to them under the agreement. One result of all this was a concentration of Roman Catholic converts in the south and of Protestant refugees in the north of this New World.

Pilgrim fathers. Not all those with Reformed sympathies in England were able to accept the new arrangements for the governance of the Church of England. It was, for this generation, a realistic ambition not just to leave the country and hide in Europe as the Marian exiles had done a generation earlier, but to emigrate to a New World. Trading companies were being formed with royal approval (in the form of charters) and with the purpose of founding trading colonies in the Americas. The companies were licensed by their charters to govern these colonies on behalf of the monarch. So there were exciting possibilities of experiment in creating new kinds of Christian commonwealth.

When the Mayflower left Plymouth in 1620 to found a cod-fishing enterprise, it carried a hundred would-be emigrants. Most were what

---

[52]The papal bull *Inter Caetera* (1493), in *Early Modern Catholicism: An Anthology of Primary Sources*, ed. Robert S. Miola (Oxford: Oxford University Press, 2007), pp. 482-83.

would now be called "economic migrants," looking for a better life financially than they could hope for in England. One group of the passengers were to become the Pilgrim fathers, and their purpose was to found communities in which they could lead the Christian life as they believed it should be lived.

The first sight of land at Cape Cod in November was discouraging. This did not look like country where a good living could be made. The emigrants divided into two factions, with the "pilgrims" and the ordinary migrants making different demands about what to do next. It was dangerous to have potentially violent disagreement on a small ship. An agreement was brokered known as the Mayflower Compact, under which the "free men" on board were to choose a governor by election and create an assembly (a "civil body politic"). This approach was derived from the combination of the city-government experience already embedded in the Swiss Reformed tradition and the new political sophistications of the late Tudor period in England. The democratic one-man, one-vote approach to dispute resolution did not extend to the servants and the women.

Within a decade, other Protestant settlements followed the one that begun in the new Plymouth in America. The Massachusetts Bay Trading Company was granted rights over the band of land stretching from the Atlantic to the Pacific, a distance more immense that was understood at the time, and by 1629 the company was under the control of John Winthrop (1587/1588-1649), a leader of Puritan persuasion. He had a vision of building a New Zion in America so that Puritans in exile could create there the Church of England as they believed it should be. Puritans enthusiastically streamed across the Atlantic to join in, and by the mid-1640s there were said to be sixteen thousand of these Puritan settlers, substantially outnumbering the settlers from England who were merely intent on trade and a better quality of life. Winthrop was eager that his settlers should be well educated, and his letters indicate that he also took seriously the importance of education for the native peoples, who had been called Indians at the period when there was confusion as to whether the New World which had been discovered was really the far coast of India.

A church covenant was soon under construction. In 1636 a draft letter on the best way to do it went from Winthrop to Henry Painter (c. 1583-1644), future member of the Westminster Assembly, noting that it will be difficult to ensure that the covenant is biblical because there is "neither precept nor patterne of any suche Covenant in Scripture." The answer he received was that "yet there is warrant sufficient for gatheringe of Churches, & therefore all things necessarily incident therto are warrantably implied." For if there was to be no Covenant how were they formally to constitute a church?

> Suppose 10 or 20 Christns were desirous to constitue a Churche, these being mett together, everyone of them makes confession of his faith, will this make them a Churche? I conceive it will posle [puzzle] a good ligitian to make these a churche, without some Contract or agreemt.... [I]f a man enters no covent, then is he not tyed to one Churche more then another [and can just leave when he feels like it].[53]

We see the settlers working out their politics along with their religion, from first principles. It turned out to be no simple task. In 1644 Winthrop wrote that "Arbitrary Governmt is, where a people have men sett ouer them, without their choice, or allowance: who have power to governe them, & Judge their Causes without a Rule."[54]

The Puritan settlers were respectful to the native Indians and paid them when they took their land, but they did not seek to open their communities to other needy would-be settlers. They tended to be exclusive. Nor were they designing a truly open democracy. The Massachusetts Bay Company conferred the right to vote on individual settlers as it chose, and sometimes it did not choose. Winthrop wrote to his son that it is important to be careful whom you admit, or "newe opinions" will "gett into or churches."[55] Freedom of religion primarily meant freedom for the Puritans to be Puritans, as they claimed was impossible for them in England, not freedom for all to believe and worship as they chose.

Winthrop's leadership did not go unchallenged. He had rivals, and there was a great deal of disagreement and much squabbling. He was

---

[53]Robert C. Wintrop, *Life and Letters of John Winthrop (1630-49)* (London, 1867), 2:417.
[54]Ibid., p. 440.
[55]Ibid., p. 418.

voted in and voted out as governor of Massachusetts again and again, twelve times in a decade. In the end Winthrop was impeached. His speech challenging his impeachment underlines a number of the problems that were found to have arisen in the course of this experimental attempt to create a Puritan Christian state:

> The great questions that have troubled the country, are about the authority of the magistrates and the liberty of the people . . . the covenant between you and us is the oath you have taken of us, which is to this purpose, that we shall govern you and judge your causes by the rules of God's laws and our own, according to our best skill.[56]

Remember your governors are human and fallible and doing their best, he says. He distinguishes two kinds of liberty. One is "incompatible and inconsistent with authority, and cannot endure the least restraint of the most just authority." The other is "civil or federal" and is "the proper end and object of authority, and cannot subsist without it."[57]

This was a community with a mission, taking its religion seriously, encouraging participation in theological debates. On September 25, 1632, Winthrop was entertained by the governor of Plymouth—"Mr. William Bradford, (a very discreet and grave man)"—and gave an account of what happened.

> On the Lord's day there was a sacrament, which they did partake in; and, in the afternoon, Mr. Roger Williams (according to their custom) propounded a question, to which the pastor, Mr. Smith, spake briefly; then Mr. Williams prophesied [preached]; and after the governor of Plimouth spake to the question; after him the elder; then some two or three more of the congregation.[58]

Yet it is apparent that strongly Puritan though the settlers' ideals were, they had not succeeded in stripping from themselves all habits of thought of earlier ages. On August 15, 1648,

> Mr. Allen of Dedham preached out of Acts 15, a very godly, learned, and particular handling of near all the doctrines and applications concern-

---

[56]Ibid., pp. 339-40.
[57]Ibid., p. 341.
[58]Ibid., p. 105.

ing that subject with a clear discovery and refutation of such errors, objections, and scruples as had been raised about it by some young heads in the country.

Then suddenly a snake appeared in the seat "where many of the elders sate behind the preacher." One of the elders trod on it and it was killed.

> Nothing falling out but by divine providence, it is out of doubt the Lord discovered somewhat of his mind in it. The serpent is the devil; the synod, the representative of the churches of Christ in New England. The devil had formerly and lately attempted their disturbance and dissolution; but their faith in the seed of the woman overcame him and crushed his head.[59]

Quakers and Amish. The Anabaptists were a second strand of reforming opinion that found itself uncomfortable with the Elizabethan Settlement and the other positions Reformers had adopted in Europe by the end of the sixteenth century. The wilder extremists among them were less in evidence. But gentler idealists were still calling for freedom from organized church life, ordained ministry and formal sacraments.

George Fox (1624-1691) was apprenticed as a shoemaker in Leicestershire, where he was born, though he did not complete the apprenticeship; so we may take it that he was not highly educated. When he was nineteen he ran away to London, but in a year he was home again, still restless, ready to argue about politics with supporters of the Parliament and about religious matters with the local minister, and any others he found on his continuing travels in the Midland Counties. He describes in his *Journal* how he came to understand this personal pilgrimage in biblical terms:

> During all this time I never joined any religious group, but gave up myself to the Lord forsaking all evil company and leaving my father and mother, and all other relatives; I travelled up and down as a stranger in the earth, as the Lord had inclined my heart, taking a rented room to myself in the town where I came, and staying sometimes more, sometimes less in a place.[60]

---

[59]Ibid., p. 377.
[60]George Fox, *The Journal of George Fox*, ed. Thomas Ellwood (1800; reprint, New York: Cam-

Keen though he was to discuss religion and politics, he was also nervous of being misled, either by the "ungodly" or by those who held strong views and "professed" their belief in a particular way: "for I dared not stay long in a place, being afraid both of professors and the ungodly persons; being a tender young man, I feared I should be hurt by conversing much with either."[61]

His idea was that he should allow God to explain things ("open" them) to him. On his way into Coventry in 1646 it was opened to him that salvation did not depend on being a Protestant or a "Papist" but on having been converted and having "passed from death to life." On another occasion, on a Sunday morning, he was walking in a field when the Lord opened to him the idea "that being educated at Oxford or Cambridge was not enough to fit and qualify men to be ministers of Christ." This rejection of the need for formal study of theology was to mature into the Quaker belief that simplicity was enough.[62] It also encouraged him to regard or respect priests less and dissenters more. But still he found none "that could speak to [his] condition." It was then that he "heard a voice which said, 'There is one, even Christ Jesus, that can speak to your condition,'" and was converted.[63]

Armed with his new certainty, he became active in a new way:

> We had great meetings in those parts; for the power of the Lord broke through in that side of the country. Returning into Nottinghamshire, I found there a company of shattered Baptists, and others. The Lord's power formed mightily, and gathered many of them. Afterwards I went to Mansfield and the area; where the Lord's power was wonderfully manifested both at Mansfield, and other towns in the area. In Derbyshire the mighty power of God formed in a wonderful manner. At Eton, a town near Derby, there was a meeting of Friends, where appeared such a mighty power of God that they were greatly shaken, and many mouths were opened in the power of the Lord God. And many were moved by the Lord to go to steeple houses, to the priests, and to the people, to declare the everlasting truth unto them.[64]

---

bridge University Press, 1952), www.hallvworthington.com/wjournal/gfjournal1.html.
[61]Ibid.
[62]Ibid.
[63]Ibid.
[64]Ibid.

He also began to develop a concern for what would now be called social justice. At Mansfield on one occasion, he felt God urging him ("it was upon me from the Lord") to speak to the local justices about the oppression of servants "in their wages."[65] He was "moved" to make representations elsewhere too, not only about treating servants well but also about oaths. He exhorted particular individuals known for their bad behavior and sometimes won them to change their ways:

> I was moved to go and speak to one of the wickedest men in the country, one who was a common drunkard, a noted whore master, and a rhyme maker; and in the dread of the mighty God I reproved him for his evil courses. When I was done speaking and left him, he came after me, and told me that he was so smitten when I spoke to him that he had scarcely any strength left in him. So this man was convinced, turned from his wickedness, and remained an honest, sober man, to the astonishment of the people who had known him before.[66]

This practice of casting oneself upon the direct leading of God had, as had been realized in earlier centuries, the great practical difficulty that the mentally ill may also believe that God is telling them what to do. The inward guide may be divine or a fantasy.

The new community tried out various names for themselves: Children of the Light, Friends of the Truth. They settled in the end on the Religious Society of Friends. The name Quaker was apparently first used by a local justice to describe the way the Friends shook or quaked during their meetings. It was Fox's personal decision to be a practicing pacifist, a notion more startling in a man living through the English Civil War with its distinctly military approach to ecclesiastical reform.

James Nayler. Among those Fox converted was James Nayler (1618-1660). From 1643 to the early 1650s Nayler fought in the Parliamentary Army during the English Civil War and then as a supporter of Cromwell and the Protectorate. He became a preacher during this time, although he was not a highly educated man. The New Model Army, in which he served, was strongly interested in the theological debates of

---

[65]Ibid.
[66]Ibid.

the time, and he may have advanced his knowledge in this way. Then he met George Fox. His own description of his conversion described how in 1652, while he was ploughing, he heard a voice that ordered him "Get thee out from thy kindred, and from thy father's house."[67] So he took up the life of a wandering preacher. He became involved with the emerging Children of Light movement, which became the Quakers, and spread through the north of England.[68] As a preacher Nayler was in the anticlerical tradition, railing against hierarchy in the Church. Rather than placing Scripture at the center, he placed the emphasis on the continuation of the prophetic ministry among believers of the present time, of the early church. He had confidence that simplicity would steer the believer right; he was hostile to learning and the learned. He and other preachers could be aggressive, bursting in and interrupting worship in parish churches. They did not ask for permission but preached enthusiastically to the local people in the open air. Nayler and Fox were eventually arrested and imprisoned in Westmorland until the spring of 1653, but once released Nayler went back to work, not only speaking but increasingly writing, making the case for a faith which was opposed to both Rome and the magisterial Reformers, yet retained some radical Protestant features.

He pulled no punches. He was a tough disciplinarian and set high standards for the flock. In 1659 he was writing "To the Gathered Churches": "Give ear you gathered churches, so called, in England and Ireland, and hear what truth says of you concerning your dealing towards God; for the day has discovered you: And God is coming to inquire for his own among you."[69]

He called on his readers to realize how profoundly they have failed to grow as they should and to bear fruit.

> But now stand still, and behold what is become of this plant; and what the fruits are you bring forth, and how you are turned into a degenerate Plant of yourselves, since the Lord took away kings, bishops, and all the

---

[67]James Nayler, *Saul's Errand to Damascus* (London, 1654), p. 30.

[68]James Nayler, *The Railer Rebuked* (1655), p. 7.

[69]James Nayler, *To the Gathered Churches* (1659), www.strecorsoc.org/jnayler/gatheredchurches .html.

whole body of opposition; compare your spring and your harvest together, and see what was sown, and what is now to reap among you for God.

In letters written between 1653 and 1660 he was equally reproving.[70]

> Now what are you about to do, who have been called, and once enlight-ened to see the vanities of the world, and the evils of its customs and fashions, ways and worships, and have been touched with judgment for your consenting thereto, and now are turning back to settle and build therein, and there to take up your rest, seeking to get a peace to your-selves in that which judgment has once entered upon you, shall this your building stand? Shall not your peace be broken? Ask your own hearts, if they condemn you not herein, and of unfaithfulness to His faithful Wit-ness in you.[71]

Nayler's "deathbed testimony" summed up his rigorous and demand-ing approach to the living of the Christian life:

> There is a spirit which I feel that delights to do no evil, nor to revenge any wrong, but delights to endure all things, in hope to enjoy its own in the end. Its hope is to outlive all wrath and contention, and to weary out all exaltation and cruelty, or whatever is of a nature contrary to itself. It sees to the end of all temptations. As it bears no evil in itself, so it conceives none in thought to any other. If it be betrayed, it bears it, for its ground and spring is the mercies and forgiveness of God. Its crown is meekness, its life is everlasting love unfeigned; it takes its kingdom with entreaty and not with contention, and keeps it by lowliness of mind. In God alone it can rejoice, though none else regard it, or can own its life. It is con-ceived in sorrow, and brought forth without any to pity it; nor doth it murmur at grief and oppression. It never rejoiceth but through suffer-ings; for with the world's joy it is murdered.

He says he discovered this view of things through his own sense of being "forsaken," which has given him a sense of fellowship with those who live "in dens and desolate places of the earth."[72]

---

[70]James Nayler, *An Epistle to Several Friends About Wakefield* (1653), www.strecorsoc.org/jnayler/epistles.html#1.

[71]James Nayler, *To Some That Were Backslidden*, www.strecorsoc.org/jnayler/epistles.html#4.

[72]*Christian Faith and Practice in the Experience of the Society of Friends* (London: London Yearly Meeting, 1960), www.strecorsoc.org/docs/nayler.html. See also J. Gough, *A History of the People Called Quakers*, 4 vols. (1789-1790).

Theologically distinctive views began to emerge as the implications of the new way of Christian living became clear. The rejection of formal theological study encouraged the Quakers to avoid explicitly advocating of a number of doctrinal conclusions that had been definitive for Christian orthodoxy for many centuries, which were not directly contained in the words of Scripture, such as use of the terms "Trinity" or "persons" to describe God the Father and his Son and Spirit. Further, if Christ is present in the community of believers, the traditional view that he had completed once and for all a necessary work of atoning sacrifice for sin through his death on the cross seemed less central. Nor did Quakers embrace the view that humanity is so pervasively sinful that the key questions were what is to be done about sin, how many are to be releived of its painful and eternal consequences, and how.

The Quaker movement spread west and south, especially to Bristol. Nayler reached London by the summer of 1655. There he began to generate an opposition. Some of the local Quaker women, led by Martha Simmonds (1624-1665), attached themselves to him, and their male relatives were perhaps jealous. Nayler's group began to break into Quaker meetings as they had done into church services. Phenomena were noted, including "quaking and trembling," and put down to recurrences of the kind of thing testified to in Scripture. Nayler was seen entering Bristol on a horse with his followers—bareheaded, though the Quakers would as a rule not take their hats off for anyone—casting garments before him in imitation of Christ's entry into Jerusalem on Palm Sunday. One of his female companions wrote him letters (endorsed by her husband) in the language of the Song of Songs, calling him the Bridegroom. There were stories that he had raised the dead. It seemed to his enemies that Nayler had come to believe that he was himself the Son of God, yet he may have seen himself merely as enacting the implications of the Quaker belief that Christ is in every believer. Nevertheless, there were abundant grounds for putting him on trial. The Parliament of the Protectorate appointed a committee of fifty-five to try him. Despite his denials they found him guilty of impersonating Christ and claiming to be divine. He could be convicted under the Blasphemy Act of 1650, but it was felt that that did not allow a sufficiently severe punishment for

"the ungodding of God."[73] There was discussion of the possibility of in-
troducing legislation allowing a more severe punishment, even the death
penalty, but there was the problem that it would have to be applied
retrospectively. "I propound it to you to proceed against him as an actual
disturber of the public peace. . . . Haply, you may find a lesser punishment than death, which may discourage him and the generation of
them" (Colonel White).

> Cursing of God is treason, but the making ones-self equal with God or
> Christ is treason.
>
> Observe how careful they are not to give honor to any authority. You
> saw how he behaved himself at the bar. Not a cap to you; . . . yet he will
> take cap, knee, kisses, and all reverence. (Mr. Downing)[74]

The Quakers now seemed a threat to public order and Cromwell's
policy of toleration began to be seriously questioned. "The growth of
these things is more dangerous" than "foreign wars or threats of invasions," said Major-General Skippon. "Their principles strike at both
ministry and magistracy."[75] Nayler escaped execution by a whisker on a
vote, but he was pilloried, bore three hundred lashes and a brand was
burned into his forehead. The mainstream Quakers now rejected Nayler,
and he died not much later.

In August 1671 Fox left for the New World with a group of thirteen
Quakers. They landed first in Barbados. There he put forward various
proposals which were later to prove highly controversial in England;
for example, that women's meetings should oversee marriages. In the
West Indies too he encountered slavery at first hand and came to the
view that it was unacceptable. He encouraged slaves to attend Quaker
meetings and learn to be sober and charitable. His efforts did not start
a movement for real change, but it gave the Quakers a name for encouraging slaves to be rebellious. William Penn's (1677-1718) eventual
settlement in Pennsylvania—land given him by the Duke of York in
1682—ruffled further feathers.

---

[73]December 8, 1556, ed. John Towill Rutt (History of Parliament Trust, 1828), 1:59,
    www.british-history.ac.uk/report.aspx?compid=36742.
[74]Ibid., 1:60.
[75]Ibid., 1:24 (extracts from the Journal of Guibon Goddard of the Parliament of 1654).

The Mennonites and the Amish. The Mennonites were originally the followers of Menno Simons (1496-1561), who had been a Dutch priest. He became disillusioned with aspects of the life of the institutional churches as he came into contact with the Anabaptists. In the 1530s he became the leader of a splinter group who took his name. The Mennonites of the United States did not arrive there directly from these early movements. They mostly migrated to America only from the eighteenth century, from the surviving Swiss and German communities, settling first in Pennsylvania and then across the Midwest.

In 1693 a schism among the German-speaking Anabaptists in Switzerland, Alsace and parts of Germany separated off the followers of Jakob Ammann (1644-before 1730), who called for a return to the strict standards of Menno Simons. The Mennonites have not remained notably separatist, but the Amish are as a rule strongly exclusivist and hold staunch views on the spiritual dangers of allowing modern dress, especially for women, and admitting modern technology into their lives.

This, however, was a puritanism of simplicity, not Puritan iconoclasm. Nevertheless, this more serene doctrine was to have its influence among the Reformed too, in the form of the conviction that Christ expected his true disciples to lead lives which were simple. Simplicity consisted not only in resisting overcleverness and self-indulgence, but also in eschewing wealth, elaborate dress, fine living. So such groups affected plainness of dress and simplicity of life. They were frequently pacifists, notably so in a warlike age.

20

The Counter-Reformation

Responding to the Challenge:
Reforming Moves in Rome

Meanwhile, what was Rome doing about this proliferation of challenges? Even if the papacy and its Curia were not of a mind to consider that what the Reformers were saying might be correct, even helpful, they were forced to take seriously what had become a major movement, one which was threatening to take away from its spiritual jurisdiction considerable tracts of the population of Europe.

The Spirituali. Rome had its own internal reformers. Many who remained loyal to the Roman Catholic Church were not blind to the fact that reforms were needed. Among them were the Spirituali, members of a movement that flourished from early in the century until about the 1560s, boasting notable figures in different areas of public life. One was the artist and sculptor Michelangelo (1475-1564), who was sufficiently in good the good graces of the Curia to be commissioned to decorate the Sistine Chapel. Gaspar Contarini (1483-1542) was another and also Reginald Pole (1500-1558), the English cardinal who played so significant a role in the reign of Mary Tudor on the English throne. Their inspiration was the idea of bringing about a spiritual resurgence, a reawakening of living faith in individuals, with an emphasis on Bible study and even a version of the doctrine of justification by faith. There were those who sympathized somewhat with Calvin too.

The Spirituali were not marginal, but included leading figures in the

Roman Church. In Contarini they had a Renaissance figure, learned in the new studies, including Greek as well as in theology. He wrote many books and treatises on subjects both philosophical and theological (such as *On the Immortality of the Soul, On Predestination*); on topics of current controversy in the governance of the Church (*On the Power of a Pope, On the Office of Bishop*); on Protestant ideas (*On Justification, A Confutation of the Articles or Questions of Luther*); and commentary on Scripture (on the Pauline Epistles). He was a practical man, too, an "operator" who was employed as a diplomat and ambassador at the court of the Emperor Charles V and in an embassy to Francis I, king of France, and in many other positions of trust in protecting the Church's position in the high politics of Europe.

The Spirituali were not, however, successful in countering the influence of conservatives who considered the only right response to the Protestants an adversarial one.

The call for a general council. When the divisions of the sixteenth century began to cause serious disquiet, there were calls for a general council. These seem to have been strongest from the Reformers themselves. Luther was appealing for at least a German council as early as 1520, within a few years of making his ninety-five theses challenge.

Yet such was the confidence of the Church that disturbances could only be temporary and dissidents would always be silenced in the end that it took a considerable time for the mounting clamor for a council to bring one about. Pope Clement VII (1523-1534) was hostile to the very idea of holding a council. Despite continued opposition from many cardinals, his successor Paul III (1534-1549) joined the emperor in an attempt to call one, to begin in Mantua in 1537, but it never took place because France and Germany were again at war, and the French bishops would not come. However, as time went on and it became clear that the Reformers and their various movements were gaining ground and were unlikely to die away naturally, attitudes began to change in the Curia.

A treatise on the power and primacy of the pope. The Reformers themselves not only wanted a meeting with the status and authority of a council to be held, at which it could all be talked through by the magisterium; they were anxious to participate, and got themselves ready to do so. An attempt was made to call a council in the 1530s. The Lutherans in particular had repeatedly called for a general council. They prepared for it in various ways, producing reports and papers explaining their position, ready for this proposed meeting of the whole of Christian Europe to consider, should it actually meet. These included documents such as the Lutheran *Treatise on the Power and Primacy of the Pope* (1537) and the Smalcald Articles (1537), which contain the call "O Lord Jesus Christ, do Thou Thyself convoke a Council, and deliver Thy servants by Thy glorious advent!"[1]

The Lutherans anticipated no such respectful treatment as had been accorded to the Eastern Orthodox a century before. They were unsure where the council was to be held, and they were afraid that they would be condemned without being summoned to address it at all. (Melanchthon tried to get the Elector of Saxony to broker an agreement that he would send representatives on condition that they would be treated as full participants in the council.) This was the main reason for preparing a written document stating their position in a series of articles, for fear the Lutherans would be "condemned unsummoned." The preface to the articles accuses the pope of being afraid to hold a truly free general council. It complains that false stories are being spread about the Lutherans and their teachings.

Papacy and council from the Reformers' point of view. Despite their lack of real hope that they would be listened to, the Lutheran theologians who met at Smalcald in 1537 took trouble over compiling an account of papal claims to power. They noted that the pope claims supremacy by divine right over all God's ministers throughout Christendom; that he claims to have both "swords," secular as well as spiritual, so he may bestow kingdoms and depose kings; that he claims power from God to define doctrine and lay down the requirements for sacraments, and when he does so his decisions have the authority of Scripture and the creeds. He says he is Christ's vicar on earth, and not to accept this is to be denied salvation. These were added to the fundamental objection Luther articulated (as discussed on p. 102), that in myriad ways "the

---

[1]"The Smalcald Articles," *The Book of Concord*, http://bookofconcord.org/smalcald.php.

people are led astray by the delusion that their piety and salvation depend upon their own works."[2]

The theologians accordingly assembled the relevant texts of Scripture that seem to weigh against these papal claims. In Luke 22:25 Jesus tells his disciples that no one should exercise lordship among them, and in Matthew 18:2 he places a little child before them as an example. In John 20:21 he sends the disciples out as equals, with no hierarchy. In the epistles, Galatians 2:6-7 has Paul stating that he was not humanly ordained and in 1 Corinthians 3:6 he considers other ministers as his equal. Then they attempted to deal with the passages that seem to point the other way, such as Matthew 16:18, "You are Peter, and on this rock I will build my church"; and John 21:15, "Feed my lambs"—with the aim of persuading the reader that the "keys" were entrusted by Jesus not to a single figure of authority in the church but to the church as a whole.

The Lutherans saw no reason not to refer to the early councils (where they found no assumptions of Roman primacy) and to patristic authorities too. For example, "Jerome says: If the question is concerning authority, the world is greater than the city. Wherever there has been a bishop, whether at Rome, or Eugubium, or Constantinople, or Rhegium, or Alexandria, he is of the same dignity and priesthood."[3]

The accusation is that the papacy has usurped the dominion over the church which he enjoys, and that it cannot be right for him to be allowed to hold councils that are not allowed to contradict him, and far from its being necessary to salvation to accept his primacy, he is to be regarded as antichrist. He is the author of a series of grievous errors: that good works earn remission of sin; that they add to the merit of Christ; that saints are to be worshiped, which is idolatry.

It is hard to see from this distance of time what the Lutherans hoped to achieve at a council by such a broadside attack. But their attention was less on the political realities than on the task of working out such ecclesiological implications as the idea that it will be "especially incum-

---

[2]Martin Luther, sermon at Erfurt, April 7, 1521, *Reformation Writings of Martin Luther*, trans. Bertram Lee Woolf (London: Lutterworth, 1956), 2:111.
[3]*Of the Power and Primacy of the Pope* 9 (1537), www.iclnet.org/pub/resources/text/wittenberg/concord/web/smc-pope.html.

bent on kings" (the Christian magistrates) to check papal powers on behalf of the church.[4]

The council becomes a reality. The series of colloquies or miniature meetings at which Melanchthon and others had attempted reconciliation in the next few years had been achievements in that they were actually held as meetings, but they had not achieved much by way of results. A general council to address the challenges was ordered to be convened at last only in 1545; then it was transferred to Bologna, then postponed because of an outbreak of plague, then delayed again in 1549. By now the politics were running high. The council finally met at Trent in 1551, under a new pope, Julius III (1550-1555). Almost at once it had to cease its work because of yet more war in Europe.

A determination to have no truck with what the Reformers were saying probably gained momentum only toward the end. At the stage of the second period of the council (1552-1553), the Protestants were invited to come and put their case, and the Reformers were guaranteed safe conduct. Melanchthon even set out to attend in 1552 with some of the Lutherans from Germany. But it was made clear that this was not to be a consensus-forming council. Those who attended to put the Protestant case were not to be allowed to vote. This was to be no meeting of minds, no grand colloquy, but an exercise in condemnation of the upstarts and their challenges. The Council of Trent met again under Pope Pius IV (1559-1565), and this time it sat from 1562-1563 and did much of the work for which it has since been known.

Trent defends the Vulgate. The Council of Trent found it hard to accept the implications of the mistakes which had recently been found to litter the Vulgate, for the Vulgate had been accepted as the standard Latin translation since the fifth century. It had—for all practical purposes—lost sight of the fact that the original text of the Bible had been written in Greek and Hebrew, not Jerome's (admittedly uninspired) Latin.

From this point of view it must have been disquieting to watch the effects of the widespread scholarly study of Greek and Hebrew in the Reformers' universities in Germany and elsewhere. The Pontificia Uni-

---

[4]Ibid.

versita Gregoriana in Rome was founded in 1553 with the aim of providing a traditional and conservative counterbalance to the trendy new universities of northern Europe, with their reformed syllabuses and their new styles of Bible study.

Robert Bellarmine (1542-1621) received part of his university education at Louvain and had a better acquaintance than many contemporary Roman Catholic theologians with the views of the "heretics." He was made Professor of Controversies at the Roman College in 1576 and wrote *On Controversies* (*De Controversiis*) based on his lectures there. Here was a *Contra Gentiles* for its time, an attempt to present the disputes of the day under a systematic arrangement to enable those who found themselves engaged in them to find their way among the pros and cons. Some of the Protestant universities of Europe were prompted to found chairs in which the incumbents could work on counter-arguments.

The council affirmed that the Vulgate was the true text of Scripture. Bellarmine sat on the commission established to revise the Vulgate, at the wish of the council in token of its awareness that serious concerns had been raised. The council affirmed the Apocrypha's place in the canon. It also took a view of the Church's right and duty to provide official and normative teaching on Scripture.

The topics of Trent. The council produced the decrees which might be expected of a council, but also canons anathematizing the contrary or different views of the Protestants. The syllabus was largely set by the need to rebut these opinions.

Luther, it was acknowledged, had proposed a very successful doctrine of "justification by faith," successful in winning an uncomfortable amount of support. In response Trent defined the traditional position about the need for good works if a person was to be justified—understood as "made righteous" rather than "declared righteous"—in the sight of God. Effort was worthwhile, it maintained; there was nothing, it insisted, in the Reformers' claim that human free will is so damaged by sin that the sinner can do good only by grace.

Among the chief architects of these rebuttals was Girolamo Seripando (1493-1563). He was an Augustinian friar and superior general of the order from 1539. He was present at the sessions of the Council of

Trent in 1546, where he presented his views on original sin and on justification, and proposed the argument that both conceptions of justice in
the sight of God are valid, the unmerited acceptance by God and the
place earned by being good.

Much of the rest of what Trent had to say consisted in obstinate resistance to change and dogged reassertion of former positions, some of
which became the firmer in the process. The doctrine that there are
seven sacraments was reasserted. The Eucharist was stated to be a sacrifice of the true body and blood of Christ (although Trent did not insist
on the full medieval definition of the doctrine of transubstantiation).
Priestly power was confirmed to be sacerdotal. The laity were not to
have Communion in both kinds. Ordination was stated to imprint an
indelible character on the person ordained. Celibacy for the priesthood
and the indissolubility of marriage for laity who entered into it were
both reasserted.

The practices traditionally beloved of the faithful and fostered by the
church but fought against by Reformers of almost every stamp were
also endorsed: the veneration of the Virgin Mary and of saints and relics,
going on pilgrimages, indulgences. The Council sought to consolidate
these renewed insistences by banning books which said anything to the
contrary. Pius IV's List of Prohibited Books (*Index Librorum Prohibitorum*), which appeared in 1559, was amended and promulgated by the
Council of Trent beginning in 1564.

Ignatius Loyola and the Jesuits. At the period of the Council of Trent
a new "army" was being formed for missionary work on behalf of what
we must now call the "Roman" Church. The Spanish nobleman Ignatius Loyola (1491-1556) had his military career interrupted by a leg in-
jury on the battlefield in 1521. He passed the time in pious reading
while he waited to recover. The *Life of Christ* attributed to the Carthusian Ludolph of Saxony (1300-1378) presented him with a new understanding of the way he could live so as to "imitate Christ." He experienced a conversion to a way of life not unlike that which had fired the
imagination of Francis of Assisi. He was filled with spiritual longings,
but he was also keen to live an active life for Christ. He went to the
Holy Land with a convert's zeal to bring it back to Christianity, but the

Franciscans there were discouraging, and he returned to Europe to train in theology.

That took him and the movement he was to found in the direction of a high-powered intellectuality. He went from university to university in Spain and then to Paris, where he almost coincided with John Calvin. He was winning followers who encouraged him to found a society, which he named the Society of Jesus. Its growth was rapid and enormous, with about a thousand members by the time he died.

Members of the Society subjected themselves to rigorous spiritual discipline and community rules, practicing daily spiritual exercises, emphasizing obedience to the church, with regular confession and frequent participation in the Eucharist. This was to be an active conservatism, a loyal adherence to the old ways of the late medieval church, by intelligent and educated men. For example, the sixth rule was "to praise relics of the Saints, giving veneration to them and praying to the Saints; and to praise stations [of the cross], pilgrimages, indulgences, pardons, crusades, and candles lighted in the churches." The seventh rule was to praise "fasts and abstinence." The eighth rule was to praise "images, and to venerate them according to what they represent." Members of the Society were to foster "scholastic learning" and to obey the church "because by the same Spirit and our Lord Who gave the ten Commandments, our holy Mother the Church is directed and governed" (thirteenth rule).[5]

Loyola desired to maintain a careful doctrinal balance among the Jesuits, such as between the teaching of predestination and free will, or between emphasizing the grace of God and maintaing a healthy fear of him, between faith and the merit of good works (rules 14-18).

John Jewel responds to Trent. As a well-respected theologian Jewel found himself commissioned to write a defense against Trent on behalf of the Church of England. The work was begun in response to the papal bull of 1560 summoning the important third session of the Council of Trent. The English Church, like other reforming churches, would not be allowed to participate because it no longer accepted the ultimate juris-

---

[5]Ignatius Loyola, *The Spiritual Exercises of St. Ignatius of Loyola*, trans. Elder Mullen (New York: P. J. Kennedy, 1914).

diction of Rome. This offical *Apology* (*Apologia*, something not in the least "apologetic" in the modern sense) was begun at the instigation of the queen's secretary and the archbishop of Canterbury, and finished with considerable expedition, in the spring of 1561, though it was not published until the beginning of the following year.[6] It was written in Latin and intended to be read in reforming circles on the Continent where sympathizers would be able to see why the Church of England stood where it did and why it claimed not to be in any way heretical.[7] It was well received there, though some thought it too strongly expressed.[8]

The *Apology* prompted rebuttals, and a pamphlet warfare began between the recusant English exiles, especially at Louvain, and the theologians at home. In 1564 Thomas Harding (1516-1572) entered the lists with a book denouncing Jewel's work, one of several bitter exchanges to come. A few years older than Jewel, Harding had followed a remarkably similar path from grammar school in Devon to Oxford, where he became a fellow of New College and was for a time Regius Professor of Hebrew in the university, where he stood with the Reformers during the reign of Edward VI, before returning to Roman Catholicism under Mary Tudor. He was exiled after Elizabeth I ascended the throne. The controversy with Harding made Jewel the champion of the Elizabethan Settlement, and for a time the most famous bishop in the Church of England.

Trent's impact was felt throughout Europe. The areas which had remained predominantly Roman Catholic accepted the decrees of the Council. These were mainly in southern Europe—Italy and Portugal, with a limited acceptance by Philip of Spain (who was insistent that the decrees ran in Spain only insofar as they did not diminish his royal authority). In the Netherlands too Philip's writ ran, and the German

---

[6]John Jewel, *The Apology for the Church of England Works*, ed. John Ayre, Parker Society (Cambridge: Cambridge University Press, 1848), 4.1247.

[7]An English translation of the work, which first appeared in 1562, was superseded by the more famous translation made by Ann, Lady Bacon, published in 1564 as an *Apologie or Answere in Defence of the Churche of Englande*, with a preface by Parker.

[8]By January 24, 1562, a copy of the *Apologia* was in the hands of Nicholas Throckmorton, the English ambassador in Paris, who expressed pleasure that the "papists were very well answeryd" but regretted that the Calvinists were not addressed and wished the language were toned down (John E. Booty, *John Jewel* [London: SPCK, 1963], p. 50).

princes in the areas which had not gone over to the Reformers accepted Trent at the diet held at Augsburg in 1566. Poland also accepted Trent.

Western Europe's divided religious future was set by these events. In the Roman Catholic regions, the Counter-Reformation took root and with it the authority of a reinvigorated Rome. In the Americas, Spanish and Portuguese settlements were Roman Catholic, and a similar division of the Americas into Roman Catholic and Reformed went with the countries of origin of conquerors and settlers.

SCIENCE AND THE BIBLE FROM
A ROMAN CATHOLIC PERSPECTIVE

Nicolaus Copernicus (1473-1543) spent his career mainly as a Polish civil servant and diplomat, an adviser to the king on monetary reform. That left him time and inclination to dabble as a polymath in various subjects, including astronomy. It was he who proposed the possibility that the sun, not the earth, lay at the center of the universe. Why was that such a dangerous idea?

In 1514 he had published an exploratory *Little Commentary* (*Commentariolus*), which he shared with only a few friends and fellow inquirers, and did not intend for printing. His ideas got about, however, and there was a degree of excitement and concern all over Europe about the implications of his ideas. He received encouraging letters from senior figures, both Roman Catholic (the archbishop of Capua) and Protestant. Philipp Melanchthon sent him a pupil, in the person of Georg Joachim Rheticus from Wittenberg. Rheticus published a book of his own, the *Narratio Prima*, setting out something of what he understood to be Copernicus's theory.

Copernicus was slow to publish the book in which he finally put his developed theory forward, the *De Revolutionibus Orbium Coelestium* (*On the Revolutions of the Celestial Spheres*). It appeared just before his death in 1543. (Legend has it that a copy was finally put into his hands on his deathbed.)

It was some years before the book caused serious controversy, and then it was primarily Roman Catholic not Protestant apologists who complained that it contradicted Scripture. The Dominican Giovanni Martia Tolosani (c. 1471-1549) said so in 1546 in a book that asserted that Scripture was absolutely true. And paradoxically, it was at the Lutheran university of Wittenberg, and with the approval of Melanchthon, that Copernicus's work was allowed to be studied.

The supporters of Copernicus argued that it had never been God's intention as he dictated Scripture to include instruction in science. The Jesuit Giovanni Battista Riccioli (1598-1671) would later attempt to distinguish the question whether the Bible contains teaching on physics and astronomy from the question whether those remarks on the subject which the Scriptures contain are really about the faith and not about science. The Council of Trent's session 4 was cited by those hostile to this position.[9]

Galileo di Vincenzo Bonaiuti de' Galilei (1564-1642) was born in Pisa. He was the eldest of six children, two of whom died in infancy. His father, Vincenzo Galilei, was famous as a lute player, but was also interested in the theory of music, which was then still regarded—as it had been since classical times—as a branch of mathematical study. After several years under private tutelage, Galileo was sent to the school in the monastery of Camaldolese monks at Vallombrosa. These was the regular way of educating a promising boy, and although Galileo seems to have considered becoming a priest, an education by monks did not necessarily lead in that direction. His father wanted him to become a physician, so he began to study medicine at the University of Pisa. There he became interested in mathematics and natural philosophy and proved so outstanding that he was given a university teaching post in mathematics in 1589, in his mid-twenties.

In 1592 Galileo moved to Padua to teach mathematics and astronomy in the university there. Galileo's father had died in 1591, and Galileo then had responsibility for the future of his little brother Michelangelo. Michelangelo (or Michelagnolo) was to become a composer and a lutenist like his father. From the 1590s Galileo was also acquiring family responsibilities of his own. He lived with a mistress, Marina Gamba, and had

---

[9]Alfredo Dinis, "Giovanni Battista Riccili and the Science of His Time," *Jesuit Science and the Republic of Letters*, ed. M. Feingold (Cambridge, Mass.: MIT Press, 2003), p. 211ff.

two daughters by her. Virginia was born in 1600, and Livia the next year. These two could not hope for marriage in an age when their illegitimacy was a barrier to social acceptance, so both were sent to become nuns at San Matteo in Arcetri. Livia suffered from poor health all her life and Virginia died in 1634. Galileo also had a son with Marina, Vincenzo, born in 1606. Steps were eventually taken to have him made legally legitimate, and he was able to inherit his father's estate and to marry.

In 1610 Galileo published his results from observing the moons of Jupiter by telescope. His book *The Starry Messenger* included some reflections on the theory advanced by Copernicus that the sun, not the earth, is at the center of the universe. Galileo's position on the question was still provisional. He was making a name and was now able to move from his lecturing position at the university and enjoy the patronage of the grand Duke of Tuscany, living in his household as his personal "philosopher and mathematician." He spent the rest of his life in this post, exposed to attack, but to some degree protected.

In 1611 he traveled to Rome to make some demonstrations of the telescope to the scholars of the Collegio Romano, which was run by the Jesuits. He wanted them to see for themselves the four moons of Jupiter he had discovered. Meanwhile Galileo's vacated professorship of mathematics at Pisa was filled by Benedetto Castelli (1578-1643), a friend and supporter of Galileo.

Now the Roman Church began to take an interest. Christina of Lorraine (1565-1637), the Grand Duchess Dowager of Tuscany, had an exchange with him in 1613 in which she challenged him to show that the Bible did not contradict what he and Galileo were saying. In particular, she cited Joshua 10:12-13:

> Then spake Joshua to the Lord. . . . Sun, stand thou still upon Gibeon; and thou, Moon, in the valley of Aijalon. And the Sun stood still, and the moon stayed, Until the nation had avenged themselves of their enemies. And the sun stayed in the midst of heaven, and hasted not to go down about a whole day. (RV)

Steteruntque sol et luna, "the sun and the moon stood still," says the Vulgate, and "and the sun stood still in the midst of the heavens" (*stetit itaque sol in medio caeli*). This was still the text being relied on as though Jerome's Latin represented God's exact words.

This seems to have been quite a good-humored encounter, but it led to trouble for Galileo in the long term. Galileo unwisely wrote a long letter to Castelli in 1613 detailing his heliocentric views and their perfect compatibility with the nonscientific intentions of Scripture, which began to circulate and to trigger debates.[10] His enemies settled in for a long battle.

Galileo suffered a similar fate to the one Charles Darwin (1809-1882) met two and a half centuries later, in that his name became attached to a certain understanding of views attacked as running counter to the teaching of the Bible. One of the strongest impressions to emerge from the letters is that Galileo was frightening influential people. He drew the fire of many who were fearful of the consequences of allowing it to be widely believed that the earth was not at the center of the universe. It was a campaign that would not die away. Thommaso Caccini (1574-1648), a Dominican, preached against Galileo in Santa Maria Novella in Florence in December 1614, accusing him, along with other mathematicians, of heretically contradicting the teaching of the Bible. Here was the Roman Catholic Church, at the end of a century of reformation and counter-reformation, fighting, as it saw it, for the supreme authority of Scripture. Yet Galileo was struggling honestly with exactly the question of how the Bible's teaching was to be reconciled with the new scientific conclusions. These arguments have a very modern ring when set beside the controversy about apparent conflict with the account in Genesis, which was excited by the publication of Darwin's *Origin of Species* in 1859, and is still raging in debates about the content of school courses.

In 1615 Niccolò Lorini (1544-c. 1617), also a Dominican, delated Galileo to the Inquisition, lodging a complaint in writing accompanied by a copy of Galileo's ill-advised letter to Castelli. Galileo's response was once more to write—and publish—lengthy explanations in the hope of persuading his opponents by rational argument. The result was the cre-

---

[10]*The Galileo Affair: A Documentary History*, ed. and trans. Maurice A. Finocchiaro (Berkeley: University of California Press, 1989), pp. 47-54.

ation of more hostages to fortune. The first was the document that became known as his "Letter to the Grand Duchess Christina," which
expanded on what he had said in his dangerous letter to Castelli. The
second earned the title of Galileo's "Considerations on the Copernican
Opinion." The third was his "Discourse on the Tides."

The Inquisition did not find much fault with Galileo on this first occasion, though it exacted an undertaking from him about what he would
and would not say in future. But there was sufficient concern about
where all this might be leading to prompt a review of the Church's position on Copernicus and his ideas.

In 1620-1621 Galileo was writing more books. The first, *The Assayer*
(*Il Saggiatore*), appeared in 1623. The second, *Dialogue Concerning
the Two Chief World Systems*, came out in 1632. They both brought
down further disapproval on Galileo. The first was about the behavior of materials, how they stood up to stresses and alternations, and
so on. This was taken by his enemies as an attack on the Roman
Catholic doctrine of the Eucharist, which had at its center a particular view of what happened to the bread and the wine when the words
of consecration were spoken. The second book, *The Dialogue*, was
alleged to have been published without obtaining proper permission
and in flagrant disobedience to the papacy. By now he was alert to
the wider implications of what he was writing and was being distinctly more challenging.

This time the Inquisition was merciless. Galileo had made influential
enemies. In 1633, condemned by the Inquisition, Galileo was forced to
abjure what he had written. He spent the rest of his life from 1634 under
arrest in his country house. The Roman authorities organized the publication of books which argued against Galileo in an attempt to diminish his influence, but visitors came to see him, and he was not left without avenues of influence. By 1638 he was blind and suffering from other
painful ailments. He died in 1642.

Censorship. In the story of Galileo are illustrated patterns of repressive response to challenge that came not from uprisings of the faithful
but from individual thinkers. Galileo founded no ecclesial community
and threatened no schism. But his ideas were held to be dangerous to

the faithful, and the Church's response was censorship of the ideas and condemnation of their originator. This had begun before Galileo became controversial, of course, and the "Tridentine Index" of forbidden works was only formally abolished in 1966.

21

CHURCH AND STATE AGAIN

New Political Dimensions of the Idea of Order

POLITICS AND RELIGION WERE AS INSEPARABLE in the sixteenth century as they had always been, but new pressures were felt. The Ottoman Turks were pressing westward, to the consternation of Eastern Europe and the concern of the empire in the West. Luther had mentioned this danger in 1518, presenting it as a divine punishment of Christendom, which fully deserved it.[1] The Turks might, he suggested, turn out to be forerunners of the apocalypse, come to destroy the antichrist, driving him out of his usurped position in the papacy. The siege of Vienna in 1529 frightened Luther enough to cause him to write a prayer for the victory of the emperor.

Within Europe itself the story of the Reformation is entangled everywhere with the strands of the local and European politics of the times. Powerful men and women made decisions to protect their political positions that did not always accord with their public statements of religious attitude.

Medieval orderliness. In front of this thorn hedge of pragmatism stood the beautiful idea of "order," a notion very old and durable, but now undergoing one of its periodic historical mutations. Aristotle had set out most of the ground rules; Christianity had added its own dimension. In the Middle Ages the idea of order had been cosmic in scale. A hierarchy of being stretched down from the Creator himself, through

---

[1]Martin Luther, *Explanation of the Ninety-five Theses* (1518).

angels and men, to animals and vegetables and insensate rocks and
stones. The arrangements for running things within human society ran
in parallel, with the right to rule accorded to those God had made for
the task, and the duty to obey falling to those born at God's choice into
lowlier levels of society. These assumptions were very slow to fade.

The New Testament image of the church as a body was adapted to fit
the state too. In the feudal northern Europe of the Middle Ages, the idea
that each part of the body has its natural place and its natural function
was attractive to rulers. That assumed that peasants should be content to
stay in their allotted role in life and not aspire to upward social mobility.

In the Italian city-states and the cities of some parts of northern
Europe, varied conceptions of citizenship and liberty challenged that
presumption. By the sixteenth century the idea of a "commonwealth"
had developed a new flavor. The underlying principle was the same, but
a notion of the common good was emerging. As Hooker put it: "The law
of a commonweal, the very soul of a politic body, the parts whereof are
by law animated, held together, and set to work in such actions as the
common good requireth."

Augustine's idea that order in society had to be enforced only because
in fallen humankind sin always tends to make people behave badly persisted throughout these changes. Hooker too comments that law and its
enforcement are needed because the will of man is "inwardly rebellious."[2]

The civil magistrate: The relations of church and state in Lutheranism.
Lutheran thinking on all this was influenced by early encounters with
the Anabaptists and their disruptive tendency to anarchism. Lutherans
settled on a moderate political position. The Augsburg Confession contains a series of statements that are clearly meant to accord with Scripture's encouragement to Christians to accept their place in society and
the government set over them, unless it conflicts with their duty to God,
rendering to Caesar what is Caesar's (art. 16). Lutherans "condemn the
Anabaptists who forbid these civil offices to Christians."

> For the Gospel . . . does not destroy the State or the family, but very
> much requires that they be preserved as ordinances of God, and that

---

[2]Ibid., 1.9.1.

charity be practiced in such ordinances. Therefore, Christians are necessarily bound to obey their own magistrates and laws save only when commanded to sin; for then they ought to obey God rather than men. Acts 5, 29.

A distinction is made between the powerlessness of sinful human beings to behave well in the sight of God and their capacity to act rationally and for the good in secular affairs and "civil life":

> Man's will has some liberty to choose civil righteousness, and to work things subject to reason. But it has no power, without the Holy Ghost, to work the righteousness of God, that is, spiritual righteousness; since the natural man receiveth not the things of the Spirit of God, 1 Cor. 2,14; but this righteousness is wrought in the heart when the Holy Ghost is received through the Word. These things are said in as many words by Augustine in his Hypognosticon, Book III. (Article 18)

Obedience to ecclesiastical authorities is not at all a straightforward matter in the Augsburg Confession. The New Testament instruction is to obey lawfully constituted authority. But does that extend to the authorities of a corrupted church? The Augsburg Confessions speak uneasily of the "power of Bishops, in which some have awkwardly confounded the power of the Church and the power of the sword." "From this confusion very great wars and tumults have resulted" because popes, "emboldened by the power of the Keys," not only have instituted new services and burdened consciences with reservation of cases and have tried to grasp secular authority too and "take the Empire from the Emperor." The Lutheran position adopted here is that spiritual authority must not creep into secular affairs; "the power of the Church and the civil power must not be confounded."

Calvinist politics and society. Calvin too had had negative experiences with civic disturbances. He wrote in his *Institutes* against the more disruptive Anabaptists and in favor of civil magistrates. Anarchism under the guise of Christian freedom is certainly frowned on: "For some, on hearing that liberty is promised in the gospel, a liberty which acknowledges no king and no magistrate among men, but looks to Christ alone, think that they can receive no benefit from their liberty so long as they see any power placed over them."[3]

Calvin's basic position was that rulers have their legitimate authority from God, who is the source of all power, and are indeed, within certain parameters, "the ministers of God." Good subjects have nothing to fear. Rulers are "not a terror to good works, but to the evil" (Rom 13:1, 3).[4] Those who deserve punishment must remember that "the magistrate, in inflicting punishment, acts not of himself, but executes the very judgements of God."[5]

Calvin assumed the irrelevance, and irreverence, of democratic discussion of political change: "And certainly it were a very idle occupation for private men to discuss what would be the best form of polity in the place where they live, seeing these deliberations cannot have any influence in determining any public matter."[6]

> Should those to whom the Lord has assigned one form of government, take it upon them anxiously to long for a change, the wish would not only be foolish and superfluous, but very pernicious. If you fix your eyes not on one state merely, but look around the world, or at least direct your view to regions widely separated from each other, you will perceive that divine Providence has not, without good cause, arranged that different countries should be governed by different forms of polity.

A compelling reason for discouraging political debate is the fear that it will lead to Anabaptist-like anarchy. The most important thing of all is not to disrupt public order. People should obey even a bad ruler.[7] "This feeling of reverence, and even of piety, we owe to the utmost to all our rulers, be their characters what they may."[8]

The Scottish Confession which resulted from Knox's transportation of Calvinism to Scotland accepted that "empires, kingdoms, dominions, and cities" and their government are "ordained by God" for "manifestation of his own glory, and for the singular profit and commodity of mankind." It follows that civil disobedience is not allowed: "So that

---

[3]Calvin, "Of Civil Government," *Institutes* 4.20, 4.20.1.
[4]Ibid., 4.20.4.
[5]Ibid., 4.20.10.
[6]Ibid., 4.20.8.
[7]Ibid., 4.20.26.
[8]Ibid., 4.20.29.

whosoever goes about to take away or to confound the whole state of civil policies, now long established; we affirm the same men not only to be enemies to mankind, but also wickedly to fight against God's expressed will." It also follows that persons in positions of authority ought to be respected and that to resist them was to resist "God's ordinance": "We further confess and acknowledge, that such persons as are placed in authority are to be loved, honored, feared, and held in most reverent estimation because they are the lieutenants of God, in whose sessions God himself does sit and judge."[9]

Erastus and the lay elders. A debate was provoked by the ideas of the Swiss theologian Thomas Erastus (1524-1583). Erastus had been a Zwinglian, especially in supporting Zwingli's ideas on the Eucharist at the series of meetings that continued the debates of the earlier sixteenth century in 1560 (Heidelberg), 1564 (Maulbronn). He was hostile to the introduction of a Reformed presbyterian polity at Heidelberg in 1570, though he was ineffective in preventing it. The leaders of the newly reconstituted church promptly excommunicated Erastus as a Socinian. He continued under the ban of excommunication until 1576, though that did not prevent his forwarding his academic career.

He had been involved in correspondence with Heinrich Bullinger and others, and had developed a series of theses in the late 1560s, discussing whether sinners should be punished by the state rather than by the church. The prompter for the treatise that made his name and created the term *Erastian* was a doctoral disputation at Heidelberg in 1568, where the candidate was an English Puritan, George Wither. He had wanted to defend a thesis about vestments, a matter which was to become highly divisive in England as the century wore on. The University of Heidelberg did not allow that, but it permitted him to defend the thesis that the presbyterate could excommunicate.

The resulting *Treatise of Erastus* was not published until 1589, well after his death. It was published by his widow's new husband, Giacomo Castelvetro (1546-1616), with supporting material and further discussion. It appeared as a discussion of the serious question of the authority

---

9"The Scottish Confession," *Still Waters Revival Books*, www.swrb.com/newslett/actualNLs/Scot-Conf.htm#Preface.

to excommunicate and the effect of excommunication.[10] Erastus argues
that the civil authorities may punish sins, not by cutting the sinners off
from the sacraments but by means of civil punishments. To allow the
state to punish sinners would equate sin with crime, and it was by no
means agreed among Reformers that that was acceptable. On the other
hand, the old disciplinary structures of the church were principally those
of the penitential system, with much of which the Reformers wanted to
dispense. The most important counter-blast, maintaining that excommunication was for ecclesiastical authorities alone, came from Beza in
his *De Vera Excommunicatione et Christiano Presbyterio* (1590).

One proposal was that the excommunication of serious sinners
should be entrusted to a panel of elders and "a part of that Eldership to
be of necessity certain chosen out from amongst the laity for that purpose" (Hooker, *Laws*, preface, 2.9). This suggestion went to the heart of
a doctrine of ministry in which the power to bind and loose, the power
of the keys, had been strictly reserved for the ordained ministry and to
priests (absolution) and bishops (absolution and excommunication) at
that. People are taught, Hooker notes, "that an *Elder* doth signify a layman admitted only to the office of rule or government in the Church; a
Doctor one which may only teach and neither preach nor administer the
Sacraments; a *Deacon* one which hath charge of the alms box and of
nothing else." The question, of course, was whether these strict demarca-
tions were biblical, or provided an acceptable solution to the need to
revisit and review the traditional hierarchy of bishop, priest and deacon.

Anglicanism and order: Richard Hooker takes stock. Hooker, born in
1554, was a small child when Elizabeth came to the throne of England
in 1558.[11] He therefore grew up during the decades when the Church of
England was fixing its official position on many of the points of belief
that had occupied Reformers for more than a century. England had
moved from the broad Protestantism of the reign of Henry VIII to the
Reformed sympathies of Elizabeth's reign, experienced a series of

---

[10]*Explicatio gravissimae quaestionis utrum excommunicatio, quatenus religionem intelligentes et am-
plexantes, a sacramentorum usu, propter admissum facinus arcet, mandato nitatur divino, an excogitata
sit ab hominibus.*
[11]Walton's *Life* of Hooker was first published in 1665.

voltes-face in between and endeavored to settle itself at last in a socially stable way which would enable church and society to work together in the long term.

Hooker respected John Jewel, who acted as his patron and whom Hooker described as "the worthiest Divine that Christendome hath bred for the space of some hundreds of yeres,"[12] but he had other patrons after Jewel's death in 1571, for example the bishop of London, Edwin Sandys. He spent his early career as an academic and a cleric whose church was situated among the Inns of Court, and was therefore well equipped for the task he addressed himself to from 1593 to his death, as the crown of his life's work. He called his book *Of the Laws of Ecclesiastical Polity;* in it he sets out an infrastructure for the church. Hooker was not gifted with eloquence. As a preacher he lacked gesture and movement and even volume, saying what he had to say—which tended to concentrate on the finer technicalities of the theological matters in issue—in a low voice and without delivery.[13] The written style of his *Laws* is similarly dense and remorseless in the demands it makes on the reader's powers of concentration. Nonetheless, he had the support of Whitgift, archbishop of Canterbury in writing it, his license to publish, and apparently the use of the Lambeth Palace Library for his research. Whitgift, a sponsor of the strongly Calvinistic Lambeth Articles (1595), did not regard the Reformed as a threat in the way that his successor Richard Bancroft (1544-1610) did. Before becoming archbishop Bancroft was bishop of London from 1597-1604, and active in the Marprelate affair (see pp. 348-49). As early as the mid-1580s he had made a name for himself as an anti-Puritan preacher and writer, and a defender of episcopacy.

Hooker was well aware that these were dangerous times, as English opinion polarized. In 1570 the pope excommunicated the queen, and a strong antipapalism made itself felt. He observed Reformed sympathizers begin to press for the end to the episcopal system which the Church of England had maintained throughout the changes of the Tudor era, and their demands from the same quarter for an altogether more Puri-

---

[12]Hooker, *Laws*, 2.6.4.
[13]Hooker, *Laws*, 5.22.19.

tan style of church life, which would presumably do away with images, along with such frippery as surplices.

Like so many of his forebears, Hooker liked order. *Discipline* is a favorite term with him. In such tightening up he thought lay the solutions to the problems that were arising with these challenges. His most urgent task, as he came to see it, was to hold off the Presbyterian challenge and make a case for the survival of episcopacy. This he set in the context of a theory of government in which secular and spiritual jurisdictions were at one, and where secular authority was granted by the whole body of the people so that they acted as the body of the Church did, as one body, under its head. The result was a highly original treatment of the relationship of church and state, theology and politics.

> The rule of ghostly or immaterial natures, as spirits and Angels, is their intuitive intellectual judgement concerning the amiable beauty and high goodness of that object, which with unspeakable joy and delight, doth set them on work. The rule of voluntary agents on earth is the sentence that reason giveth concerning the goodness of those things which they are to do.[14]

In running human societies, laws derive in a similarly ordered way, from the ultimate law of God down through natural law to "positive" or civil law, the laws which individual communities make for themselves, and which can vary from place to place. Hooker said, "Laws whether mixedly or merely human are made by politic societies." He distinguishes civil from spiritual societies and their laws. "Only as those societies are civilly united; some as they are spiritually joined and make such a body as we call the Church."[15]

Right reason and the importance of preserving order. "The laws of well-doing are the laws of right reason" (*Laws*, 1.7.4). Hooker was confident in the power of the reasonable argument to carry sensible men's judgments with it. He was always balanced, judicious, even where he was fundamentally opposed to a position. He mentions Calvin with approval in his preface, for like him, Calvin had had his "bringing up" in "the study of the

---

[14]Hooker, *Laws*, 1.8.4.
[15]Ibid., 1.10.10.

Civil Law" (pref., 2.1). But it is to be regretted, says Hooker, that his followers have become caught up in the polarization of opinion in England, "the people's" frightening "sudden attempt for abolishment of popish religion." And the problem is the greater if, as Hooker observes, it becomes a competition when communities of opinion have "endeavoured to be certain degrees more removed from conformity with the Church of Rome, than the rest before had been" (pref., 2.2).

Then there are the dangers of fostering an unquestioning loyalty to a religious leader or human authority: "Of what account the Master of the sentences [Peter Lombard] was in the Church of Rome, the same and more amongst the preachers of reformed Churches Calvin had purchased: so that the perfectest divines were judged they which were skilfullest in Calvin's writings" (pref., 2.8). This can lead to the people being led astray. They do not fully understand how complex theology is: "Let the vulgar sort amongst you know that there is not the least branch of the cause wherein you are so resolute, but to the trial of it a great deal more appertaineth than their conceipt doth reach to" (pref., 3.3). They do not understand how complex politics is either:

> He that goeth about to persuade a multitude, that they are not so well governed as they ought to be, shall never want attentive and favourable hearers; because they know the manifold defects whereunto every kind of regiment is subject, but the secret lets and difficulties, which in public proceedings are innumerable and inevitable, they have not ordinarily the judgement to consider.[16]

A demagogue willing to play up claims of the misbehavior of leaders of other factions or enemies in the church, "the faults especially of higher callings," can always win respect among the people as a leader of opinion (pref., 3.6). Simpy propose your "own form of Church government, as the only sovereign remedy of all evils" (pref., 3.8), Hooker quips, and the people will follow admiringly.

Constitutional monarchy. Hooker was well aware of the link between the Lutheran practice of treating the magistrate as a replacement for the pope as civil "head" of the church and what had now happened in Eng-

---

[16]Ibid., 1, 1.1.

land under Elizabeth. He makes the link ("that the *Civil Magistrate* being termed *Head* by reason of that authority in Ecclesiastical affairs").[17] He discusses the question from many angles.[18] In book 8 he sets about justifying the royal supremacy as a mode of civil magistracy. This takes him to the question where to draw the line between secular and spiritual authority of the monarch.[19] Hooker supports the divine right of kings and the idea that kings have dominion by that right. He discusses what is meant by *head* when a monarch is head of the church?[20] A king as head of the church and the way Christ is head of the church "differeth in order, measure and kind."[21] For one thing the king is head only "within his own dominions."[22] That is a key principle of civil magistracy.

At the same time, Hooker believed that authority to rule, though from God, comes through the consent of the people.[23] Whether this is the case or whether the only legitimate exercise of secular power came directly from God through hereditary rights had been a repeating topic of debate in the later Middle Ages. Hooker held that the natural tendency of human beings to want to get to know others and to form united groups or bodies was fundamentally important. He had new evidence on this point. The recent discoveries of the New World were, he suggests, prompted by this human desire to get to know and unite with others. He gives the biblical example of the desire of the Queen of Sheba to visit Solomon.[24]

The unity of human groups operates best, he thinks, through their lawfully appointed representatives. "As in parliaments, councils, and the like assemblies, although we be not personally ourselves present, notwithstanding our assent is by reason of others agents there in our behalf."[25] These ideas could seem natural only to a writer who had been born in late Tudor times, when the medieval monarch Henry VII had

---

[17]Ibid., 8.4.6.
[18]Ibid., 8.2.1.
[19]Ibid., 8.1.2.
[20]Ibid., 8.4.
[21]Ibid., 8.4.5.
[22]Ibid., 8.4.7.
[23]Ibid., 1.10.8.
[24]Ibid., 1.10.12.
[25]Ibid., 1.10.8.

essentially been had mutated through the tyrannies of Henry VIII and the controlling committee of Edward VI's time, to the precarious constitutional monarchy of Elizabeth I. Styles of government had moved on throughout northern Europe as feudalism was modernized into new polities and new theories of government.

22

BIBLE QUESTIONS CONTINUE

WRESTLING WITH THE HUMANITY
OF SCRIPTURE

Historicity and inspiration. The rediscovery of the Bible in its original languages had been the great transforming moment of Reformation Bible study. The task of establishing which is the most reliable text took on new dimensions at the Reformation, when scholars began trying to recover the best versions of the original texts by going back to the original languages (*ad fontes*; see pp. 231-48). But that had raised many new difficulties that were not easily resolved.

The discovery that it was not straightforwardly possible to resolve all Bible problems by looking backward to the sources had many ramifications once it was realized not only that the text had apparently taken subtly different forms over the centuries but also that the role of human authors had not necessarily been merely to sit with pen in hand and the Holy Spirit whispering in their ears, as the Evangelists were traditionally portrayed in pictures. Reformers often found they could not sustain the classical and medieval assumption that the oldest is always best, or that in biblical interpretation there could be nothing new that was good. This was true of practice as well as doctrine. There were no alms houses, parishes or tithes in the early church, "which the Apostles' times could not have," pointed out Richard Hooker—but we have them now and they are a good thing.[1]

---

[1]Hooker, *Laws*, pref., 4.4.

The question, as revived in the seventeenth century, grew more subtle. Exactly how did God employ the human authors of his Scriptures? Daniel Whitby (1638-1726) provided his *A Paraphrase and Commentary on the New Testament* with a general preface in which he discusses "the divine authority of the Scriptures of the New Testament"; his argument being that if this can be established it must follow that "the Doctrines and Instructions delivered in them, are to be owned as the Rules and Doctrines of our Lord, and so are necessary to be believed and practiced by all that bear the name of Christians." He distinguishes between prophets, who experienced "an immediate Suggestion and Representation in their Fancy and Imaginations of the things which they delivered as from the Mouth, and in the Name, of God," and the Holy Writers who were inspired by the Holy Spirit in such a way as to leave them "to the use of their own Words, and to the exercise of their Reasons." "I can by no means grant any slips of Memory in the Compilers of these Sacred Books of the New Testament," he adds. He ends confidently with the idea that if the earliest Christians, who had met the apostles and seen original copies of the Scriptures, were confident that they had divine authority that is in itself a testimony.[2]

The Bible itself indicates that there were several different ways in which God worked with human authors in its composition. Luther was willing to admit the difficulty. In his *Table Talk* he comments on the well-known puzzle of the way in which the early events of the creation of the world and what followed could have been known to Moses:

> Many things were written and described where Moses was born. Doubtless, Adam briefly noted the history of the creation, of his fall, of the promised seed, etc. The other patriarchs afterwards, no doubt, each set down what was done in his time, especially Noah. Afterwards Moses, as I conceive, took and brought all into a right method and order, diminishing therefrom, and adding thereunto, such things as God commanded: as, especially, touching the seed that should crush the serpent's head, the history of the creation, etc.; all which, doubtless, he had out of the sermons of the patriarchs, that always one inherited from another.[3]

---

[2]Daniel Whitby, *A Paraphrase and Commentary on the New Testament* (London, 1703), 2:i-xv.
[3]Luther, *Table Talk* 19.

This humanizing of the process of writing Scripture made Reformers think afresh about the role of the human authors who had brought the Bible into being, the realities of transmission, even the possibility that the Bible had been an evolving text in human hands. In another passage of Luther's *Table Talk*, it is recorded that "Forsheim said that the first of the five books of Moses was not written by Moses himself," and that "Dr. Luther replied: What matters it, even though Moses did not write it? It is, nevertheless, Moses's book, wherein is exactly related the creation of the world."[4] That sort of position was becoming difficult to sustain without provisos and a closer look at the roles of Moses and other human authors of the Scriptures.

We have noticed already that the Bible is not a textbook of systematic theology. It does not set out its teaching in the order of a school syllabus. It was remarked in the patristic period that it was, on the face of it, not always consistent. It was undeniable that the Bible sometimes seemed to contradict itself. Augustine had attempted a harmony of the Gospels, and Calvin made an attempt to add to Augustine's attempt to harmonize the Gospels. In the dedicatory letter to his *Harmony of the Gospels*, Calvin described it as: "a Harmony arranged out of Three Evangelists, and has been prepared by me with the greatest fidelity and diligence. What toil I have bestowed on it would serve no purpose to detail; and how far I have succeeded must be left to others to decide."[5]

Others have found this difficult too, he explains. "Faithful and learned commentators spend a very great portion of their labor on reconciling the narratives of the three Evangelists." And "persons of ordinary abilities find the comparison to be no easy matter." Martin Bucer has provided Calvin with a model, and one who has made use of the learning of those of earlier ages "who had travelled this road before him." Calvin has borrowed from him judiciously, but not slavishly: "Where I use the liberty of differing from him, (which I have freely done, whenever it was necessary,) Bucer himself, if he were still an inhabitant of the earth, would not be displeased."

---

[4]Luther, *Table Talk* 36.
[5]John Calvin, "Harmony of the Evangelists," *Commentary on Matthew, Mark, Luke*, vol. 1, www .ccel.org/ccel/calvin/calcom31.vii.html.

Yet the magisterial Reformers shared a traditional commitment to the normative authority of the canonical Scriptures and the Creed that narrates its trinitarian scope (see pp. 37-42, 48-51), highlighting the unity in the Bible's diversity. Calvin argued that the purpose of John's writing is one reason why his Gospel "differs widely from the other three Evangelists: for he is almost wholly occupied in explaining the power of Christ, and the advantages which we derive from him; while they insist more fully on one point, that our Christ is that Son of God who had been promised to be the Redeemer of the world." Mark, likewise,

> does not everywhere adhere to the order which Matthew observed, and from the very commencement handles the subjects in a different manner. Some things, too, are related by him which the other had omitted, and his narrative of the same event is sometimes more detailed. It is more probable, in my opinion—and the nature of the case warrants the conjecture— that he had not seen Matthew's book when he wrote his own; so far is he from having expressly intended to make an abridgment.

This is an approach that respects the possibility that the Four Evangelists made a contribution to the work that went beyond simply holding the pen for God. The Evangelists "intended to give an honest narrative of what they knew to be certain and undoubted, [while] each followed that method which he reckoned best." On the other hand they did not make these choices without divine direction:

> Now as this did not happen by chance, but by the direction of Divine Providence, so under this diversity in the manner of writing the Holy Spirit suggested to them an astonishing harmony, which would almost be sufficient of itself to secure credit to them, if there were not other and stronger evidences to support their authority.

Appeals to authoritative tradition. "Does the Bible contain everything necessary to salvation?" is the ancestor of the question posed by Luther and other sixteenth-century Reformers who wanted to insist that "only Scripture" was authoritative and on Scripture alone could the Christian rely for salvation. It did not lose its topicality after the Reformation. The shift from "no salvation outside the Church" to "no salvation without Scripture" is therefore of central importance to the historical progress of the question of the authority of the Bible. Luther had an eye on both when he remarked that "It is not necessary for salvation to believe that the Roman Church is superior to all others. . . . I know that Gregory Nazianzus, Basil of Caesarea, Epiphanius, Cyprian, and numerous other Greek bishops are among the redeemed, even though they did not believe this article."[6]

Zwingli says, "Where I have not now correctly understood the Scriptures I shall allow myself to be taught better, but only from the Scriptures."[7] And as noted earlier, Zwingli's *67 Conclusions* 5 condemns "All who consider other teachings equal to or higher than the Gospel. . . . [They] do not know what the Gospel is."[8] For Roman Catholics all this made it necessary to rethink what was "other than Scripture" or "additional" to it and to define its authority or its contribution to Scripture's authoritativeness.

The contrary conservative position is nowhere better exemplified than in the attitude of the Council of Trent, which in its fourth session produced a decree concerning the canonical Scriptures. This links together as authoritative "traditions" several streams of revelation—"as well those appertaining to faith as to morals"—which were either dictated by Christ himself or by the Holy Spirit to the prophets and apostles, or were orally "preserved in the Catholic Church by a continuous succession." The council fathers defended the Vulgate "which, by the lengthened use of so many ages, has been approved of in the Church." It is to be "held as authentic" in "public lectures, disputations, sermons and expositions."[9]

Does Scripture contain all that is necessary to salvation? No, said Portuguese polemicist Diego de Paiva de Andrada (1528-1575) at the Council of Trent. It needs interpretation, and officially approved interpretation at that. He maintained that Christ's intention was solely to provide a kind of aide-mémoire, a brief summary of key points, and that

---

[6]Luther, *Disputatio I, Eccii et M. Lutheri Lipsiae Habita*, 1519, WA 2, p. 279ff. Translated in *The Reformation in Its Own Words*, ed. Hans J. Hillebrand (London: SCM Press, 1964), p. 67.
[7]Zwingli, *Zwinglis Sämtliche Werke*, 1:458-61. Translated in *The Reformation in Its Own Words*, ed. Hans J. Hillebrand (London: SCM Press, 1964), p. 132.
[8]Ibid., p. 133.
[9]*Canons and Decrees of the Council of Trent*, trans. J. Waterworth (London: Burns & Oates, 1888), pp. 17-18.

he meant the whole story to be written on the church's innermost heart and not the pages of a book. His evidence is that Christ's teaching was oral and that (as he alleges) there was a wish on God's part to distinguish it clearly from the Old Testament era, when things had been written on tablets of stone. Andrada claims, says Chemnitz, that the settled view of the Catholic Church is the ultimate authority because there are preserved the echoes of many things the apostles said that were not written down in the canon of Scripture. This makes the authority of the Church, its customs and traditions, equal with that of the text of the Bible and even superior, because it is fuller and more detailed.[10]

If the Bible needs authoritative professional commentary to be fully understood, the boundary between Scripture and not-Scripture, divine authorship and human authorship, becomes hard to fix. Among the problems for the academic commentator was what weight to attach to an official Church position as against the authority of earlier commentary. The issue as it restated itself by the end of the sixteenth century was whether and how the Catholic Church's authority stands over against that of Scripture. For Luther the Church was, for these purposes, the papacy. He insists that the Roman pontiffs have been mere human beings, and fallible at that, judges in their own cause, some of them ignorant time servers. It seems to Luther that it follows that their decrees, condemnations and approvals are without authority and "Do not prove anything."[11]

TEXTUAL DIFFICULTIES AND TRANSLATION ISSUES

Textual difficulties. An increasing awareness of variant readings and ambiguities in the biblical manuscripts, though these rarely impinged upon matters of faith and practice, contributed to the difficulty the Reformers and their heirs faced in asserting the divine authority and reliability of Scripture. For example, sixteenth-century Jewish scholar Elia Levita (1469-1549) had controversially asserted that the vowel points and accents in the Hebrew text of the Old Testament were not original. This

---

[10]Martin Chemnitz, *Examination of the Council of Trent*, trans. Fred Kramer (St. Louis: Concordia Press, 1971), pp. 44-45. This work was written primarily against Andrada.

[11]Melanchthon, *De corrigendis*, p. 15, as translated in *The Reformation in Its Own Words*, p. 60.

controversy was revived in 1624 with the publication of a work in support of Levita by a Huguenot scholar Louis Cappel (1585-1658). Cappel did not stop there; by the middle of the century he was raising questions about the respective authority of the Hebrew and the Septuagint versions of the Old Testament (regarding the former as inferior), and being confrontational on the subject of variant readings.[12] This was, in its way, independent scholarship that did not allow itself to be impeded by the author's personal confessional position, and so successful was Cappel in this respect that even the Roman Catholic authorities became eager to publish his work in order to undermine the inherent authority and clarity Protestants claimed for the Bible. Other, often more radical, critics piled in behind.[13]

The polyglot projects, which had begun in the sixteenth century, also helped to throw wide open the question of which text of the Bible was authoritative, that is, which actual words could be relied on as constituting the Word of God. The proliferating vernacular versions that were being made available throughout Europe compounded the problem. Was the German Bible's choice of words to be treated safely as the Words of God? Which of the English translations—Coverdale, Tyndale, King James Version—had got it right and could claim divine approval?

The Complutensian Polyglot edition of the New Testament, begun in 1502, was completed in 1514, but not licensed for distribution until 1520, by which time Erasmus's Greek New Testament of 1516 had already been available for some time. But the Complutensian version reflected other ideals than Erasmus's notions of the authoritativeness attaching to the Greek text. The archbishop gave his support to the project of publishing a polyglot Bible partly because he was concerned that systematic theology had moved too far from the old methodology of exegesis of Scripture with the aid of patristic commentary and too far in the direction of analysis by means of Aristotelian logic. He also believed that the best method of resolving the numerous problems

---

[12]R. A. Muller, "The Debate Over the Vowel Points and the Crisis in Orthodox Hermeneutics," *Medieval and Renaissance Studies* 10 (1980): 53-72.
[13]Thomas Hobbes's *Leviathan* (1650) includes an attack on the belief that Moses was the author of the Pentateuch.

about what the Latin text ought to say was to provide Greek and Hebrew for comparison.

In the mid-seventeenth century, Brian Walton (1600-1661) and his coworkers believed the texts they were laying before the public were more authentic than those made available in earlier polyglots such as that of Antwerp (1569-1572) and Paris (1628-1645). Walton's polyglot, which collated text and variants from nine ancient languages and ran to six large folio volumes (the last of which were published in 1657), received hostile reviews from both sides. It was put on the Roman *Index Librorum Prohibitorum*; it was attacked by John Owen in *Of the Divine Original of Scripture* (1659) for tending to undermine faith in the integrity of the biblical text.

Martin Chemnitz reflected on the way mistakes could get into the text in his *Examination of the Council of Trent.* The devil has been cunning over the centuries in adulterating the purity of the Word of God; God himself, on the other hand, has been careful to restore that purity, for he knows well how easily oral traditions become distorted. For that reason, he made provision for a special period of revelation in which an utterly trustworthy written text was created, and from that time onward oral tradition takes second place and must be checked against this authoritative version. It is no longer appropriate to seek new and special revelations every time a point becomes the subject of dispute.

Chemnitz's approach to all this is historical in conception. The way to clear up the present controversy, he suggests, is to trace the way in which the Bible came into existence. His narrative is geared to his argument. God instituted the written text as a method of preserving the purity of doctrine and practice. By his own act and his own example he initiated and dedicated and consecrated this written record by inscribing the words of the Ten Commandments on the tablets of stone which were given to Moses. This historical approach does not extend to the history of the noninspired Apocrypha.

Translation issues. Textual issues now had to be considered in the context of the existence and availability of many versions in many languages, some original, some translations. Was the Greek, the Hebrew, the Latin or some vernacular translation to be regarded as the authentic Scripture? And if the Bible's authenticity did not lie in the actual words, where did it lie? Because Jerome's text was regularly analyzed for centuries as though it were the very Word as spoken by God, many of the problems of interpretation that had arisen turned on his particular choice of words. For example, Jerome usually translated the Greek command *metanoiete* into Latin as *paenitentiam agite*, "Do penance," as in Matthew 4:17, "Do penance! For the kingdom of heaven is at hand." Protestants pointed out that the Greek denotes a deep change of mind and heart—"Repent!"—rather than a requirement to perform specific penitential acts. While repentance clearly does not exclude external actions, such texts certainly could no longer be taken so readily to undergird the elaborate medieval penitential system.

William Tyndale's preface to the New Testament (1526) reflects this realization of the complexity of the task of arriving at a true text of Scripture from the sources. "I have looked over again . . . with all diligence, and compared it unto the Greek, and have weeded out of it many faults. . . . If ought seem changed, or not altogether agreeing with the Greek, let the finder of the fault consider the Hebrew phrase or manner of speech left in the Greek words." He was distressed to learn that George Joye was similarly engaged in making corrections to his work (see pp. 301-2). Tyndale says that he restrained himself from entering into a dispute with him as to which should do it or whether they might not collaborate, until someone brought him a copy of Joye's work,

> and showed me so many places, in such wise altered that I was astonied and wondered not a little what fury had driven him to make such a change, and call it a diligent correction. . . .
>
> If that change . . . be a diligent correction, then must my translation be faulty in those places, and St. Jerome's. . . .
>
> The straunge maner of phrase and often tymes the troublous spekynge of dyvers croked figures and tropes be of so great diffyculte that often tymes we our selfe also muste labour right sore before we can perceive them.

Valla remarked that it was a "great mystery" how Latin had been religiously preserved as a holy language for so many centuries among strangers and barbarians and enemies of the Romans.[14] It remained the common language of scholarship in the West throughout the Reformation period and beyond. Nevertheless, the enlargement of academic language study to include Greek and Hebrew had shaken up presuppositions radically and in various ways, and encouraged the combination of traditional academic approaches with something quite new. This newness included the emergence of the notion of Oriental languages and the value of their wider study.

To Augustine nearly a millennium and a half earlier, Greek was not an Oriental or even an Eastern language, but merely the other main language of educated people in the Roman Empire, and he perhaps barely thought of Hebrew as remote from his own world of Romano-Christian thought. Quite different was the perception of William of Auvergne (c. 1180-1249) in the thirteenth century, to whom Islam was a challenge without antique precedent, and distinctively Eastern.[15] Seventeenth-century critics display still more new dimensions of cultural awareness, because of the emerging early modern consciousness that Eastern or Oriental languages came from a cultural context different in many ways from that of the West. The study of Hebrew ultimately led to an interest in Arabic. New Oriental language professorships in the universities reflected a trend, a developing interest in a wider world and the dawning realization that there were quite other cultures, especially in Asia.

In Oxford there was a contention that Hebrew studies required a knowledge of Arabic, and many competent in one also studied the other.[16] So by the seventeenth century the netful of ancient languages considered requisite for the study of the Bible included Chaldaic, Syriac and Arabic. This meant that provision needed to be made in universities

---

[14]*Magnum igitur Latini sermonis sacramentum est . . . quod apud peregrinos, apud barbaros, apud hostes, sancte ac religiose per tot saecula custoditur.* Lorenzo Valla, *De Linguae Latinae Elegantia* I, ed. Santiago López Moreda (Càceres: Universidad de Extremadura, 1999), 1:58.

[15]William of Auvergne, *De Legibus* I, in *Opera Omnia* (1674; reprint, Frankfurt-am-Main: Minerva, 1963), p. 22. Chapter 18 contains a hostile life of Muhammad with the usual accusations. Chapter 19 criticizes Muhammad's idea of paradise with its fleshly pleasures. Chapter 20 compares the Judaic law (*lex fortunae*) with the Muslim (*lex naturae*) and the Christian (*lex gratiae*).

[16]*History of the University of Oxford,* ed. L. S. Sutherland and L. G. Mitchell (Oxford: Oxford University Press, 1986), 5:538.

to study Oriental languages as a group. Two professorships at Oxford were established, with the requirement that lectures be given on Arabic. The chair established by Archbishop of Canterbury William Laud (1573-1645) in 1640 required the professor to lecture for an hour a week on Wednesdays in the university vacations, so as to explain the similarities of Arabic, Syriac and Hebrew.

The emphasis on assistance with the study of Hebrew for the purposes of Bible study began to be complemented during the later seventeenth century by the recognition that the study of Arabic could give access to an enormous body of literature and learning in the field of philosophy. It was recognized that the Arabs had been invaluable custodians of the learning of ancient Greece, in centuries when the Greek language had fallen out of use in the West.

Laud and others started to collect many manuscripts. Edward Pocock (1604-1691) was chaplain at the Levant Company from 1630. He seized his chance to study Hebrew, Syriac and Ethiopic as he traveled in connection with his pastoral duties, and to collect manuscripts, forming lasting friendships in the Middle East. From October 1631, Laud arranged that all ships of the Levant Company entering English ports must bring at least one manuscript with them. Laud's plan was to build up the collection in the Bodleian Library and to establish a professorship of Arabic in Oxford, with Pococke his choice for its first holder.

John Milton likewise stressed the value of formal academic study of languages:

> Though a linguist should pride himselfe to have all the tongues that Babel cleft the world into, yet, if he have not studied the solid things in them as well as the words and lexicons, he were nothing so much to be esteem'd a learned man, as any yeoman or tradesman competently wise in his mother dialect only.[17]

But this study did not necessarily make comprehension or appreciation any easier. The coupling of Hebrew and Arabic as Oriental, together with a related interest in other Eastern languages, led to an awakening of

---

[17]John Milton, *Of Education, Complete Prose Works*, ed. D. Bush et al. (New Haven, Conn.: Yale University Press, 1959), 2:369-70.

awareness that there were features of such languages, and assumptions underlying their use, which were identifiably non-Western.[18]

Robert Boyle (1627-1691) even admitted that what seemed to Western sensibilities a lack of eloquence, "their Dark and Involv'd Sentences, their Figurative and Parabolical Discourses; their Abrupt and Maimed way of expressing themselves. . . often leaves us at a losse for the Method and Coherency of what they write."[19] Discussing the "Style of the Scriptures," Boyle was quite sensitive to such differences among languages:

> There are in Hebrew, as in other Languages, certain appropriated Graces and a peculiar Emphasis belonging to some expressions, which must necessarily be impaired by any/Translation, and are but too often quite lost in those that adhere too scrupulously to the words of the Original. And as in a lovely face, though a Painter may well enough express the cheeks and the nose and the lipps. Yet there is often something of splendor and vivacity in the Eyes which no Pencil can reach to equal.

He speaks of the "helps to understand the sense of many passages that may be afforded by skill in the original languages."[20]

Awareness of such things is especially important in the translation of the Bible, Boyle believed. "It is more difficult to translate the *Hebrew* of the Old Testament, than if that Book were written in *Syriack* or *Arabick*, or some such other Eastern Language." This is not because "the Holy Tongue is much more difficult to be learned than others" but because there is no surviving literature of texts with which it may be compared. It is the unique surviving work in ancient Hebrew. So if it uses a word only once, it is hard to be sure we have correctly understood that word.[21]

Richard Hooker thought it best to approach translation issues that affected the church's preaching and teaching with reverence and flexibility: "The fittest for publique audience are such as [follow] a middell course between the rigor of literall translators and the libertie of para-

---

[18]Mordechai Feingold, "Oriental Studies," in *The History of the University of Oxford*, ed. Nicolas Tyacke (Oxford: Oxford University Press, 1997), pp. 449-503.

[19]Boyle, *Style of the Scriptures*, in *Works*, ed. Michael Hunter and Edward B. Davis (London: Pickering & Chatto, 1990), p. 453.

[20]Ibid., p. 404.

[21]Ibid., p. 396.

phrastes," so as to "with greatest shortnes and plainenes delibver the meaning of the holie Ghost." And "everie little difference should not seme an intolerable blemish necessarily to be spoonged out."[22]

John Dryden (1631-1700) tried to tease apart the various difficulties involved in translation,[23] but with limited success:

All Translation I suppose may be reduced to . . . Metaphrase, or tourning an Authour word by word, . . . Paraphrase, or Translation with Latitude, where the Authour is kept in view by the Translator so as not to be lost, but his words are not so strictly followed as his sense . . . [and] Imitation, where the Translator (if now he has not lost that Name) assumes the liberty not only to vary from the words and sense, but to forsake them both as he sees occasion.[24]

The translator has his sympathy and his respect: "The Verbal Copyer is incumber'd with so many difficulties at once. . . . He is to consider at the same time the thought of his Authour, and his words, and to find out the Counterpart to each in another Language."[25] He notes the different demands different writers create, for example Pindar, "so wild and ungovernable" that he cannot be translated literally. "His Genius is too strong to bear a Chain, and Sampson like he shakes it off."[26]

THE STYLE AND OBSCURITY OF SCRIPTURE

Appeals to exegesis in light of tradition. There was by the sixteenth century a long tradition of commentary on the Bible, consolidated in the twelfth century into the *Glossa Ordinaria*, or standard gloss, to which there had been further additions in the late medieval centuries. A printed Bible in this tradition would show these glosses in concentric rectangles around a small portion of Scripture positioned in the center

---

[22]Hooker, *Laws*, 5.19.2.
[23]Daniel Hopkins, "Dryden and His Contemporaries," in *The Oxford History of Literary Translation in English (1660-1790)*, ed. Stuart Gillespie and David Hopkins (Oxford: Oxford University Press, 2005), 3:55-67. See too Donald Mackenzie, "Biblical Interpretation and Paraphrase," in *The Oxford History of Literary Translation in English (1660-1790)*, ed. Stuart Gillespie and David Hopkins (Oxford: Oxford University Press, 2005), 3:453-69.
[24]John Dryden, *Preface to Ovid's Epistles (1680), The Works of John Dryden* (Berkeley: University of California Press, 1956), 1:114.
[25]Ibid., p. 115.
[26]Ibid., p. 117.

of the page. Their content consisted mainly of extracts from patristic and medieval authors.

The study of the Bible, whether in homily or in reading and teaching, was bound to involve commentary. One important question for the Reformers was whether it was still acceptable to use the huge body of existing gloss and commentary. The glosses and commentaries of the existing academic and ecclesiastical tradition are dangerous and likely to mislead in their deceitful gloss, Tyndale seems to warn (*Preface to the New Testament*):

> I thought it my duty (most dear reader) to warn thee before, and to show thee the right way in, and to give thee the true key to open [the Scripture] withal, and to arm thee against false prophets and malicious hypocrites, whose perpetual study is to leaven the Scripture with glosses.

The typical Protestant ways of forming the people into good readers of Scripture were robust preaching and catechetical instruction (and often, as in the Church of England, a Bible-saturated liturgy; see pp. 334-35, 344-47). Sermons on portions of Scripture were automatically exegetical, even while the formal medieval "art of preaching" maintained a lingering influence on the mainstream Latin scholarly tradition. Johannes Reuchlin (see pp. 242, 252) published an *Art of Preaching* in 1503. He found himself drawn into a wider dispute between the humanists and the scholars who were defending a traditional scholasticism and disputed the right of these newcomer amateurs to dabble in theology at all.[27] Willibald Pirckheimer (1470-1530), a fellow humanist, defended Reuchlin in 1517:

> A theologian ... in addition to grammar ... must know Latin, Greek and Hebrew ... [and] dialectic. Furthermore, if a theologian knows nothing about rhetoric, I do not see how he can communicate the word of the Truth to the Christian people, if at any rate he intends to teach in a way that is intelligible to the people and if he wants to engage them emotionally, so that his message sticks in people's minds like the tip of an arrow.[28]

Reuchlin's manual on preaching was therefore one of the first to

---

[27]Erika Rummel, *The Case Against Johann Reuchlin* (Toronto: University of Toronto Press, 2002).
[28]Ibid., pp. 136-40.

break with the medieval model and advocate an approach of a humanist sort, at a date before the truly controversial nature of his opinions had become apparent and he had become notorious. Some of his supporters moved on to support Luther—as discussed earlier, Reuchlin's grand-nephew Melanchthon was to become one of Luther's greatest friends and supporters.

Reformers might prefer to study the text directly in the original lan-guages and in translations, but they also regularly employed the tradi-tional forms of textual analysis. The corpus of medieval work in the universities was enormous, subtle, refined, sophisticated and hard to abandon without something adequate to replace it. For academics studying the Bible in the light of this material, the Bible was more likely to appear a mere outline, embodying a core of essential material, but requiring elaboration for its meanings to be fully understood.

The Reformers and the fathers. Protestants had divergent views on the fathers. The Anabaptist Thomas Münzer portrayed the scholars of an earlier age as thieves, stealing words from the Bible as Jeremiah describes (Jer 23:30) in a way which resembles taking the bread from one's neigh-bor's mouth. His own researches suggested to him that after the death of the first generation of followers of the apostles, the pure and virgin church became a harlot. Scholars always want to sit on top, and they have led the church and the Scriptures into prostitution.

The magisterial Reformers' views on the fathers were mixed. On the one hand, they were better than the scholastic authors of the Middle Ages. On the other hand, they were not inspired in the same way as the human authors of Scripture. Zwingli was described by Heinrich Bull-inger as very widely read. Luther's opinion, as recorded in his *Table Talk*, was that

> The student of theology has now far greater advantages than students ever before had; first, he has the Bible, which I have translated from Hebrew into German, so clearly and distinctly, that any one may readily compre-hend it; next, he has Melancthon's *Common-place* Book (*Loci Communes*), which he should read over and over again, until he has it by heart. Once master of these two volumes, he may be regarded as a theologian whom neither devil nor heretic can overcome; for he has all divinity at his fingers'

ends, and may read, understandingly, whatsoever else he pleases. Afterwards, he may study Melancthon's *Commentary on Romans*, and mine on Deuteronomy and on the Galatians, and practice eloquence.[29]

On the question of normative authority Luther was adamant. "No faithful Christian can be forced beyond the Sacred Scripture, which is alone the divine law, unless new and approved revelation is added," he says. Yet he immediately linked his assertion with fifteenth-century authority: "This principle was lately asserted by Gerson in many places."[30] Despite differences, among Lutherans and Reformed there was a shared commitment to canonical authority, the Creed and the best of the patristic exegetical tradition (however "best" was to be defined).

Seventeenth-century divines such as the Irishman James Ussher (1581-1656) took a serious interest in the editing of patristic texts, especially the Greek. Ussher was ordained to the ministry and taught as professor of sacred theology at Trinity from 1607 to 1621, when he became a bishop. He understood the importance of creating a good library for the new university at Trinity College, Dublin, and he did more than anyone else to build up what would now be regarded as a research library, an innovative notion at a time when universities saw themselves primarily as teaching institutions. He also made regular journeys to England (Oxford, Cambridge and London) every few years in order to buy books. This led him into research of his own.[31]

INCREASINGLY RADICAL DIVERGENCES OF OPINION AND PRACTICE

Kinds of radical divergence. The desirability of encouraging believers to read the Bible for themselves still had to be balanced against the drawback that they might then form and try to propagate heretical opinions, which seemed alarmingly on the rise in the seventeenth century. The new reality in the early modern era was not an appeal to proper interpretive approach or practice, but a gradual abstraction of these from a

---

[29]Luther, *Table Talk* 45.
[30]Luther, *Disputatio I*, p. 67.
[31]On Ussher see Alan Ford, *James Ussher: Theology History and Politics in Early-Modern Ireland and England* (Oxford: Oxford University Press, 2007).

commitment to the authority of the Bible and the creedal rule of faith. The radical Jewish philosopher Benedict de Spinoza (1632-1677), for example, appeals to the right of private interpretation in a very different way than someone like Luther:

> I would not charge the sectaries with impiety for adapting the sayings of Scripture to their own opinions, for as they were originally adapted to the understanding of ordinary people, so it is permissible now for each individual to adapt them to his own opinions, if he finds by so doing that, in matters requiring justice and charity, he can obey God with a greater unity of mind and heart.

Spinoza's interpretive keynote here is obedience. "That men are saved only by obedience" is "the basic doctrine of theology."[32] So the reader may be highly selective in discerning what is or is not important in Scripture. "The only knowledge commended in Scripture is that which everybody needs in order to be able to obey God in the way required by that precept [of love of one's neighbor]." "It is evident, then, that so far as Scripture is concerned, we are under obligation to believe only what is indispensable for carrying out that command."[33]

That the Bible had a complex history was not widely in dispute by the end of the sixteenth century. It was increasingly difficult to not give equal weight to the fact that the Bible was a book with a real human history as well as a product of divine inspiration. A new question in the seventeenth century was how far it could be studied in the same way as any other book which had been written in a particular time or context. Conyers Middleton's (1683-1750) *A Letter to Dr. Waterland Containing Some Remarks on His Vindication of Scripture: In Answer to a Book, Intituled, Christianity as Old as the Creation . . .* (London, 1731) is in part a debate about the difficulty of making Scripture accord at some points with the conclusions of contemporary historical or scientific research. The identity and roles of the human authors of particular books were also reexamined in the light of concerns about things which were diffi-

---

[32] Benedict Spinoza, *Tractatus Theologico-Politicus*, 15.26, in *Spinoza on Freedom of Thought: Selections from Tractatus Theologico-Politicus and Tractatus Politicus*, ed. and trans. T. E. Jessop (Montreal: Mario Casalini, 1962), p. 35.

[33] Ibid., 14.13, p. 27.

cult to explain and the possibility that when there were perceived short-comings they could be imputed to the human authors and not the divine. The underlying question was whether these kinds of studies could be senior to the evidence of Scripture itself, and they are questions arising with a new force as scholarly studies took themselves more seriously and deemed themselves to have greater rigor.[34]

This uncomfortable century in which independent personal Bible-reading first became widespread was also the century in which higher education moved from the clerical classes to become the province of gentlemen, laymen who had sufficient family wealth to be able to afford a period at university studying for a degree. It should be emphasized that this opportunity was also available to the poor but ambitious through a system of bursaries and sizarships (which allowed a student to pay his way as a servant to a richer student).

For the first time, theological expertise came within the perceived reach of the ordinary graduate and was no longer to be regarded as a study so advanced that only a few rare individuals proceeded as far as a doctorate in the subject in middle age, after many years of study, as had been the case in the medieval universities. The resulting university-educated lay theologian who felt quite capable of putting himself on a level with the professionals when it came to Bible study was a new phenomenon of the seventeenth century.

Not only was it possible for such scholars to sit more loosely to the received tradition of Christian belief and practice, but to inherited patristic interpretations as well. Milton became convinced his own *De Doctrina Christiana* was needed when his reading showed him not only that the authorities were often wrong but also that the citadel of Protestant doctrine had places where the walls might be breached. He describes how he began as a young man to read the Bible carefully with reference to the theologians, before coming to his present position.[35]

---

[34]See for example the concerns expressed in Richard Baxter, *The Arrogancy of Reason. 'gainst Divine Revelations* (London, 1655).

[35]*Coepi igitur Adolescens . . . cum ad libros utriusque Testamenti lingua sua perlegendos assiduous incumbere, tum Theologorum Systemata aliquot breviora sedulo percurrere: ad eorum deinde exemplum, locos communes digerere, ad quos omnia quae ex scriptures haurienda occurrissent, expromenda cum opus esset, referrem.* John Milton, *The Works of John Milton;* and *Complete Prose Works of John Milton,* ed. and

Others were much more dismissive. Jean Barbeyrac's (1674-1744) account of the history of morality pays particular and disparaging attention to the views of the fathers.[36] The preface to the 1722 English translation suggests that "the Pains are not worth taking" when it comes to reading patristic literature: "Nor was there ever anything more insolent and dishonest than to refer us for the Knowledge of the Scriptures to the Fathers." Barbeyrac went on to claim the fathers "perpetually confound the Duties of a Man, and the particular duties of a Christian" and lists their worst errors: Athenagoras praises virginity and Cyprian is against marriage; Clement of Alexandria offers "a confused Heap of Precepts without Order, without Connexion." Tertullian misled his hearers into "extravagant Austerities"; Origen was too allegorical and took literally the instruction to make selves eunuchs for the kingdom of heaven's sake. And Gregory the Great indisputably wrote on morals but was tedious and prolix.[37]

The seventeenth-century graduate, while still orienting himself somewhat with reference to the traditional framework of problems and explanations, often felt free to be more radical and to identify wholly new approaches to the text. This was at least partly on the supposition that the Bible might be susceptible to the same critiques as any other book, and is best encountered outside the traditional parameters of Creed and tradition.

Appeals to tradition for interpretive restriction. Tyndale warned that "if it were lawful . . . to every man to play boo peep with the translations that are before him, and to put out the words of the text at his pleasure, and to put in everywhere his meaning or what he thought the meaning were; that were the next way to stablish all heresies and to destroy the ground wherewith we should improve them."[38] This was one reason Thomas More was suspicious of translation, not only because it could so easily result in the choice of the wrong word and mislead the unwary

---

trans. Maurice Kelley and John Carey (New Haven, Conn.: Yale University Press, 1973), 6 (Columbia edition 14:4-5).

[36]Jean Barbeyrac, *The Spirit of the Ecclesiasticks of all Sects and Ages as to the Doctrines of Morality* (London: J. Peele, 1722).

[37]Ibid., pp. 14, 17, 19, 35.

[38]William Tyndale, *Preface to the New Testament* (1526).

with insufficient education, but because it allowed everyone, educated or not, to take a personal view of the meaning of Scripture.

This was a perennial concern. Under a law of the reign of Henry IV in 1401 ("On the Burning of Heretics"; see pp. 217-18), it was forbidden to make a translation of the Bible into the language of the people or even to own one. The punishment was to be burned at the stake as a heretic. The Act was not repealed until 1559, in the Act of Supremacy of Elizabeth I. Reading the Bible for yourself in your own language (or having it read to you if you were illiterate) was at times automatically taken to be an act of defiance against the church and at the same time a politically dangerous act, constituting a threat to civil order.

The traditional way of ensuring that personal eccentricities of opinion were not actively spread was to require the licensing of preachers. In the Middle Ages only those with a license from the diocesan bishop could preach, and the punishment for disobeying this rule was severe. A canon law applicable in the diocese of Oxford in 1407 says that, if anyone preaches the Word of God without first having been authorized by a diocesan endorsement and without being able to show his bishop's letter with a seal, he shall be excommunicated.[39]

The general thrust of the sixteenth-century Reformation was toward making the Bible accessible to ordinary readers and trusting that a reasonable person would be able to make sense of it (and the *right* sense of it). Tyndale, who was so concerned about eccentric interpretations, commented in his *Preface to the Pentateuch* (1530): "I had perceived by experience how that it was impossible to establish the laypeople in any truth, except the Scripture were plainly laid before their eyes in their mother tongue, that they might see the process, order and meaning of the text."

Yet it was not easy to separate in reality, in the actual events, a number of strands which tended to plait themselves together. Popular preaching and private reading, and the habit of getting together to study Scripture in groups, depended on the availability of Bible texts

---

[39] *"Aliquis . . . non auctorizatus, praedicans Verbum Dei, priusquam fuerit approbatus a diocesano"*: *Convocation of Canterbury, 1472, Records of Convocation* 6, ed. Gerald Bray, Church of England Record Society (Woodbridge, U.K.: Boydell Press, 2005), p. 212.

in the people's own language. These frightened the authorities because they observed a tendency for a particular set of antiestablishment views to be embraced by those who heard such sermons and read the Bible for themselves, especially when they met in their houses or elsewhere for Bible study and shared their ideas.

The Council of Trent sought to ban private reading of the Bible by ordinary individuals, restricting direct access to the text to professionals, academically trained clerics who could read it in Latin with supporting information from approved early Christian and medieval sources. In session 4 it agreed to a decree on the "use of the sacred books," saying that "no one, relying on his own skill" shall presume to interpret Scripture for himself, "wresting the sacred Scriptures to his own senses" or contrary to the sense in which the Catholic Church holds the passage in question. The Council of Trent also censored the indiscriminate printing of copies of the Bible with commentaries, sometimes anonymous and sometimes without the imprint of the publisher being identifiable, and the keeping of such books for sale in bookshops. The most that might be allowed was that the Bible should be made available to ordinary people in select extracts, that is the portions read aloud in church, rather than put into their hands in its entirety.

These misgivings were not restricted to Roman Catholics. "Prophesyings" were a popular exercise in the 1570s and later in England, and equally mistrusted by the authorities. They took the form of the preaching by members of the local clergy of two or more sermons on a chosen theme. A congregation of laypeople might be present for the actual preaching, but afterward all the clergy would retire to discuss the theological issues arising among themselves as professionals, with a senior cleric acting a moderator. Such occasions often had the approval of the local bishop and were seen as a useful opportunity for what would now be described as the continuing professional development of the clergy.[40]

An example of a regular meeting along these lines was that held in

---

[40] *Conferences and Combination Lectures in the Elizabethan Church: Dedham and Bury St. Edmunds, 1582-90*, ed. Patrick Collinson, John Craig and Brett Usher, Church of England Record Society 10 (2003), p. xxix.

Kidderminster on the first Thursday of every month in the 1660s, at Richard Baxter's instigation. A topic was agreed in advance, sometimes a disciplinary matter. The group ate together, and after the meal they held their debate. Baxter published some of these disputations and kept records of others among his papers. He gave a lecture each week in addition, after which some of the circle would retire with him to his home to discuss it. Baxter described these as "comfortable" meetings and he saw them as building up the pastoral community. We see here a sense of equality of contribution, where any moderator or lecturer was not necessarily seen as the leader and everyone felt entitled to express and even publish his thoughts.

Such occasions had a direct precedent in Zurich, where Bullinger used to arrange "combination" lectures, making use of the local library resources to enhance the educational value of this social and participative exercise. At Geneva the English who were living there in exile spoke up, every one, "as God shall move his heart."[41] John Hooper (d. 1555) had seen this done in Switzerland, and he tried out something similar in his diocese of Gloucester in the reign of Edward VI, strictly as a closed session, with the "unlearned" excluded.[42]

The concerned authorities nonetheless made moves to suppress the prophesyings and their like. Queen Elizabeth disapproved of them but Archbishop Grindal wanted them to continue, and he would allow the laity to be present, but he did not wish to see them taking part.[43] There were sound reasons for allowing the laity to remain in the room. Secret meetings, such as those of whose proceedings a record survives for the 1580s, which were held at Dedham in East Anglia, could easily (it was feared) become seditious.[44] So nervous did the English ecclesiastical hierarchy become that prophesyings conducted by ministers who were not licensed for the purpose were banned in the canons of 1604.

---

[41] W. D. Maxwell, *John Knox's Genevan Service Book, 1556* (Edinburgh: Oliver & Boyd, 1931), p. 104.

[42] John Hooper, *Later Writings* (Cambridge: Parker Society, 1852), p. 132.

[43] *Conferences and Combination Lectures in the Elizabethan Church: Dedham and Bury St. Edmunds, 1582-90*, ed. Patrick Collinson, John Craig and Brett Usher, in Church of England Record Society 10 (2003), p. xxxii.

[44] Ibid., p. xxix.

This kind of thing had parallels not only in Switzerland but all over Europe, where it was in many places the object of official censure. Repression continued into the seventeenth century, and if anything it grew more determined. The late-seventeenth-century Roman Catholic Church forbade meetings of Quietists, because they involved laypeople but also because they were gatherings which provided opportunities for such people to mislead one another.[45] On November 12, 1660, John Bunyan (1628-1688) was going to a meeting where he had been invited to give some teaching. "The justice hearing thereof . . . forthwith issued out his warrant to take me, and bring me before him, and in the mean time to keep a very strong watch about the house where the meeting should be kept, as if we that was to meet together in that place did intend to do some fearful business to the destruction of the country." The constable entered the room and, as Bunyan reports in his autobiography, he "was taken and forced to depart the room."[46] The Conventicle Act of 1664 and the Conventicles Act of 1670 outlawed religious meetings of more than five persons if they were not organized by the Church of England.[47]

Appeals to proper interpretive approaches. Augustine had long ago admitted that he had been put off the Christian Scriptures as a young man with an educated taste for fine language, because he found them so badly written. The loyal educated Christian of late antiquity made an effort to find in this crudeness of style evidence of a profound divine subtlety and kindly accommodation to human limitations.[48] Erasmus too acknowledged in an English version of his *Enchiridion* that a great deal of hard work needed to be done to understand the Bible aright, proposing that some educated men should extract the essentials and put them into a form plain enough for general comprehension.[49]

---

[45]Owen Chadwick, "Indifference and Morality," *Christian Spirituality: Essays in Honor of Gordon Rupp*, ed. Peter Brooks (London: SCM, 1975), p. 217.

[46]John Bunyan, *Grace Abounding and Other Spiritual Autobiographies*, ed. John Stachniewski and Anita Pacheco (Oxford: Oxford University Press, 1998), p. 98.

[47]See R. L. Greaves, *Deliver Us from Evil: The Radical Underground in Britain, 1660-1663* (Oxford: Oxford University Press, 1986).

[48]Erich Auerbach, *Literary Language and Its Public*, trans. R. Manheim (London: Routledge, 1965), p. 45ff.

[49]Erasmus, *Enchiridion militis Christiani* (1533; reprint, Amsterdam: Theatrum Orbis Terrarum, 1969), n.p.

How does this concern, expressed many times in the ten centuries and more between Augustine and Erasmus, sit with the belief of the Reformers that the Bible cannot err, is directly inspired, and tells the believer all he or she needs to know to be saved?

The danger that when the uneducated read the Bible they will misunderstand it was apparent to Reformers as well as to the Roman authorities. Cranmer insisted that God has thought of that and

> the holy ghost hath so ordered and tempered the scriptures, that in them as well publicans, fishers, and shepherds may find their edification, as great doctors their erudition. For those books were not made to vain glory, like as were the writings of the gentile philosophers and rhetoricians, to the intent the makers should be had in admiration for their high styles and obscure manner and writing, whereof nothing can be understood without a master or an expositor. But the Apostles and prophets wrote their books so that their special intent and purpose might be understood and perceived of every reader, which was nothing but the edification of amendment of the life of them that read or hear it.[50]

There are, of course, technical and other theological difficulties. The reader should not wade in to "such matters of difficulty" beyond his or her knowledge or capacity and should avoid "over[ly] hard questions" and getting into "contention and debates about scriptures and doubts."

The typical way of dealing with the longstanding fear of the authorities that if theologically uneducated people could read the Bible for themselves unorthodox opinions might run riot was to insist that the Holy Spirit could be trusted to guide the faithful soul in reading the Bible. The problem was that independent Bible readers were also likely to be hearing sermons by independent reforming preachers. Still at the end of the century Richard Hooker was nervous about what would happen if "the liking of an ignorant multitude . . . have power to change whatsoever itself listeth" (*Laws*, pref., 2.1). For "they had no laws at all agreed upon, but did what the Pastors of their souls by persuasion could win them unto."

---

[50]Thomas Cranmer, *Preface to the Great Bible*, in Documents of the English Reformation, ed. Gerald Bray (Cambridge: James Clarke & Co., reprint 2004), p. 237.

Hooker made a practical suggestion based on the assumption that the faith is one and there is only one Christian truth. Read for yourself if you wish, but be prepared to think again if you find that your views do not accord with the accepted orthodox view:

> They whose hartes it possesseth ought to suspect it the more, in as much as if it did come from God and should for that cause prevaile with others, the same God which revealeth it to them, would also give them powers of confirming it to others, either with miraculous operation, or with stronge and invincible remonstrance of sound reason.[51]

Richard Baxter made a seventeenth-century suggestion for a way forward:

> If we could only prove that the holy Ghost was given to the Penmen of holy Scripture, as an infallible guide to them in the matter, and not to enable them to any excellency above others in the method and words, but therein to leave them to their natural and acquired abilities this would be no diminution of the credit of their testimony, or of the Christian Faith.[52]

Baxter was one of many seventeenth-century scholars to try to defend the Scriptures against critics who condemned them for looseness of thought and expression. They say "there are contradictions in the Scripture, and great weaknesses in stile and method; how then can we believe they were sealed by God?" His answer is that this means the readers who say this "do but half understand" the Scripture. The fault is the reader's not God's.[53] But Baxter did not consider that the ordinary reader should be put off, still less prevented from, trying. This is an early modern counterpart of the patristic and late medieval confidence that God had designed the Bible carefully to meet human needs, but it allowed in the possibility that in some respects the Bible might be a text like any other and contain flaws.

One of the results of the new educated gentlemanly confidence in the layperson's capacity to join the professionals in biblical interpretation was that a similar kind of criticism of Scripture to that advanced by

---

[51]Hooker, *Laws*, 5.9.10.
[52]Baxter, *Arrogancy of Reason*, p. 58.
[53]Ibid., p. 57.

Augustine began to be heard again. In seventeenth-century England, notably in Royal Society circles, gentlemen dared to suggest that perhaps the style of Scripture left something to be desired to the educated eye and ear. This claim came from stylistic purists who respected classical models. According to Boyle, many complained "that the reading of the Bible untaught them the purity of the Roman Language, and corrupted their Ciceronian style."[54]

It is an irony that a very similar assault by a challenging *intelligentsia* had been parried by Augustine in his *De Doctrina Christiana* and *The City of God* (see pp. 55-56). As trained orators and philosophers they were admirably placed to sneer at the simplicities of Scripture's style, and Augustine had done so himself as a young man, as he admits in the *Confessions*.

But in the early modern era this challenge also, and importantly, reflected a complete shakeup from truly new assumptions about what constituted the actual text, which had been brought about by studying it in Greek and Hebrew and translating it into many vernaculars. And it overlapped with other areas of interest to educated lay circles, often at the point where physics and metaphysics were being separated in contemporary work on the sciences. The manifest imperfections of the text, in point of style and content and inconsistency, had to be explained afresh in terms that would be meaningful to highly educated early modern readers and in the much wider world of the many versions now available. It was also beginning to be recognized that critical scholarship since the sixteenth century had created its own exigencies, and that its contents must be read against the findings of a growing body of contemporary scientific research. Augustine's question of a millennium and a half earlier—"Why is the Bible so badly written?"—seemed to require completely new answers.

Edward Stillingfleet (1635-1699) responded to Spinoza and others by appealing to the divine authority of Scripture, even as a human production. In an unedited fragment, he asserts, "The Question is not, whether the Books of Moses were written by himself or by others according to

---

[54]Boyle, *Style of the Scriptures*, p. 447.

his Appointment or Direction. It is not, whether the Writings of Moses were preserved free from all literal mistakes," the question is whether Moses is complete or abridged, "for then the Certainty of our faith doth not depend on the Authority of Moses or the Prophets, but on the Credibility of those Persons, who have taken upon them to give out these Abridgements instead of their original writings."[55]

Other commentators tried further devices for reconciling the discrepancies. Hooker suggested it was best not to worry too much about contradictions on minor details in the Bible. "Although there be in theire wordes a manifest show of jarre" (Lk 5:6-7 says the fishing net broke; Jn 21:11 says it did not).[56] According to Baxter, critics say "there are contradictions in the Scripture, and great weaknesses in stile and method; how then can we believe they were sealed by God?" His answer is that this means "they do but half understand them."[57]

By the seventeenth century it was realized more deeply that the Bible was not only composed of many books but of many different kinds of book. There was a growing literary sensitivity to the fact that the Bible is a collection of writings in different genres. As Boyle explains in his *Style of the Scriptures*, "We must not look upon the Bible as an Oration of God to men or as a Body of Lawes, like our English Statute-Book, wherein it is the Legislator that all the way speaks to the people." There are many "composures" where the Holy Spirit "both excited and assisted them in penning the Scripture," yet many others are "introduced speaking" besides the "Author [God] and the Pen-men," such as soldiers, shepherds and women "from whom witty or eloquent things are not [especially when they speak *extempore*] to be expected," so Scripture should not be blamed for a want of eloquence on their account.[58]

Boyle, a man more highly educated in formal terms than Baxter, and approaching these questions as a scientist as well as a theologian, nevertheless relies upon a similar insistence that it is all for the best and God knew what he was doing, and any apparent imperfections must be put

[55]Gerard Reedy, ed., *The Bible and Reason: Anglicans and Scripture in Late Seventeenth-Century England* (Philadelphia: University of Pennsylvania Press, 1985), p. 147.
[56]Hooker, *Laws*, 5.19.3.
[57]Baxter, *Arrogancy of Reason*, p. 57.
[58]Boyle, *Style of the Scriptures*, p. 399.

down to human inadequacies, not those of the divine Author:

> Nor does it misbecome God's Goodnesse any more than his Wisdom, to
> have so tempered the Canonical Books, as therein to leave all sorts of
> readers an exercise for their Industry, and give even the greatest Doctors
> continual inducements to implore his Instruction, and depend on him for
> his irradiations, by leaving amongst many passages that stoop unto our
> weaknesse, some that may make us sensible of it . . . like a River, wherein
> a Lamb may quench his thirst, and which an Elephant cannot exhaust.[59]

Boyle, therefore, argues that

> We must not look upon the Bible as an Oration of God to men, or as a
> body of Lawes, like our English Statute-Book, wherein it is the legislator
> that all the way speaks to the people, but as a Collection of composures
> of very differing sorts, and written at very distant times; and of such
> composures, that though the Holy Men of God . . . were acted by thye
> Holy Spirit who both excited and assisted them in penning the Scrip-
> tures, yet there are many others besides the Author and the Pen-men
> introduced speaking there.

For these purposes God is the Author, and "The Omniscient Author
of the Scripture foreseeing" that many members of the church would be
illiterate ensured that the Bible would be "written in such a plain and
familiar way as may befit such Readers."[60] It is right and a benevolent
dispensation of God that readers should have to make an effort to understand the obscurer passages. But he is willing to set this whole familiar debate in the context of new critical theories.

Boyle's work is perhaps the most comprehensive and extended attempt of the age to meet the new challenge on a number of fronts, but
he too proceeds by trying to integrate the old academic answers in the
design of the new, freer, gentleman-scholar ones. "Diverse witty men,"
he admits, "who freely acknowledge the Authority of the Scripture take
exceptions at its Style."[61] They take this to include a wide range of alleged flaws.

---

[59]Ibid., p. 409.
[60]Ibid., pp. 401-2.
[61]Ibid., p. 393.

Some of them are pleased to say that Book is too obscure, others, that
'tis immethodical, others, that it is contradictory to it self, others, that
the neighboring parts of it are incoherent, others, that 'tis unadorned,
others, that it is flat and unaffecting, others, that it abounds with things
that are either trivial or impertinent, and also with useless Repetitions.[62]

These "objectors" (whom Boyle is seeking to answer) "choose rather
to study Other Books of Devotion and Morality, as containing more full
and Instructive Precepts of Good Life."[63]

Boyle was a member of an extensive class of seventeenth- and eigh-
teenth-century figures, corresponding with one another throughout
Europe, often still using Latin as a convenient common language for
the purpose, who wrote upon both science and theology. He was a layman and proud of the fact that he did not speak as theologians were
accustomed to:

Severer Divines may safely Pardon some Smoothnesse in a Discourse
Written Chiefly for Gentlemen, who would scarce be fond of Truth in
every Dresse, by a Gentleman who fear'd it might misbecome a Person of
his Youth and Quality Studiously to Decline a fashionable Style.[64]

Boyle suggested that his "being a secular parson" might "the better
qualify" him and also make his writings more acceptable to readers
who "have a particular pique at the clergy, and look with prejudice
upon whatever is taught by men, whose interest is advantaged by having what they teach believed."

For the more intelligent and better educated, he suggests, as many
approved interpreters of old had done, that God has deliberately created
the difficulties to understanding the Bible presents "to exercise such
mens abilities, and to reward their industry, there should be some abstruse Texts of Scripture fitted to the capacities of such speculative wits,
and above the reach of vulgar Apprehensions."[65]

But equally—and again Boyle is using an explanation which had
been advanced in earlier centuries—God has provided for the simple

[62]Ibid., p. 394.
[63]Ibid., p. 430.
[64]Ibid., p. 391.
[65]Ibid., p. 403. On industry and its rewards see also p. 409.

and uneducated reader too. "The Omniscient Author of Scripture foreseeing that it would follow from the condition of mankind that the greatest part of the members of the Church would be . . . many of them very weak or illiterate" ensured that parts "should be written in such a plain and familiar way as may befit such Readers." The Bible was "designed for . . . numberless differences of humour."[66]

One must not rate a Hebrew text by a translation which "misseth the Propriety both of the Hebrew Speech and of the Latin," insists Boyle.[67] It was also important to him that a translation may render the text less elegant than it is in the original, and he saw from the wider perspective of his age that "not appearing Eloquent to European judges" is not the only consideration, for "the Eastern Eloquence differs widely from the Western":[68]

> Now scarce any but a Linguist will imagine how much a Book may lose of its elegancy by being read in another tongue than that it was written in, especially if the Languages from which and into which the Version is made be so very differing as are those of the Eastern and these Western parts of the world.[69]

Once vernacular translations were so commonplace in the Protestant world as to have become the main route by which most people knew the text, it became as easy to lose sight of the fact that the King James Version (for example) was a mere translation as it had once been to forget that God had not originally dictated the Bible in the Vulgate's Latin. As Boyle points out, it is only too easy for the ordinary reader to forget that the text with which he or she is familiar is a mere translation, and even to regard as Scripture items conventionally printed and bound with the Bible. Isaac Watts (1674-1748) later noted the same phenomenon: "It is for the same reason that the bulk of the common people are so superstitiously fond of the Psalms translated by Hopkins and Sternhold, and think them sacred and divine, because they have been now for more than a hundred years bound up in the same covers with out Bibles."

---

[66]Ibid., p. 403.
[67]Ibid., p. 449.
[68]Ibid., p. 451.
[69]Ibid., p. 448.

"Cavilers" tend to judge of the Bible "by the Translations wherein alone they read it."[70]

Boyle therefore points out that this very reverence for the text has encouraged scrupulous, wooden translations with the disastrous result "that for fear of not keeping close enough to the sense, they usually care not how much they lost of the Eloquence of the passages they translate." In ordinary translating "the Interpreters are wont to take the liberty to recede from the Author's words, and also substitute other Phrases instead of his, that they may express his meaning without injuring his Reputation."[71] Did the criticisms of the rude style still apply, though, when the text was translated? Yes, it seemed. They were not eradicated by the translator's skill; they went deeper. Style was not the only reason that among the rising generation of academics and professionals the Bible was increasingly accused of obscurity.

Ultimately, Boyle urged that the Bible should be studied on its own terms, as a whole. Otherwise readers would be tempted to collect a pile of pebbles, quotations they could throw at their adversaries rather than using them to build a coherent doctrinal position for themselves.[72] Despite the strength of the tradition that the Bible was all true and formed a coherent whole, centuries of liturgical tradition brought the Bible before the worshiping congregation in short portions, selected from the complete text of the Bible, so that the Bible as a whole was not necessarily heard by the people even if they faithfully went to church every time there was a service and were fortunate enough to have a parish priest who would conscientiously explain to them in homilies the texts they had heard.[73]

---

[70]Isaac Watts, *Logic; Or, the Right Use of Reason in the Inquiry After Truth*. . . . 3.5 (1724; reprint, London, 1845), p. 187.

[71]Boyle, *Style of the Scriptures*, p. 395.

[72]Ibid., pp. 381-488.

[73]See Owen Chadwick, *The Early Reformation on the Continent* (Oxford: Oxford University Press, 2001), p. 14.

CONCLUSION

The church of the people. "Great mischief on earth is mounting up fast" had been Langland's conclusion as he gazed at the social and spiritual disarray of fourteenth-century England spread before him on the great plain below the Malvern Hills. His disillusioned "nouveau middle class" readers represented the articulate front line of a popular revolt against unsatisfactory behavior by the leaders of church and state.

Some medieval theologians discussing ecclesiology—the question of what constitutes the church—still took the view that the church comprised only the clergy, and not the clergy and people. That view became unsustainable by the sixteenth century. A number of the strands of discontent that had been prompters of medieval dissidence had plaited themselves together now into a cable of some strength.

New concepts of social order. The first of these strands involved people's wish to be done with their sense of exclusion, the feeling that they were treated largely as passive recipients of a work done in them for their salvation through the instrumentality of the institutional church. Sixteenth-century reform restored to its supporters a sense of being able to make their own direct response to God. But they wanted a say in secular affairs too, at least at the level where their own lives were affected.

Much of the awareness of reasons to be dissatisfied in the Middle Ages had lain in local perceptions and local grumbles. Something of the lived texture of the Reformation at the local level is captured in Eamon Duffy's intimate studies of local life and the ways in which ordinary people who were not themselves leaders of thought were affected by the flowing of the great tides of the times.[1] The new reforming churches were almost all "people's churches," and the power of popular opinion had become something to be reckoned with.

Comparatively few medieval people were able to travel. Paradoxically, the stability of the new enlarged European and global society of the sixteenth century was protected by the fact that it was still relatively unusual to move away from the place where one was born. Local society was able to keep an eye on the behavior of local people and to identify strangers. The Elizabethan Poor Law of 1601 depended on local knowledge to assist in classifying the "deserving" poor who got social support and the "undeserving," the idle and the vagrants, who were liable to be sent to prison.

Yet some glimpsed a larger problem in the government of the state in which they lived or in the Western and New World order. It seemed to a few resentful individuals who felt hemmed in, their ambitions curtailed, that they were suffering under corrupt governments in league with a corrupt church. Among the indignant this frequently moved up a notch higher still, so that the alleged bad behavior of human authorities, secular and spiritual, became identified with satanic activity and the struggles of dissidents with the cosmic war of good and evil. Modern analogies will spring to mind.

This complex interpenetration—of resentments of unworthy and sometimes unlawful exercise of authority and dissatisfactions with the way things were run—was an important starting place for the story of what happened in the Reformation. If the ideas and the complaints were not much different from the old ones, the reasons for the startlingly different result must be partly social. "Religion being the chiefe Band of humane Society, it is a happy thing, when it selfe, is well contained, within the true Band of Unity," as Francis Bacon put it.[2]

The *Essays* of Francis Bacon were written between 1597 and 1625, and

[1] Eamon Duffy, *The Voices of Morebath: Reformation and Rebellion in an English Village* (New Haven, Conn.: Yale University Press, 2001); and Eamon Duffy, *The Stripping of the Altars: Traditional Religion in England c. 1400–c. 1580* (New Haven, Conn.: Yale University Press, 1992).
[2] Francis Bacon, "Of Unity in Religion," *The Essayes or Counsels, Civill and Morall*, ed. Michael Kiernan (Oxford: Clarendon Press, 1985), p. 11.

it was as apparent to him, as it was to his contemporary Richard Hooker when writing his *Laws*, that in their day and age religion was a social as well as a spiritual bond. Unity makes for peace. An appropriate disposition of the two swords, spiritual and temporal, help the community avoid what may be "tending to the Subversion of all Government."[3] The "heathen," suggests Bacon, did not quarrel about religion as Christians do, because they had a religion which "consisted rather in Rites and Ceremonies; then in any constant Beleefe." For them there was less at stake. Christians too should not allow themselves to quarrel over points "to small and light, not worth the Heat, and Strife about it" and even over bigger ones when "driven to an over-great Subtilty, and Obscurity."[4]

Something was happening here which began to make Europe look recognizably modern to our later eyes, and it was connected with a changing mindset. One of the most important changes signaled by all this lay in the balance of power. Those who asked awkward questions seem to have had much more success in starting movements in northern Europe than further south. This may be a consequence of social change in Germany and parts of northern Europe where the feudal system was giving way to an era in which princes could be seen as "civil magistrates," and cities enjoyed a degree of self-government.

The central complaint of the (in the main) socially rather lowly dissidents of the Middle Ages was about alleged abuse of power, spiritual and social. The Waldensians had voiced complaints in the twelfth century that had been repeated more loudly by the Lollards and others later in the Middle Ages. They all objected to the conspicuous consumption and neglect of duty by some of the clergy, especially those most highly placed and powerful. This led them to ask whether they could disregard the claims of the powerful and still save their souls. For the most important of the implications for ordinary people was the church's claim that it had the power to decide who went to heaven, or at least how speedily a soul could arrive there, through its control of forgiveness and the discharge of penances. Some asked whether it was possible to get to heaven without the assistance of the institutional church and thus challenged the Augus-

---

[3]Ibid., p. 14.
[4]Ibid., p. 13.

tinian doctrine *nulla salus extra ecclesiam.* Some questioned the need for the sacraments. Some said they saw no reason why ordinary believers should not read the Bible for themselves, and began Bible study groups.

The essential complaint rising up from the grassroots in this way was that the institutional church had overextended itself and was making excessive claims, requiring the faithful to comply with human impositions which were not God's requirements at all. So this was at root an ecclesiological challenge as well as a personal one. Luther's doctrine of justification by faith was a bold attempt to cut through layers of complexity and detailed requirements, and to offer believers a simple promise. They did not have to earn their way to heaven by doing penances or good works. Anyone could hope for heaven who took hold of Christ as his or her Savior. But to adopt that view was to reject much of the apparatus of the medieval church, by which it set much store and in which it had a large investment, financial as well as spiritual.

The hatred of the religious orders that characterized reforming thought in the sixteenth century was already to be found in Wyclif. Wyclif objected that these "sects" were claiming a superior form of membership of the church, a sort of baptism beyond that which was available to the ordinary faithful. He objected that they were claiming that they had a second baptism and were privileged and special Christians. The sixteenth century saw a strong reaction against them, especially in England, where monasteries were dissolved and their property seized by the crown. Wealth and privilege were ripe to be grabbed in the name of righteous indignation.

Meanwhile, popping up again and again in protest and debate ran declarations of outrage that the church was encouraging the faithful to worship what was lower than God, mere creatures—or worse, mere depictions of creatures. This was idolatry, was the cry, though not everyone thought so. Thomas More said he saw no difference between images in pictures and images in words: "Since all names spoken or written be but image, if ye set aught by the name of Jesus spoken or written: why should ye set nought by his image painted or carven that representeth his holy person to your remembrance, as much and more too, as doth his name written?"

Academics learn to be popular. Other strands making up the change were intellectual rather than social. An uneducated population had had little choice but to accept their need for priestly ministrations. If people could not read the Bible for themselves and understood only the barest minimum of theology as conveyed to them by the parish priest—whose own education might be slight—it was hard for them to know what to believe. The narratives acted out in mystery plays and pictures on the church wall were of limited help in providing a theologically more advanced education, except to those who already understood the implications of the way they put things. An ecclesiastical senior figure such as Pecham, aware of the need to ensure adequate teaching of the laity, seems to have been something of a rarity. The great shift of expectation that got the Bible into people's hands in their own languages meant that even the illiterate could hear it read and make something of it. With it went a quite new process of popularization of at least the essentials of academic writing and debate.

Although they flourished in particular localities, universities had always been international, pan-European, their scholars peripatetic and freely exchanging ideas. The universities of Europe continued to run their theology courses as higher degree subjects and only for a privileged few. Peasant uprisings and bourgeois claims for attention could never have become the vehicles of Renaissance, although they underpinned the Reformation. The medieval dissidents had usually been groups of peasants or townspeople, with the occasional prominent and controversial academic. Rarely in the Middle Ages was an academic's name closely linked with a popular movement as John Wyclif's came to be after his death, and it may be wondered whether that would have happened if he had lived on in his cantankerous eccentricity and not died and left the Lollards to look after their own affairs.

From the end of the fifteenth century, largely independent scholars and academics began to alter things. Academics got among the people, wrote popular theology and provided clear instruction in catechisms and manuals on theology.

Some sixteenth-century Reformers had a sense of humor—sometimes a coarse one by modern standards of good taste. Luther was particularly notable for guffaws of that sort. In fact this was an age of variegated humor, challenging old securities, with a rich vocabulary of mockery, laughing down the nose, derision, scurrility, irreverence. Satire and farce were popular. Dramatic monologues performed at feasts of the church could include risqué jokes: in drama, a pretend preacher could be a woman; macaronic games lowered the prestige of the learned languages by mixing them mischievously with the vernacular. Melanchthon taught his students to approach their studies with a smile, speaking of "games with words" as a *ludus*.

A series of individuals with university educations and sometimes connections with powerful patrons were able to strut the small stages of northern European cities and dukedoms and become prominent by name, as Martin Luther did. Patrons and princes alike warmed to the suggestion that civil authorities (magistrates) should supervise the running of ecclesiastical affairs, even if they still had to stand back from interference in the church's spiritual and sacramental life. The invention of printing made it possible to decide to write a book and see it become a runaway success in providing a manual for the reference of large numbers of sympathizers, as John Calvin did with his *Institutes*.

The popularity of public disputations between protagonists with opposing views made them a tempting way of trying to settle disagreements, although it turned out again and again that the only result was to throw up new points of dispute and make it necessary to set up yet another meeting for yet another public debate. The people seem to have enjoyed theological disputations as theater. A public disputation could become a popular entertainment, an opportunity for the audience to cheer and boo and throw rotten eggs.

Styles of churchmanship and new conceptions of what matters. The Roman Catholic Church had long been a monolith in the West. If asked, it would simply have called itself "the *Catholic* Church," meaning "universal." But now the varied social styles of Europe were able to print themselves more thoroughly on local church life, especially where Reformers were dominant.

Differences of style in language had their counterpart in the ways local preferences expressed themselves in religious differences across Europe, so that in some places one thing seemed essential and another indifferent, while in other regions the priorities were different. For example, the building of St. Peter's in Rome, funded by active marketing to sell indulgences, had caused sufficient offense in Germany to set Luther and then Zwingli off on their respective courses of reform. Among some wings of reforming opinion, that led to a determination to avoid having church buildings at all, with worship held in private houses. Some accepted the need for special places of worship, but insisted that they must be plain, stripping out pictures and statues in those they took over.

What Stayed the Same?

What would Langland have made of the world and its religious tensions as it all stood at the end of the sixteenth century? It was a considerably bigger world, now including the New World. Its social parameters had altered beyond recognition. Langland includes in his visionary landscape a tower or castle on a hill and a dungeon in the valley as images of heaven and hell, familiar notions in medieval feudal England. But now the feudal order had broken down in much of northern Europe and with it a good deal of the hierarchical ordering of the church. Social mobility had increased, and the intellectually talented young who did not wish to make careers in the church could now get degrees, seek patrons and make their way upward in society by other routes. One of the most favored of these in late Tudor England was to study law and then enter Parliament.

Langland, looking down from the Malvern Hills on the "fair field of folk," or walking the streets of London, would have seen different "undesirable characters" mingling with the populace. Among them would be vagrants, some of them refugees cast out from religious houses that had been closed and finding no easy place to be in society outside. Much of the later part of Langland's poem is concerned with the search for Dowel (Do-well), Dobet (Do-better) and Dobest (Do-best). He might have had to rethink the characteristics of the good man or woman in an era when Reformers had shifted the emphasis decisively away from officially prescribed good behavior as marking out the true road to heaven.

Since the fourteenth century the influence of this poem had entered into the very process of the changes a latter-day Langland could have observed. A mythology, created by references in the writings of the rebel leader John Ball, helped to associate *Piers Plowman* with the Peasants' Revolt of 1381, as though he had been a real person and not a character in a story. This meant the emergence of a popular association of the poem with Lollardy. The way the poem has been understood has since been affected by that connection, while the poem may itself have contributed to the emergence of Lollard ideas. It certainly lacked the respectability which might have got it printed early in the history of printing, though it went on being copied in manuscript form. By the time Robert Crowley (c. 1518-1588) published the poem in 1550, it had an accepted place as a Protestant tale, but times were very different by then. And even so it was a Protestant text of a particular color, approved in a Marprelate tract. The political complexion of its message was still perceived to be strong. Though the Tudor monarchs faced different challenges from their fourteenth century predecessors, power and the abuse of power were still great preoccupations, and there William Langland would have felt quite at home in the later reforming landscape. And beneath this turbulent surface ran a continuity of belief and practice in the essentials of the Christian faith.

WHAT WAS THE ESSENTIAL
CHARACTERISTIC OF THE CHANGE?

We have seen the emergence of a Western Europe in which there was no longer to be one monolithic institutional church but a seemingly endless variety of churches, each claiming to be the only one preserving the truth. We place the Reformation at the beginning of the modern world, but contemporaries had no idea that they were participating in the end of the Middle Ages. They lived lives which did not seem to them to be crossing a bridge in a world in transition, for how could they begin to glimpse what *modern* has come to mean?

One big difference between the medieval dissidents and the sixteenth-century Reformers lay in the effect they had. During several late medieval centuries, very similar complaints had been heard, but the church and the secular authorities actively suppressed the complaints and punished individuals who voiced them, and the challenge never rose much above the level of a sustained grumble. In the sixteenth century, dissidents became public Reformers.

Accusations of heresy still flew in both directions during the six-teenth century, and still on many of the points which had been contro-versial for centuries, but somehow with more equal force. Now the com-batants could sometimes claim comparable standing in terms of the areas of Europe they could call their own; the rebels often had the local support of the secular authorities, such as the civil magistrates the Lu-therans looked to. Erastus's perception of the consequences of associat-ing *regio* (the local government) and *religio* (the complexion of belief) was turning out to be profoundly important.

Those who still held firmly to the view that there was only one church and it was theirs were nevertheless faced with the undeniable reality that others were able to sustain their similar claims elsewhere. In parts of north-ern Europe the church was no longer the Church of Rome but perhaps the Church of England or the Church of Scotland. From the mid-century the church could be seen as divided rather than threatened with extinction. What had happened has left Western Christendom divided until now.

That does not mean the debate ended or that the adversarial posi-tions became fixed in the sixteenth century. It has been one of the char-acteristics of Christian conflict that dissent leads to further fragmenta-tion of opinion, often with a single key point being fixed on as essential and therefore potentially church-dividing. 'Brethren,' for example, have taken their identities from several traditions—the sixteenth century Anabaptists, the late eighteenth century Methodists, the nineteenth century Plymouth brethren movement—and have broken into further sects: the modern Amish may be Old or New Amish.

The early modern period saw a shift of concern and interest to-wards revivals of some very old disputes, such as the seventeenth and eighteenth century Socinian and Unitarian debates about the Trinity. The confidence of the eighteenth century Age of Reason or Enlighten-ment that humanity might be capable of perfecting itself by its own efforts also had its day. In the modern world revivals of traditional con-cerns continue, with a present-day period of polarization in some parts of the world between an extreme literalist reliance on Scripture and an extreme confidence that science will in the end answer all questions.

HANDLIST OF REFORMATION CONCERNS AND THEIR HISTORY

CHRISTIAN THEOLOGY HAS ITS PERENNIAL THEMES and areas of concern. In each generation the same topics have become subjects for impassioned debate, though the emphasis has shifted with the fashions of the time. At the Reformation certain concerns clustered. The Christian community in the West was broken into separated and mutually hostile pieces. Taking a particular position came to seem a matter of spiritual life or death, for heaven was at stake. This book has traced the threads in the discussion of these perennial themes as they wove their way toward the Reformation's moment and as they entwined (and began to unravel) afterward.

They form a complex tapestry. This handlist of themes and topics offers a summary of the aspects that chiefly triggered Reformation convictions and actions and helps the reader recognize the repeating patterns in the fabric as it unrolled over the centuries.

THE BIBLE AND BELIEVING

Justification by faith alone. Why did Luther insist so forcefully—in one of the great defining challenges that set the Reformation going—that only faith could justify the sinner in the sight of God?[1] Of course he

---

[1]Alister E. McGrath, *Iustitia De: A History of the Christian Doctrine of Justification* (Cambridge: Cambridge University Press, 2005).

felt the insight was fundamentally biblical; but it also seems to have been his way of cutting through the mass of requirements which made the faithful feel so heavily burdened. He knew that feeling personally. He had been terrified himself.

Then he began to be angered by the knock-on effect of a series of connected beliefs: that Christians must make up for their sins by hard work, doing penance, as though repenting and being forgiven were not enough; and that even if they were spared an eternity in hell, they were likely to have to serve a sentence in purgatory before there was any hope of heaven. He also grew indignant about what seemed to him a theologically chaotic doctrine of indulgences attached to this teaching; this encouraged the faithful to think they could buy remission of the penalties the church taught sinners still had to pay even when they had confessed their sins and been absolved.

Luther, like Wyclif before him, came to regard all these as "human impositions." Wyclif had concentrated his resentment on the abuse of power in the institutional church. Luther's primary aim was to proclaim the free mercy of God in Christ, and the freedom of the Christian from anxiety over religious performance.

This clear, simple idea had immense attractions. It eased the pain of what Luther called the "terrified conscience." Yet the doctrine of justification by faith also had built into it a particular attitude to the existing church structure and its by now extensive requirements.

> FOR FURTHER READING
> On these topics see "One Faith and Different Rites" (chap. 3), "John Wyclif" (chap. 14), "The Conversion of Martin Luther and Its Consequences" (chap. 16).

The content of faith and Scripture alone. Luther's cry *sola scriptura* (Scripture alone) stood side by side with his claim that only faith justifies, for it is only Scripture that could tell the believer *what* to believe, and it is through Scripture that the Spirit works repentance and faith. Having faith is an affective act, a commitment, but it also involves believing something (and not believing other things). Faith has a *content* too. There has been a long history of discussion of the content of the faith as well as of what believing really means and what it does. All this still had to be fitted in, in the background of Luther's transformative leading idea. For the Reformers found a great deal to disagree about.

Other Reformers tended to follow Luther's lead and favor reliance on the Bible as the sole source of knowledge about the content of the faith. For some this meant trusting Scripture *instead of* the church's "teaching." But the Bible is not a textbook of systematic theology in the sense that it sets out a comprehensive set of points of belief in an orderly way. For most reforming communities the solution lay in reliance on a combination of Scripture and subordinate authorities such as the ancient creeds, or confessional statements such as the Augsburg Confession, or both. Many found the older aids to study of the faith, such as the writings of Augustine of Hippo, still useful—if not indispensable.

FOR FURTHER READING
On these topics see "What Do We Believe? Trying to Put the Faith in a Nutshell" (chap. 3), "The Invention of Universities" (chap. 11), "The Conversion of Martin Luther and Its Consequences" and "Creating a Lutheran Doctrinal System" (chap. 16).

Which books make up God's Word?
Any attempt simply to rely on Scripture as the Word of God was complicated by longstanding debates about the inclusion or exclusion of certain books from the canon (the normative content of the Bible). This had been a live question among some until as late as the fourth century, but it settled down through the Middle Ages, largely no doubt because the completion of Jerome's Vulgate ("common") translation provided a fixed and widely accepted Latin version and supplanted the numerous Latin versions of variable quality then in circulation. Jerome himself expressed doubts about the authenticity of books not found in the Hebrew version of the Old Testament, but versions of these apocryphal books later tended to be included with the rest of the books and regarded as part of the Vulgate.

Most of the leading Reformers were well aware of the growing sophistication of contemporary biblical scholarship, and many were taking part themselves in its development. Some of the sixteenth-century Reformers raised once more the question of which books were truly scriptural. Martin Luther included (in one of his attempts to put down Johannes Eck) a robust dismissal of 2 Maccabees 12 on the grounds that this and other apocryphal books were not cited by the New Testament writers as other Old Testament books were.

But Luther went further. He also argued that certain books which seemed to counter the doctrines that justification is by faith alone (*sola fide*) and that only Scripture (*sola scriptura*) was a reliable source of teaching for the Christian could not be canonical. This included several New Testament books. He tried to get Hebrews and the epistle of James as well as Jude and Revelation removed from the canon, although very few Protestants followed Luther in this particular desire.

Part of the problem was the difficulty of establishing common ground as to what constituted proof or authority when it came to defining the canon. In other words, who decided what was the Word of God and what was not? For Rome the answer was straightforward. The church had decided. The Reformers tended to find the basis for biblical authority in the Bible's own witness to its prophetic and apostolic authority, a reality confirmed by the testimony of the Holy Spirit.

Interpreting the Bible: The complications of popular access. There were many other dimensions to the apparently simple idea of relying straightforwardly on what the Bible says under the guidance of the Holy Spirit. It implied that ordinary people ought to have access to Scripture for themselves, in their own language, so that they could hear or read God's teaching

> FOR FURTHER READING
> On these topics see "A New Idea" (chap. 2).

and respond to it directly. When Jerome translated the Vulgate, the Latin "common" version, he was providing the vernacular version of his day. It was only in later centuries, as Latin ceased to be the common language of Western Europe, that it became a clerical preserve.

By the later Middle Ages and the sixteenth century, Europe had Christian populations in many languages, and vernacular translations now unavoidably introduced variety where the Vulgate had offered a more or less uniform text. Different languages, of course, are not exactly equivalent in grammar or vocabulary. It is not simply a matter of turning a word in one language into its counterpart in another. So translators had to make choices of style and emphasis as well as to find ways of being as faithful to the original as they could.

And which was the original text, the *fons* (spring) from which the Word of God flowed? The New Testament had been written in Greek. For the Old Testament there was the Hebrew and also the Septuagint, an early Greek version. But since the Vulgate had become the standard Bible text throughout the West from the fifth century, all the apparatus of scholarly criticism had been created to interpret and explain it. Although Jerome said that he did not consider he had been inspired as a translator, the Vulgate was commonly treated by scholars with the respect it would have merited if God had spoken Latin when he gave his Word.

Making translations into the languages ordinary people now spoke implied that teaching should move out of the hands of the church, away from official instruction by a parish priest—or conveyed in a sermon by a preacher licensed by the local bishop—and under the direct control of the Holy Spirit, illuminating the minds of the laity as he chose. That turned theology from a *disciplina arcani*, a secret code known only to experts, into a study open to all and where individual members of the laity might hold personal views. "Private reading" could lead to the holding of opinions which did not conform with the church's official teaching.

Long-running problematic topics that had been the subject of scholarly and ecclesiastical dispute did not become less so with the widespread Reformation belief that because Scripture alone sufficed, Scripture would explain itself clearly to the individual reader who would be guided to the right understanding by the Holy Spirit. The problem was that some passages of Scripture appeared to be in conflict with others, or at least not to match exactly. Even the Gospels did not all tell the story of Jesus in the very same way.

Certainly ontradictory statements cannot both be true—yet God cannot lie or be mistaken and both statements are the Word of God. This difficulty had been tackled down the centuries by various sophisticated means designed to reconcile seeming contradictions. Augustine had attempted harmonies of the Gospels, and Calvin did the same. But most devices involved taking one or both of the apparently conflicting passages in a figurative sense. Some Reformers found this unacceptable because it seemed to sit uncomfortably with the idea that God had made his meaning plain. The Reformers' preference was to take the

Bible literally and simply live as it told them to. Any such resolve proved hard to keep to, and Reformers sometimes found themselves expounding Scripture figuratively.

So *sola scriptura*, Scripture alone, was by no means a straightforward claim. And with disputes about which books were to be included, and in which versions, came areas of further debate about the *content* of the faith as set out in the Bible.

Despite these difficulties, most sixteenth-century Reformers did not need convincing that the Bible ought to be accessible to ordinary people through translations in their own language, or that the huge apparatus collected over the centuries to assist with its interpretation needed to be overhauled, possibly abandoned, and replaced with a new emphasis on the study of the Bible in Greek and Hebrew. This necessitated accepting that individuals should be free to read for themselves, trusting in the Holy Spirit to guide their understanding, and perhaps to expound the Bible for the edification of others in sermons and Bible study groups.

These changed attitudes derived from the rejection of the Roman Catholic Church's claims to be the sole approved authority able to maintain custody of the sacred text, which it usually considered was safer kept in Latin away from uneducated people. The Church had further protected the Bible by licensing only those regarded as holding safe opinions to preach on it, and the main academic endeavor of the Middle Ages had gone into the compilation of the glosses and commentaries whose significance the Reformers now wished to relativize. Instead of glossed Bibles they now designed and published polyglot Bibles.

FOR FURTHER READING
On these topics see chapters 14, 15 and 22.

Creeds. Very early on the church developed creeds, short statements of the faith summarizing the storyline and trinitarian scope of Scripture, to be used at baptism and in regular worship. From these emerged the Apostles' Creed, though it probably took its present settled form only some centuries later.

Controversies about challenges from dissidents, subsequently defined as heretics, also prompted the drafting of an official statement, approved by a council, in the Niceno-Constantinopolitan Creed of the fourth century. The clauses of this creed, while foundational and universal in scope, are also strongly marked by the preoccupations of the time and the need to rebut particular views. The creed omits many of the topics which were to become controversial later, and which were preoccupations of the Reformation. Though radicals did occasionally challenge Trinitarian and Christological orthodoxy during the sixteenth century, the Reformers had different concerns about what they alleged were slippages in beliefs about Christ and his work, in which attempts by the institutional church and its ministers to act *in persona Christi*, "in the person of Christ," to attempt to supplement in any way his once-for-all sacrifice on the cross were prominent.

FOR FURTHER READING
On these topics see "What Do We Believe? Trying to Put the Faith in a Nutshell" (chap. 3), "Creating a Lutheran Doctrinal System" (chap. 16), "The English Reformation Turns Reformed" (chap. 19).

And Reformation churches often created creeds of their own in the form of confessions of faith containing lists of articles defining orthodoxy for their own community.

THE IDEA OF CHURCH

"Scripture alone" and "faith alone" made essentially the same assault on the power claims of the institutional church of the time. In Luther's claim that faith alone justifies the sinner before God, the antithesis is between faith and works, between simply receiving Christ for justification and striving to please God by human effort. The doctrine of the efficacy of good works had come to mean relying on the Roman Church's teaching that there was no salvation apart from fellowship with that ecclesial body, and that in its turn meant trusting the efficacy of the sacraments as that church understood and administered them. Completing the penitential process involved performing required works, such as fasting, almsgiving, prayer. So in rejecting the teaching of the Church about the necessity of good works, Luther saw himself as also rejecting the immense apparatus of what he saw as additions to Scripture carrying no authority but human authority. And with that rejection he was rejecting the Church itself, in the institutional form it had developed by the end of the Middle Ages in the West.

The perception of the church as power broker. Reformers of the sixteenth century frequently expressed their anger about what they saw as the power-brokering habits of the Western Church and its leaders.[2] The polemical literature—and there is plenty of it—is full of fury on this point. Resentment showed itself in several ways in the arguments of various Reformers. Some focused on the pope as tyrant or usurper, an idea already lively in the writings of John Wyclif at the end of the fourteenth century (see pp. 214-15). Some wanted to try again—as had been attempted in the fifteenth century—to shift power to a council of bishops in preference to a monarchical papacy (see pp. 98-102). Some said that the problem lay in claiming that the church was a single visible institution outside which there was no salvation; they asserted that the church is invisible in its fullness and only small outcrops can be seen in the form of local gathered congregations (see pp. 277-78). Among those who took this view there was sometimes a more extreme reluctance to use the word *church* at all, which may explain the preference for *congregation* in some Protestant communities.

> FOR FURTHER READING
> On these topics see chapter 2, "The Idea of Church."

> FOR FURTHER READING
> On these topics see chapters 14 and 18.

THE PROBLEM OF MINISTRY

In modern ecumenical dialogue agreeing to a doctrine and practice of ministry has proved again and again to be the point on which talks break down. There were problems in the first centuries in the form of clashes between those who put the emphasis on the direct calling of the Holy Spirit (the "charismatics") and those who said the church must also approve and commission those who believed they had heard God's call and were chosen to minister to the people. Those who thought this way held that it was not safe to rely on un-

---

[2]Again, the "West" meant something different from its modern sense. It referred to the part of Europe where the descendants of the Latin-speakers of the Roman Empire lived, in contrast to the part where the heirs of the Greek-speakers lived.

authenticated claims and that institutional approval provided some
security. Lunatics could believe they were God's chosen, and they
could sometimes win a following with their preaching of strange
ideas. So from an early stage in the evolution of the doctrine of ministry it came to be accepted that there should be three elements in
the making of a minister: God's personal calling of the individual
(vocation), the calling or welcome by the congregation where he was
to serve, and the action of the church in ensuring that he understood
and held the one faith, then authorizing him, by ordination, to carry
out the duties of a minister.

The balance among these shifted during the medieval period toward
an emphasis on the part played by the church, specifically ordination,
which came to be included among its sacramental powers; this was a
power reserved to the bishops as leaders of the church. Ordination was
held to confer a *character*, a permanent stamp, which made a man a
bishop—the same thing applied to a priest—until he died. Only bishops could ordain deacons or priests or participate in the ordaining of a
new bishop, which formally required three bishops.

With the emergence in the later Middle Ages of a more elaborate
doctrine of the sacraments as various channels for a process conferring
grace from God, the idea that an ordained priest or bishop had personal
powers seemed to strengthen too. One effect of the development of a
doctrine of ministry in which sacramental ordination and sacramental
functions were prominent was to heighten the idea of the minister not
as shepherd (*pastor*) but as priest (*sacerdos* rather than *presbyter*), exercis-
ing a ministry whose distinctive feature came to be seen as the power to
sacrifice Christ at the celebration of the Eucharist. It began to be accepted that only priests could grant absolution to the penitent sinner
and validly celebrate the Eucharist.

This emphasis made the validity of ordination hugely important, for
only a properly ordained priest could, it was believed from the late eleventh century, make bread and wine truly the body and blood of Christ.[3]
Any perceived glitch in the process of handing on the commission

---

[3]On the development of this doctrine, known as "transubstantiation," see pp. 86-90.

granted to the apostles to their successors down the ages could form an unbridgeable gap, cutting off one community from another in a schism. This is what happened in the case of the Donatists, a sect which caused Augustine much trouble while he was a bishop in North Africa.[4] The same idea presented many difficulties in mending division in the Reformation period as doctrines of ministry developed and ecclesial communities fragmented. The orders of Anglican priests and bishops are still today officially regarded as null and void by the Roman Catholic Church.

These medieval developments took control of their spiritual lives away from ordinary members of the faithful, or, at any rate, so many began to claim. They were encouraged to see themselves as passive recipients of what the church did to them through the sacraments, able to act for themselves only by way of repenting their sins, confessing to a priest and accepting and carrying out the penances or penalties he imposed. The pastoral side of a priest's ministry thus became entangled with the church's power and its control of the lives of the laity. And the people most often could not read the Latin Bible or engage in theologizing for themselves. That too was for priests and bishops alone. These were trends still apparent in the early sixteenth century, which the Reformers became insistent on reversing.

Anticlericalism became a consistent driving force among Reformers from at least the twelfth century. People could of course see for themselves that not all priests and bishops were exemplary. Movements of resistance arose, complaining about corruption and excess among the clergy. Wyclif challenged the settled idea, accepted in the early church, that ministerial functions were not thwarted by the unworthiness of the minister because this did not nullify God's gracious actions. He claimed that certain behaviors could make the ministry of the sacraments of no effect. These ideas persisted and recurred in the Lollard movement and among the Hussites in the fifteenth century, and it took little time for connections to be made when the Reformation of the sixteen century began, so as to integrate these older resentments into the new debates.

---

[4]On the Donatists, see William Frend, *The Donatist Church* (Oxford: Clarendon Press, 1971); see also pp. 59-60.

Luther was particularly strong on the subject of papal excesses. For example, the Thirty-Nine Articles of the Church of England eventually settled on the Augustinian statement that "in the visible Church the evil be ever mingled with the good," but with the proviso that even where "the evil have chief authority in the Ministration of the Word and Sacraments, forasmuch as they do not the same in their own name, but in Christ's, and do minister by his commission and authority, we may use their Ministry, both in hearing the Word of God, and in the receiving of the Sacraments," the faithful may be confident that sacraments thus administered "be effectual, because of Christ's institution and promise, although they be ministered by evil men."

The Lutherans did not want to insist—at least not all Lutherans everywhere—on the abolition of the episcopate or a comprehensive replacement of the traditional relationship of local churches with their dioceses. It was Calvin's followers who tended to concentrate their indignation on episcopacy, crying that bishops were instruments of the Catholic Church's conspicuous wealth and corruption, and that by their life and doctrine they were claiming powers inappropriate in a Christian ministry of service. The Reformed called for a presbyterian or presbyteral ministry, arguing that the New Testament gives no warrant for two separate orders. They claimed that *episkopos* and *presbyteros* were merely alternative terms for the leaders of the early Christian communities.

Other Reformers, including those who said that the only visible church was the local gathered congregation, went further still. The Congregationalists believed that ministry in the church depended solely on the calling of the Holy Spirit and acceptance by the congregation of which the minister was to be pastor. No hierarchical process of ordination was needed. At the far extreme were some Anabaptists and other groups who would have no truck with ministry in their communities at all.

These basic positions have consistently thrown up differences so irreconcilable that ecumenical experiments have failed ever since. But other shifts have also proved problematic. The idea that a pastor was better than a priest because there would be no claims to power from pastors proved illusory. Pastors could—and still can—become hero figures to their congregations, leaders of opinion, respected to the point of adoration.

Membership of the church and the hope of heaven. Since the time of Augustine a great dilemma had remained unresolved. Augustine believed that there is "no salvation outside the church" (*nulla salus extra ecclesiam*),[5] but he also believed, and increasingly strongly the longer he lived, that only God knows whom he has chosen. His *City of God* has a good deal to say about this problem. Something of the duality of Augustine's position lingered in medieval twofold use of the imagery of the bride of Christ either as the soul or as the church. Christ was portrayed as joining himself as bridegroom to the community of the visible church and to the individual person.

> FOR FURTHER READING
> On these topics see "The English Reformation Turns Reformed" (chap. 19).

During the Middle Ages in the West, it had come to be accepted that individual membership of the visible church began when an infant was baptized, and every infant was baptized except those born into the relatively small communities of Jews and in some parts of Europe, Muslims. Yet the visible church was not a pure community of the saved. It was recognized that not all these members by any means would find their way to heaven.

Lutheran and Reformed churches accepted this distinction, although cast somewhat differently in the light of the doctrine of justification by faith alone. Calvin presented a challenge of a differ-

> FOR FURTHER READING
> On these topics see "The Doctrine of Baptism Emerges" and "Insiders and Outsiders: Cyprian and the Rigorist Approach to the Problem of Apostasy" (chap. 5), "The Conversion of Martin Luther and Its Consequences" (chap. 16), "John Calvin" (chap. 19).

ent sort when he also appealed to a strong Augustinian doctrine of double predestination. These two rationales have their implications for the idea of membership of the church as well as for the individual's hope of a place among God's people in the world to come.

---

[5]Cyprian probably originated this phrase. It is found in "Letter 73," in *Ad Jubajanum de haereticis baptizandis*, ed. G. F. Diercks, CCSL 3.C (Turnhout: Brepols, 1996), p. 529ff.

How Many Sacraments?

The great Lutheran cry "faith alone" pushed the sacraments into a role in the Christian life that, while still significant, was always subordinate to the word. The Reformed generally shifted this focus still further, although not nearly as far as many Anabaptists who sought to do away with the idea of ordained means of grace altogether.

A substantial area of sixteenth-century debate was concerned with the number of sacraments there are: two (the ones Jesus instituted) or seven (the number recognized in the West at the end of the Middle Ages)? The Protestant Reformers held to the two instituted by Christ himself: baptism, confirmed through his own baptism by John the Baptist and commanded in the Great Commission; and the Eucharist, enjoined by the celebration of the Last Supper with his disciples.

FOR FURTHER READING
On these topics see chapter 7.

Article 25 of the Church of England's Thirty-Nine Articles neatly summarizes the distinction and the Reformers' reasons for their objection:

> Those five, commonly called Sacraments, that is to say, Confirmation, Penance, Orders, Matrimony, and Extreme Unction, are not to be counted for Sacraments of the Gospel, being such as have grown, partly of the corrupt following of the Apostles, partly from states of life allowed in the Scriptures; but yet have not like nature of sacraments with Baptism and the LORD'S Supper, for that they have not any visible sign or ceremony ordained of GOD.

The insistence that only those initiated by Jesus are truly sacraments continued to be important in the sixteenth century.

Baptism. In the early church the doctrine of baptism grew very important. Baptism, it came to be believed, purged the sinner of the guilt of the inherited original sin that afflicts all humanity since the fall of Adam; it also took away the reparation due to a just God for all the particular sins each person had committed up to that moment. This was not the end of sinning of course, but in the first Christian centuries the emphasis of concern about sins committed after baptism was on the serious sins of apostasy, murder and adultery. These were sins likely to be visible to the rest of the community and to set a bad example to others.

It was agreed that baptism could not simply be repeated. That would allow Christians to put their hands to the plough and then turn back (Lk 9:62). The church saw a series of fierce disputes about the very possibility of restoring the lapsed and other serious sinners to the community of the faithful, between the rigorists and others.

Infant baptism was a point of controversy for some. In the earliest years, Christians were converts who had heard the good news and believed. We have no sure record, however, of what the standard practice in apostolic times was for handling the spiritual welfare of these converts' children. Some argued against the practice of infant baptism; most seem to have assumed it. Some also argued against the misguided practice of waiting until the last possible moment to be baptized (for safety's sake, so that there was less risk of sinning gravely again).

By the end of the fourth century, it became official practice to baptize infants as soon as possible after they were born in order to spare the many who died in infancy the otherwise inevitable eternity shut out of heaven. Once the doctrine of baptism's efficacy for salvation developed to a certain point, this made good sense, especially in a period of high infant mortality. It affected the requirements of baptism, however. The validity of baptism in separated or heretical communities had been the subject of debate, and it had been agreed that provided the baptism was carried out in the name of the Trinity and with water, it was both valid and efficacious. But clearly the expectation that those coming to be baptized would spend a period as catechumens learning about the faith and then profess their faith before the community at their baptism could not be a requirement in the baptism of infants. This difficulty was adressed by allowing the parents and godparents to affirm the faith on the child's behalf and undertake to bring it up to know the faith for itself.

A different balance of concerns was in evidence in the sixteenth century. Some Reformers rejected the uneasy compromise about infant baptism and insisted that only adult believers could be baptized. Some claimed that infant baptism was not baptism at all and required baptism to be undergone again ("anabaptism") by adults. Many Anabaptists insisted that baptism must involve total immersion in water as a token of dying to the old life and being reborn in Christ. Some radicals claimed baptism was unnecessary or that it did not affect a Christian's chances of salvation. Most Reformers sought to strengthen the assumption that children would be taught the faith through catechism, and be brought to a bishop or the elders to be confirmed when they could affirm their faith for themselves.

FOR FURTHER READING
On the topics see "The Doctrine of Baptism Emerges" and "Insiders and Outsiders: Cyprian and the Rigorist Approach to the Problem of Apostasy" (chap. 5).

The legacy of the ideal of purity. A doctrine of the importance of purity in the community remained of paramount importance in certain communities, which often became sects, those who regarded themselves as the remnant of the true church, the sole remaining few true believers. Such sects took it to be their duty to purge themselves of any members who appeared to be "leaven," so that the sect could remain pure unleavened bread of "sincerity and truth" (1 Cor 5:8). Others were somewhat gentler, such as the Mennonites and the Amish (see "Quakers and Amish" [chap. 20]), though equally determined to keep to themselves and to preserve simplicity of life and strict scriptural standards.

FOR FURTHER READING
On these topics see "Insiders and Outsiders: Cyprian and the Rigorist Approach to the Problem of Apostasy" (chap. 5), "Guibert of Nogent: Monk and Social Commentator" (chap. 10), "Exemplary Individuals and Being an Example to Others" (chap. 13), "John Calvin" and "Puritans Leave for the New World" (chap. 19).

The penitential process. At the outset of his protest movement, Luther's indignation was strongest in the area of penitential requirements and the apparatus which had grown up around indulgences. It was here that it seemed to him the church had gone much too far. His own personal experience of the "'terrified conscience" was perhaps the greatest prompter, with its huge burden of living with the consciousness of one's sinfulness and the certainty of a God who will give us what we deserve.

There was widespread rejection by the Reformers of the swollen and onerous penitential system and of the system of indulgences which had increasingly become associated with it from the late eleventh century.[6] To the eyes of sixteenth-century Reformers, the penitential manuals, which had been created to enable priests to calibrate the penances to be imposed for each type of sin, were highly undesirable because they exacerbated the problem of religious performance,

> FOR FURTHER READING
> On these topics see chapter 6.

and promoted an intense anxiety to ensure that one had done all that was necessary to make up for one's sins.

Yet the changes the Reformers proposed did not seek to diminish belief in God's just judgment upon sin. Luther took that very seriously. But the Reformers sought to place the remedy elsewhere by reminding believers that when Christ died on the cross he had done everything that needed to be done. His sacrifice was more than enough for all the sins of humanity, so that God's love and forgiveness for his sake are as just as his judgment.

The Eucharist and Christ's sacrifice on the cross. The doctrine of the Eucharist that developed in the medieval West led to a great deal of conflict in succeeding centuries. This doctrine—known as transubstantiation from the twelfth century—articulated the belief that when an officiating priest said Jesus' words of consecration, "This is my body" and "This is my blood," the bread and wine literally became, in substance though not in appearance, his body and his blood.

The one sacrifice on the cross thus easily became merged in this theology with the daily offering of Christ's body and blood in the Eucharist. So a key reforming theme was the insistence that Christ's sacrifice on the cross was sufficient for salvation, and no repetitions or additions were needed (or possible). Martin Bucer in his *Commonplaces* expressly denies the doctrine of transubstantiation's claim that the bread and wine became at consecration the actual body and blood of Christ. In our "participation in the body of Christ which was given for us," "bread and wine ... remain unaltered in their nature and substance."[7]

---

[6]A. C. Piepkorn, *Profiles in Belief: The Religious Bodies of the United States of America*, 3 vols. (New York: HarperCollins, 1977-1979).

[7]Martin Bucer, *A Brief Summary of Christian Doctrine* (*Commonplaces*), trans. D. F. Wright (Abingdon, U.K.: Sutton Press, 1972), p. 87.

"Masses" eventually began to be celebrated by priests alone, without any congregation present, paid for by the pious who wanted to add to the hopes of heaven for themselves or their dead relatives by making sacrifices for them in this way. Reformers protested again that this had led to a general belief that the Eucharist was a repeating of, or addition to, Christ's sacrifice on the cross. That diminished the sacrifice. It made it look as though it had not been sufficient.

The same doctrine involved a view of the saints that the Reformers also quarreled with. Saints, it had come to be held, had spare holiness. The pious could purchase some of it through praying at the holy shrines of saints, or honoring their relics, bones and objects, which were holy things. Invoking the saints in this way was seen as something akin to borrowing from their surplus sanctity to add to the level of one's own.

Reformers changed the emphasis drastically, from the holiness of saints to the holiness of Christ. Luther and Calvin taught the "real presence" of Christ in the Eucharist, feeding his people on himself, but not as a substantial change in the consecrated bread and wine. Other reforming themes included the shift to the idea of a community celebration, outlawing the saying of private Masses.

Reformers sought to return to an emphasis on thanksgiving (the meaning of the word *eucharist*) and the community (nonprivate) character of the celebration. So Martin Bucer said in his *Commonplaces* that the Holy Supper is a "remembrance . . . held in an assembly of the people, and its ministers and participants be such that noone can fail to recognise them by their fruits as other than true Christians." It is, he insists, not a sacrifice but serves "to strengthen faith and life in Christ."[8]

FOR FURTHER READING
On these topics see "Eucharist" (chap. 7).

THE UNITY OF THE CHURCH AND ITS RELATION TO SOCIETY

The concerns of the early church were chiefly about the way to ensure that the faith remained one and disagreements could be resolved with-

[8]Ibid., pp. 86-87.

out fragmentation of the church's unity. Acts 15 describes the first experiments. The initial solution relied on holding councils, but in succeeding centuries there arose a counter-ploy of power claims by metropolitan bishops. These were the bishops of leading sees, often the churches of metropolitan cities. The ancient patriarchates of Alexandria, Antioch, Constantinople, Jerusalem and Rome divided geographically into four Eastern areas, where the liturgy was in Greek, and one Western patriarchate, held by the bishop of Rome. The struggle to establish whether there should be a universal primacy of authority and if so, to whom it should go, took much political effort from the sixth century until the schism of 1054 decisively divided Greek East and Latin West, and the pope as bishop of Rome was left in sole supremacy in the West. Important ecclesial decisions were ultimately arbitrated by the pope, sometimes relying on a council to bolster his authority, as in the case of the Fourth Lateran Council of 1215.

The Reformers of the sixteenth century were more or less at one in their rejection of papal authority, and with it the authority of the institutional church of which he was head. That structure, which had become predominantly monarchical by the end of the Middle Ages, had the advantage of ensuring a high degree of institutional unity. It made it possible for decisions to be taken and to be treated as binding on the faithful.

The fifteenth century saw a conciliarist attempt to wrest power back into the hands of the bishops of the West, making the government of the church collegial instead of monarchical. In the bull *Execrabilis* (1460), Pope Pius II (1405-1464) claimed that there can be no right of appeal from a pope to a council.[9] By the beginning of the sixteenth century it looked as though the Conciliarist movement was going to be defeated. Papal claims to plenitude of power did not, however, cease to cause offense, and it was not going to be long before the call to put council above pope would arise again, from new quarters.

The Fifth Lateran Council ended only in 1517, and it concerned itself with the need for reforms, though mainly on points of clergy discipline.

---

[9]From "Execrabilis," in *A Source Book for Mediaeval History*, trans. O. J. Thatcher and E. H. McNeal (New York: Charles Scribner's, 1905), p. 332.

It was not thinking the sort of thoughts about reform that were occurring to Luther. It also had a good deal to say about preaching. "Preaching is of the first importance, very necessary and of great effect and
utility in the church, so long as it is being exercised rightly, from genuine
charity towards God and our neighbour." But some present-day clergy
are not imitating Christ the teacher; they are merely showing off. People, especially the uneducated, are attracted to these performances and
are easily misled by the private interpretation of these preachers who are
given to "twisting the sense of scripture in many places, often giving it
rash and false interpretations, they preach what is false." The council's
solution was to decree that no one should preach without being examined by a superior and duly licensed, and that what is taught should be
in accordance with agreed orthodoxy. Certain topics are to be avoided,
the coming of antichrist and criticism of the clergy, and preachers are
not to claim to be directly inspired by the Holy Spirit.[10] There are strong
hints here of stirrings with a Reformation flavor. So the bid to restore
the older conciliar method of decision-making in the fifteenth century
had been unsuccessful, though many of the Reformers still had hopes of
mending breaches in a general Council.

On the face of it, the Reformers' claim that there was no intrinsic
need for official institutional decision-making, that the community of
the faithful could rely on 'Scripture alone," ought to have lightened the
pressure. But private reading of Scripture bred variety of opinion; and
the formation of groups of believers, who often re-formed in order to
distinguish themselves on some point from others within the original
groups, lent an air of fissiparousness to the decision-making of Protestant communities. The church became the churches.

Some communities tried to resolve the problem of divergence in doctrine and practice by creating lists of "commonplaces," axiomatic statements representing the official position of their churches on the most
important biblical matters. The Lutherans did this in the Augsburg
Confession and its successors, and the Church of England in the series

[10]"Fifth Lateran Council," *IntraText*, www.intratext.com/ixt/ENG0067. See also Norman P. Tanner, *Decrees of the Ecumenical Councils* (Washington, D.C.: Georgetown University Press, 1990),
p. 605ff.

of articles which culminated in the Thirty-Nine Articles. The Reformed communites throughout Europe composed a host of confessional statements. Although all of these show strong family resemblances, they had the effect of consolidating difference rather than restoring unity.

Such a set of settled convictions could be treated among a particular confessional group as a requirement for Christian identity. Only those who would formally accept them might be allowed membership. There could be political and social consequences too. In England

> FOR FURTHER READING
> On these topics see "Local Churches and the Universal Church" (chap. 2), "Councils and Other Ways of Making Decisions" and "The Fifteenth-Century Bid for Conciliarism Instead of Primatial Government of the Church" (chap. 8).

until the Universities Tests Act of 1871, subscription to the Thirty-Nine Articles was required of every would-be student at Oxford or Cambridge. Established institutions of higher education were closed to everyone who was not a practicing member of the Church of England.

The church and the state. From the earliest centuries the powerful in the state proved reluctant to allow Christian believers freedom of worship. The Roman Empire adopted a syncretistic approach to the multifaith environment that had been created as it expanded across Europe and into Africa and Asia. Most of the peoples in the conquered territories were polytheistic, or even if they had loyalties to a particular god or gods they did not insist that these were the only deities. Local or household deities were often the objects of special affection. It was also comparatively easy in such a religious climate for people to accept the convention that notable persons and emperors would often be installed in the pantheon of gods upon their death and should be venerated (worshiped) by the people.

But Jews and Christians were different. (Islam had not yet been founded.) These were monotheist religions, and their adherents refused to worship any but the one true God of Israel. This constituted a political challenge, and repeatedly in the early centuries Christians were persecuted and those who refused to apostatize were martyred. Even when, at the beginning of the third century, Constantine became the first emperor to call himself a Christian, there were many details to be worked out about what was the church's business and what it belonged to the state to administer.

This became a major preoccupation during the medieval centuries from the Investiture Contest of the late eleventh century until the sixteenth century, when Reformation leaders were faced with a fresh challenge. During the Middle Ages *church* was monolithic though *state* could mean any of a number of politically distinct secular entities: empire, kingdom, Italian city-state. With the sixteenth century and the growing numbers in different parts of Europe who declared themselves Lutherans or Reformed, church ceased to be a single jurisdictional and political entity. Many of the new religious communities presented an essentially local phenomenon. The disputes and battles that followed encouraged secular leaders to take a position in relation to their local Reformers. The Lutherans were willing to accept a Christian magistrate as the secular local head of a Lutheran community instead of the spiritual hegemony of the papacy. That reopened some of the questions provisionally settled in the twelfth century when the Concordat of Worms of 1122 decided to allocate the temporalities to the secular authorities and the spiritualities to the ecclesiastical. Perhaps the most significant idea to emerge from all this was the principle articulated by Erastus, that the realm adopts the religion of the ruler.

FOR FURTHER READING
On these topics see chapters 9 and 21.

Monastic life, monastic education and awakening social concerns. Reformation resentments of the religious orders were prompted by some of the same perceptions as anticlericalism. To skeptical eyes, monks, nuns and friars could appear wealthy, lax, self-indulgent. There was particular dislike of the mendicant orders, especially the Dominican and Franciscan friars, with their confessors at court, enjoying influence and the ear of the powerful.

In the parts of Europe where Protestant opinion was gaining ground, local nobles sometimes disbanded and plundered monasteries. In England the wealth of the monasteries was a strong temptation to Henry VIII. Thomas Cromwell sent around Visitors who found evidence of corrupt practices, vice and excesses of various kinds.

FOR FURTHER READING
On these topics see chapter 10.

Between 1536 and 1541 a series of legislative acts made it possible for monasteries to be dissolved and their assets seized to the royal coffers.

The beginning of academic theology and the invention of universities.
Universities were a creation of twelfth- and thirteenth-century Europe.
They came formally into being as self-governing communities of scholars, with some of the twelfth-century schools whose masters were peripatetic and often in competition with one another developing an institutional stability as corporations (*universitates*). So valuable were they as
training grounds for the royal and papal civil services, and for potential
candidates for the episcopacy, that the papacy and the local secular authorities took a lively interest in them from the beginning, and their
subsequent history is marked by episodes of conflict in which the academics fought to defend their independence. Individual academic freedom seems less important at that time than institutional autonomy.

The most able minds were stretched in medieval universities. Standards were high. The teaching was demanding and the courses lengthy.
The Reformers of the sixteenth century depended on the universities to
maintain standards of scholarship and to provide a forum for debate or
disputation. The arrival of academic study of the biblical languages of
Greek and Hebrew was found to require such support, and a series of
trilingual institutions of which the first, the Complutensian University
in Madrid, appeared in 1499.

In Germany in particular a number of universities founded late in the
Middle Ages were disposed to try novel syllabuses and new approaches.
Heidelberg was founded 1386, Freiberg in 1457, Tübingen in 1477, and the
University of Wittenberg, where Luther and Melanchthon taught, in
1502. Marburg (founded as a Protestant university from the outset) began
in 1527. Switzerland had a university at Basel from 1460.

With the Reformation many of the most ancient European universities, those in France and Italy, found themselves in territories which
remained predominantly Roman Catholic. In England, Oxford and
Cambridge had their painful battles with state authority as England
swung from Roman Catholic to Protestant under Henry VIII and Edward VI, back to Rome under Mary Tudor, to settle down with a Prot-
estant-established Church of England under Elizabeth I. Scotland's late
medieval universities were to be challenged to some extent by Scottish
Calvinism under the inspiration of John Knox.

But perhaps the most striking Reformation development was the emergence of the secular scholar. Throughout the Middle Ages clerks were essentially also clerics. But now individuals with interests in the new theology and in a range of related studies formed groups of correspondents or met socially for discussion, rather in the spirit of the Romans in Cicero's time.

LAY MOVEMENTS

Popular preaching. Popular preaching became a problem for the secular and ecclesiastical authorities in the later Middle Ages. The old assumption had been that preaching required an episcopal license, and that was the best way to ensure that preachers were orthodox and under the control of the church. Preaching in local parishes was allowed only by invitation of the local priest.

FOR FURTHER READING
Links: On these topics see chapters 5, 11 and 15, "Melanchthon, Moderation and Building a Bridge Between the Academic and the Popular" (chap. 16) and "Science and the Bible from a Roman Catholic Perspective" (chap. 20).

From the late twelfth century, unlicensed popular preachers had begun to appear, with the rise of dissident movements such as the Waldensians. Some of the experimental preaching groups—the mendicant orders of the Franciscan and Dominican preachers—won papal approval to preach outside this structure and both orders developed a rigorous training regimen for their preachers.

The Franciscans in particular became skilled in winning popular interest. Preaching became a popular entertainment as well as a vehicle of spiritual instruction. Popular preachers offering sermons in the vernacular began to spring up in the later Middle Ages. Some of these were political demagogues, some preaching on spiritual matters but in unorthodox terms. People might not find it easy to tell the difference, and the secular authorities became worried.

FOR FURTHER READING
On these topics see chapters 12 and 14.

From the point of view of the sixteenth-century Reformers, two things were especially important. One was that their sympathizers should have freedom to preach and evangelize. The other was to maintain the link between preaching and the ministry of the Word, so that preachers could expound Scripture to the people in their own language.

Theological education for the laity. The mainstream medieval church had implicitly placed the laity in a category of inferior membership of the church. Some theologians seem to have held that only the clergy were fully members.[11] Anticlericalist movements naturally wished to challenge such ideas, and as the articulate middle classes expanded in the later Middle Ages the demand from the laity to have a say grew louder.

Some bishops responded by seeking to improve the religious education of the laity (see pp. 201-5). But the culture of the times meant that there were pervasive features of popular life and assumptions in the minds of ordinary people which made them both deeply religious and superstitious. This was not at all a new phenomenon. The leaders of the early church had battled constantly against the persistence of superstitious practices, the clinging to the old gods for safety's sake or the substitution of saints for these comfortingly familiar and local deities. Augustine records how his Christian mother Monica used to sacrifice at such shrines with no real sense of its inappropriateness.[12]

In the later Middle Ages, popular religion had some of this character of a debased Christianity. The cult of saints still met many of the needs it had met for Monica, and the church seemed to encourage it. There was an income to be gained from pilgrims by the owners of shrines. The Reformers were determined to root out accretions and irrelevancies and all the panoply of practices which could get in the way of a believer looking to Christ alone for forgiveness and redemption.

> FOR FURTHER READING
> On these topics see chapter 13.

REBELS, DISSIDENTS AND REPRESSION

The Reformers were initially not primarily concerned about the problem of dealing with dissidents. They *were* the dissidents. Awareness of

---

[11]G. R. Evans, *The Church and the Churches* (Cambridge: Cambridge University Press, 1994).
[12]Augustine, *Confessions* 6.2.2, ed. James J. O'Donnell (Oxford: Clarendon Press, 1992), pp. 58-59.

the dangers of the local presence of activists with different views was to grow as a result of challenge to their own orthodoxies from extremists, sometimes involving violence. Among the extremists, exclusivist positions were common, with all relations with outsiders shunned. The dissident community could set itself up as the only true church or the remnant and prove as inflexible and repressive as the official church had ever been.

Nor were they necessarily actively aware of the teachings which had caused official concern in the fourteenth and fifteenth centuries. These were histories yet to be written, except where they had entered the church's own record, for example in the proceedings of the Council of

FOR FURTHER READING
On these topics see chapters 14 and 18.

Constance. It seems likely that though Luther was aware of the ideas of John Hus, for example, he knew little or nothing of Wyclif and the Lollards.

In the lands where it took root, the Reformation domesticated dissent and made it normal. The Lutherans, with the cooperation of some of the local electors in Germany, designed a solution to the problem of bringing the secular authorities to accept Protestants as the new orthodoxy. The Christian magistrate was identified as the appropriate officer to head a church in all but sacramental matters. After the to-ing and fro-ing of the Tudor monarchs, England settled to a similar arrangement in which the monarch was the head of the church, a church established by secular law and having its ecclesiastical legislation ratified by Parliament. For Calvin it was acceptable for the secular law to punish Christians for certain spiritual offenses, thus partly—and controversially—conflating sin and crime.

It was not until the nineteenth century that the tide of divergence began to be stemmed by the suggestion that concerted efforts should be made to reunite the Churches. The Anglican Lambeth Conferences began in the mid-nineteenth century in an endeavor to keep the Anglican communion together, but the early conferences included an ecumenical effort to bring together the divided Protestant communions. One of the fruits was the World Council of Churches, founded in the wake of the world missionary conference held in Edinburgh in 1910. The Orthodox joined in too, though cautiously, with the Constantinople encyclical of 1920 which proposed a fellowship of churches. Only with the twentieth century and the groundbreaking Second Vatican Council (1962-1965) did the Roman Catholic Church begin to enter seriously into ecumenical dialogue. The bilateral and multilateral dialogues of the second half of the twentieth century seemed promising, but foundered on the old problem of ministry—and the world waits still for that to be resolved.

SELECT BIBLIOGRAPHY

PRIMARY SOURCES

Abelard, Peter. *Collationes*. Edited and translated by John Marenbon and Giovanni Orlandi. Oxford: Oxford University Press, 2001.

———. *Dialogue of a Philosopher with a Jew and a Christian*. Translated by Pierre J. Payer. Toronto: Pontifical Institute of Mediaeval Studies, 1979.

———. *Ethics (Scito te ipsum)*. Edited by David Luscombe. Oxford: Clarendon Press, 1971.

———. *Historia Calamitatum*. Edited by J. Monfrin. Paris: Vrin, 1967.

———. *Sic et Non*. Patrologia Latina 178.1339. Edited by B. Bouer and R. McKeon. London: University of Chicago Press, 1976-1977.

Aelred of Riveaulx. *De institutione inclusarum*. EETS. Edited by John Ayto and Alexandra Barratt. Oxford: Oxford University Press, 1984.

Alighieri, Dante. *Purgatory*. Translated by Mark Musa. Bloomington: Indiana University Press, 1981.

Ancrene Wisse. *The English Text of the Ancrene Riwle: The "Vernon Text."* Edited by Arne Zettersten and Bernhard Diensberg. EETS 310. London: Oxford University Press, 2000.

Augustine. *Confessions*. Edited by James J. O'Donnell. Oxford: Oxford University Press, 1992.

———. *De doctrina Christiana*. Edited and translated by R. P. H. Green. Oxford: Oxford University Press, 1995.

———. *Homilies on the Psalms*. CCEL. www.ccel.org/ccel/schaff/npnf108.ii.i.html.

Bacon, Francis. "An Advertisement Touching the Controversies of the Church of England." In *An Introductory Sketch to the Martin Marprelate Controversy*. Edited by Edward Arber. London, 1880.

Baxter, Richard. *The Arrogancy of Reason Against Divine Revelations.* London: T. N. for Tho. Underhil, 1655.

Bede. *Ecclesiastical History* 3.25. Edited by B. Colgrave and R. A. B. Mynors. London: Oxford University Press, 1969.

Bernard of Clairvaux. *Opera Omnia.* Edited by J. Leclercq, H. Rochais and C. H. Talbot. 8 vols. Rome: Editiones Cisterciensis, 1957-1974.

The Book of Common Prayer (1559). Edited by John E. Booty. Charlottesville: University Press of Virginia, 1976.

The Book of Concord: The Confessions of the Evangelical Lutheran Church. Edited by Theodore G. Tappert. Philadelphia: Fortress, 1959. http://bookof concord.org/treatise.php.

Bossuet, Jacques-Bénigne. "Introduction." In *Politics Drawn from the Very Words of Holy Scripture.* Translated and edited by Patrick Riley. *Cambridge Texts in the History of Political Thought.* Cambridge: Cambridge University Press, 1990.

Boswell, James. *Life of Johnson: An Edition of the Original Manuscript.* Edited by Marshall Waingrow. Edinburgh: University of Edinburgh Press, 1994.

Boyle, Robert. *The Style of the Scriptures, Works.* Edited by Michael Hunter and Edward B. Davis. London: Pickering & Chatto, 1990.

Brooks, Douglas A. "This Heavenly Boke, More Precious than Golde: Legitimating Print in Early Tudor England." In *Tudor Books and Readers.* Edited by John N. King. Cambridge: Cambridge University Press, 2010

Bucer, Martin. *A Brief Summary of Christian Doctrine (Commonplaces).* Translated by D. F. Wright. Abingdon, U.K.: Sutton Press, 1972.

Bunyan, John. *Grace Abounding and Other Spiritual Autobiographies.* Edited by John Stachniewski and Anita Pacheco. Oxford: Oxford University Press, 1998.

Burton, Thomas. *Diary of Thomas Burton.* Edited by John Towill Rutt. History of Parliament Trust, 1828. www.british-history.ac.uk/report.aspx?compid= 36742.

Caesarius of Heisterbach. *Dialogue on Miracles.* Translated by C. C. Swinton Bland. London: G. Routledge, 1929.

Calvin, John. *Concerning the Eternal Predestination of God.* Translated by J. K. S. Reid. London: James Clarke, 1961.

———. *Institutes of the Christian Religion.* Edited by John T. McNeill. Translated by Ford Lewis Battles. 2 vols. Philadelphia: Westminster, 1960.

Canons and Decrees of the Council of Trent. Translated by J. Waterworth. London: Burns & Oates, 1888.

Carruthers, S. W. *The Westminster Assembly: What It Was and What It Did.* Manchester: Manchester University Press, 1943.

Chemnitz, Martin. *Examination of the Council of Trent.* Translated by Fred Kramer. St. Louis: Concordia Publishing, 1971.

Collinson, Patrick. *Conferences and Combination Lectures in the Elizabethan Church: Dedham and Bury St. Edmunds, 1582-90.* Edited by Patrick Collinson, John Craig and Brett Usher. Church of England Record Society 10 (2003).

Corso, Giovani. *Life of Ficino.* 1506.

de Lubac, Henri. *Exégèse médiévale.* 2 vols. Paris: Aubier-Montaigne, 1959-1964.

de Nebrija, Elio Antonio. *Apologia.* 1516.

De Sanchez Caro. Edited by J. M. Herrera García. Avila-Salamanca: University of Salamanca, 2008.

De Vitry, Jacques. *The Historia Occidentalis of Jacques de Vitry: A Critical Edition.* Spicilegium Friburgense 17. Edited by J. F. Hinnebusch. Fribourg: University Press, 1972.

Donne, John. *The Sermons of John Donne.* Edited by G. R. Potter and Evelyn M. Simpson. 10 vols. Berkeley: University of California Press, 1953-.

Dryden, John. *The Life of St. Francis Xavier* (1688). In *The Works of John Dryden.* Edited by Alan Roper and H. T. Swedenberg. Berkeley: University of California Press, 1979.

Engen, John H. Van, ed. *Devotio Moderna: Basic Writings.* Classics of Western Spirituality. Mahwah, N.J.: Paulist Press, 1988.

Erasmus. *Antibarbarorum liber.* Edited by K. Kumaniecki. *Erasmi Opera Omnia* 1-1. Amsterdam: North Holland Publishing, 1969.

———. *De pueris statim ac liberaliter instituendis.* Edited by J. Margolin. *Erasmi Opera Omnia* 1-2. Amsterdam: North Holland Publishing, 1971.

———. *Paraphrasis seu potius epitome in Elegantiarum libros Laurentii Vallae.* Edited by C. L. Heesakkers and J. H. Waszink. *Erasmi Opera Omnia* 1-4. Amsterdam: North Holland Publishing, 1973.

Fox, George. *The Journal of George Fox.* Edited by Thomas Ellwood. 1800. Reprint, New York: Cambridge University Press, 1952.

Francis of Assisi. *The Writings of St. Francis of Assisi.* Translated by Paschal Robinson. Philadelphia: Dolphin, 1906.

Fulbert of Chartres. *The Letters and Poems.* Edited and translated by Frederick Behrends. Oxford: Clarendon Press, 1976.

Galilei, Galileo. *The Galileo Affair: A Documentary History.* Edited and translated by Maurice A. Finocchiaro. Berkeley: University of California Press, 1989.

Gilbert of Poitiers. *Commentaries on Boethius*. Edited by N. M. Häring. Toronto: Pontifical Institute of Mediaeval Studies, 1969.

Gregory the Great. *Moralia in Job*. Edited by M. Adraien. CCSL 143, 143A, 143B. www.lectionarycentral.com/GregoryMoraliaIndex.html.

Guibert of Nogent. *De Vita Sua*. Edited by G. Bourgin. Paris: Picard, 1907.

Higden, Ralph. *Polychronicon*. Rolls Series. Edited by J. B. Lumby. 1886.

Hillebrand, Hans J., ed. *The Reformation in Its Own Words*. London: SCM Press, 1964.

Hooper, John. *Later Writings*. Cambridge: Parker Society, 1852.

Hugh of St. Victor. *De Sacramentis Ecclesiae*. PL 176.

———. *Didascalicon*. Edited by Charles Henry Buttimer. Washington, D.C.: Catholic University Press, 1939.

Hugonis de Sancto Victore Didascalicon de Studio Legendi: A Critical Text. Studies in Medieval and Renaissance Latin 10. Washington: Catholic University Press, 1939.

Ignatius Loyola. *The Spiritual Exercises of St. Ignatius of Loyola*. Translated by Elder Mullen. New York: P. J. Kennedy, 1914.

Isidore of Seville. *El "De viris illustribus" de Isidoro de Sevilla*. Edited by Carmen Codoñer Merino. Salamanca: Colegio Trilingüe de la Universidad, 1964.

———. *Etymologiae*. Translated by Stephen A. Barney. Cambridge: Cambridge University Press, 2006.

Isidore, Ps. *Decretales Ps-Isidorianae*. Edited by P. Hinschius. Leipzig, 1863.

Jerome. *Commentarius in Ecclesiasten*, CCSL.

———. *Commentary on the Pauline Epistles*. PL 26.

———. *Letters*. www.newadvent.org/fathers/3001002.htm.

John of Paris. *On Royal and Papal Power*. Translated by Arthur P. Monahan London: Columbia University Press, 1974.

John of Salisbury. *Historia pontificalis*. Edited and translated by Marjorie Chibnall. Oxford: Oxford University Press, 1986.

———. *Policraticus*. Corpus Christianorum Continuatio Medievalis 118. Edited by K. S. B. Keats-Rohan. Turnhout: Brepols, 1993.

Joye, George. *An Apology Made by George Joye, to Satisfy, If It May Be, W. Tindale*. Birmingham, 1882.

Kempe, Margery. *The Book of Margery Kempe*. Edited by Lynn Staley. Kalamazoo, Mich.: Medieval Institute Publications, 1996.

Knighton's Chronicle, 1337–1396. Edited and trans. G. H. Martin. Oxford: Oxford University Press, 1995.

Langland, William. *Piers Plowman: A New Translation of the B-text.* Translated by A. V. C. Schmidt. Oxford: Oxford University Press, 1992.

Libellus de diversis ordinibus. Edited by Giles Constable and Bernard Smith. Oxford: Oxford University Press, 1972.

The Life and Times of Anthony Wood. Edited by Andrew Clark. 1891.

Little, A. G., and Decima Douie. "Three Sermons of Friar Jordan of Saxony, the Successor of St. Dominic, Preached in England, A.D. 1229." *English Historical Review* 54 (1939).

Logica Modernorum. Edited by L. M. De Rijk. 2 vols. Assen: Van Gorcum, 1967.

Lollard Sermons. EETS 294. Edited by Gloria Cigman. Oxford: Oxford University Press, 1989.

Lollards of Coventry, 1485–1522. Camden Fifth Series. Edited and translated by Shannon McSheffrey and Norman Tanner. Cambridge: Cambridge University Press, 2003.

Ludus Coventriae. EETS. Edited by K. S. Block. Oxford: Oxford University Press, 1922.

Luther, Martin. *Reformation Writings of Martin Luther.* Translated by Bertram Lee Woolf. London: Lutterworth, 1956.

Madrigal, Alfonso de, el Tostado. *Introduccion al Evangelio segun San Mateo.* Edited by José Manuel Sanchez Caro, Rosa Maria Herrera García and Inmaculada Delgado Jara. Avila-Salamanca: University of Salamanca, 2008.

Maitland Club. *The Proceedings and Legislation of the Church of Scotland in the First Decades After the Reformation.* 3 vols. London: Institute of Historical Research, 1839-1845.

Maxwell, W. D. *John Knox's Genevan Service Book, 1556.* Edinburgh: Oliver & Boyd, 1931.

Melanchthon, Philipp. *De corrigendis adulescentiae studiis.* In Corpus Reformatorum 11, edited by Karl Gottlieb Bretschneider. Halle, 1843.

———. *On Christian Doctrine: Loci Communes, 1555.* Translated and edited by Clyde L. Manschreck. New York: Oxford University Press, 1965.

———. *Supplementa Melanchthoniana* (1510-1528). Edited by O. Clemen. Vol. 1. Leipzig: M. Heinsius, 1926.

Milton, John. "Of Education." In *Complete Prose Works of John Milton.* Edited by Douglas Bush et al. Vol. 2. New Haven, Conn.: Yale University Press, 1959.

Mirc, John. *Instructions for Parish Priests*. EETS. London: Oxford University Press, 1868.

More, Thomas. *The Complete Works of Thomas More*. Vol. 6.1, *A Dialogue Concerning Heresies*. New Haven, Conn.: Yale University Press, 1981.

Morison, J. L. *Reginald Pecock's Book of Faith*. Glasgow, 1909.

Nayler, J. *The Railer Rebuked*. 1655.

———. *Saul's Errand to Damascus*. 1654.

Neatby, William Blair. *A History of the Plymouth Brethren*. London: Hodder & Stoughton, 1902.

Nève, Félix. *La Renaissance des lettres en Belgique*. Louvain, 1890.

Nicholas of Cusa. *Sermones*. Edited by H. D. Reimann, H. Schwaetzer and F. B. Stammkötter. Hamburg: Meiner, 2005.

Norwich Heresy Trials. Camden Fourth Series. Edited by Norman Tanner. London: Royal Historical Society, 1977.

The Paston Letters. Edited by Norman Davis. Oxford: Oxford University Press, 1963.

Pecock, Reginald. *The Book of Faith*. Edited by J. L. Morison. Cambridge, Trinity College, MS B.14.45.

———. *Repressor of Overmuch Blaming of the Clergy*. Edited by Churchill Babington. Rolls Society. London: Longman, Green, Longman & Roberts, 1860.

Peter the Chanter. "Prologue." In *Verbum Abbreviatum*. Edited by F. Guisberti. Naples, 1982.

Petri Cantoris Parisiensis. *Verbum adbreviatum. Textus conflatus*. CCCM 196. Edited by Monique Boutry. Turnhout: Brepols, 2004.

Pierre de Langtoft. *Chronicle*. Rolls Series. Edited by T. Wright. London: Longman, Green, Reader & Dyer, 1868.

Piltz, Anders, ed. *Studium Upsalense: Specimens of the Oldest Lecture Notes Taken in the Mediaeval University of Uppsala*. Uppsala: University of Uppsala, 1977.

A Repertorium of Middle English Prose Sermons. Edited by Veronica O'Mara and S. Paul. Turnhout: Brepols, 2007.

Rolle, Richard. *The Incendium Amoris of Richard Rolle of Hampole*. Edited by Margaret Deanesley. Manchester: Manchester University Press, 1915.

The Schleitheim Text, Brotherly Union of a Number of Children of God Concerning Seven Articles. Translated and edited by John Howard Yoder. www.anabaptists.org/history/the-schleitheim-confession.html.

Tanner, Norman P. *Decrees of the Ecumenical Councils*. Washington, D.C.: Georgetown University Press, 1990.

Thatcher, O. J., and E. H. McNeal, trans. "Execrabilis." In *A Source Book for Mediaeval History*. New York: Charles Scribner's, 1905.

Thomas de Chobham. *Summa de arte praedicandi*. CCCM 82. Edited by F. Morenzoni. 1987.

Thoresby, John. Prologue to *The Lay Folks' Catechism*. EETS 118. Edited by T. F. Simmons and H. E. Nolloth. 1901.

The Towneley Plays. EETS. Edited by Martin Stevens and A. C. Cawley. Oxford: Oxford University Press, 1994.

A Treatise on the Power and Primacy of the Pope: A Treatise Compiled by the Theologians Assembled at Smalcald (1537), *Triglot Concordia: The Symbolical Books of the Evangelical Lutheran Church: German-Latin-English*. Edited by F. Bente et al. St. Louis: Concordia Publishing, 1917.

Valla, Lorenzo. *Collatio Novi Testamenti*. Edited by A. Perosa. Florence: Sansoni, 1970.

———. *Collatio*. In *Opera Omnia*. Edited by E. Garin. Turin: Bottega d'Erasmo, 1962.

———. *In Novum Testamentum annotationes*. Basel, 1527.

———. *De linguae latinae elegantia*. Vol. 1. Edited by Santiago López Moreda. Cáceres: University of Extremadura, 1999.

Visitation Articles and Injunctions of the Early Stuart Church. Edited by Kenneth Fincham. Church of England Record Society 5. Woodbridge, U.K.: Boydell Press, 1998.

Watts, Isaac. *Logic; Or, The Right Use of Reason in the Inquiry After Truth with a Variety of Rules to Guard Against Error, in the Affairs of Religion and Human Life, as well as in the Sciences* 3.5. 1724. Reprint, London, 1845.

Whitby, Daniel. *A Paraphrase and Commentary on the New Testament*. London, 1703.

William of Auvergne. *De legibus* 1. In *Opera Omnia*. 1674. Reprint, Frankfurt-am-Main: Minerva, 1963.

William of Newburgh. *The Sermons of William of Newburgh*. Edited by A. B. Kraebel. Toronto: Pontifical Institute of Medieval Studies, 2010.

Willoughby, Harold R. *The First Authorized English Bible: And the Cranmer Preface*. Chicago: University of Chicago Press, 1942.

Wintrop, Robert C., ed. *Life and Letters of John Winthrop (1630-49)*. London, 1867.

Workman, Herbert B., and R. Martin Pope, eds. *The Letters of John Hus*. London: Hodder & Stoughton, 1904.

The Zurich Letters, Second Series (1558-1602). Edited by Hastings Robinson. Parker Society Cambridge: Cambridge University Press, 1845.

Secondary Sources

Arber, Edward, ed. *An Introductory Sketch to the Martin Marprelate Controversy.* English Scholar's Library 8. London, 1880.

Aston, Margaret. *England's Iconoclasts.* Oxford: Oxford University Press, 1988.

Auerbach, Erich. *Literary Language and Its Public.* Translated by R. Manheim London: Routledge, 1965.

Backus, Irene. *The Reception of the Church Fathers in the West: From the Carolingians to the Maurists.* Leiden: Brill, 1997.

Baldwin, John W. "Peter the Chanter: An Edition of the Long Version of Peter the Chanter's *Verbum Abbreviatum,* Review Article." *Journal of Ecclesiastical History* 57 (2006).

Bale, Anthony. "A Norfolk Gentlewoman and Lydgatean Patronage," *Medium Aevum* 78 (2009).

Bennett, J. A. W. "Chaucer's Contemporary." In *Piers Plowman: Critical Approaches.* Edited by S. S. Hussey. London: Methuen, 1969.

Bentley, Jerry H. *Humanists and Holy Writ: New Testament Scholarship in the Renaissance.* Princeton, N J : Princeton University Press, 1983.

Blair, Ann. "Ovidius Methodizatus: The Metamorphoses of Ovid in a Sixteenth Century Paris College." *History of Universities* 9 (1990).

———. "The Teaching of Natural Philosophy in Early Seventeenth Century Paris: The Case of Jean Cécile Frey." *History of Universities* 12 (1993).

Bluhm, Heinz Siegfried. *Martin Luther: Creative Translator.* St. Louis: Concordia Publishing, 1965.

Cameron, Euan. *The European Reformation.* Oxford: Oxford University Press, 1991.

Chadwick, Owen. *The Early Reformation on the Continent.* Oxford: Oxford University Press, 2001.

———. "Indifference and Morality." *Christian Spirituality: Essays in Honor of Gordon Rupp.* Edited by Peter Brooks. London: SCM Press, 1975.

Chambers, Katherine. *The Rich and Poor in Twelfth-Century Paris: The Social Thought of Peter the Chanter.* Ph.D. thesis. University of Cambridge, 2006.

Chazelle, Celia. "Exegesis in the Ninth-Century Eucharist Controversy." *The Study of the Bible in the Carolingian Era.* Edited by Celia Chazelle and Burton Van Name Edwards. Turnhout: Brepols, 2003.

————. "Figure, Character, and the Glorified Body in the Carolingian Eucharistic Controversy." *Traditio* 47 (1992).

Coolman, Boyd Taylor. *The Theology of Hugh of St. Victor: An Interpretation.* Cambridge: Cambridge University Press, 2010.

Courtenay, William J., and Katherine H. Tachau. "Ockham, Ockhamists, and the English-German Nation at Paris, 1339-1341." *History of Universities* 2 (1982).

Davies, Joan. "Student Libraries in Sixteenth Century Toulouse." *History of Universities* 3 (1983).

de Jonge, Henk J. "The Study of the New Testament in the Dutch Universities, 1575-1700." *History of Universities* 1 (1981).

Diller, Aubrey. "Petrarch's Greek Codex of Plato." *Classical Philology* 59 (1964).

Dix, Dom Gregory. *The Question of Anglican Orders.* Revised ed. Westminster: Dacre Press, 1956.

Duffy, Eamon. *Catholic England Under Mary Tudor.* New Haven, Conn.: Yale University Press, 2009.

————. *The Stripping of the Altars: Traditional Religion in England c. 1400-c. 1580.* New Haven, Conn.: Yale University Press, 1992.

————. *The Voices of Morebath: Reformation and Rebellion in an English Village.* New Haven, Conn.: Yale University Press, 2001.

Dvornik, Francis. *Pope Gelasius and Emperor Anastasius.* München: C. H. Beck'sche, 1951.

Eisenstein, Elizabeth. *The Printing Press as an Agent of Change: Communications and Cultural Transformations in Early Modern Europe.* Cambridge: Cambridge University Press, 1979.

————. *The Printing Revolution in Early Modern Europe.* Cambridge: Cambridge University Press, 1993.

Evans, G. R. *The Church and the Churches.* Cambridge: Cambridge University Press, 1994.

————. *Fifty Key Medieval Thinkers.* London: Routledge, 2002.

————. *The Language and Logic of the Bible.* 2 vols. Cambridge: Cambridge University Press, 1984-1985.

————. "*Ponendo theologica exempla*: Peter the Chanter's *De Tropis Loquendi*." *History of Universities* 2 (1982).

Evans, R. W. J. "German Universities After the Thirty Years War." *History of Universities* 1 (1981).

Finucane, R. *Miracles and Pilgrims: Popular Beliefs in Medieval England.* London: J. M. Dent, 1977.

Fletcher, John M. "Chance and Resistance to Change: A Consideration of the Development of English and German Universities During the Sixteenth Century." *History of Universities* 1 (1981).

Ford, Alan. *James Ussher: Theology, History and Politics in Early-Modern Ireland and England*. Oxford: Oxford University Press, 2007.

Frend, William. *The Donatist Church*. Oxford: Clarendon Press, 1971.

Frieensburg, W., ed. *Urkundenbuch det Universitat Wittenberg*, I, 1502-1611. Magdeburg: Selbstverlag der historischen Kommission für die Provinz Sachsen und für Anhalt, 1926.

Furey, Constance M. *Erasmus, Contarini, and the Religious Republic of Letters*. Cambridge: Cambridge University Press, 2006.

Goertz, Hans-Jürgen. *The Anabaptists*. London: Routledge, 1996.

Gough, J. *A History of the People Called Quakers*. 4 vols. 1789-1790.

Grafton, Anthony. "Teacher, Text and Pupil in the Renaissance Class-Room: A Case Study from a Parisian College." *History of Universities* 1 (1981).

Greaves, R. L. *Deliver Us from Evil: The Radical Underground in Britain, 1660-1663*. Oxford: Oxford University Press, 1986.

Guppy, Henry. *Miles Coverdale and the English Bible, 1488-1568*. Manchester: Manchester University Pres, 1935.

Guy, J. A. *Thomas More*. London: Arnold, 2000.

Gwyn, Peter. *The King's Cardinal. The Rise and Fall of Thomas Wolsey*. London: Pimlico, 1992.

Haller, William. *The Rise of Puritanism*. New York: Columbia, 1938.

Hammerstein, Notker. "The University of Heidelberg in the Early Modern Period: Aspects of Its History as a Contribution to its Sextenary." *History of Universities* 6 (1986-1987).

Howell, Wilbur Samuel. *Logic and Rhetoric in England 1500-1700*. Princeton, N.J.: Princeton University Press, 1956.

Hudson, Anne. *The Premature Reformation*. Oxford: Oxford University Press, 1988.

———. "The Sermons of MS Longleat 4." *Medium Aevum* 53 (1984).

———, ed. *Two Wycliffite Texts*. EETS 301. Oxford: Oxford University Press, 1993.

Hunter, Michael. *Robert Boyle, 1627-1691: Scrupulosity and Science*. Woodbridge, U.K.: Boydell Press, 2000.

Iserloh, Erwin. *Johannes Eck (1486-1543): Scholastiker Humanist Kontroverstheologe*. Münster: Verlag Aschendorff, 1981.

James, William. *Varieties of Religious Experience*. Cambridge, Mass.: Harvard University Press, 1985.

Jones, L. *The Discovery of Hebrew in Tudor England*. Manchester: Manchester University Press, 1983.

Judges, A. V. *The Elizabethan Underworld*. London: Routledge, 1930.

Kelly, J. N. D. *Early Christian Creeds*. 3rd ed. London: Continuum, 2006.

————. *Jerome: His Life, Controversies and Writings*. London: Duckworth, 1975.

Kugler, Robert A. "Tyconius's Mystic Rules and the Rules of Augustine." In *Augustine and the Bible*. Edited by Pamela Bright. Notre Dame, Ind.: University of Notre Dame Press, 1999.

Kusukawa, Sachiko. "Law and Gospel: The Importance of Philosophy at Reformation Wittenberg." *History of Universities* 11 (1992).

Lambert, Malcolm D. *Franciscan Poverty*. St. Bonaventure, N.Y.: Franciscan Institute, 1998.

Lapidge, Michael. *The Anglo-Saxon Library*. Oxford: Oxford University Press, 2006.

Lawless, G. *Augustine of Hippo and His Monastic Rule*. Oxford: Clarendon Press, 1987.

Le Goff, Jacques. *The Birth of Purgatory*. Translated by A. Goldhammer. London: Scolar Press, 1984.

Leader, D. R. *A History of the University of Cambridge*. Cambridge: Cambridge University Press, 1988.

Leclercq, J. "Un traité *De fallaciis in theologia*." *Revue du Moyen Age Latin* 1 (1945).

Lindberg, Conrad, ed. *The Earlier Version of the Wycliffite Bible*. Vol. 7. Uppsala: Almqvist & Wiksell, 1997.

Luscombe, David. *The School of Peter Abelard*. Cambridge: Cambridge University Press, 1970.

MacCulloch, Diarmaid. *Reformation: Europe's House Divided, 1490-1700*. London: Allen Lane, 2004.

Marenbon, John. *The Philosophy of Peter Abelard*. Cambridge: Cambridge University Press, 1997.

McConica, James, ed. *History of the University of Oxford*. Vol. 3. Oxford: Oxford University Press, 1986.

McGrath, Alister E. *Iustitia Dei: A History of the Christian Doctrine of Justification*. Cambridge: Cambridge University Press, 2005.

Minchamp, Georges. *Le Cartésianisme en Belgique*. 1886.

Minnich, Nelson H. "The Voice of Theologians in General Councils from Pisa to Trent." *Theological Studies* 59 (1998).

Miola, Robert S., ed. *Early Modern Catholicism: An Anthology of Primary Sources.* Oxford: Oxford University Press, 2007.

Mitchell, W. Fraser. *English Pulpit Oratory from Andrewes to Tillotson.* London: Russell & Russell, 1962.

Mohrmann, Christine. *Mélanges.* Utrecht: Het Spectrum, 1973.

Morgan, Nigel, and Rodney Thomson, eds. *The Cambridge History of the Book in Britain.* Cambridge: Cambridge University Press, 2008.

Mouron, Anne. *"The Manere of Good Lyving:* The Manner of a Good Translator." *Medium Aevum* 78 (2009).

Murray, Stuart. "Biblical Interpretation Among the Anabaptist Reformers." In *A History of Biblical Interpretation.* Edited by Alan J. Hauser and Duane F. Watson. Grand Rapids: Eerdmans, 2009.

Nauta, Lodi. *In Defense of Common Sense: Lorenzo Valla's Humanist Critique of Scholastic Philosophy.* Cambridge, Mass.: Harvard University Press, 2009.

Nock, A. D. *Conversion.* Oxford: Oxford University Press, 1933.

Oberman, Heiko. "Luther and the *Via Moderna*: The Philosophical Backdrop of the Reformation Breakthrough." *Journal of Ecclesiastical History* 54 (2003).

Ocker, Christopher. *Biblical Poetics Before Humanism and Reformation.* Cambridge: Cambridge University Press, 2002.

O'Donnell, James J. *Cassiodorus.* Berkeley: University of California Press, 1979.

Pearsall, Derek. "The Idea of Universal Salvation in Piers Plowman B and C." *Journal of Medieval and Early Modern Studies* 39 (2009).

Pellistrandi, Benoît. "The University of Alcalá de Henares from 1568-1618: Students and Graduates." *History of Universities* 9 (1990).

Phidas, V. "Hermeneutique et patristique au concile de Florence." *Christian Unity: The Council of Ferrara-Florence, 1438/9-1989.* Edited by G. Alberigo. Louvain: Louvain University Press, 1991.

Piepkorn, Arthur Carl. *Profiles in Belief: The Religious Bodies of the United States and Canada.* 3 vols. New York: HarperCollins, 1977-1979.

Poschmann, B. *Penance and the Anointing of the Sick.* London: Herder & Herder, 1964.

Potter, G. R. *Zwingli.* Cambridge: Cambridge University Press, 1976.

Rebholz, Ronald A. *The Life of Fulke Greville.* Oxford: Clarendon Press, 1971.

Reedy, Gerard. *The Bible and Reason: Anglicans and Scripture in Late Seventeenth Century England.* Philadelphia: University of Pennsylvania, 1985.

Ridley, Jasper. *Thomas Cranmer.* Oxford: Clarendon Press, 1962.

Rubin, Miri. *Corpus Christi: The Eucharist in Late Medieval Culture*. Cambridge: Cambridge University Press, 1991.

Rummel, Erika. *The Case Against Johann Reuchlin*. Toronto: University of Toronto Press, 2002.

Ryrie, Alec. *The Gospel and Henry VIII: Evangelicals in the Early English Reformation*. Cambridge: Cambridge University Press, 2003.

————. *The Origins of the Scottish Reformation*. Manchester: Manchester University Press, 2006.

Ryrie, Alec, and Peter Marshall, *The Beginnings of English Protestantism*. Cambridge: Cambridge University Press, 2002.

Schüssler, Hermann. *Der Primat der Heiligen Schrift als theologisches und kanonisches Problem in Spätmittelalter*. Wiesbaden, 1977.

Sharpe, Richard. "The English Bibliographical Tradition from Kirkestere to Tanner." *Britannia Latina: Latin in the Culture of Great Britain from the Middle Ages to the Twentieth Century*. Warburg Institute Colloquia 8. Edited by Charles Burnett and Nicholas Mann. London: Warburg Institute, 2005.

Smalley, Beryl. *The Study of the Bible in the Middle Ages*. 3rd. ed. Oxford: Basil Blackwell, 1983.

Stupperich, Robert. *Melanchthon*. Translated by Robert H. Fischer. London: Lutterworth, 1966.

Sutherland, L. S., and L. G. Mitchell, eds. *History of the University of Oxford 5*. Oxford: Oxford University Press, 1986.

Tierney, Brian, and Peter Lineham, eds. *Authority and Power: Studies on Medieval Law and Government Presented to Walter Ullmann*. Cambridge: Cambridge University Press, 1980.

Tillard, J.-M.-R. *Eglise d'églises: L'ecclésiologie de communion*. Paris: Cerf, 1987.

Torrell, J. P. *Théorie de la prophétie et philosophie de la connaissance aux environs de 1230*. Etudes et Documents 40. Louvain: Spicilegium Sacrum Lovaniense, 1977.

Weber, Christoph Friedrich. "Ces grands privileges: The Symbolic Use of Written Documents in the Foundation and Institutionalization Processes of Medieval Universities." *History of Universities* 19 (2004).

Whiteside, D. T. "Patterns of Mathematical Thought in the Later Seventeenth Century." *Archive for History of Exact Sciences* 1 (1960-1962).

Author Index

Abelard, Peter, 149, 152-53, 157, 161, 162, 171, 233, 268
Aelfric of Eynsham, 138, 140
Aelred of Riveaulx, 195, 196
Alan of Lille, 175, 176, 260
Albertus Magnus, 188
Ambrose of Milan, 86, 236, 241
Andreae, Jakob, 291
Andrew of St. Victor, 150, 233
Ann, Lady Bacon. *See* Bacon, Lady Ann
Anselm of Canterbury, 138-40, 142, 168-69
Anselm of Laon, 152
Aquinas. *See* Thomas Aquinas
Aristotle, 87-88, 118, 153, 157, 158, 256, 258, 379
Arnold of Brescia, 152, 172
Arundel, Thomas, 90, 205-6, 217, 219, 222
Astley, John, 256
Aston, Margaret, 295n3
Athanasius, 47, 203
Athenagoras, 408
Augustine of Canterbury, 167
Augustine of Hippo, 19, 32, 38, 40, 46n1, 48, 49, 51, 52-53, 54-56, 57-59, 61, 65, 66, 67, 69-70, 71, 72-74, 90, 132, 137, 140, 144, 146, 149, 150, 153, 161, 162, 163, 165, 167, 170, 175, 179, 204, 218, 224, 225-26, 235, 236, 238, 241, 252, 256, 267, 270, 277, 284, 287, 307, 322, 330, 380, 381, 392, 399, 412-13, 415, 432, 434, 439, 441, 453
Aurifaber, John, 42, 278, 281
Bacon, Francis, 351, 422-23
Bacon, Lady Ann, 372n7
Baldus de Ubaldis, 118, 119
Bale, Anthony, 208n21
Barbeyrac, Jean, 408

Bartolus of Sassoferrato, 118
Basil, 236, 394
Baxter, Richard, 411, 414, 416
Bede, 19, 35, 82, 146, 161, 165, 167, 303
Bellarmine, Robert, 369
Berengar of Tours, 87, 88
Bernard of Clairvaux, 114-15, 116, 117, 131, 154, 169, 170-71, 178, 196, 198, 199, 206
Beza, Theodore, 338-39, 348, 384
Birgitta of Sweden, 200, 207-8
Boethius, 154, 157, 238
Bolsec, Jérôme-Hermès, 321
Bonaventure, 83, 188, 212, 264
Booty, John E., 372n18
Boyle, Robert, 241, 401, 415, 416-20
Briggs, Charles F., 206n18
Bucer, Martin, 31, 67, 69, 76, 290, 298, 302, 317, 335, 392, 445, 446
Bullinger, Heinrich, 328, 336, 338, 339, 383, 404, 411
Bunyan, John, 412
Caesarius of Heisterbach, 89
Calvin, John, 31, 42, 45, 50, 51, 69, 246, 261, 271, 291, 315-24, 325, 328-29, 330, 331, 333, 336, 341, 364, 371, 381-82, 386-87, 392, 393, 426, 434, 441, 446, 454
Campensis, 301
Cappel, Louis, 396
Cartwright, Thomas, 338, 348
Cassiodorus, 149
Castelvetro, Giacomo, 383
Caxton, William, 208
Chaucer, Geoffrey, 15, 85, 131

Chemnitz, Martin, 261, 291, 395, 397
Chrysostom, 224, 271, 303
Cicero, 55n12, 56, 157, 165, 175, 238, 250, 256, 258
Clement of Alexandria, 60, 408
Clement of Rome, 30
Colet, John, 251, 256
Contarini, Gaspar, 232, 364-65
Copernicus, Nicolaus, 244n27, 373, 374, 375, 377
Corso, Giovani, 238
Coverdale, Miles, 273, 299-303, 336, 396
Cranmer, Thomas, 244, 295, 296, 297-99, 300, 302, 303-4, 328, 334-35, 346, 413
Crowley, Robert, 428
Cyprian, 69-72, 74, 241, 394, 408, 441n5
Cyril of Jerusalem, 86
D'Ailly, Pierre, 235
Dante Alighieri, 79, 80, 116, 117, 122
Dionysius, 30, 198
Donatus, 157
Donne, John, 250
Dryden, John, 250, 402
Duffy, Eamon, 421
Duns Scotus, John, 188, 241, 249-50
Eck, Johann Maier von, 50, 266-68, 290, 432
Eckhart, Meister, 199
Erasmus, Desiderius, 193, 240, 247-48, 251-52, 254, 256, 273, 293, 303, 307, 316, 396, 412, 413
Erastus, Thomas, 383-84, 429, 450
Eriugena, John Scotus, 86, 128
Euclid, 259
Eutyches, 94, 95, 105, 106
Everard of Breteuil, 133, 134

Subject Index

Scripture Index